THE

PROGRESS

OF

RELIGIOUS IDEAS,

Through Successive Ages.

BY

L. MARIA CHILD.

God sends his teachers unto every age,
To every clime, and every race of men,
With revelations fitted to their growth
And shape of mind, nor gives the realm of TRUTH
Into the selfish rule of one sole race:
Therefore, each form of worship that hath swayed
The life of man, and given it to grasp
The master-key of knowledge, REVERENCE,
Enfolds some germs of goodness and of right.
J. R. LOWELL.

IN THREE VOLUMES.
VOL. III.

New York:

C. S. FRANCIS & CO., 554 BROADWAY.
LONDON: S. LOW, SON & CO.
M. DCCC. LV

CONTENTS OF VOL. III

———— ◆•◆ ————

Publishing Statement:

This important reprint was made from an old and scarce book.

Therefore, it may have defects such as missing pages, erroneous pagination, blurred pages, missing text, poor pictures, markings, marginalia and other issues beyond our control.

Because this is such an important and rare work, we believe it is best to reproduce this book regardless of its original condition.

Thank you for your understanding and enjoy this unique book!

PROGRESS

OF

RELIGIOUS IDEAS.

———◄•►———

CHRISTIANITY.

"Whatever errors may have crept in among the simple, yet sublime
views, published by Christ, the practical *moral character* of his Gospel has
always stood prominently above the abstract *doctrines.* From the first
publication of Christianity, to this very day, it may be safely asserted that
no sincere convert has embraced it allured by its *creed.*"—J. BLANCO WHITE.

FROM THE TIME OF CONSTANTINE.

WHILE internal changes were being gradually wrought in
Christianity, by the previous opinions of its converts, and
by the various sects and schools, with which it was constantly engaged in controversy, important changes were
also taking place in its relations to the government. The
emperor Constantius, one of the colleagues of Diocletian,
had been uniformly tolerant, and even friendly toward the
Christians, either from humanity, or from motives of policy;
they being numerous in the part of the empire which he
governed. His son Constantine had been left as a hostage
at the imperial court, and suffered much from the jealousy
and tyranny of Galerius. He is said to have been in Nico-

media at the first furious outbreak of persecution, and to
have witnessed the heroic endurance of the Christians. He
afterward commanded the army in Gaul, and, on the death
of his father, in the year three hundred and six, when he
was nearly forty years old, the troops proclaimed him emperor; but rivals were in the way, and battles must be
fought to decide who should wear the imperial purple. He
was at that time a worshipper of the gods, and the Sun was
his tutelary deity. In consequence of the successful termi-
nation of a war with one of his rivals, he gave public thanks
in a celebrated temple of Apollo, presented magnificent offerings, and had coins stamped with *Soli, Invicto Comiti:* To
the Sun, the Invincible Companion. His situation at that
period was perplexing. Adherents of the old religion, if
not the most numerous, were still in possession of power.
On the other hand, Christianity had become an important
element in state affairs. The numerous communities, scattered throughout the empire, were united by the strongest
of all bonds, that of a persecuted faith, and might be expected to serve zealously the interest of any ruler who
would espouse their cause. The political enemies of Constantine were also the enemies of Christianity. His rival,
Maxentius, was diligently employing every means of worship and of magic to secure the protection of the gods of
Rome; and Constantine had great dread of the effect of
such rites. If advantage was to be gained by pursuing an
opposite course, it would be exclusively his own. He felt
the need of assistance from some powerful Deity; and he
reflected that emperors who had persecuted the Christians
had generally ended miserably, while his father, who protected them, had a happier fate. A recent example had
occurred in the painful death of Galerius. This was continually urged by the Christians; and Constantine appears
to have been in a state of mind similar to Ahaz, king of
Judah, who sacrificed to the gods of Damascus; saying:
"The gods of the kings of Syria help *them,* therefore will
I sacrifice to them, that they may help *me.*" Eusebius, the
historian, represents him as in a state of conflict; and the

fluctuating course he pursued for some time afterward, indicates the uncertainty of his faith.

A short time before the great battle, which was to decide his destiny, he prayed to the Christians' God that he would reveal himself, and protect him from his enemies. It is not easy to imagine a state of mind more favourable for the appearance of omens. It is recorded that, in the course of his march, he saw, about noon, a Luminous Cross above the Sun, which heretofore had been his tutelary deity. On it was inscribed the motto: "Under this sign thou shalt conquer." He and his army gazed at the brilliant phenomenon with astonishment. The following night, he dreamed that Christ appeared to him, and showed him a cross bearing the monogram of his name, with the assurance that, if he assumed it for a standard, he would march to certain victory. He sent for Christian teachers, and inquired of them concerning their God, and the import of the symbol. He then caused a standard to be made according to his dream, and, under its protection, he conquered Maxentius, entered Rome in triumph, and was proclaimed emperor. This occurred in the year three hundred and twelve.

The story is told by Eusebius, Bishop of Cæsarea, in his Life of Constantine, written after the death of that emperor, which occurred twenty-five years after the battle. He asserts that Constantine made the statement to him, in familiar conversation, many years after the event, and affirmed it with an oath. Rufinus, a celebrated Christian writer of the fourth century, states that Constantine saw a flaming cross in a dream, and waking up in a fright, found an angel by his side, who exclaimed: "By this conquer!" Cotemporary history is silent; which is remarkable, considering that a whole army were astounded by the extraordinary vision. It is also singular that Eusebius himself, in his Ecclesiastical History, makes no allusion to such a wonderful intervention of Deity to change the religion of the Roman Empire. It, however, remained an unquestioned miracle for many centuries. But, in modern times, the scientific have ventured to inquire of what nature such a luminous apparition in the sky could be; and many of the religious have felt that Jesus could not have assumed the entirely new character of a military protector, without a manifest departure from his own pacific maxims. At the present day, the miracle is very generally rejected. Some consider it a fiction, invented either by Constantine or Eusebius, to throw supernatural interest round the first union of Christianity with the State. Others more reasonably suppose that the emperor really saw some uncommon meteor, and that, as years passed on, the account of it became greatly exaggerated. Being in an anxious state of mind, having prayed that the Christians' God would reveal himself, and living at a period when everything was construed into an omen, or a miracle, the imagination of Constantine would doubtless have been easily excited, either by northern lights in the evening, or a solar halo at noon; and it would be very natural that his dreams should be connected with what he had seen. If he subsequently adopted the motto, it would readily be added to the marvellous story in process of time. The probability that meteors were actually seen is increased by the statement of Nazarius, a Roman orator, and a votary of the old worship. He pronounced a panegyric on Constantine, nine years after his decisive victory, long before Eusebius wrote his account of the miracle. He describes a troop of beautiful Spirits in the sky, clad in refulgent armour, who were heard and seen by the whole army. He says: "It is the report throughout all Gaul that armies were seen, who professed to be divinely sent; saying, We want to find Constantine. We are sent to his assistance." The flattering orator adds that even Divine Beings were ambitious of such distinction, and glorified themselves with the idea of fighting for Constantine. Among the fantastic forms of the Aurora Borealis, none are more common than shooting streams of light, resembling lances hurled across the sky. In that age of the world, a supernatural cause would of course be assigned for such appearances; and where Greek and Roman imagination saw deities descending with brilliant spears, Christians in the army could quite as easily perceive a luminous cross.

Whatever might have been the real origin of the story, the emperor caused a standard to be made in the form of a cross; and, according to tradition, it was an exact copy of the one seen in his dream. The shaft was cased with gold, and it was surmounted by a golden crown, on which were inscribed a monogram, signifying the name of Christ. Beneath the crown was a small purple banner, and the bust of Constantine, which shared the homage paid by the soldiers to their consecrated standard, without necessarily bringing them under the charge of idolatry. This standard was called the Labarum, the meaning of which is now unknown. It was for a long time carried at the head of the imperial army, intrusted to the care of fifty faithful guards; and a belief prevailed that no weapon could harm them while they were employed in guarding the sacred emblem.

After the victory over Maxentius, Constantine adopted the cross as a kind of amulet, to which he ascribed supernatural powers of protection. It was always carried with him on important occasions, and he was often observed to make the sign of the cross upon his forehead. But his proceedings indicate a prolonged uncertainty in his mind, as if he were waiting for events to decide what deity would prove most powerful to advance his own interests. It is likely that during the first years, the old and the new were mixed in his mind; reverence for the ancient worship remained to a considerable degree, and struggled with the conviction that Jehovah was the greatest of all gods. He pursued a very liberal policy toward Christians; but many of his actions were obvious violations of their precepts. He set at liberty those who were unjustly imprisoned, and pardoned most of those who had taken up arms against him; but he caused many of his enemies to be executed, and put to death the infant son of his rival Maxentius. Many of his German captives, whom Roman pride designated as barbarians, were exposed to contests with lions and tigers in the circus, for the amusement of the populace; as had been the custom with previous emperors. In the year three hundred and thirteen, he published an edict of unlimited toleration, in which Christianity was recognized as one of the forms in which Deity might be lawfully worshipped. The church property, confiscated during previous reigns, was restored, and he gave large sums of money to the Christians in Africa to rebuild their ruined edifices. Those who had meanwhile come into legal possession of the land were indemnified. A regular allowance of corn was granted in each city, to meet the demands of ecclesiastical charity. His pious subjects received permission to bequeath land or money to the church to an unlimited extent. The clergy were exempted from taxes, contributions, and certain municipal services, which pressed heavily on other citizens. Thus the nucleus of an ecclesiastical power, distinct from the civil, was introduced into the Roman Empire, which had hitherto never known an established priesthood. The emperor, in a letter to the Bishop of Carthage, assigns, as a reason for these privileges, that the Christian Clergy ought not to be withdrawn from the worship of God, on which the prosperity of the state depended.

But while so much favour was shown to the long-persecuted faith, entire freedom was secured to other forms of religion. The old temples and altars were not only left undisturbed, but in many cases were repaired at the expense of government; and orators lauded him for the munificence of his donations. His medals and coins still bore the image of the Sun, and other emblems of the old religion. He did not offer sacrifices to the gods himself, or cause it to be done for him by representatives in the provinces; but he followed the custom of his predecessors in accepting the title of Supreme Pontiff of the old religion, and performed many of the public functions of that office.

In three hundred and nineteen, he published laws in which it was declared: "They who wish to remain slaves to their superstition, have liberty for the public exercise of their worship." "You, who consider it profitable to yourselves, may continue to visit the public altars, and observe the solemnities of your usage. We do not forbid the ancient rites to be performed, provided it be done in the open light." This prohibition against secresy grew out of the fact that his colleague, Licinius, was disposed to head a party in opposition to him and Christianity. Itinerant magicians and soothsayers were forbidden to exercise their arts; for Constantine was always unable to overcome his dread of having magical rites practised against himself. From the same fear of treasonable designs, private consultation of Augurs was forbidden, and people were not allowed to offer sacrifices in houses. If the Augurs visited each other's dwellings, they were to be burned, even if they urged the plea of friendship. Whoever summoned an Augur to his house was banished, and his goods confiscated. But public auguries were consulted by priests at the temples, the same as formerly. As late as three hundred and twenty-one, he passed a law that in case lightning struck the imperial palace, or any of the public buildings, the Augurs should be consulted, according to usage, as to what it might signify; and that a careful report of their answer should be drawn up for his own use. He also gave public permission to use magical ceremonies for good purposes; such as the prevention of storms, and the preservation of harvests. Oracles convicted of fraud were silenced; but otherwise they were not interfered with; and it is even said that he sometimes availed himself of their services. Some popular festivals, connected with midnight revels, and licentious practices, were interdicted, as dangerous to public morals. But, with these exceptions, rites endeared to the people by ages of reverent observance, were performed by the priesthood as usual. Offices of trust were impartially distributed between adherents of the old and the new religion. All the measures of government indicated the prudent policy of a statesman, adapting himself to a transition state in public opinion, rather than the fresh zeal of a thorough proselyte.

It has been already stated that most of the ancient nations had a series of seven days, named for the seven planets known to them, in which the sun and moon were included. This does not appear to have been a division of time, but to have grown out of certain ceremonies and invocations successively offered to the Seven Spirits of the Planets, who were universally supposed to have a very powerful influence on human affairs. The Romans, following a very ancient custom, called our first day of the week Dies Solis, the Day of the Sun; the second, Dies Lunæ, the Day of the Moon; the third, Dies Martis, the Day of Mars; the fourth, Dies Mercurii, the Day of Mercury; the fifth, Dies Jovis, the Day of Jupiter; the sixth, Dies Veneris, the Day of Venus; the seventh, Dies Saturni, the Day of Saturn. Apollo had gradually become more popular, as an object of worship, than Jupiter the Thunderer. As god of poetry and eloquence, he was attractive to cultivated minds; as god of prophecy, he had strong hold of the reverential and superstitious; and as god of medicine, he wore a friendly aspect to the populace. He was originally god of *intellectual* light, the divine *archetype* of the sunlight of this world; but in the latter days, his worship had become gradually mingled with Helios, god of the material sun. Therefore, it is likely that peculiar ceremonies were appropriated to him on Dies Solis. The sun had always been the chosen emblem of Constantine. Apollo was his tutelary deity; and, until he was forty years old, had always been honoured by him as his invincible protector and benefactor. The Sun's Day was therefore consecrated both to his heart and his imagination; and men do not suddenly outgrow long-cherished ideas. One of the earliest acts of his reign was to add that day to the list of public Festivals; and the following edict was passed: "Let all the people in towns, judges, mechanics, and tradesmen, rest on the venerated Day of the Sun. But those who are in the country may freely cultivate their fields; since it often happens that on no other day can grain be more suitably sowed, or the vines set." A large proportion of the soldiers adhered to the old worship. A form of prayer was written for them, such as a person of any religion might offer for the health of the emperor and the welfare of the state. They were required to go into the fields and repeat this, at the word of command. In this edict no allusion was made to the Sun's Day as connected with Christianity. The increasing humanity of the age, to which Christ, his Apostles, and those who reverenced their kind and gentle morality, had contributed so very largely, was indicated by one feature in the law: the courts were closed on that day for all purposes, except the manumission of slaves. Military exercises were also prohibited.

Licinius, who married the sister of Constantine, governed the Eastern part of the empire. Jealousy between the two emperors resulted in war. Licinius was defeated, and peace remained unbroken for several years. He is said to have been avaricious and sensual, while Constantine was generous, temperate, and virtuous, in all his habits. The strict morality enjoined by Christian bishops was probably an uncomfortable restraint upon the debaucheries of Licinius, while, at the same time, jealousy of Constantine's power led him to seek popularity with a large class of his subjects by throwing his whole influence in favour of the old religion. He allowed no one to retain rank in his army unless he consented to offer sacrifices to the gods. He confined bishops to the care of their own dioceses, and forbade them to meet in councils; probably fearing such opportunities might be used to his disadvantage. On the ground of salutary moral regulations, he ordered that women belonging to Christian communities should be religiously instructed only by deaconesses; that men and women should assemble for worship in the open air, and not meet together in churches. He forbade Christians access to the prisons, which they had been in the habit of visiting frequently for purposes of charity and devotion. Finally, he ordered their churches in the province of Pontus to be closed, and in some cases destroyed. Acts of personal violence, and even of martyrdom occurred. The terrified Christians fled from the cities, and hid themselves in woods and caves. In consequence of these outrages, Constantine again took up arms against his brother-in-law. Political rivalry was the real cause of strife, but, by force of circumstances, it became a struggle for mastery between the old and new religions. Licinius solemnly invoked the gods, offered sacrifices, and consulted oracles and divinations, from which he received promises of universal empire. Constantine marched to the contest with his standard of the cross, and accompanied by bishops. He gained the victory, which Christians attributed to the prayers of their bishops, and the presence of the holy Labarum. Eusebius declares that Constantine himself told him that one man, who, in terror, gave up the standard of the cross to another, was immediately transfixed by a spear in his flight, while the bearer of the cross passed on unhurt amid a shower of javelins, and not a man in its immediate neighbourhood was even wounded. This battle gave Constantine undivided mastery of the Roman world. He gave orders to spare the lives of his enemies, and offered rewards for all captives who were brought to him alive; an improvement on the old customs, probably owing to the humanizing influence of the bishops. Licinius was permitted to retire to private life, and it is said Constantine took a solemn oath to spare the life of his sister's husband; which, however, he failed to keep.

The adulation of the bishops was excessive; but much may be excused in men who had found an imperial protector, after such frequent and fierce storms of persecution. Eusebius of Cæsarea represents him as giving orders for battle under the influence of direct inspiration from heaven, in answer to his prayers. When the bishops in attendance upon him congratulated him as ruler over this world, and destined to reign with the Son of God in the world to come, he admonished them rather to pray for him, that he might be deemed worthy to be a servant of God, both in this world and the next.

He recalled the exiled Christians, restored their confiscated property, and the honours of those who had been degraded in state or army. He rebuilt the churches at his own expense, and empowered the clergy to receive donations of land, as he had previously done in the Western parts of the empire. In the proclamations announcing these decrees, he expresses the conviction that the only true and Almighty God, had, by special interposition in his favour, given him victory over the Evil Powers, in order that his own worship might, by his means, become universally diffused. In one of them he says: "I invoke thee, Lord of the Universe, holy God! for by the leading of thy hand, have I undertaken and accomplished salutary things. Everywhere, preceded by thy sign, have I led on a victorious army. For this reason, I have consecrated to thee my soul, deeply imbued with love and with fear. I sincerely love thy name, I venerate thy power, which thou hast revealed to me by so many proofs, and by which thou hast confirmed my faith."

With regard to the adherents of the old worship, he says: "Let the followers of error enjoy the liberty of sharing peace and tranquillity with the faithful. The improving influence of intercourse may lead them into the way of truth. Let each act according to the dictates of his own soul. Let no one molest his neighbour concerning that which is according to his convictions. If possible, let him profit him by the knowledge he has gained; if not possible, he should allow him to go on in his own way. It is one thing to enter voluntarily into the contest for eternal life, and another to force one to it against his will. Let those who remain strangers to the holy laws of God retain their temples of falsehood, since they wish it." He adds that "the mighty dominion of error was too firmly rooted" to admit of the universal prevalence of Christianity.

The first instance in which he caused any temples to be destroyed, or old forms forcibly suppressed, was in the case of certain temples of Venus, where licentious rites were practised. The site of one of these, in Phœnicia, was occupied by a new church. There were no Christians in the place; but he sent bishops and a body of the clergy there,

and bestowed large sums on them for the support of the
poor; on the ground that the people might be converted
to the new faith by doing good to their bodies. The famous
old Temple of Æsculapius, at Ægæ, was destroyed, on the
charge that impositions were practised on the people by
cures pretended to be miraculous. He took many objects
of Art from these temples to adorn the imperial palace, or
bestow upon his friends. Some of the images were found
to be so constructed that the priests could enter and speak
through them. These were exhibited to convince the people of the deceptions that had been practised upon them.
In order to advance Christians to office, a law was not long
after passed forbidding public functionaries to sacrifice to
the gods. The erection of any new images was likewise
prohibited.

The letters and proclamations of Constantine, after his
victory, generally betray that temporal success was to his
mind the strongest evidence of the truth of Christianity.
With this view of the subject, his recent good fortune could
not do otherwise than increase his zeal for his adopted faith.
He studied the Hebrew and Christian Scriptures, delivered
theological discourses, and considered himself competent
to decide controverted points of doctrine. In this kind of
warfare it may be fairly presumed that the successful soldier was guided by his bishops. In his discourses, he
quoted the Sibylline Prophecies in proof of Christianity;
and placed peculiar reliance upon the one purporting to be
composed six hundred years after the Deluge, in the form
of an acrostic, making the words, Jesus Christ, Son of God,
Saviour.

Virgil, who died nineteen years before Christ, was a sort
of poet laureate to the imperial family of Augustus, from
whom he received munificent presents. The poets, from
time immemorial, had sung of a Golden Age, under the
reign of Saturn. They said when the Iron Age commenced, Astrea, Goddess of Justice, departed from this
earth, and was placed in the Zodiac, as the constellation of
the Virgin; they predicted that the reign of Saturn would

return, and the Virgin Astrea again live upon the earth. During the peaceful and prosperous reign of Augustus, Virgil wrote an Eclogue, dedicated to his friend Pollio, embodying this universal prophecy. He coupled it with the birth of a wonderful child; which scholars suppose to be a complimentary allusion to some infant about to be born in the imperial family. He says: "The last age, prophesied by the Cumæan Sibyl, comes. The great procession of centuries begins anew. Now the reign of Saturn and the Virgin returns. Now a new race is sent from the high heaven. Only be thou propitious, O chaste Lucina,* to the infant boy, by whom the Iron Age shall first cease, and the Golden shall begin throughout the world: then may we say thy own Apollo reigns. In thy consulship, Pollio, this grace of our time shall enter, and the great months shall set forward. * * * * * * He shall partake the life of the gods, shall see heroes and demi-gods associated, shall himself be seen by them, and shall rule the tranquillized world with his father's virtues. For thee, boy, the earth shall spread out her offerings. * * * Goats shall of themselves bring home their distended udders, and herds shall not fear the huge lion. Thy cradle shall yield fragrant flowers. Serpents and treacherous herbs of poison shall perish. When thou shalt be able to read the deeds and praises of thy father, and know what virtue is, the plain shall become yellow with waving grain, purple grapes shall hang on the rough thorn, and rugged oaks distil honey, clear as the dew. * * Every land shall produce everything. The soil shall not feel the harrow, nor the vine the pruning-hook; the fleece shall no more cheat with artificial hues, but the ram shall imbue his wool with rich purple, or glowing saffron, and the grazing lambs shall be clothed with scarlet. The Fates have said to their distaffs: 'Run off these ages!' Loved offspring of the gods, great child of Jupiter, advance to the exalted honours! for the time is at hand."

* The goddess who presided over birth

The general features of this Eclogue obviously resemble prophecies found in all the Sacred Books, and ancient poems, of the world; while others clearly imply the expected birth of some Roman child of regal rank; and the empress Scribonia was about to become a mother at the time it was written. But Constantine assumed that it predicted the advent of Christ, and the establishment of his kingdom upon earth. The return of the Virgin he supposed to be a prophetical allusion to the Virgin Mary. This idea was adopted by the Fathers of that age, and zealously propagated for centuries.

At that time a very hot controversy was raging between the partisans of Arius and Athanasius, concerning the persons of the Godhead. Constantine, or some mild and judicious bishop, who dictated his epistle, wrote to the contending parties, rebuking them for disturbing the unity of the church by agitating such unimportant questions. He advised them to copy the prudence and moderation of philosophers, who agreed to differ amicably upon abstruse questions, and never discussed them in presence of the ignorant multitude. He reminded them that as they all believed in the same God, and worshipped him after the same manner, they ought to meet in a friendly synod, and not fall into discord about exactness of expression concerning minute distinctions; that each should allow the other individual freedom, and agree to remain united in the common bonds of Christian brotherhood. He soon after issued a mandate summoning bishops from various parts of the empire to meet in council at Nice, in Bithynia, for the purpose of settling disputed questions. He himself met with them, dressed in imperial costume, and took an active part in the proceedings. "He exhorted the bishops not to lay the foundation of schisms, by mutual jealousies, lest they should give occasion to their enemies to blaspheme the Christian religion. He reminded them that unbelievers would be most easily led to salvation if the condition of Christianity was made to appear in all respects enviable. Some might be drawn to the faith by being seasonably supplied with the means of subsistence; others were accustomed to repair to that quarter where they found protection; others were won by an affable reception; others by being honoured with presents; few loved the exhibitions of religious doctrine; few were the real friends of truth. For this reason, they should accommodate themselves to the characters of all; as skilful physicians gave to each man what was likely to contribute to his cure." He acknowledged the supremacy of the ecclesiastical power, in all matters connected with the church, by taking a seat lower than the bishops. Eusebius even goes so far as to say that he waited for their permission to be seated. He invited them all to a sumptuous banquet at the palace, where they were received with the utmost deference, as representatives of the Deity. Eusebius, Bishop of Cæsarea, who was one of the guests, describing the scene, says: "One might easily imagine that he beheld a type of Christ's kingdom." Constantine declared that the decrees of this council ought to be regarded as the decisions of God himself; "since the Holy Spirit, residing in such great and worthy souls, unfolded to them the divine will." From this time, the coins and medals of the empire began to be stamped with the Standard of the Cross, bearing the monogram of Christ.

This complete revolution in the wheel of fortune elated some of the bishops beyond the bounds of moderation; and it could not have been otherwise, unless they had been more than human. In their gratitude for such complete security from persecution, and their joy at such rapid and unexpected advancement of power, they seem to have regarded Constantine as more than a mortal. But his faith in Christianity had been confirmed by external means, and it must be confessed that it was rather external in its character. Though he had pledged himself not to put to death Licinius, his sister's husband, he caused him to be executed about a year after he was defeated. The motives for this violation of his oath are variously assigned by his friends and enemies. Not far from the same time, and after he

had manifested so much interest in Christianity at the
Council of Nice, he caused the young Licinius, his sister's
son, to be put to death, from motives of political jealousy.
Crispus, his own son, by his first wife, a young man of distinguished talent and bravery, was also suddenly executed,
without public trial.   Secret treason was the excuse given
for this dark deed; but of that there was no proof.   Some
attributed it to the emperor's jealousy of his son's great
popularity; others said it was domestic jealousy, the empress Fausta having accused her step-son of avowing a passion for her.   Fausta herself disappeared soon after.   The
rumour went abroad that Helena, mother of Constantine,
discovered that she had brought a false accusation against
Crispus, in order to advance the interests of her own sons;
and that the emperor had revenged himself by causing her
to be suffocated in a hot bath.   This last crime is doubted
by some historians, who find traces of Fausta's existence
some time after her alleged death.   A veil of mystery was
thrown over these transactions at the time, and the truth
cannot now be discovered.   It is, however, certain that
they produced an effect on the public mind very unfavourable to Constantine.   Of course, his own enemies, and the
enemies of Christianity, were ready to utter sarcasms on
the religion of a man who had put to death his brother-in-
law, his nephew, his son, and his wife, while making the
greatest professions of piety.   The populace of Rome betrayed signs of disapprobation; and some went so far as to
fasten on the gates of the palace verses in which he was
compared to Nero.   These indications of unpopularity are
supposed to have caused his determination to remove the
seat of government to Byzantium; to which he gave a
Greek name signifying the City of Constantine; in English, Constantinople.   In the embellishment and consecration of this new Capital, there was the same intermixture
of the new and the old, which had characterized the beginning of his reign.   Statues of the gods were brought
from all parts of the empire.   Images of Castor and Pollux
surmounted the Hippodrome.   The Goddess of Fortune

was placed in a shrine on one side of the Forum; and on the other was Cybele, deprived of her symbolic lions, and in the attitude of a suppliant, as if praying for the public prosperity. When the city was consecrated, the emperor, accompanied by a vast procession, rode through the principal streets in a splendid chariot, carrying a golden statue of Fortune with a cross in her hand; and it was decreed that his own statue, thus holding the golden image, should be annually brought to the foot of the throne to receive homage from the reigning emperor. In one part of the city, a statue of Apollo stood on a column of three intertwisted serpents. Another, of colossal size, was placed on a tall column of marble and porphyry, with a globe and sceptre in its hands. The head of Constantine himself was substituted for that of the deity who had been regarded as the guardian of his youth. No new temples were erected, but the old ones remained open for worshippers. Some Christian churches were built, but he did not manifest so much zeal in the work, as at a later period of his reign. When Rome was a republic, she had dedicated temples to Faith, Modesty, and Peace. Constantine imitated the example, by dedicating one of his new churches to Sophia [Wisdom], and another to Eirene [Peace]; names with which no fault could be found by the votaries of any religion. One of the most splendid was dedicated to the Archangel Michael.

A distinguished philosopher, named Sopater, who had been a disciple of Jamblichus, and afterward head of the same school, took up his residence in Constantinople, soon after it became the Capital. Some of the Christian bishops were the intimate friends of Constantine; and one of the most learned of the Fathers, named Lactantius, had been chosen to educate Crispus, his unfortunate son. The Platonist was soon admitted to equal intimacy; and it was said he cherished hopes of retarding, if not averting, the downfall of the old worship. Constantine delighted in his conversation, and on public occasions often caused him to sit by his side. This soon excited jealousy on the part of

the Christian leaders, lest his influence should be success-
fully exerted over the emperor, if not decidedly in favour
of the old religion, at least in favour of an eclectic impar-
tiality between the old and the new. Constantinople depended on foreign countries for grain, and it chanced that
adverse winds long detained the Alexandrian ships, on
which reliance was placed for a supply. Theurgy was at
that time much practised by the degenerated school of philosophers; and a murmur arose among the populace that
Sopater chained the winds by magical arts. Famine threatened the city, and it was a favourable opportunity to exaggerate any report to his disadvantage. The favourite became so odious, that when the emperor entered the theatre,
the people received him without their usual acclamations.
Whether he believed that magic had power over the winds,
or whether alarm for his own popularity induced him to
sacrifice a friend, is unknown. History merely records that
the unfortunate Platonist was forthwith beheaded.

The fluctuating course pursued by Constantine gave rise
to doubts concerning the depth and earnestness of his convictions, of which votaries of the old worship were exceedingly ready to avail themselves. It was currently believed
and reported by them that remorse for the hasty murder
of his innocent son was what finally settled the question in
his mind. In his affliction, they said he began to lean
toward the religion of his youth ; but when he consulted
the priests, they told him the gods had prescribed no rites
by which such a crime could be expiated. Others said he
sought the same relief from Sopater; but the doctrines of
Platonism offered no atonement for the guilty. But Christians, they said, assured him that the blood of Christ was
sufficient to wash away all sin; and that however criminal
he might have been, faith in its efficacy would secure to
him an immortal crown.

Little is known concerning Helena, the mother of Constantine. Some say she influenced him in favour of Christianity, others that he was the cause of her conversion.
However that might be, her zeal in the cause became very

conspicuous. Pilgrimages to holy places were favoured by
the example of all the East. Attended by a devout train
of men and women, she undertook a pilgrimage to Jerusalem. An empress, who was seeking for interesting localities to endow with her wealth, could not fail to find them
in abundance. Christian devotees in Jerusalem eagerly
pointed out to her where Christ was born, where he performed various miracles, where he was crucified, and where
he ascended. The footsteps of the patriarchs, the prophets,
and the apostles, were traced with equal precision. The
empress-mother gazed on them all with undoubting reverence, and gave munificent donations to erect churches and
chapels on the consecrated spots.

Constantine also made a visit to the Holy City, with
Eusebius, Bishop of Nicomedia. Romans had built a temple to Venus on Mount Calvary, which he ordered to be
immediately demolished. When the earth and stones were
removed, it was said and believed, that the workmen discovered the identical tomb of Joseph of Arimathea, in
which Jesus had been buried. Near by, was found not
only the cross on which Christ had suffered, but also the
crosses of the two thieves, and the inscription written by
Pilate, in three languages. It was not the tendency of that
age to inquire whether such large and heavy instruments
of punishment were likely to be buried with the criminals.
The True Cross, thus discovered, was consigned to the care
of the Bishop of Jerusalem, who put a portion of it into a
silver case, and divided the remainder into small fragments
to be sold to pilgrims. The nails of the cross, the crown
of thorns, and the spear that pierced the side of Jesus were
likewise found. It is said that Constantine placed these
holy nails round the head of his colossal Apollo, at Constantinople, so arranged as to form a glory, in imitation of
the halo usually represented round the God of the Sun.
Over the place where the tomb was discovered, he caused
a magnificent church to be erected; at first called the
Church of the Resurrection, afterwards of the Holy Sepulchre. The interior was inlaid with costly marbles. The

dome was supported by twelve pillars, surmounted with
silver vases, in commemoration of the Twelve Apostles.
The roof was overlaid with gold, which shed a resplendent
light. A court within the church contained the tomb, over
which was erected a chapel blazing with gold and gems.
Near Hebron, an oak tree was pointed out as the spot
where Abraham had an interview with the angels. Some
polytheistic worshippers had sacred traditions connected
with it, and had been accustomed to perform religious
ceremonies there in honour of the Spirits that appeared to
Abraham; whose name was held in reverence by several
Asiatic nations. Constantine caused the place to be purified, and a church to be erected there. He also built
splendid churches at Antioch and Alexandria. At Rome,
he erected a superb church on the Vatican Hill, occupying
the site of the circus and gardens of Nero, where early
Christians had died of lingering tortures. According to
current tradition, the edifice stood on the very spot where
Peter suffered martyrdom. Within the enclosure of the
imperial palace at Rome, called the Lateran, he built a
church dedicated to the memory of the Apostle John. In
his zeal to propagate the new faith, it is said he offered a
white baptismal garment, and twenty pieces of gold to
every convert; and that twelve thousand men, with a proportionate number of women and children, were baptized
in one day at Rome. He granted an appeal from the civil
courts to the bishops, whose decisions were to be in all
cases binding. He frequently invited the clergy to his own
table, even when they were very meanly clad. He never
went a journey without taking a bishop with him; thinking it made him more secure of prospering in his undertakings. He was accustomed to say that if he should see
a bishop engaged in any sinful or unbecoming action, he
would cover him with his own imperial robe, rather than
have others see him. He affirmed that even Grecian oracles were compelled to testify in favour of Christians; that
after the advent of Christ, Apollo no longer presumed to
speak through a human voice in the temple, but spoke

from a deep dark cavern, as if he had hidden himself. Being asked why he did this, he replied: "Because of the just men who are now on the earth." When Diocletian inquired who those just men were, one of the priests of Apollo, who stood by, answered: "They are Christians." Constantine declares he was one of the company, and heard it; and he calls upon God to witness it.

He passed a law to defend Christian converts from Judaism, but he found it more difficult to shield them from their own dissensions. Council after council was called to settle theological disputes, and still the strife went on. He wrote to the Bishop of Alexandria, exhorting him to pursue a peaceful and charitable course toward those who differed from him with regard to the Trinity. But he satisfied the demands of the bishops by passing very severe laws against Manicheans, Marcionites, and other Gnostic sects, whose property was confiscated. For many years before his death, he would not allow his image to be placed in any of the temples. He caused his statue to be made with a cross in his hand, inscribed with the motto: "By this he conquered." Medals and pictures representing him in a devout attitude of Christian worship were distributed throughout the empire. Other and better fruits of Christianity are also recorded of him. In times of public distress, it had been common to expose young children, to sell them into slavery, or put them to death. By advice of Lactantius, it was proclaimed that the emperor considered himself the father of all such children, and would support them at his own expense. He encouraged the sending of missionaries to distant lands. He diminished taxation, ameliorated the penal laws, and made regulations for the health and comfort of prisoners; saying it was his duty to secure a man who was accused of crime, but not to injure him. When slaves were divided among the heirs of a deceased person, he forbade the separation of husbands and wives, parents and children; a humane regulation, which had been previously neglected.

Though his adhesion to Christianity was finally unquali

fied, he did not partake of its sacraments till his last illness.
No one was allowed to taste the Lord's Supper till he had
passed through the purifying process of baptism; and as
that was supposed to wash away all sin, perhaps Constantine thought to make sure of eternal salvation by deferring
a rite so efficacious until he was past the danger of committing further sin.   Whatever might have been his motive, he was not baptized until a short time before his
death; which took place when he was sixty-three years
old, after a reign of thirty-one years.

In the honours paid to his memory, there was the same
mingling of religions which had characterized a large portion of his life.   His polytheistic subjects followed the old
custom of placing the emperor among the deities by solemn
ceremonies.   The medals issued after his apotheosis bore
his name, with his title "God;" and on the reverse side
was the monogram from the Labarum, forming the name
of Christ.   Some of the medals represented him seated
in the chariot of the Sun, drawn by four horses, while a
hand issued from the clouds to take him up among the
demi-gods.   Cotemporary Christian writers, very naturally
blinded by gratitude, exaggerated his really great merits,
and eulogized him without limit, and without discrimina-
tion.   The eastern churches kept an annual festival in
honour of his memory, and added to his name: "Equal to
the Apostles."

Niebuhr, in his History of Rome, says: "Men judge
him by too severe a standard, because they look upon him
as a Christian; but I cannot regard him in that light.   The
religion he had in his head must have been a strange compound.   The man who had on his coins, Sol invictus, [The
Sun invincible,] who worshipped polytheistic deities, and
consulted the haruspices, while at the same time he shut
up temples, built churches, and interfered with the Council
of Nice, certainly was not a Christian."   Mosheim, in his
History of Christianity, supposes that Constantine at first
regarded Christ merely as one of the gods, who had power
to confer prosperity and happiness on those who honoured

him, and to punish those who contemned and persecuted him; but that being afterward better instructed in Christianity, he became a sincere convert.

The outward benefits he conferred on the Christian religion were perhaps balanced by the rapid degeneracy they induced. It became a matter of policy to profess Christianity. All classes, princes and beggars, flocked into the church, without serious conviction, or proper instruction; and all supposed that the magical waters of baptism had washed away their sins. Eusebius reckons as one of the greatest evils of that period the indescribable hypocrisy of many who pretended to be Christians merely to advance their own interests, and who abused the confidence of the emperor by their false show of zeal.

CHRISTIAN SECTS.

Having thus rapidly traced Christianity from its obscure origin, through outward perils, I will, as briefly as possible, describe the dissensions which arose among themselves.

At the outset, Christians had no creed. In the time of Irenæus and Tertullian, formularies of faith were written, on purpose to exclude the Gnostics; and catechumens were required to give public assent to them before they were baptized. The Gnostic sects were therefore outside the church. They formed a link between Christianity and the old Egyptian, Persian, and Grecian ideas, and were one of the agencies by which many of those ideas glided into the new religion, and became permanently incorporated with it. The heterogeneous elements heaved and tossed wildly, before they could be definitely settled into a theological form. It would fill volumes to explain all the subdivisions of sects on minor points of faith or practice. Asceticism, growing out of the old Oriental idea that Matter was the origin of evil, began to manifest itself very early in various forms. There was a sect called Abelites, who abstained from matrimony, in order to avoid propagating original sin. They adopted the children of others, and brought them up in their own principles. They had great reverence for Abel, because he died unmarried, and childless. The Aquarians used water instead of wine, at the Lord's Supper, and abstained from animal food, because they thought it wrong to stimulate or please the senses. The Apostolics were also called Renouncers, because they considered it wrong to possess any property, and therefore held all things in common. They allowed no married person to belong to their churches.

QUARTODECIMANS.—One of the earliest and most troublesome schisms in the church, after the question of circumcision was at rest, related to a mere external observance. The first Christians continued to keep the Passover as a Jewish custom. They ceased to sacrifice a lamb, because they observed the festival in commemoration of Christ, of whom the Paschal Lamb was supposed to be a type; thus Paul says: "Christ, our Passover, is sacrificed for us." Jews observed the first day of the first full moon, after the vernal equinox, on whatsoever day of the week it happened to fall; and Christians, in the Eastern part of the Roman empire, long continued to do the same. In the Western part, they formed the habit of keeping it the Sunday following the first day. They did this partly because Christ rose on Sunday, and partly because there was an increasing disposition to distinguish themselves from the Jews. Thus it happened that while some churches were mourning for the crucifixion, others were rejoicing over the resurrection. In the second century, the dispute grew very warm. The Bishop of Rome excommunicated the Eastern churches. Polycarp remonstrated with him, and alleged that the day they kept was the same he had himself observed with the Apostle John. Synods were in vain called to settle it. Those who kept the fourteenth day were called Quartodecimans, and regarded as heretics by the churches of Italy. It was considered a question grave enough for the intervention of the emperor; and Constantine sustained the Council of Nice in deciding that it should always be kept on the Sunday following the full moon.

MONTANISTS.—In the middle of the second century, Montanus, an illiterate bishop in Phrygia, preached a stern and fervid kind of spiritualism, which attracted many followers. In most respects, his doctrines were the same as those of the Christian Church. But he differed in maintaining that every true believer in Christ, whether man or woman, received direct inspiration from the Holy Ghost; in support of which he quoted Joel's prophecy: "I will pour out my Spirit upon all flesh; and your sons and your daughters shall prophesy." He considered Judaism as the infancy of religion, Christianity as its youth, and the more advanced state, attained by full and general reception of the Holy Ghost, was its manhood. He himself claimed to be an inspired prophet, sent by God to lead the church into a stricter life, and prepare it for the millennium, which he painted in glowing colours, and as nigh at hand. He had prophets and prophetesses in his train, whose wild and passionate preaching excited paroxysms of devotion in themselves and their hearers. This pouring out of the Spirit upon Christians of all conditions, they regarded as one of the strong proofs that the end of the world was approaching. Maximilla, the associate of Montanus in his preaching, said expressly: "After me, no other prophetess shall arise; but the end shall come." Tertullian thus describes one of these inspired women: "There is a sister among us indued with the gifts of revelation by an ecstasy of spirit, which she suffers in the church, during the time of divine service. She converses with angels, and sometimes also with the Lord. She sees and hears mysteries, knows the hearts of some, and prescribes medicines to those who need them." After the assembly was dismissed, her visions were taken down in writing; and much information concerning the invisible world was supposed to be gained from them. Montanus, when describing the prophetic power, represented the Lord as taking away the souls of men, and giving them souls; as saying: "The man is a lyre, and I sweep over him like a plectrum. The man sleeps, I wake." To him, and to his two leading prophetesses, he said God had imparted the fulness of his Spirit; whereas Paul confessed that he only knew in part, and prophesied in part. Epiphanius charges a branch of the Montanists with making women bishops and presbyters; sustaining the custom by Paul's words: "In Christ Jesus there is neither male nor female."

The morality of this sect was very rigid. They considered all recreations and pleasures of the senses sinful. They lived abstemiously, and kept prolonged fasts. Those who devoted themselves to prophecy generally left their wives and husbands; considering a life of celibacy the only way to become perfect recipients of the Holy Spirit. They regarded marriage as a spiritual union, to be continued in another life; therefore second marriages were considered unlawful. They likewise deemed that a marriage was not valid unless performed in a church, in the name of Christ. While they thus reverenced the union of souls, they regarded the earthly relation as a necessary evil, which ought to be conscientiously restrained within certain limits. They considered the rite of baptism so important that they even baptized the dead.

Their preachers were accustomed to make rousing appeals to sinners, denouncing upon them the vengeance of God, and making terrific pictures of eternal torment, in contrast with the most luxurious pictures of Christ's kingdom upon earth. They held human learning in great contempt, and considered the study of philosophy, or classic literature, as a participation in idolatry.

Their leaders forbade them to avoid persecution, or to hold communion with any who did. Those who fled from the storm, or purchased safety by any concession, however slight, were regarded as recreant to Christianity, and enemies of Jesus. Their preachers said: "Let it not be your wish to die on your beds, in the pains of child-birth, or in debilitating fever; but desire to die as martyrs, that he may be glorified who suffered for you." This, combined with eloquent descriptions of the glory and happiness of martyrs, to which the soul could attain by no other process, produced among them such a rage for martyrdom, that they rushed needlessly into danger. They considered themselves the only genuine Christians, and carried on hot controversy with all others, by whom they in their turn were much disliked. Tertullian became a Montanist, and abused, in unmeasured terms, the church he had left. They were subdivided into sects; one of which was accustomed to use bread and cheese at the sacrament. They were for some time a very troublesome element in the church. They encountered a good deal of persecution, and had almost disappeared in the fourth century.

DONATISTS.—The leading characteristics of the Montanists reappeared in a sect which caused far more deadly strife than any that had yet been excited. Donatus, a Numidian bishop, agreed with the church in most matters of faith, but took the ground that no one could be a Christian who had at any time, or in any way, evaded persecution; that no ordination was valid, if performed by such a person; and no person was free from stain who had received the sacraments from such hands. All the bishops of Europe and Asia were pronounced more or less infected with this sin, and thus the true apostolic succession was broken. On this ground, they disputed the election of the Bishop of Carthage, and refused to submit to his authority. They maintained that they were the only true Christians; being the only ones who had not in some way connived at apostacy. Councils were called to decide the matter, but the Donatists treated their decisions with scorn. An imperial decree from Constantine met with the same fate. A military force was sent to compel them to submit to the laws. They were driven into exile, their property was confiscated, and their churches sold or destroyed. Persecution had its usual effect, to increase zeal and strengthen obstinacy. The Donatists defied the army, as they had the bishops and the emperor. Now, for the first time, Christians began to shed each other's blood. The African cities became scenes of massacre and licentious outrage. The Donatists were treated with horrible cruelty, and retaliated with savage barbarity. They exulted in their sufferings, and eagerly rushed upon martyrdom. The church was bent upon subduing or exterminating them, and justified excessive cruelties by the example of Moses and Elijah, who had slain unbelievers by thousands. When Donatists took possession of churches that had been used by their opponents, they washed the pavements, scraped the walls, burnt the altars, and melted the plate; if they found any of the consecrated bread, they threw it to the dogs, with as much horror as if they had been purifying a temple of Venus. They even cast out of their burying-grounds the bodies of those whose practice had not conformed strictly to their views. All who joined them were re-baptized; if bishops or presbyters, they were re-ordained; if men or women pledged to celibacy, they were obliged to renew their vow. In vain Constantine tried to heal the schism by an edict of peace. The warfare continued during his lifetime, and for a long time after. One hundred and seventy-two bishops of Africa belonged to this stern sect. Their discipline and style of preaching resembled the Montanists. They sang fervid hymns to wild and passionate melodies, and fiery outbursts of scriptural eloquence excited their hearers to the highest pitch of enthusiasm. There were at that time swarms of devotees, or monks, called Circumcellions, who wandered about, obtaining subsistence by begging from the peasants. These joined the Donatists in large numbers, and spread consternation throughout the African provinces. At first, they took only what was necessary for their subsistence; but growing bolder, they plundered at will, and punished the slightest opposition with death. Christian priests, whom they took prisoners, were tortured with every refinement of cruelty; churches were demolished, dwellings burnt, and whole provinces desolated with murder and pillage. As monks, they were vowed to perpetual chastity; but the doctrine of spiritual perfection produced the same results as in other ages and countries. The resistance of nature to the arbitrary constraint imposed upon her, combined with the idea that saints could not be polluted by any external actions, resulted in paroxysms of furious licentiousness. Captives taken in war were subjected to the most brutal outrages, and their army was followed by troops of women raised above earthly contamination by their state of perfected sanctity. Several of the Donatist bishops, finding remonstrances altogether fruitless, applied to the civil power for aid against these lawless allies, who refused to be governed or restrained by the church. The government resorted to various modes of treatment at different times. Constantine, having in vain tried to compel them to submit, had recourse to a system of complete toleration, and wrote to them in a strain of kind, paternal advice. His successor attempted to win them over to unity with the established church by expostulation and liberal distribution of money; to which they scornfully replied: "What has the emperor to do with the church?" The members of their party were forbidden to receive any present from the reigning powers. The corruptions resulting from the union of the church with the state became the favourite theme of their eloquence. They traced all degeneracy to the splendour and luxury of the times, and railed at bishops whose ambition or avarice led them to flatter princes. They declared that the Lord had sent them as his delegates to purify the church, and redress the wrongs of the oppressed. Their leaders were called Captains of the Saints, Sons of the Holy One. Sometimes they dropped their own names, and took religious ones; such as Deum Habet, God with him. Each carried a huge club, which they termed an Israelite, and their battle cry was, Praise be to God! The Christian doctrine of human equality and brotherhood, they attempted to enforce with blind and reckless violence. They released all debtors from prison, and cancelled all debts. Any creditor who refused to comply with their demands, was sure to have his property destroyed, and was fortunate if he escaped with his life. They gave freedom to all slaves who resorted to them, and revenged whatever cruelties they had suffered. If they met a wealthy man riding, they compelled him to walk, and placed his slave in the chariot.

All conciliatory measures having failed, force was again employed against them, but only served to kindle their zeal into a more furious blaze. Many of their bishops and clergymen were put to death, and horrible tortures were inflicted on the Circumcellions who were taken prisoners in battle. These outrages were fiercely retaliated on all of their opponents who came into their power. They rushed upon danger with savage joy, impatient for the glorious crown of martyrdom. They profaned temples by unclean acts, interrupted festivals, broke statues, demolished churches, and carried off the church plate, on purpose to get executed. If other means failed, they sometimes resorted to self-inflicted martyrdom. Having indulged awhile in feasting, and all kinds of revelry, they appointed a day, and in the presence of assembled friends, they burned themselves, or threw themselves from a steep precipice, or employed some one to kill them. They justified these proceedings by the example of Razis, as recorded in the Book of Maccabees. They never used swords, because Peter was commanded to put up his sword; therefore, they beat out the brains of their victims with a club.

In process of time, the Donatists split into sects; the small fractions still claiming to be sole depositories of religious truth, the only faithful disciples, whom Christ would find worthy to share his kingdom, at his second coming. This schism raged, more or less furiously, in Africa, for three hundred years, and ceased only with Christianity itself in those regions.

THE LOGOS.—Another schism, more universal, and which became scarcely less virulent, seemed for a time destined to rend the church into fragments. It has been already stated how the doctrine of the Logos conflicted in many minds with preconceived ideas of the unity of God. Christians called Ebionites, who retained the original Jewish ideas, did not accept the doctrine at all; nor does it appear that they ever heard of it. The idea of The Word of God, by which creation was produced, was familiar to every reader of Genesis; and Jews were accustomed to speak of him under the name of Memra; but they never seem to have associated him with their ideas of the Messiah. Some of the Ebionite Christians thought Christ was a reappearance of Adam, who was the Son of Adam Kadman, the Primal Man; and in that sense, perhaps, they called him the Son of Man. But they generally considered him like other mortals in all respects, except superior holiness and stricter adherence to the Law of Moses. This idea of a merely natural birth appeared also among various Gentile sects. The Gnostics supposed that Jesus was a man, but so pure that some great Spirit, emanating from the highest existences, had descended and united with his soul at baptism. About a century before the time of Constantine, Artemon, at Rome, gave name to a sect who denied the divinity of Christ. Theodoret says: "Artemon taught that Christ was a mere man, born of a virgin, and excelling the prophets in virtue. He said the Apostles taught this; but those who came after them made a God of Christ, who was not God." His followers spread into Syria, and continued to propagate their doctrines till far into the third century.

Paul of Samosata, Bishop of Antioch, in the middle of the third century, maintained that the Logos bore the same relation to God, that reason did to man; that it was a divine attribute, not a person. The doctrine of the incarnation he rejected altogether. He said that the divine reason, or wisdom, operated in Christ in a more perfect manner than it ever had in any other man; so that he was the Son of God in a sense that no other medium of divine wisdom had ever been. He denied that he existed before his human birth. By his being with God before all time, he merely understood that his existence was predes-

tined in the reason, or wisdom, of God. Paul had powerful opponents and zealous friends. After a contest of a
few years, he was finally obliged to yield to the decision
of the Bishop of Rome, by whom he was deposed for
heresy.

Marcellus, Bishop of Ancyra, and Photinus, Bishop of
Sermium, were deposed for teaching similar doctrines in
the fourth century. Athanasius says: "Their followers
denied the preëxistence of Christ, his divinity, and his
everlasting kingdom." Other Fathers describe them as
teaching that the "Logos was in God, as his reason or
wisdom;" that "he was a divine energy inhabiting him
who was the son of David; not a subsisting person." Eusebius says: "They gloried in acknowledging but One
God." Photinus is eulogized as a man of genius, learning,
and powerful eloquence. He was persecuted and condemned solely for his doctrines. His moral character stood
very high. Hilary says: "Though excommunicated, he
could not be removed, on account of the affection the people had for him." Sozomon says: "Though banished, he
continued to defend his opinion, and wrote books in Greek
and Latin, to prove all opinions false except his own."
Jerome says: "He endeavoured to revive the Ebionite
heresy, and wrote many volumes, chiefly against the heathen." Basil requested that persons might be sent from
Rome to condemn the heresy of Marcellus, which had infected some of the leading men in his own diocese, and was
gaining many proselytes in Asia Minor. The Fathers
record that heretics boasted the number of books written
by these men. But none of them have come down to our
times; being diligently destroyed, according to the usual
practice. There was also a sect founded by one Theo-
dotus, a leather-dresser. They believed that Christ had
grown up from the beginning under the special guidance
of the Holy Spirit; but they complained that the distance
between him and God had not been sufficiently marked by
the church; that he was a man, on whom God had bestowed his wisdom in larger measure than on any other

messenger he had sent, and therefore he was preëminently called the Son of God.

Against those who maintained Christ was merely a holy man, their opponents cited passages to prove that Peter, Paul, and John, acknowledged him as God, and that he himself declared he was one with the Father. They sustained the extreme antiquity of the doctrine by reference to the oldest church teachers and the most ancient hymns. Pliny's letter is also evidence that the Christians in Bithynia worshipped Christ as God, in the time of Trajan. Some went so far as to assert that Christ was the one undivided, Supreme God; that he was called the Son merely with reference to his manifestation in a human body; that Jehovah was God invisible, and Christ was the same God visible. In proof of which they quoted the words of Jesus: "He that hath seen me hath seen the Father." This doctrine was as shocking to many pious minds, as the total denial of his divinity; because it involved the inference that God himself was buffeted, scourged, and crucified. In controversy with these opposite modes of preserving the unity of God, the doctrine of the Trinity gradually grew up and unfolded itself.

SABELLIANS.—Sabellius, a Christian teacher at Ptolemais, in the year two hundred fifty, was a zealous advocate for the unity of God; but he differed from his predecessors in admitting the Holy Ghost into his theory. He said, Father, Son, and Spirit, were not persons, but merely different manifestations of the Godhead: a three-fold relation of God to the world. He compared the Father to the substance of the sun; Christ to its illuminating power; and the Spirit to the warmth of life imparted to believers. His followers laid great stress on Christ's saying: "I and my Father are one." This view of the subject attracted many minds, and excited great opposition. Athanasius complains that in some places Sabellians prevailed so much, "the Son of God was hardly preached in the churches." Epiphanius says that "Sabellians, in their zeal for the unity

of God, would ask plain simple men, 'Well, my friends,
have we one God, or three Gods?' And when a pious
person, not sufficiently on his guard, hears this, he is
alarmed, and, by assenting to their error, denies the Son
and the Holy Spirit."

In their eagerness to refute Sabellius, and at the same
time preserve the unity of God, some took the ground that
there was an essential difference between the Father and
the Son; that the Son was inferior in power, and less in
glory. This was substantially the same doctrine taught
by Origen, and other early Fathers of the church.

ARIANS.—Arius, a presbyter in the church at Alexandria, about the year three hundred and eighteen, striving
to refute Sabellius, maintained the distinct personality of
the Son, and the Holy Spirit; but wishing to preserve the
unity of Deity, he maintained that the Father alone was
self-existent; that there had been a time, inconceivably
remote, when he dwelt alone, and undeveloped. That by
an effort of his will, he created his only Son, out of nothing, ages before the world was made. He was the Logos,
the "express image of God," and all other beings were
immeasurably beneath him; but he was inferior to the
Father, and was employed by Him in the creation of the
Universe. He said the Holy Spirit was the first Being created by the Logos, and was as subordinate to him as the
Son was to the Father. The term Logos had been originally
applied to the Word, or Wisdom of God, and was of course
a portion of God. In the time of Arius, it had become generally applied to Christ; and he, adopting it as he found it,
represented the Logos as a distinct created being. Tertullian had declared, half a century before, that there was a
time when God could not be called Father, because there
was a time "when the Son was not." But Arius lived at
a period when the church was coming into established
power; when learned, acute, and energetic men were
labouring with all their ability to lay firmly and securely
a corner-stone of doctrine that would settle forever the

perplexing question, how a being who ate and drank, was tempted and troubled, suffered and died, like mortals, could be a man, and be at the same time God. The statement of Arius brought all the elements of controversy into intense activity. He very soon numbered two bishops, seven presbyters, and twelve deacons, among his followers, and their doctrines spread rapidly throughout Egypt and Syria. In their progress, they gave rise to curious questions whether the Son of God was begotten, or made; whether he was of the same substance with the Father, as Gnostics, and other believers in emanations, had always said, or whether he was of a dissimilar substance. The clergy were greatly annoyed by these new impediments to the unity of the church; and they were the more vexed with Arius, because in controversy with the Gnostics they had very particularly guarded against *separation* of the Godhead; all the Gnostics being ready to admit that Christ was a powerful and glorious Being, but subordinate to God. Those who wished to avoid participation in the quarrel found it exceedingly difficult to pursue a neutral course. Hilary, Bishop of Poictiers, says: "If I preach God according to the Law, the Prophets, and the Apostles, Sabellius is upon me, ready to devour me whole. If, preaching against Sabellius, I acknowledge that the Son of God is truly God, the new.heresy waits for me, and tells me that I preach two Gods." Most of the clergy were bitter in their animosity. Alexander, Bishop of Alexandria, promulgated an anathema against "the impious Arius, the forerunner of Antichrist, who had dared to utter blasphemies against the Divine Redeemer."

After a struggle of six years, the famous Council of Nice was called, in three hundred twenty-five, to settle the question. The public establishment of post-horses was placed at the disposal of the clergy. Three hundred and eighteen bishops assembled, besides a large company of presbyters and deacons; and great was their exultation when the emperor Constantine signified his intention to be present and take part in the discussion. In the course of the argument, some of the members, striving to prove that the Son was not a separate Being from the Father, applied to him the Greek word Homoousios, meaning of the same substance. This proved a battle-cry. The controversy it excited seemed interminable. Discussions concerning the substance of God, and whether the Son was begotten or made, shocked some pious minds, who feared they might tend to produce very material views of Deity. Every wind of doctrine was astir. The Council was in session two months. At last it was decided that Christ was "the only Son of God; begotten, not made; consubstantial with the Father; through whom everything has been made in heaven and on earth; that he was God of God, light of light, very God of very God;" that there was a substantial, indissoluble union between the perfect God and a perfect man; that this mode of existence could not be explained by human language, or illustrated by human ideas; it was to be believed, not understood.

The opponents of Arius were completely triumphant. His confession of faith was torn to pieces in his presence; his writings were condemned, and an imperial edict was issued commanding every one, on pain of death, to deliver them up to be burned. He was solemnly anathematized by the Council, banished by the emperor, and especially forbidden to enter Alexandria. The verdict was signed by nearly all the bishops. Three, who refused at first, were intimidated by Constantine. Two who persevered in refusal, were condemned with him, and followed him into exile. Eusebius of Cæsarea yielded reluctantly, and finally sent the creed to his diocese with a careful explanation of the word Homoousios, to guard against material ideas of God. This was the first warfare in the church strictly on points of faith; and from this time may be dated the practice of requiring the unquestioning assent of every Christian to articles of belief established by votes of the clergy.

But notwithstanding Arianism was discountenanced by the emperor, and formally condemned by such a powerful

Council, it still continued to spread. Synod after synod was in vain called to suppress it. The emperor's sister, Constantia, was an Arian, and exerted her influence to convince him that Arius was a good man, and ought to be recalled from banishment; and in this she was aided by his friend, Eusebius, Bishop of Nicomedia. Arius also sought to conciliate him by writing another confession of faith. It was principally composed of texts of Scripture; and every one engaged in polemical controversy soon learns that the same words of Scripture may be used by several individuals, to each one of whom they convey a different significance. The string of texts was considered by Constantine a satisfactory acceptance of the creed established by the Council of Nice. Arius was recalled to Constantinople, where a Council had been held in which his party predominated. Alexander, Bishop of that city, refused to allow him to commune with his church. Constantine commanded him to administer the Eucharist to Arius on the following Sunday. The bishop manifested a strong inclination to disobey the imperial mandate. The Arians threatened to force their way into the church. The Homoousians, no longer sustained by the civil power, in which they had lately exulted, prayed to God for the scattering of their enemies. While the bishop was thus kneeling in prayer before the altar, Arius was triumphantly escorted through the principal streets of the city toward the church. On his way, being suddenly seized with pain, he was obliged to leave the procession for a few moments. His friends, after awaiting his return for a time, sought for him, and found him dead. His enemies ascribed it to the vengeance of God, for his "blasphemous heresies;" while his friends whispered of poison. From some of the circumstances, it appears not unlikely to have been a deadly attack of cholera. Athanasius, Bishop of Alexandria, the able leader of the Homoousian party, compared his disease to that of Judas, whose treacherous example he accused him of having imitated, in his readiness to degrade Christ. He was accustomed, ever after, to bring forward the sudden

death of Arius as a sufficient refutation of his heretical
doctrines; an argument likely to have great weight, when
all such visitations were regarded as direct punishments
from Heaven.   The Bishop of Constantinople, relieved
from the presence of his popular rival, set apart a day for
thanksgiving in the churches; but it professed to be for
escape from external violence, not for the death of an
enemy.

The mind of Constantine, though habitually credulous,
was not so affected by this event as to turn again in favour
of the Homoousians.   He became displeased with Athanasius, whom he accused of arrogant behaviour.   He sent
him into banishment, from which he refused to recall
him, till he was on his death-bed; and he then manifested his own predilections by receiving baptism from the
hands of his friend Eusebius, the Arian Bishop of Nicomedia.

Arius seems to have been inadvertently drawn into this
warfare by his zeal to establish the personality of the Logos, in opposition to the theory of Sabellius.   His enemies
have recorded that he was a man of learning, and of blameless morals, graceful in person, fluent in conversation, subtle
in argument, and eloquent as a public speaker; but they
add that ambition and craftiness were concealed under his
quiet and simple manners.   Even if no more than the
favourable portion of the statement were correct, he might
well be considered a formidable antagonist.

For forty years after his death, Arianism and Athana-
sianism were alternately patronized by the government.
Arianism received the sanction of several numerous councils, and during two reigns it was the religion of the imperial court.   The scales of destiny seemed to fluctuate in
deciding whether or not it should be the established creed
of the Christian world.   Which ever party was in power,
the strife went on.   Both aimed at supremacy; and the
extensive power and wealth now employed in the control
of the Christian church was a prize too important to be
divided or risked by mutual toleration.   Sometimes, differ-

ent portions of the empire were divided between the factions. While Athanasius ruled supreme in Alexandria, Antioch and Constantinople were under the sway of Arian bishops. Rival councils were held, one denouncing what the other had decreed. Every election of bishops occasioned popular tumults, which the emperor was often obliged to quell by military force. Athanasius was sometimes hiding himself in deserts and tombs, sometimes escorted through the illuminated streets of Alexandria in triumphal procession.

That the leaders of the two theological parties should have been strongly interested in such abstract questions is easily accounted for, whether we believe they were entirely actuated by a sincere conviction of their importance to the spiritual welfare of the church, or whether we suppose them to have been influenced, more or less unconsciously, by ambition to win a game where the patronage of emperors was the prize. But it seems marvellous that questions so purely metaphysical, so entirely above the reach of human reason, should have proved so exciting to the populace. Gregory, Bishop of Nyssa, describing the state of Constantinople, says: "Every corner and nook of the city is full of men who discuss incomprehensible subjects; the streets, the markets, the people who sell old clothes, those who sit at the tables of the money-changers. If you ask a man who deals in provisions, how much you are to pay for his articles, he replies by dogmatizing on generated and ungenerated being. If you inquire the price of a loaf of bread, you are answered that the Son is subordinate to the Father. If you ask whether the bath is ready, you are told that the Son of God was created out of nothing."

Everything, great or small, was pressed into the service of this polemical war. There were old Greek tunes much in vogue with the populace. Sailors, millers, and almost every class of artisans, had some of these airs, which they habitually sung in the streets, with words appropriate to their various trades. When Christianity began to prevail, some of these tunes were naturally used as vehicles of the new form of religious sentiment. Arius composed hymns adapted to them, which became very popular. Half a century later, Chrysostom found the streets of Constantinople still resounding with his praises of the self-existent Father and the created Son. The heretical sounds were so offensive to his ears, that he trained a band of choristers to attract the populace by singing hymns to the co-equal dignity of the Father, Son, and Holy Ghost.

Adherents of the old worship of course exulted in these dissensions, which betrayed so much uncertainty of faith, and were carried on in a manner little calculated to sustain the claim of a superior moral standard among Christians. These incessant disputes between sects, often about mere hair-splitting distinctions, and the mutual disposition to blacken each other's characters, became such a laughing-stock with the unbelieving portion of the populace, that comic representations of them were given in the theatres of Alexandria, Constantinople, and other cities.

But so many tragic scenes were connected with this prolonged dissension, that one has no heart to smile at such a melancholy waste of intellect and feeling. Constantinople was the stronghold of Arianism. When the Arians were in power, they tolerated all the smaller sects, but maintained unalterable animosity against the Homoousians, whose religious meetings were interdicted. Gregory of Nazianzen, being invited to that city, held meetings at the house of one of his kinsmen. The Arians were provoked by this intrusion on their premises. After much skirmishing of words had mutually passed, each party accusing the other of preaching a plurality of Gods, a crowd of Arians, joined by such portions of the populace as are always ready to mingle in some affray, broke into the meeting and dispersed it by their violence. According to the description of the scene given by their opponents, there issued from the church of Sophia [Wisdom], then an Arian cathedral, a mob of "common beggars, who had forfeited their claim to pity; of monks, who had the appearance of goats, or satyrs; and of women more terrible than so many Jezebels." Much damage was done with sticks and stones, and one man was killed.

An Arian bishop was sent to take the place of Athanasius, in Alexandria. The people opposed him with violence. Military force sustained his claims, and the streets became a scene of tumult and bloodshed. The adherents of Athanasius, compelled by government to submit, avoided any connection with the bishop thus imposed upon them. Vexed by their obstinacy, he sought to compel them to receive the sacrament from his hands. To effect this purpose, he sent many into banishment, and caused some, among whom women were included, to be scourged with rods, or beaten with clubs.

Paul, an adherent of the Athanasian party, claimed to be rightfully elected Bishop of Constantinople. The Arians, who constituted a majority, denied his claims, and supported Macedonius. The dispute spread till the whole city was in an uproar. The Arian emperor Constantius sent troops to expel Paul. The Homoousian portion of the populace rose against them, and fought so savagely, that their commander took refuge in a house. The mob immediately set it on fire. They afterward murdered him, and dragged his mangled body by the heels through the streets. After heaping all manner of insults upon the corpse, they threw it into the sea. When Macedonius, the Arian bishop, came guarded by soldiers, Arians and Athanasians rushed pell-mell to see which could first obtain possession of the cathedral. Three thousand one hundred and fifty persons were killed. Streams of blood overflowed the porticoes and courts of the church, and Macedonius was compelled to pass over heaps of bodies to ascend the episcopal chair. Paul, the deposed bishop, was carried in chains to a wild town in the deserts of Mount Taurus, where he is supposed to have died. The Homoousians sought to avoid all relations with the detested bishop, as they had done in Alexandria. But children were seized and baptized. The virgins of the church were burned with hot iron, or cruelly pressed between boards, to compel them to partake of the sacrament from the hands of an Arian bishop. Other reluctant victims had their mouths forced open with a wooden machine.

Arian bishops, assembled at Sardica, were accused of burning churches, of imprisoning Athanasian bishops, making them suffer with cold and hunger, and wounding them with swords. They published a protest against these charges, in which they, in their turn, accused Athanasius of pillaging Arian churches; slaying the people, even bishops; compelling them, by various modes of torture, to partake of "his sacrilegious communion;" of "raging in a tyrannical manner during the holy season of Easter," and inciting the magistrates to scourge and imprison all who kept it on the day of the Jewish Passover.

It is painful to dwell on these scenes of outrage, so often repeated and so long continued. Behind them seems to rise the mild, benevolent countenance of Jesus, his eyes suffused with tears. And all this was done to settle a question concerning the substance of God! A question forever placed beyond the comprehension of finite minds. If the struggle had been for toleration, the principle of freedom involved would have done much to ennoble the contest, though not to excuse the excesses. But both parties insisted on supremacy, and disdained to accept of anything short of that. Both were zealous, obstinate, intolerant, and violent. We have a more full record of Arian outrages; for they were eventually the conquered party, their writings were generally destroyed, and their story is mainly told by theological enemies. Many good men, on both sides, mourned over scenes so humiliating and injurious to the Christian name. There were various attempts to obtain a truce; and concessions would perhaps have been made and received, had not the unfortunate word Homoousios stood in the way. The inflexible Athanasius would not listen to changing a single letter of the Nicene Creed. If one grain of sand were let into the wall, he foresaw that a stream would pour in and upset the embankment. To preserve the unity and authority of the established church was the ruling object of his life; and he pursued it with a remarkable degree of ability, courage, and perseverance.

The Arians were more pliable. Before the year three hundred and sixty-six, they had published sixteen professions of faith; but none of them satisfied the demands of the Athanasian party. Various shadings of opinion, concerning the degree of resemblance between the Son and the Father, crept in among them; partly originating in a desire to find some ground to meet upon for cessation of hostilities. At last, there arose a party called Anomæans, from Greek words meaning no similarity. They not only denied that the Son was of the same substance as the Father, but declared that there was no similarity between them; that Christ was merely the most perfect of creatures, whose mission it was to conduct other creatures to God. The opponents of Arians cried out exultingly that such a result was the natural consequence of the principle they had established at the outset. Arians themselves were shocked, as sects always are, when any of their members venture to go a little further than themselves have gone. They publicly disclaimed the Anomæans altogether; but they continued to be reproached none the less for the doctrines taught by them. Sects multiplied, and different branches of Arians vilified each other as heartily as they had ever denounced the Homoousians.

THE HOLY GHOST.—At the Council of Nice, the doctrine concerning the Third Person of the Trinity was expressed in very vague and general terms; for it had not as yet taken shape in the minds of men. The Montanists gave him prominence by the continued inspirations they professed to receive directly from the Holy Spirit; and the Arian controversy whether the Son was generated by the Father, and consequently of the same substance with him, naturally gave rise to similar queries concerning the Holy Ghost. Arius regarded him as the first being created by the Son, and as far removed from him in dignity and power, as the Son was from the Father. Afterward, many of the Semi-Arians supposed him to be a sort of Archangel, created by the Son, as an agent for carrying into effect the divine purposes. Some sects regarded him merely as "the sanctifying energy of the Father and the Son;" but he was generally regarded as a personal Being. Gregory of Nazi- anzen, who wrote near the end of the fourth century, says: "Some of our theologians consider the Holy Spirit to be a certain mode of the Divine agency; others a creature of God; others God himself. Others say they do not know which of the opinions they ought to adopt, out of reverence to the Holy Scriptures, which have not clearly explained this point." Macedonius, a Semi-Arian Bishop, denied that the Holy Ghost was any portion of God. He averred that he was a creature; and that the Scriptures contained no sufficient evidence of his divinity. He sustained himself on Paul's assertion: "There is one God, the Father, *of* whom are all things; and one Lord Jesus Christ, *by* whom are all things." The Athanasians denounced him and his followers, as "impugners of the Spirit." The Macedonians maintained their ground, and the sect increased. The con- troversy waxed warmer and warmer, and the church saw in it another warning to establish rigid formulas, and allow reason no room to move in the close fetters of ecclesiastical authority. Before the Council of Nice, the Doxology, "Glory be to the Father, Son, and Holy Ghost," had not been introduced into the churches; but in some places, it had been customary to ascribe "Glory to the Father, *through* the Son, and *in* the Holy Spirit." Indeed, up to this period, ideas concerning the Third Person of the Christian Trinity seem to have been as indefinite as those of the New Pla- tonists concerning the third principle of *their* Trinity, which they called The Soul of the World, and defined to be the animating and pervading principle of all things. A Council of Bishops was called at Constantinople, in three hundred and eighty-one, to define more closely the doctrine of the Trinity. To the Creed of Nice they added: "I believe in the Holy Ghost, the Lord and Giver of life, who proceedeth from the Father; who, with the Father and the Son together, is worshipped and glorified." During the warmth of this controversy with Macedonius, Flavianus of Antioch shouted out, in the midst of the church service: "Glory to the Father, to the Son, and to the Holy Ghost!" The celebrated Basil, Archbishop of Cæsarea, likewise commenced the practice of singing, "Glory to the Holy Spirit!" in his churches; but he complains that he was much blamed for it. He says of his opponents: "They would sooner cut out their tongues, than say, Glory to the Holy Spirit. This is the cause of the most violent and irreconcilable war with us. They say glory is to be given to God, *in* the Holy Spirit; not *to* the Holy Spirit." He adds that it was the subject of universal discussion, "even by women and eunuchs."

After the Council at Constantinople had decided what ought to be believed, it was deemed as heretical to doubt the divinity of the Holy Ghost, as it was that of the Son. Chrysostom says: "He who halts with regard to the Spirit, cannot walk upright with respect to the Son." Gregory of Nazianzen says: "Whoever maintains that any of the Three Persons is inferior to the others, overturns the whole Trinity." Basil the Great says: "To deny the divinity of the Holy Spirit is the sin against the Holy Ghost." The Macedonians, though generally denounced, were admitted to be of exemplary character. Gregory of Nazianzen says: "We admire their lives, though we do not approve their faith."

APOLLINARIANS.—Apollinaris, ordained Bishop of Laodicea, in three hundred and sixty-two, was highly esteemed for his virtues as a man, and his acquisitions as a scholar. He entered zealously into the controversy against the Arians, and sought to explain the Trinity by comparing it with the three-fold nature of man; viz: his rational soul, his sensuous soul, and his body. Origen had taught that Jesus was a perfect man; and that the Logos of God united himself to his rational soul, and thus imbued him with supernatural power. Apollinaris thought such a union implied two persons in Christ; as indeed it was generally objected to, as making four persons in the Trinity. He therefore varied the doctrine by teaching that the Logos constituted the rational soul of Christ; that God himself was united to the sensitive soul and the material body of a man. The superior soul of Christ was the Logos, the fulness of the Godhead; his inferior soul was employed in the meaner functions of mortal life. He taught that Mary was to be revered as the spiritual mother of Christ, but he did not believe that his body was derived from her. He supposed it descended from heaven, and was consequently incapable of passion, change, or decay. His plan of redemption was also peculiar. He said the sensuous soul was always striving against the rational soul; and the *human* rational soul was too weak to subject to its own power this inferior resisting soul. To redeem mankind from sin, it was therefore necessary that an immutable Divine Spirit should enter into the sensuous soul, and take the place of the human rational soul. When the Logos ruled over the lower soul, and brought it into complete subjection to himself, harmony was restored between the higher and lower principles of man's nature, and thus the original destiny of human nature was realized. He maintained that worship was due to the sensuous soul thus united to the Logos in one person; and was accustomed to use such expressions as that "God was born," or "God died."

These doctrines were condemned by the same Council that condemned the Macedonians. Apollinaris, however, formed a congregation of his adherents at Antioch, and appointed a bishop. The sect spread into neighbouring countries, and a society of them existed in Constantinople; but they were never numerous.

PELAGIANS.—Pelagius is said by some to have been an English monk. He resided at Rome in the beginning of the fifth century, when the doctrine had begun to prevail extensively that God had predestined a certain number of human souls to be saved, and a certain number to be damned. He rejected this theory, as alike disparaging to the mercy and the justice of God. He also denied that human souls were implicated in the sin of Adam, and consequently did not admit the efficacy of baptism. He said the will of man was free, and his nature capable of attaining to all the Christian virtues, if he had an earnest purpose to do so; for Divine assistance always came to the aid of human endeavours after holiness. He sought upon all occasions to demonstrate the inefficacy of faith, unless accompanied by works. He wanted to banish mysticism, and to make religion an indwelling principle, for the practical improvement of character. In his time, both clergy and laity had become a good deal corrupted, and he exerted all his influence to raise the standard of morals among them.

Pelagius was a man of great learning, and his theological opponents bear testimony to his unspotted character. Even Augustine, whose doctrines he most diametrically opposed, admits that in conduct he was "eminently a Christian." His opinions excited a lively controversy, in which Jerome was peculiarly violent. He never attempted to form a sect, but his writings influenced many minds. They were pronounced heretical by several synods, anathematized by the Bishop of Rome, and formally condemned by the Council at Ephesus.

NESTORIANS.—After the Arian controversy gave rise to discussions concerning the substance of Christ, the name of Mary became more prominent than it had previously been; and among the emphatic modes of asserting his divinity, it became common to style her the "Mother of God." But this phrase was not pleasing to all ears. Nestorius, Patriarch of Constantinople, in four hundred twenty-eight, was highly esteemed for the austerity of his morals, and celebrated for the fervour of his preaching. One of his presbyters said, in the course of a sermon: "Let no man call Mary the mother of God; for she was human, and

God cannot be born of a mortal." This remark offended some of his hearers, and excited much discussion. When the presbyter was charged with being a heretic, Nestorius defended him, and expressed his own disapprobation of the phrase; alleging that it was unsanctioned by the Apostles, and well calculated to remind people of the genealogies of some of the Roman gods. In the course of his objections, he made the blunt statement that "a child of two months old could not be God." He began with merely disapproving of the phrase then in use, because it seemed to him irreverent toward Deity; but having roused opposition, he found himself compelled to define his position distinctly. Being a devout believer in the divinity of Christ, yet shocked at the idea that God could be born of a woman, he sought to obviate the difficulties that arose in his mind, by supposing that two distinct natures existed in Christ, the one divine, the other human; that they were not united by nature, but by his will. He admitted a spiritual union between the Logos and the mortal man, but by no means a personal union. He said Mary was to be revered, because she had prepared a temple for the Logos to dwell in. This temple was the humanity, which became exalted to divine dignity by unity with the Logos, and formed one Christ; but she was not the mother of the Logos. Thus an angel might be united to a human being at the moment of conception, but the mother of the body was not the mother of the angel.

This theory excited violent animosity. Cyril, Bishop of Alexandria, zealously maintained that the divine and human natures in Christ were indivisible from the moment of conception; consequently, Mary did give birth to God, and ought to be reverenced as the Mother of God. He summoned a synod to anathematize Nestorius. Still more violently was he assailed by Rheginus, Bishop of Constantia, who preached against him as a heretic worse than Cain and the Sodomites. He said the earth ought to open and swallow him up; fire ought to descend from heaven and consume him; the God-Logos, whom he had dared to sever, who had come forth from the flesh of Mary, the Mother of God, would condemn him to an eternity of torment, when he came to judge the wicked. He concluded by saying: "Let us worship the God-Logos, who has condescended to walk among us in the flesh without separating himself from the essence of the Father." A general Council was summoned at Ephesus, in four hundred thirty-one, which decided the question thus: "As in God, the Father, Son, and Spirit are three persons, but one God; so in Christ, the Godhead is one person, and the manhood is another person; and yet they are not two persons, but one person." Nestorius and his adherents were treated with great intolerance and harshness throughout the whole of the proceedings. He was deposed and condemned; and Cyril of Alexandria caused the verdict to be exultingly proclaimed by heralds throughout the city. Nestorius retired to a monastery in Syria. But his enemies, the bishops, fearing his influence on the Syrian churches, obtained an edict of exile from the emperor. He was dragged about by soldiers from one place of banishment to another, till, enfeebled by age and accumulated misfortunes, he died in the deserts of Thebais. The manner of his death is unknown. Persecution followed him beyond the grave. A church historian of the period recorded that "his tongue was gnawed away by worms, and that he went to another world to be gnawed eternally by the worm that dieth not." He was compared to Simon Magus, Porphyry, and Arius. The bishops demanded that all his writings should be burned. An edict was proclaimed to that effect; and any person who ventured to preserve a copy was rendered liable to severe penalties. His followers were forbidden to hold meetings for worship, and were henceforth to be called Simonians, in allusion to Simon Magus. They spread into distant countries, formed large congregations, appointed bishops of their own, and established an independent church.

Every new heresy that was broached produced an opposite new heresy, in the effort to counteract it. In opposi-

tion to Nestorius, Eutyches maintained that Christ had but
one nature; that even his body was of a divine, incorruptible substance, which existed without being created, and
was incapable of passion, pain, or change. He was reproached with believing in a phantom: and in return, he
ridiculed his opponents for ascribing the necessities of human nature, even nutrition and digestion, to the Godhead.
A Council was called at Chalcedon, by which Eutyches
was condemned and excommunicated. He had numerous
followers, who formed a sect called Monophysites, from
Greek words meaning one nature. They maintained that
the divine and human natures were "united in Christ in
one *nature*, without change, mixture, or confusion." The
church asserted that the two natures were "united in one
person, without change, mixture, or confusion:" and this
was established as orthodox doctrine by the Council held
at Chalcedon. It requires an intellectual microscope to discover a difference between the statements: but theologians
have a microscopic vision. The question whether Christ
was *of* two natures, or *from* two natures, disturbed the peace
of the churches for a long time; giving rise to fierce alter-
cations, sometimes resulting in bloodshed. When it was
announced in assembled council that the creed of the church
was settled unalterably, it was received with shouts: "On
this depends the salvation of the world!"

CHILIASTS.—During all these centuries of conflict concerning the nature of Christ's divinity, the believers in an
earthly millennium, called Chiliasts, were also a disturbing
element. Montanists, Donatists, and members of various
sects, preached the doctrine with great zeal. Nepos, a
bishop in Egypt, wrote a book against those who spirit-
ually interpreted the predictions on that subject in the
Apocalypse. His book became a prodigious favourite both
with clergy and laity in that region, and they were ready
to denounce as heretics all who refused to embrace its doctrines. It is refreshing to record some instances where denunciations were met in a spirit of Christian love. Diony-

sius, Bishop of Alexandria, visited the discontented district, in two hundred fifty-five, called the clergy together, permitted all laymen to be present, and for three days listened to all their objections with patience, and answered them with gentleness. He said to them: "On many accounts I loved Nepos. On account of his faith, his untiring diligence, his familiar acquaintance with the Holy Scriptures, and the great number of church hymns composed by him, which to this day are the delight of many of the brethren. And the more do I venerate the man because he has already entered into his rest. But dear to me, above all other things, is the truth. We must love him and agree with him wherever he has expressed truth; but we ought to examine and correct his writings where he seems to be in the wrong." The result produced by this course was very different from the usual experience of councils. The clergy thanked him for his paternal instructions, and his principal opponent acknowledged himself convinced. But Chiliasm long continued to make proselytes in various places. In the fourth and fifth centuries, there were so many prophecies of the near approach of the millennium, and the speedy destruction of the world by fire was preached so zealously, that many people were terrified into bestowing their whole estates upon the church. This happened so often, to the detriment of rightful heirs, that the emperors were obliged to prohibit it by law.

It would have been well for the church if more bishops had been guided by the moderate spirit which influenced Dionysius; for nothing did so much injury to Christianity, as the numerous sectarian contests, carried on with a mutual disposition to vilify each other's characters, and a willingness to seize almost any weapon that was likely to demolish an opponent. The Arians accused Athanasius of murder, and brought a dead man's hand into court to sustain the charge; but the appearance of the man said to have been murdered, and the exhibition of his two hands, threw them into confusion. A woman of infamous character was employed to accuse him of licentiousness; but when the case was brought for examination, she pointed out the wrong man, and thus betrayed herself. Lucifer of Cagliari was a bitter opponent of the Arians; but having started a heresy of his own, he became equally bitter against the church claiming to be orthodox; which he denounced as "the brothel-house and synagogue of Antichrist and Satan." Is it strange that the Romans and the Jews could not easily perceive the divinity of doctrines which bore such fruits as these?

COURSE OF THE ROMAN GOVERNMENT, AFTER CONSTANTINE.

Constantius pursued a less tolerant course toward the old religion, than his father Constantine had done. He destroyed many celebrated temples, and plundered others; giving the rich spoils to Christian churches, or to favourite courtiers. Some of these men, who were suddenly made rich by imperial bounty, gave themselves up to extravagance and dissipation, and brought upon themselves diseases and disasters, which adherents of the old worship were apt to quote as punishment from the gods, for the desecration of their temples. On the other hand, Christian preachers stimulated the emperor to the work of destruction, by reminding him that Jehovah commanded the utter extermination of idolatry, and the death of idolaters. But policy restrained him within more prudent limits. He ordained that certain temples associated with popular games and national festivals should be preserved uninjured; and when he resided in Rome he did not venture to take any measures against the old worship in that city, which continued to be celebrated with all its ancient splendour.

In the controversy then raging among Christians, he, and his brother Constans, who ruled the Western part of the empire, took different sides. Constantius was the patron of Arians, and Constans was the friend of Athanasius. The jealousy between Rome, the old capital of the empire, and Constantinople the new capital, was continually on the increase, and the different characteristics of the two places were perpetually manifested in the opposite sides they took in ecclesiastical disputes. Accusations were heaped up against the able and influential Athanasius. Councils in the West acquitted him; Councils in the East condemned him. Each assumed to be the genuine representatives of Christendom, and anathematized the other. Soon there was civil war between the imperial brothers; Constans was killed, and Constantius reigned supreme. When a Council was called at Milan to investigate charges brought against Athanasius, he copied the example of his father, and met with the bishops to take part in their discussions. But the pampered church had grown strong since the day it hailed the presence of Constantine with so much exultation. In vain the emperor professed to have had a vision from heaven, which commissioned him to restore peace to the distracted church. A scheme of doctrine which he laid before them, in obedience to that command, was rejected by the Western bishops, as tinged with Arianism. They went still further, and maintained that it was wrong for a layman to interfere with ecclesiastical concerns. They demanded a free Council, in which the emperor should not be present, either in person, or by proxy. In fact, they declared the church independent of the State, in all ecclesiastical matters. They refused to condemn Athanasius, or commune with Arians. Moreover, when Constantius concealed himself behind a curtain to listen to some of their debates, he heard himself denounced as a heretic and Anti-Christ. Accustomed to flattery and servility, his rage knew no bounds. He proclaimed himself the champion of the Arians, who, having their turn in power, were not slow to retaliate the wrongs they had suffered under proscription. Athanasian bishops were scourged, mutilated, and tortured in various ways to compel them to conform. Troops of banished prelates were all the time passing through the deserts, making the solitude resound with hymns expressive of their faith and courage. From those

deserts came forth writings, denouncing the emperor as a
tyrant in civil affairs, and Anti-Christ in the churches;
whose object it was to give over to the Devil the world for
which Christ had suffered and died. There was a stubborn
resistance to the imperial edicts, which exasperated the
magistrates, and heated still hotter the furnace of persecution. In the midst of this turmoil of the churches, the son
of Constantine slept with his father, and his cousin Julian
reigned in his stead. Gregory, the Arian Bishop of Alexandria, delivered a funeral oration, in which he said a choir
of angels hovered over Mount Taurus and chanted a hymn
in praise of the departed.

JULIAN.—In the will of Constantine the Great, his brother was mentioned among the heirs of the empire. He
and his family were soon after slaughtered, and Constantius was suspected of having connived at the deed, from
motives of political jealousy. Two little boys, Gallus and
Julian, were saved from the massacre, by the timely interference of a Christian bishop. Their education was intrusted to Eusebius, Bishop of Nicomedia, who appointed
Mardonius as their teacher. This man was of high moral
character, and well versed in all the learning and accomplishments of his time. He inculcated stoical simplicity,
abstemiousness, modesty, and contempt for frivolous pleasures, while he stimulated intellect, and kindled imagination, with the philosophy, poetry, and music of glorious
old Athens. Julian always held the memory of this
teacher in affectionate reverence; and at this early period
of his life he probably imbibed that passionate predilection
for Grecian literature and philosophy, which ever after
characterized him.

This course of education was pursued for eight or nine
years. But when Julian was near fifteen years old, a
change took place, probably from motives of political precaution; for Constantius had no children, and a party
might be formed to raise these young princes to the throne.
They were accordingly conveyed to a fortress in Asia

Minor, and placed entirely under the supervision of Christian priests, who prescribed implicit obedience, midnight watchings, frequent fasts, long prayers, alms to the poor, gifts to the clergy, and offerings at the tombs of martyrs. It is said they were ordained public readers in the church, with a view to prepare them for the priesthood, as the best means of.diverting their thoughts from the possibility of succession to the throne. Gallus was exceedingly obedient to the clergy, and received their instructions with unquestioning faith. But Julian, whom nature had endowed with restless activity of mind, felt the constraint to which he was subjected, and longed for the literary pursuits to which he had become so much attached under the tuition of the accomplished Mardonius. What were his real views with regard to Christianity, at that period, cannot be known. If he felt some instinctive aversion to the religion of those cousins for whose security his father and relatives had been murdered, and himself guarded like a prisoner; and if the generous sympathies of youth were shocked by the fierce recriminations and bloody contests of Athanasians and Arians, there would certainly be nothing unnatural or surprising in the fact. There were some indications that such was the case. Unlike his brother, he manifested little docility in receiving things upon the authority of bishops, and sometimes resolutely disputed their doctrines. When religious themes were given to them for discussion, Gallus defended Christianity, and Julian chose to advocate Grecian philosophy; giving as an excuse that he could better exercise his ingenuity by arguing on the weaker side. Even when the brothers were induced to undertake the pious labour of erecting a chapel over the tomb of the martyr Mammas, the work went on rapidly under the hands of Gallus, but the stones Julian laid were constantly overthrown, as if by some invisible agency. Gregory of Nazianzen says he had this fact from eye-witnesses; and he seems to regard it as a prophetic miracle. Significant of the future it certainly was, since it indicated the state of the young workman's mind.

The empress Eusebia, a kind-hearted, intelligent woman, being herself childless, exerted her influence in favour of the young princes, who had so long been excluded from the society and advantages appropriate to their rank. Gallus received the title of Cæsar, and was appointed to command some provinces in the East. Julian, when he was about twenty years old, was allowed to reside in Constantinople, and afterward in Nicomedia, where he encountered many poets and philosophers attached to the old order of things. They were at that time a depressed minority, banished from their temples, and retired from their schools. Julian was attracted toward them by the associations of his early education, and by the natural sympathy of youth with a class of men proscribed by the majority, and secretly performing those religious rites which their forefathers had celebrated with such solemn and stately pageantry. Libanius the orator, an eloquent advocate of the old religion, was at that time attracting much attention by his lectures. Julian was forbidden to hear him, and of course availed himself, with redoubled eagerness, of every stolen chance to read his writings. The philosophers with whom he formed acquaintance are accused of managing very artfully to obtain influence over his eager mind and impressible imagination. They told of the magical skill acquired by Maximus, one of the last of the New Platonists. They related how he had led them into a temple of Hecate, and when he had burned incense and repeated a hymn, the statue of the goddess smiled. Seeing them astonished by this phenomenon, Maximus told them they should see greater wonders. He uttered some words, and instantly all the lamps lighted up, as if by invisible agency. The philosophers, who described the scene, spoke lightly of magical skill, in comparison with the inward purification of the soul. But the ardent imagination of Julian was kindled, and he started off to Ephesus, to obtain an interview with Maximus, whose venerable appearance, persuasive tones, and fluent conversation, gained his heart at once. With him he drank copious draughts of Platonism, and studied into the allegorical meaning of what poets had said concerning the gods. He also became versed in astrology, and confirmed his faith in the power of the stars. He learned to consult auguries, to evoke Spirits, and to distinguish the signs of their presence. Some of the Christian Fathers relate that Maximus took him into a deep cavern at midnight, where he heard awful sounds, and saw lurid spectres; that Julian, in his terror, involuntarily crossed himself; whereupon the sounds instantly ceased and the Spirits vanished. They add that Maximus adroitly turned aside the effect of the miracle, by saying the gods disliked the presence of such a profane worshipper.

Gallus, having heard something of his brother's pursuits, sent an Arian bishop to counteract the influence of philosophers and magicians. Julian, conscious of being closely watched, dissembled to such a degree, that his enemies accuse him of having been far more zealous in outward conformity to Christianity, than he had ever been. His aversion to the religion professed by his imperial cousin was doubtless increased by a misfortune which befel him at this period. His brother Gallus was accused of treasonable designs, and thrown into prison, where he was soon after beheaded. It is said the young man had governed in a haughty and cruel manner; but whether he deserved his fate or not, Julian was fondly attached to him, and seeing him cut off thus suddenly, without public examination into his conduct, he felt that Constantius was the murderer of his brother, as he had always believed him to be of his father. He himself also was continually harassed by the consciousness of being watched. The popularity he gained by his quick talent, his varied information, his fluent utterance, and courteous deportment, was displeasing to the emperor. He caused him to be arrested, and for seven months he remained in prison, daily expecting to meet his brother's fate. But the kindly counsels of the empress saved his life. He was allowed to retire to Athens, where his wounded spirit again found solace in companionship with scholars, and the calm pursuits of literature and phi-

c*

losophy. The High Priest became his intimate friend, and
he was initiated into the Eleusinian Mysteries, which had
such a powerful effect on his mind, that he became a confirmed and enthusiastic votary of the old worship.

Surrounded by influences so congenial, it was with unfeigned regret he found himself compelled to change his
sphere of action. But Constantius, influenced by the empress, conferred on him the title of Cæsar, summoned him
to command the army in Gaul, and gave him his sister in
marriage. A young man who had lived so much apart
from courts and camps, and devoted himself to philosophy,
seemed likely to gain but few laurels as a warrior. But
it was Julian's nature to enter with all his soul into whatsoever he undertook; and the emperor's jealousy was soon
alarmed by the fame of his military exploits. The ardent
attachment of the army placed him in a dangerous position,
from which he could neither advance or retreat with safety.
Constantius marched to attack him, but died on the way,
and named him his successor.

While Julian commanded the army, fear of his imperial
cousin induced him to attend the Christian festivals, while
he secretly performed the old rites with a few of his attendants. But when he became emperor, his first act was to
proclaim himself a worshipper of the gods, and his first
employment of the treasury was to rebuild and embellish
the temples. Enormous sums were expended to purchase
hecatombs of cattle, and to import rare birds, to be offered
in sacrifice. He was zealous in his attendance on the numerous religious ceremonies, and often performed in person
the most menial offices of the temples; blowing the fire,
bringing the wood, and examining the entrails of victims
with his own imperial hands. The oracles were again consulted with solemn ceremonies. The old festivals were
restored with great magnificence; and being vain of his
eloquence, he delighted in making florid orations to the
people on such occasions. Prayers were offered in the
temples three times a day, and bands of choristers trained
to chant hymns to the gods. He ordered that reverential

silence should be observed in all places of worship. The people were forbidden to receive him with acclamations when he entered a temple, and all persons in authority were required to leave their guards at the door. He received a baptism of blood, called the Taurobolia, the observance of which was supposed to be conducive to the welfare of the state. On this occasion, an ox was sacrificed to the gods, and the sacred blood, passing through a perforated floor, flowed copiously over the person standing beneath to receive it.

The Sun was his tutelary deity, and he believed there was some mysterious affinity between his own soul and the Spirit of that luminary. When a boy he was always singularly attracted by the sunlight, and he regarded it as an unconscious longing after the God to whom he was related. The private chapel in his palace was consecrated to the Sun; but his gardens were filled with altars and statues of all the gods. Many times in the day he might be seen there, employed in acts of worship. Morning and evening, he offered sacrifices and prayers to the Sun, and he rose in the night to worship the Spirits presiding over moon and stars.

There is every indication that these things were done from a sincere conviction of their importance. He always resented any irreverence towards the gods far more than disrespect toward himself. He was accustomed to say "that if he could make every individual richer than Midas, and every city greater than Babylon, he should not consider himself a benefactor to mankind, unless he could reclaim his subjects from their impious revolt against the gods."

His doctrines were the same as those taught by the New Platonists. The poetic stories concerning the gods he regarded as fables, but he supposed they contained a spiritual treasury, which philosophers could unlock by the key of allegorical interpretation. He believed that Spirits of the Stars, and others, employed as messengers between God and man, sometimes inhabited temples on this earth, and even animated their statues, when invoked with suitable prayers and ceremonies. He affirmed that he lived in constant companionship with those Spirits. He said they often waked him by their touch, and he could easily distinguish them by their voices, as well as by their forms. He spoke reverently of the immortality of the soul, concerning which he adopted the Platonic theory; but he alluded to it with timidity, very unlike the triumphant certainty of Christian martyrs. He says: "I am not one of those who disbelieve the immortality of the soul; but that is a secret, which man can only conjecture; the gods alone can know."

He attributed the rapid spread of Christianity to the charity toward the poor, manifested by its adherents; to their burial of the dead; their kindness to strangers; and the general sobriety of their clergy. He strongly urged this example upon the priests of his own religion. He took unwearied pains to seek out men eminent for virtue to fill the office of High Priest, and superintend the inferior priesthood. He gave them orders that in all the towns men most conspicuous for reverence toward the gods, and justice toward their fellow beings, should be selected for priests, without any reference to rank or fortune. They were enjoined not to frequent theatres or taverns; not to appear at public festivals, where women were mixed with the crowd; to associate only with those of virtuous and discreet behaviour; to avoid all reading calculated to inflame the passions; and to abjure the writings of Epicureans, Pyrrhonists, and all other schools of philosophy calculated to produce scepticism on religious subjects. Priests who were guilty of any unworthy conduct, or who "allowed their wives, sons, or servants, to unite with the Galileans" were to be immediately deposed.

He levied a tax in every province for the maintenance of the poor. He distributed large supplies of grain among the priests, and what was left from their own support was to be devoted to charitable purposes. He ordered hospitals to be erected for the sick, and asylums for strangers of all religions, where whosoever needed might find relief; and he so far profited by the ideas he had derived from Christian teachers, that he formed a plan for the general instruction of the people, by means of preachers and schools. In a letter to the High Priest of Galatia, he writes: "That which hinders our Grecian worship from making as much progress as we could wish is the manners of those who profess it. The success so far certainly surpasses our hopes; but we must not stop on our good way. How has this new atheism established itself? It has been by hospitality; by care of the sepulchres, and by all the appearances of an honest and pious life. Order thy priests to keep away from shows, not to get intoxicated in the public places, and to abstain from all infamous trades and professions. Build hospitals. Is it not disgraceful to us to leave our poor without resources, while we cannot see a single mendicant Jew, and while the Galileans collect our poor with their own?"

Julian's aversion to Christianity was manifested in all manner of ways. Though aiming to establish a character for philosophic candour, he could not refrain from an unseemly tone of biting irony, whenever he alluded to them. He excluded Christians from all high offices of the state or army, saying their religion forbade them to bear the sword, either for justice or war. He passed an edict that they should be always called Galileans; and described them as a set of fanatics contemptible to gods and men, by whose obstinate impiety the empire had been well nigh reduced to the brink of destruction. He wrote a book against Christianity, in which he ridicules the Festivals of Martyrs and the reverence for their relics, as "the worship of dead men's bones." He considered the Sun as the glorious representative of the Platonic Logos, and he expressed surprise that Christians should "prefer an invisible to a visible Logos." He continually reproached them for "making a dead man of Palestine their God." He says: "None of the Apostles call Christ God; and he himself does not say it plainly." He ridicules the great efficacy which Christians ascribed to baptism. He says: "It cannot remove leprosy, gout, warts, or any other greater or lesser bodily defects; but lo! it is able to wash away all

the sins of the soul!" He dwelt with stinging sarcasm on
the bitter animosity which different sects manifested toward
each other, and the relentless persecution they practised.

For some centuries, there had been gradually increasing
attention to education in the Roman Empire. In all the
principal towns, professors were appointed to teach gram-
mar, rhetoric, and philosophy. In many places, learned
Christians filled these offices; but Julian forbade them to
teach Greek literature without express sanction from the
magistrates. He assigned as a reason, that Hesiod, Homer,
and all the old historians and orators, had dedicated themselves to the worship of the gods; and that it must be
either shameful hypocrisy, or unprincipled avarice, which
induced Christians to teach what they did not believe,
merely for the sake of making money. He taunted them
with the contempt they were so fond of expressing for
human learning, and added, in his usual tone of irony:
"Let them be content with explaining Matthew and Luke
in the Galilean churches." Some of the Christians, being
thus excluded from the prevailing literature, composed
poems in imitation of Homer and Pindar, in which they
commemorated the deeds of patriarchs and apostles; and
these they taught in their schools.

The monogram of Christ was removed from the Labarum,
and representations of the gods were again placed on the
military standards. A splendid temple was built for the
statue of the Goddess of Fortune, and the Cross, which
Constantine had placed in her hand, was taken away. His
law exempting the Christian clergy from taxation and other
civil burdens, was annulled. The ample revenues, which
he had granted from the imperial treasury, for their support, and for ecclesiastical charity, were transferred to the
old order of priests. Bishops were peculiarly objects of
dislike and jealousy; their influence over the people being
a formidable obstruction in the way of restoring the old
worship.

But with all these symptoms of animosity, Julian prescribed to himself a system of toleration, and made an effort

to practise it. He ordered the governors of provinces to prefer pious men of the old religion, in the distribution of honours, emoluments, or privileges; but never to put Christians to death on account of religion, or allow any injury to be done to them. On one of these occasions, he writes thus: "I hear they do not coerce them. They might be treated like children, who are forced to do their duty; but it shall not be thus. They shall be permitted to infect themselves with this leprosy. A forced worship does not satisfy our gods. They wish to be adored with the heart." Again he writes: "Leave them to punish themselves; poor, blind, and misguided beings, who abandon the most glorious privilege of mankind, the adoration of the immortal gods, to worship mouldering remains, and bones of the dead."

As Constantine had spared neither money nor influence, to induce people to be baptized, so Julian spared neither expense nor favours to tempt them to sacrifice to the gods; both of them inquired no further, if they could but obtain the outward act. Sometimes he paid his soldiers for sacrificing; sometimes he resorted to artifice. When troops passed in review before him, he caused standards, bearing images of the gods, to be placed so near his own person, that they could not pay the customary homage to the emperor, without bowing before the images. Some were caught by this stratagem; others, who were determined to avoid even the appearance of worshipping the gods, passed without making the usual salute; and so were imprisoned and put to death for disrespect toward their prince. Upon one occasion, when he was to distribute donations to the army, he surrounded his throne with statues and consecrated emblems, and ordered a pile of gold coins to be placed on one side, and a heap of frankincense on the other. Whoever passed to receive the money was required to place a portion of the incense in a fire burning on the altar. Many Christian soldiers did this; some of them thoughtlessly, supposing they had merely paid the prescribed homage to the emperor. Afterward, when some

of them were at dinner, and made the customary sign of
the cross over their cups, before they drank, they were
asked how they could do that, when they had publicly abjured Christ. When this was explained to them, they
rushed into the market-place, proclaiming: " We are Christians! We are Christians! If our hands are guilty, our
hearts are innocent." They surrounded the palace, threw
down the coins, and cried out: " The emperor has deceived
us. Give the gold to others, who will have no cause to
repent of it. As for us, we value Christ above all things."
For this breach of discipline, they were led to execution,
and manifested the utmost eagerness for martyrdom. But
a messenger from the emperor put a stop to the bloody
scene, and they were merely punished with banishment.

When Julian commanded the reconstruction of demolished temples, he did not pay for it from the imperial
treasury, or indemnify those who had legally come into
possession of the land, or buildings erected thereon, as
Constantine had done with regard to the churches. He
gave orders that Christians accused of pillaging the temples, or of assisting to destroy them, should be compelled
to pay for rebuilding them. Nearly all the work of destruction and plunder had been done by permission of his
cousin Constantius, whom he seems to have regarded with
so much aversion; and perhaps that circumstance blinded
his usual clear sight of justice. The oppressive edict fell
very heavily on the Christians, and many innocent people
were the victims of false accusations. It required immense
sums to make the required restitution in all parts of the
empire; for during the forty years that Christianity had
basked in the sunshine of imperial favour, the old religion
had suffered much at their hands. Zealots had urged upon
the sons of Constantine the great merit of imitating God's
chosen people the Israelites, in their zeal to exterminate
idolatry. They said: "O ye most religious emperors, destroy without fear the ornaments of the temples. Coin the
idols into money, or melt them into useful metal. Confiscate all their endowments for the advantage of the govern-

ment. By your recent victories God signifies his sanction to your hostility against the temples." Where such a spirit existed, fanaticism would of course make wild work in some places, without waiting for legal authority. Indignation had lain smouldering in the hearts of the old worshippers, and now that they had a return of power, they were generally disposed to force restitution, without much consideration whether the penalty fell on the guilty or the innocent. Disputes everywhere arose concerning the execution of the edict. The passions of men were excited to a terrible degree; and in some places, the most horrible atrocities were committed against the Christians. The Fathers tell of murdered bodies dragged through the streets, pierced by the spits of cooks, and the distaffs of enraged women, and at last thrown to the dogs. Marcus, Bishop of Arethusa, was accused of having aided in the destruction of a temple, and required to make compensation. He was poor, and could not have done it, if he would. But in order to compel him to raise the money, they scourged the aged prelate, tore his beard, anointed his body with honey, and hung it up in the sunshine, a prey to tormenting insects. Even in that situation, he gloried in the destruction of idols, and insulted his persecutors. He was rescued from their hands, and was afterward almost worshipped as one of the holy Confessors. The emperor was reminded by his friends that the multiplication of such examples of constancy would be very bad policy. It is true, he did not order such barbarities, nor did he ever give them his sanction; but he did not show his characteristic energy in preventing, or punishing them. His subjects presumed on his well-known antipathy to "the Galileans;" and they did it with impunity.

Christians, on their part, had been too long accustomed to power, to bear their reverses with the patience and humility worthy of the religion they professed. Mobs overthrew the altar of Cybele at Pessinus, and at Cæsarea they destroyed a Temple of Fortune; the only one left to the polytheistic worshippers in that place. Magistrates punished the leaders, but those who suffered were almost adored as martyrs. The Governor of Phrygia, having opened temples for the observance of the old worship, a mob of Christians went in the night and shattered the statues to fragments. Fruitless search was made for the offenders, and there was such an angry state of feeling, that a general and bloody persecution seemed inevitable. In view of this, the authors of the mischief came forward and acknowledged what they had done. The judge offered to pardon them if they would sacrifice to the gods; but they replied they would rather endure anything he could inflict, than pollute themselves by such a deed. After being tortured in various ways, they were burned to death on gridirons, defying their tormentors to the last. The emperor himself did not escape annoyances from Christian zeal. One day, when he was offering sacrifice in the temple, the Arian Bishop of Chalcedon, who was old and blind, remonstrated with him for his wickedness. "Peace, blind old man!" replied Julian. "Thy Galilean God will not restore thy eyesight." "I thank God for my blindness," rejoined the bishop; "since it spares me the pain of beholding an apostate like thee." The emperor proceeded to sacrifice, without making any reply.

As if disposed in all things to dislike whatever Constantius had favoured, Julian recalled all those who had been exiled for heretical opinions, and humbled the Arians, whose intolerant use of power he had witnessed during the years that he conformed to Christianity. Receiving complaints from Edessa, that some disorders had arisen in consequence of insults and oppressions exercised by the Arians toward their theological opponents, without waiting to investigate the truth of the charge, he gave immediate orders to confiscate all the church property of the Arians. The lands were added to the imperial domain, and their money distributed among the soldiers. The edict was accompanied with threats of fire and sword, if the disorders continued. In his usual mocking tone, he wrote: "Such has been my clemency toward the Galileans, that I have left them at liberty to renounce the gods, and to live in impiety. But those whom they call Arians, being carried into culpable excesses, I resolved to assist them in accomplishing an admirable precept of their law. I have confiscated the riches with which they gorged themselves during the preceding reign, and have rendered them poor, and thus worthy to enter that kingdom of heaven which they expect."

Alexandria, always full of commotions, became a scene of tumult during the reign of Julian. A man named George, originally a contractor of bacon for the army, monopolized trade in all profitable articles, and became very wealthy. He was endowed by nature with considerable ability, but rendered himself odious with all classes of citizens by his extortionate and tyrannical proceedings. This man was professedly a Christian; probably belonging to that numerous class who are always ready to adopt any creed that is patronized by government. In the reign of Constantius, he was Arian Bishop of Alexandria, and caused the whole people to groan under his heavy taxation. Adherents of the old worship had been flattered with promises of toleration; but as soon as he was in power, he interdicted their festivals, pillaged the rich ornaments of their temples, and invented various pretexts for levying fines, and confiscating their property. They were compelled to submit to these aggressions during the reign of Constantius, but when Julian came to the throne the long suppressed rage burst forth. A furious mob surrounded the episcopal palace, murdered the bishop and two of his officers, dragged their bodies through the streets, tore them in pieces, and threw them into the sea, to prevent their bones from being honoured as the relics of martyrs. The emperor addressed a letter to the people, admitting that their indignation was just, but rebuking them severely for taking the law into their own violent hands, and for tearing men to pieces, like dogs, and then daring to lift their blood-stained hands to the gods.

In consequence of Julian's edict recalling heretics banished in the preceding reign, Athanasius had returned to

Alexandria. A majority of the numerous Christians in that city were devotedly attached to him; and in the midst of these tumults his strong character took the ascendancy which belonged to it by nature. The emperor was indignant to hear that he had presumed so far as to resume his episcopal dignity, and that he had converted some ladies of high rank. He wrote to the governor to banish forthwith that "most wicked Athanasius, by whose influence the gods are brought into contempt." He says: "Nothing will give me greater joy than to hear the godless wretch is banished from every district of Egypt, who, during my reign, has dared to baptize noble Grecian women." The people petitioned in great numbers, but in vain; and Athanasius again went into exile. In his letters to the governor, Julian assigned political motives, saying: "It is a dangerous thing for so cunning and restless a man to be at the head of the people." He reproached the Alexandrians for "neglecting to worship the God of the Sun, whose benign influence they all experienced, and devoting themselves to Jesus, the God-Logos, whom neither they nor their fathers had seen." He says: "The prelate of the Galileans ought to love me. I have treated them better than my predecessor. Under his reign, those whom they called heretics were hunted and massacred. Whole villages were sacked and destroyed. I have recalled them, and restored their property. But I put limits to their ambition; that is my crime."

He summoned a meeting of various Christian sects, and attempted to preside over their discussions. Whether he did this in a spirit of mockery, or with a proud philosophic certainty of vanquishing them by his arguments, it is not easy to decide. Whatever his motives might have been, the disputes between Athanasians, Arians, Apollinarians, Anomæans, and of Donatists with them all, became so clamorous, that he could not make himself heard; and he dismissed them with the remark: "No wild beasts are so savage and intractable as Christian sectaries."

The magnificent and richly endowed Temple of Apollo,

in the Groves of Daphne, near Antioch, has been described in the chapter on Greece. The worship at this temple, once so exceedingly popular, gradually declined. Babylas, Bishop of Antioch, had died in prison, during the Decian persecution. Gallus, the brother of Julian, who ruled the Eastern provinces about a hundred years after, found a portion of the Groves of Daphne converted into a Christian burial-place. He caused the bones of the martyred bishop to be removed thither, and a superb church was erected over his tomb. The ancient nations universally considered the presence of a dead body pollution to any consecrated place. The priests of Apollo quitted the precincts in dismay; and the old worshippers feared to enter there, to consult the far-famed oracle. The Christian Fathers said Apollo was abashed by the presence of a holy martyr; that he felt himself vanquished, and his oracle dared not break silence. The temple, thus deserted, fell into decay. Julian had the same predilection for Apollo that had been manifested by his uncle Constantine. In the general restoration of temples, this far-famed edifice received early attention. Julian resolved to visit it in person, on the occasion of the ancient Festival of Apollo. On the road, he offered prayers and sacrifices at every temple and altar; often ascending steep and rugged mountains, in the midst of drenching rain, if there was a temple at the top. As he approached Antioch, his imagination was full of long processions of priests, pouring libations from golden goblets, boys in white robes waving incense, bullocks crowned with garlands, and graceful dancers moving to music's most harmonious measures. Great was his disappointment to find the beautiful Groves of Daphne full of tombs, the temple silent, and only one pale, sad old priest, who had but a single swan to sacrifice to Apollo. Upon inquiry, he found that only a few of the old people in Antioch remembered the ancient ceremonies. Julian says: "Not one brought oil for the lamp; not one brought incense, libation, or sacrifice." He severely rebuked those who held large estates attached to the temple, yet neglected its service, while they allowed their wives to lavish money on the "Galilean" bishops. He ordered the Christian church to be demolished, and the temple restored to its former splendour. As a necessary preliminary, all the dead bodies were removed to Antioch, five miles distant, and the consecrated grounds were purified according to the ancient Grecian rites. The Christians sent a chariot to receive the remains of Babylas; and an immense procession came out from the city to escort it to the burial-place. They met it with thundering acclamations, and followed it chanting alternate strains, in which they continually repeated: "Confounded be all they that worship graven images, and delight in vain idols." Julian, exasperated by this intentional insult, ordered punishment to be inflicted on some of the leaders. Sallust, the Prætorian Prefect, being characterized by moderation, subjected only one young man to torture. But he so exulted in his sufferings, and continued to shout so obstinately, "Confounded be all they who delight in vain idols," that Sallust reminded the emperor how much the Christian cause gained by such examples of constancy, and how much their own would lose by cruelty. His caution was accepted, and no further notice taken of the offence.

The restoration of the temple proceeded rapidly; and a beautiful new peristyle already surrounded it, when, at midnight, Julian received tidings that the building was on fire. The roof, the costly ornaments of the interior, and the colossal statue of Apollo, were all consumed. Christians said God had struck the impious place with lightning, at the intercession of the martyred Babylas; but the emperor and his friends believed it to be the work of incendiaries. Many supposed the fire had taken accidentally, from torches placed within the temple by a zealous worshipper in Julian's train. He was so strongly persuaded to the contrary, that he ordered the cathedral at Antioch to be closed, and its wealth confiscated.

After Julian left Antioch, the magistrate who was intrusted with the examination of the affair, adopted modes of persecution unsanctioned by the emperor. Several of

the Christian clergy were tortured, and one beheaded.
Many acts of injustice were done; and in some cases the
oppression fell on individuals who had been distinguished
for moderation and gentleness when they had the power
in their own hands. Libanius, the orator, a zealous advocate of the old worship, had written to the magistrate, to
"make those weep who had long made merry with the
better cause." But he protested strongly against the injustice he witnessed, and boldly shielded its victims. A
poor and truly religious man, named Orion, was called upon
to pay large sums of money, or submit to torture. Libanius
sheltered him in his own house, and persisted in refusing
to give him up. He wrote to the magistrate: "This man
is not one of those who can easily change with the times.
But when he was in authority, during the preceding reign,
he oppressed no one, and was never arrogant. He did not
imitate those who made a bad use of their power; on the
contrary, he always blamed them. He never made war
against our worship, or persecuted our priests; and he
saved many from misery by the mild administration of his
office. This made the man dear to me; for while he
reverenced his own religion, he never annoyed those who
swore by the name of Jupiter. I now see this man full of
distress, his family broken up, and his furniture plundered.
I know all this is not according to the will of the emperor.
He has said: 'If any man has property belonging to the
temples, require him to give it up; but if he has not, do
not allow him to be either abused or insulted.' It is manifest these men are coveting the goods of others, while they
pretend to be desirous of serving the gods." As soon as
the emperor received information of the injustice practised,
he expressed strong disapprobation, and forbade its con-
tinuance. For another Christian, Libanius intreated that
his elegant house might be spared, because it made the city
beautiful, and because "he did not, with arrogance and
impiety, plunder the temple," on whose site it was erected;
but paid for it, according to the law then established. For
another, who was called upon to rebuild a demolished tem-

ple, he petitioned that he might be permitted to pay half
the sum at once, and raise the remainder at some future
time.

Romans generally regarded Jews as less impious than
Christians, because they had an ancient and established
religion, from which they had never seceded.   In addition
to this universal feeling, Julian had various inducements
to favour them.   Being on the eve of an expensive war,
it was policy to secure the good will of a numerous and
wealthy class of citizens; and even without this motive, he
would have been attracted toward them by the fact that
Christians disliked them, and that his cousin Constantius
had oppressed and plundered them, under various pre-
tences.   "The Jews differ from us only in the exclusive
worship of one God," said he.   "Everything else they have
in common with us; temples, sacred groves, altars, lustra-
tions, and a variety of other observances, wherein we differ
but little, or not at all."   Soon after his accession, he addressed a friendly epistle to the Jews scattered throughout
his empire.   He admitted that Jehovah was a true God,
though not the only one; pitied their misfortunes, condemned those who had oppressed them, and styled himself
their protector.   Concerning the difference of religious belief between them, he argued thus: "If the God proclaimed
by Moses is the universal framer of the universe, presiding
immediately over the world, then *we* have the more correct
idea of Him, who regard him as Lord of the *whole* universe,
and the inferior gods as presiding over individual nations;
standing in relation to Him, as governors of provinces under a king; nor do we represent Him as a rival of the gods,
who are under Him.   But if Moses worshipped one of the
subordinate deities, and ascribed to him the creation and
government of all things, then it is better to follow *us*, and
to acknowledge the Universal God, who is indeed Lord
over all, without failing to recognize that other Being also,
who should be worshipped as the governor of a province,
not as the Creator of all."   He proposed to rebuild their
temple on Mount Moriah, more magnificently than Con-

stantine had built the Christian church on Calvary. He asked them to pray to their God for him; and added: "I will pray with you in the temple we are going to reconstruct." The Jews, accustomed to pillage and persecution under the preceding emperors, received this unexpected proposal with triumphant joy. They flocked from all quarters to their Holy Mountain, where the voice of Psalm and Hallelujah had been hushed for so many centuries. Women poured their jewels into the treasury, misers unlocked their hoards, and every little child was eager to contribute his mite toward rebuilding that temple whose recounted glories had so dazzled his infant imagination. Men and women of the highest rank laboured at removing the ruins with their own hands. Stones were dug out with pickaxes and shovels of solid silver, and women removed rubbish in silver baskets, or mantles of the richest silk. The aged, the lame, and the blind, competed with the strong for some share in the sacred work. All the implements employed were to be kept ever after as consecrated memorials, and transmitted to posterity. A large quantity of materials was collected, and the excavation had already proceeded to a considerable depth, when the workmen were suddenly interrupted by volumes of flame bursting from the centre of the hill, accompanied by tremendous explosions. The scorched and blasted labourers fled in terror. The Jews were discomfited and alarmed by such an evil omen; but it is likely that the undertaking would have been resumed, had not Julian gone to the war in Persia, from which he never returned. The account is given by the Pagan historian, Ammianus. It was much amplified by subsequent writers. They said a violent earthquake shook the mountain; that a horse and his rider were seen enveloped in the flames; that the fire was so fierce, it consumed even the iron tools; that blazing crosses settled on the garments of the workmen; and when they sought shelter in a neighbouring church, the doors were fast closed against them, by supernatural force.

The prophecy that the temple would never be restored,

and that another would descend from heaven with the New Jerusalem, when Christ came to establish his kingdom on earth, had been perpetually reiterated by Christians. Consequently, they exulted over the frustrated attempt to disprove this prediction, and saw in it the miraculous intervention of offended Deity. In fact, it has been generally so regarded unto the present time. But M. Guizot and Dr. Milman, suggest that these explosions may be accounted for, "on the principle of fire-damps in mines." They state that there were vast excavations under Jerusalem, which could be entered from the temple. They are supposed to have been made in the time of Solomon, for the purpose of concealing treasures and provisions, in time of siege; and also as a means of escape, in case of extreme emergencies. During three centuries of desolation, the outlet had probably become choked up, and the cavern filled with inflammable gas, which exploded with a great noise, when workmen approached the aperture with torches. Josephus relates a similar incident, as having occurred when Herod sent men to explore the sepulchre of David, in hopes of finding hidden treasures. In Julian's time, all classes of men were prone to assign supernatural, rather than scientific causes for all phenomena; and doubtless this tendency of mind discouraged the Jews, while it animated the Christians.

While Julian was so diligent in restoring religious ceremonials, he had by no means forgotten his friends the philosophers. As soon as he assumed the imperial purple, he wrote to Maximus, urging his immediate attendance at court. This was followed by invitations to others, whom he considered eminent for wisdom or virtue. The roads to the capital were now thronged with philosophers, travelling at the public expense, as bishops had done in the days of Constantine. Julian spared no pains to do them honour, and they are most lavishly eulogized in his writings. Maximus, whose magical skill had so much astonished his youth, was his chosen friend and counsellor. Imperial favour had the same effect on him that it had on some bishops, in the days of Constantine and Constantius. He became luxurious, ambitious, and arrogant. The same was true of many of the philosophers, on whom he lavished wealth and honours. The belief in magic was universal. The most enlightened Christians of that time believed in it as firmly as others; only they imputed its marvels to agency of the Devil. Most of the philosophers at that period sought to gain power over the credulous by arts deemed magical; but some of them disapproved of it. Eusebius, an able and eloquent man, a fervent admirer of Plotinus, was among the intimate friends of Julian. He believed in the wonders performed by Maximus, but discountenanced the pursuit of such knowledge; saying he deemed it far wiser to seek after the true essence of things, the ideas perceptible to enlightened reason, than to practise illusions on the senses by means of magic. Priscus, another philosophic friend and adviser of the emperor, bore prosperity with great moderation. Serious in character, and austere in morals, he despised those who embraced philosophy because it was the fashion. He continued to live very simply, and would never consent to become a courtier. Chrysanthus was another of the New Platonists distinguished for uprightness, purity, moderation, and dignity of manner. The emperor sent repeated invitations, and even wrote with his own hand, urging him and his wife Melita to come to court; but they constantly refused. Finding it useless, he appointed him High Priest of Lydia, conjointly with his wife, and invested them with full authority to erect temples, restore ancient ceremonials, and nominate priests. They performed the duties of their station with so much justice, kindness, and discretion, that the greatest enemies of their religion were constrained to respect their virtues.

Julian himself did not agree with those of his philosophers who discountenanced magic. He was a great believer in prophecies, divination, and miracles by aid of theurgy. Soothsayers and magicians flocked to him from all quarters. Many of them had been imprisoned during preceding reigns, for impositions on the people, meddling with political affairs, and connecting cruel practices with their midnight incantations. But Julian was prone to regard them with a degree of favour, which the wisest of his friends and subjects observed with regret. Chrysostom, who could not be expected to judge very impartially of Julian and his friends, and who probably classed all the philosophers with magicians, says: "Men who had grown old in prison, and in the mines, and who maintained their wretched existence by the most disgraceful trades, were suddenly advanced to places of dignity, and invested with the priesthood, and sacrificial functions."

Many were, of course, gained over by the same selfish motives which induced multitudes to be baptized in the time of Constantine and Constantius. The Fathers speak with indignation of such men, "who changed their religion as easily as their garments; who abandoned the churches, and ran to the altars; enticed to apostacy by the bait of honourable offices; pointed at by the finger of scorn, as those who had betrayed Christ for a few pieces of silver." It was, in fact, a period when men could easily lose their way, between the two extremes of scepticism and fanaticism, which always mark the dissolution of old forms. Scepticism had for a long time been at work diminishing the authority of the ancient religion. The increasing manifestation of it produced an extreme reaction of fanaticism in some, who, with terrified desperation, and redoubled zeal, sought to sustain the faith of their fathers; while those whose activity of intellect was chastened by reverence, resorted to allegorical interpretation as the only method of conciliation between the atheism and the superstition of their time. Julian undertook a hopeless task in attempting to restore the old worship. Such life as was in it in the olden time had departed; and it is always a vain effort to build temples with ashes. Himself, and others who were sincere in their reverence for it, merely wished to preserve it as a time-honoured respectability. Notwithstanding the magnificence of his temples, and the splendour of his festivals, he could not excite the people to much zeal in sacrificing; while those whom he paid for honouring the gods, often ate and drank at the banquets in a manner so excessive as to disgrace their cause.

But notwithstanding the many and powerful enemies which Julian made in his attempt to subvert Christianity, it could not be denied that he had great ability and many virtues, which, at an earlier period of history, would have placed him among the brightest and best of the emperors. He was brave by temperament, merciful in disposition, and affable in manners. He set an example of serious and almost austere virtue. He disliked amusements, and when compelled by custom to enter the theatre annually, he staid the shortest possible time necessary to fulfil his public functions. His mode of life was extremely temperate and simple. He dismissed the thousand barbers and servants of the bath, whom he found at the imperial palace, and retained but one personal attendant. A crowd of spies and informers were likewise sent away. By these and other retrenchments, he was enabled to remit to the people one-fifth part of all their taxes. He made great improvements in the courts of justice, and, with few exceptions, governed humanely. Excessive vanity may be forgiven in so young a man, endowed with showy talents and imperial power. His aversion to Christianity doubtless grew in part from personal animosity to his Christian cousin, who had murdered his family, and kept his youth under such jealous constraint. We ought, moreover, to remember that the multitudes swept into the baptismal pool by imperial influence, decidedly tended to lower the general character of Christianity. As Julian found it, it was a warfare of abstruse doctrines, a perpetual struggle for ecclesiastical power, a mass of external forms, borrowed from various quarters, encrusting the living, loving heart of Christ's religion. He verily believed that the rapid degeneracy of the Roman empire was owing to neglect of the ancient gods; therefore his zeal to renovate the old worship was in fact a religious phase of patriotism. The determined opposition

he met with increased his hostility to the new faith. His
laws grew more stringent in the latter part of his reign.
The holy water used at the temples, called lustral water,
he caused to be sprinkled on all the provisions in the market, and in all the public fountains; and Christians, who
refused to partake of food or drink, which had thus become infected with idolatry, were led to execution. Had
he lived many years, he might possibly have become a relentless persecutor; but he did not survive to prolong the
struggle.

In the year three hundred and sixty-five he became involved in a war with Persia, which cost him his life, after
an active and brilliant reign of one year and eight months.
The story has been many times repeated that when mor-
tally wounded by an arrow, he threw a handful of his
blood toward heaven, exclaiming bitterly: "Thou hast
conquered, O Galilean!" But this improbable statement
is now admitted to rest on insufficient authority. It had
been predicted to him that he would die in battle, and he
met his fate with philosophic composure. To the weeping
friends, who crowded into his tent, he spoke with a firm
and gentle voice, telling them what he wished to have done
with his private fortune, trying to soothe their immoderate
grief, begging them not to disgrace by unmanly tears the
departure of a prince who would so soon ascend to heaven,
and be united with the stars. He said: "I have learned
from philosophy how much the soul is more excellent than
the body, and that the separation of the nobler substance
should be a source of joy, rather than affliction. I have
also learned that the gods often bestow an early death, as
the best reward of piety; and I accept, as a favour from
them, the mortal stroke that secures me from the danger
of disgracing a character which has hitherto been supported by virtue and fortitude." Calmly discoursing with
his friends Maximus and Priscus, concerning the immortality of the soul, his spirit passed away. The account of
his death is given by the Roman historian Ammianus, who
was present at the scene. Adherents of the old worship

mourned over him as their last hope; and eulogized him in terms almost as unmeasured as the bishops had done Constantine. Theodoret, the Christian historian, says that when the news was received at Antioch, the Christians had festal dances in the churches, and at the cemeteries of martyrs, and that they celebrated the triumph of the cross at the theatre.

JOVIAN.—Jovian, who was proclaimed emperor, immediately announced himself a Christian; but declared that people were free to follow the old religion; that he should punish nothing but magic. It was unknown what sect he would favour, and all were eager to make a favourable impression on him. The theological warfare, which had been hushed for awhile, by a sense of common danger, was renewed. The highways were crowded with Athanasian, Arian, Semi-Arian, and Anomœan bishops, trying to outstrip each other. The new prince was almost stunned by their arguments and mutual invectives. He recommended charity toward each other, and proclaimed universal toleration to all forms of worship. Something concerning principles of freedom had been slowly learned in this conflict of centuries. Themistius, who adhered to the ancient rites of his country, in an address to the new sovereign warmly praised his liberality. He says: "You are aware that the monarch cannot force everything from his subjects; that there are things superior to all constraint, all threatening, all law. This is the case with virtue in general; but it is especially true concerning piety toward God. You have wisely considered that nothing but hypocrisy is produced, unless the unconstrained and absolutely free will of man is left to move first. Deity has implanted religious sentiments in all human beings; but his law remains forever unchangeable, that each man's soul is free in reference to his own peculiar mode of worship."

Gregory, Bishop of Nazianzen, manifested a similar spirit, though he claims it as a peculiarity of Christianity; forgetting that all men had learned somewhat, during this protracted struggle. He exhorted his people not to retaliate the injuries they had received during Julian's reign. He said : "Let us show what a difference there is between what these men learn from their gods, and the lessons which Christ teaches us. Let us promote the spread of the Gospel by long suffering, and subdue oppressors by gentleness." Of course, a worthless crowd of proselytes, ready to jump on either side, again came over to the religion of the emperor.

VALENTINIAN.—Jovian had a brief reign, and was succeeded by Valentinian, a semi-barbarian in character; ignorant, severe, and gross in debauchery. He is said to have withdrawn from Julian's army, rather than seem to worship the gods by saluting the standards. He was an Athanasian, but followed Jovian's system of toleration. Some of the estates lavishly bestowed by Julian, for the benefit of the old worship, were taken back into the imperial domain. But the priesthood remained undisturbed, and a military guard, in which Christians were not required to serve, was appointed to protect the temples from depredation or insult. Religious festivals prolonged into midnight, were prohibited, because the concourse of all sorts of people, brought together under the veil of darkness, had led to gross immoralities. Prœtextatus, Governor of Achaia, a man universally respected for his learning and excellent character, was a devout worshipper of the old deities. He petitioned the emperor to except the Eleusinian Mysteries; representing that the life of Grecians would be dreary and comfortless without the inestimable blessing of that sacred institution. Those Mysteries, ancient and venerable, had always been observed with the greatest solemnity and decorum; and his request was immediately granted. The old rites of divination at the temples were allowed, provided the Augurs were not consulted for any treasonable or bad purpose. But severe inquisition was made into the practice of magic, in consequence of complaints from one of the subordinate magistrates of Rome, who averred that

attempts had been made, by three obscure persons, to destroy himself and wife by magical arts. These, being put
to cruel torture, made confessions, which implicated many
people, of all ranks, as seeking the aid of magic for licentious purposes, for poisoning, and all manner of crimes.
From time immemorial, it had been supposed that Spirits
of the stars, the waters, the earth, and regions under the
earth, would impart their power to men and women, if
sought with mysterious ceremonies, solemn incantations,
potent herbs, and bloody sacrifices. These things, after
having been practised for centuries, not only with impunity, but generally with honour and profit, had been gradually growing into disrepute; not because the power of
magic was doubted by any class of men, but because it had
become a trade with increasing numbers of low, base itin-
erants, willing to use it for the worst of purposes. But still
many men of rank and education continued to seek its aid
in emergencies, regarding it as a true science, though perverted and misused by the wicked. Therefore, when it
came to be treated as a crime, punishable with death, it
seemed to throw a pall over the whole empire; especially,
as it furnished a ready means of gratifying personal hatred
and revenge. Valentinian authorized the Præfect of Rome
to extort evidence by the most cruel tortures. Spies and
informers were everywhere on the alert. There was an
extreme reluctance to acquit any one who was accused. A
species of insanity seemed to prevail on the subject. The
most improbable charges were proved against individuals
of the highest character. Senators, matrons, and philosophers were dragged to prison in chains, scourged, racked,
and put to death in the most ignominious manner. The emperor kept two fierce bears chained near his bed-chamber,
to tear criminals in pieces for his amusement. One of these
animals was afterward turned loose into the forest, as a reward for his services to the state.

In the Eastern part of the empire, governed by the
emperor's brother, Valens, the persecution raged still more
terribly; his fears having been excited by a rumour that

D*

magical arts had been employed to spell out, by a circle of letters, the name of him who would succeed him on the throne. Suspicions that a treasonable plot was therewith connected made him extremely anxious to ascertain what name the circle had indicated. Several philosophers, some of them Julian's personal friends, were implicated in the transaction; being suspected of wishing to restore his order of things. One of them was horribly tortured to induce him to give evidence against a suspected magistrate; but no agony could induce him to say otherwise than that the man was innocent. Another, very young, but of austere philosophy, acknowledged that he knew the secret of the name, but declared that no power should compel him to divulge it. He was burned alive, and met his fate with stoical calmness. Maximus made a similar confession, but declared it unworthy of a philosopher to divulge a secret intrusted to him. He was executed, and many others with him. The excellent Priscus was accused and imprisoned for a short time, but had the rare good fortune to be dismissed as blameless. He retired into Greece, where he lived solitary in the temples, till he was eighty years old. Eunapius cites him as "a rare example of longevity, at a time when so many distinguished men killed themselves in despair, or had their throats cut by barbarians." A Roman youth suffered death merely for copying an old book of magical incantations. So strict was the search for such books, that many men of learning burned their entire libraries, fearing lest some sentence they contained might be construed into magic. Few Christians suffered from this persecution; for believing that magical skill was derived from Evil Spirits, they were rarely tempted to consult it.

Valens had been baptized by an Arian bishop, and always retained his predilection for that sect. Patronized by the government, it maintained the ascendancy it always had in the East. In almost every city, there were two rival bishops, each claiming to be legitimate authority, and regarding the other with watchful animosity. Valens, a weak-minded man, often lent himself as an instrument of episcopal jealousy. Being at Edessa, he commanded the Governor to break up all assemblies of the Athanasians. The Governor was an Arian, but he pitied the people, and gave them private information of the orders he had received; hoping they would refrain from meeting. But the next morning, they flocked together in greater numbers than ever. Seeing a woman hurrying along, leading a little child, he inquired: "Whither goest thou in so much haste? Knowest thou not that the Governor has orders to kill all he finds in the church?" She replied: "I know it very well. Therefore, I make so much haste, lest I should arrive too late to secure the crown of martyrdom." Being asked why she was dragging her little son along with her, she answered: "That he also may have his share of the reward." Grieved to see people thus led like sheep to the slaughter, the Governor went back to the palace, and succeeded in dissuading the emperor from his bloody design.

It had become very fashionable for the wealthy to seek salvation for their souls by leaving large estates to the church. In this way, the ecclesiastical revenues had become immense; though scarcely half a century had elapsed since Constantine passed the law empowering his subjects to make such bequests. Devout women, especially, were easily induced to build churches, or leave their wealth for charitable purposes, at the disposal of the clergy. The evil became so great, that Valentinian forbade ecclesiastics to frequent the houses of widows, or receive testamentary donations; confining them to their own natural and legal rights of inheritance.

THEODOSIUS.—In three hundred and seventy-eight, Gratian became emperor of the Western part of the empire. He was a very young man, entirely under the influence of Ambrose, Bishop of Milan. The East was ruled by Theodosius the Great, an hereditary Christian, educated in the Athanasian creed. He soon announced his determination to exterminate the old worship, root and branch.

Human sacrifices had never been a custom with the Romans, and they uniformly forbade them in the nations they conquered. But in some provinces, the barbarous rite was practised, though very rarely, and usually in obedience to the command of some oracle. Theodosius abolished it, under penalty of death. Magical arts, and the inspection of the entrails of victims, for purposes of divination, were forbidden under the same penalty. All property belonging to the temples was confiscated, for benefit of the army, and the churches; the priesthood were deprived of all their privileges; sacrifices were forbidden, either within or without the temples; and any magistrate who entered a temple was fined fifteen pounds of gold. Hitherto, all the Christian emperors had followed the old custom of assuming the office and title of Pontifex Maximus, and of acting on state occasions as High Priest of the worship they had deserted. But when the Senate of Rome sent a solemn deputation to Gratian, to perform the usual ceremony of inauguration, he rejected the intended honour with contempt. The Goddess of Fortune, with whose worship the welfare and glory of Rome was supposed to have been intimately connected for ages, was ordered to be taken from her pedestal, and her altar destroyed. Sorrow and unfeigned alarm took possession of all the people, who retained any reverence for the old order of things. Deputations were sent to remonstrate earnestly with the youthful emperor, imploring him to be cautious how he thus endangered the safety of the state; but the Christians sent in a counter petition, through Damasus, their bishop, and his influence prevailed.

Monks, who had become numerous at this period, were everywhere the fiercest and most reckless enemies of the old worship. Soon after the accession of Theodosius, they began to traverse the rural districts, overturning the altars, demolishing temples, and plundering their rich treasures, wherever they found them unprotected. This desecration was regarded by many of the country people not only with deep grief, but with absolute terror. Their simple faith, rooted in the soil of centuries, had not been shaken by so many rude storms of political revolution, or slowly undermined by self-interest, as had been the case in cities. The peasant woman, when she laid her fragrant offering of blossoms on the altar, felt sure that the kind Goddess of Flowers would sprinkle her garden with dew, and fill it with honey for the bees. The farmer had undoubting faith that the altar, or image of a deity, among his grape-vines, or his wheat, was a security against drought and blight, and destructive insects. When they saw squalid-looking men, with matted hair, and dirty dresses, going about insulting the beneficent Spirits, who they verily believed had protected them and their forefathers for ages, they expected storm, pestilence, and famine, as the inevitable consequence; and their sorrow, fear, and indignation knew no bounds. In many places, the rustic population rose in defence of their sacred buildings and images, and succeeded in driving off the invaders, some of whom they put to death.

Theophilus, Bishop of Alexandria, was peculiarly zealous in finding accusations against adherents of the old worship in that city. A temple of Osiris had been granted by the emperor to the Christians, who proceeded to build a church on the ground. While digging the foundation, they found various symbols used in the worship of the god; and among them was the emblem of the generative principle, connected with many religious ceremonies in Hindostan, Egypt, Greece, and Rome. This ancient symbol was associated in their minds with reverence and gratitude to a beneficent Deity, for the mysterious reproduction of life, in all departments of the universe; but to Christians, it suggested nothing but indecency. The Bishop so far forgot the dignity becoming his office, that he exposed these symbols in the market-place, where they were examined by the crowd with jokes and scornful laughter. Those who revered the old Egyptian worship were exasperated beyond measure. They rushed upon the jesters, and a conflict ensued, in which the streets flowed with blood. The Christians who were slain, received the honours of martyrdom, and the zeal of survivors was redoubled. Conscious of power, they were not sparing of threats or accusations. Hostility between the factions daily increased. It was rumoured that beautiful women of high rank were decoyed into the Temple of Serapis, under the pretence of being chosen favourites of the god, who was in fact represented by his priests. These stories, doubtless more or less true concerning all powerful priesthoods, since the world began, were diligently circulated, and pointed popular hostility toward the Temple of Serapis. Surrounded by walls and outer courts, the building was strong as a citadel. The worshippers of Serapis, expecting an attack, collected there in great numbers, and from time to time sallied forth to seize Christians, whom they forced to offer sacrifice on their altar, or slew them and threw their bodies into a deep trench filled with the offals of victims. Magistrates came with troops, and threatened them with vengeance of the law; but they were beaten back, and obliged to wait for orders from the emperor. Olympus, a philosopher, had endeavoured to cheer his associates in those dark days, and prepare their minds for the destruction of external objects of worship, which he foresaw must come. He reminded them that "the statues of the gods were but perishable material images; that the Immortal Spirits who once dwelt within them had withdrawn to the stars." Wrought up by the excitement of present danger, he strove to stimulate his friends to obstinate resistance; saying: "Let us make a glorious sacrifice of our enemies, and then immolate ourselves, and perish with our gods." But at midnight, when the gates were fastened, and all was still, one clear, strong voice sang, "Hallelujah!" and the tones resounded through the silent temple. Regarding it either as an alarming omen, or as an indication that Christians had secret means of ingress to their fortress, his courage failed. He stole out of the temple, and embarked for Italy. An imperial edict soon arrived authorizing the destruction of the world-renowned Temple of Serapis. It was received with tumultuous shouts of joy by the Christian populace, while philosophers and priests fled to secret places. The Archbishop Theophilus, with an army of soldiers and monks, hastened with all zeal to the work of devastation. The far-famed Alexandrian Library had been partially destroyed by fire during the invasion of the city by Julius Cæsar, but the loss had been in a measure repaired by an extensive library, which Mark Anthony presented to Cleopatra. Three hundred thousand volumes were preserved in rooms within the inclosure of the Temple of Serapis. The monks from the desert who were led on to this attack by the archbishop, were generally ignorant men, with a strong contempt for human learning. They would therefore be likely to have little respect for this great storehouse of the genius and learning of ages. But they were avaricious of plunder; and as rare manuscripts were then valued as diamonds are now, it is not unlikely that many of them were preserved and sold. What proportion of them was destroyed is unknown. They were all pillaged, and it is supposed that many were burned. Orosius, a Christian historian, who visited the Library rooms, twenty-five years after, says: "I saw the empty book-cases, which were broken open; and men of these times relate that they were plundered by our people." [That is, by Christians.]

When the crowd entered the sanctuary of the temple, the colossal statue was so impressive in its majesty, and Christians were so thoroughly imbued with the idea that Evil Spirits lurked about the temples and statues, in which they had been accustomed to be worshipped, that for a moment their purpose was arrested. The archbishop seeing them thus irresolute, ordered a soldier to strike the image. He struck it first on the knee, and then climbing up chopped off the head. A large colony of rats ran out, and converted the fears of the multitude into boisterous mirth. The huge limbs of Serapis were dragged through the streets with shouts and mockery, and finally burnt in the amphitheatre. To demolish the massive architecture of the temple was the work of time. An army of monks from the desert encamped among the ruins, and a Christian church soon rose on the foundations of the ancient sanctuary.

Serapis presided over the inundations of the Nile, on which the fertility of Egypt depended; of course, many fears were entertained lest the land would be punished for the indignity offered to the god. When the time came for the annual overflow, the people watched with anxiety; and when they saw the waters remain for several days at their usual level, the alarm began to spread, and there was a loud demand that the customary sacrifices should be offered. The inflexible emperor answered that Egypt must go dry, if the inundation depended on the practice of idolatrous rites. Doubtless this answer would have excited insurrection, had not the Nile begun to swell before it arrived. The overflow was even more abundant than usual, and the fickle populace joined with the Christians in mocking the dethroned Serapis.

Christian writers were eloquent in their exultation over the downfall of idolatry; and writers on the other side were proportionably bitter in their expressions of hatred and contempt for the monks. Eunapius describes the scene thus: "Men, who had never heard war spoken of, bravely attacked the Serapeum with stones, demolished it, and scattered the offerings, which the veneration of ages had accumulated there. Having courageously given battle to statues, they made a military convention that all they had stolen was a fair prize. But as they could not carry away the land, however much they might wish it, those heroic conquerors retired, and were replaced in the occupation of the sacred soil by monks; that is to say, by beings having the appearance of men, living like the vilest animals, and giving themselves up in public to the most disgusting actions that can be imagined; for it was for them an act of piety to profane this sacred place, in all manner of ways. These monks encamped among the ruins of the Serapeum, and slaves and criminals were seen receiving worship there, instead of the gods of intellect. In exchange for the heads of our divinities, they showed the dirty skulls of miserable convicts, and knelt before them, and adored them. Infidel slaves, torn by the whip and furrowed with marks of their crimes, they call martyrs, deacons, and leaders in prayer! Such are the new gods of this earth! Whoever wears a black robe has despotic power. Philosophy, and piety to the gods, are compelled to retire into secret places, to dwell in contented poverty and dignified meanness of appearance."

The work of destruction went on far and wide. Theophilus soon after marched at the head of his party, and demolished the temple and statue of Canopus, god of humidity. Martin, Bishop of Tours, undertook the task of extirpating idolatry in Gaul. He marched all over the country with a band of monks, destroying altars and temples, and building churches in their place. He asserts positively that during these predatory excursions, Jupiter, or Mercury, or Minerva, often appeared to him, and did their utmost to turn him from his work. Marcellus of Apamea pursued the same course in Syria. A massive temple of Jupiter, standing on a lofty eminence, long resisted their attacks, but it was finally undermined and overthrown. A band of rustics, who were watching the progress of the work, waylaid Marcellus, when he was at a distance from his companions, and burned him alive. He was placed among the martyrs, and the synod of his province refrained from taking any means to punish a death, which they deemed so happy for himself, and so glorious for his family. In almost every province of the Roman world, a large portion of the temples were destroyed. Where monks were not numerous, some were left to the slow decay of time. Others, whose construction could be easily altered for the purpose, were converted into churches. The Temple of the Celestial Venus at Carthage, whose beautiful groves formed a circumference of two miles; a temple at Damascus; and another at Heliopolis, were enclosed and consecrated to the use of the Christians.

Some of the more prudent bishops tried to check the insatiable zeal of their people for destroying altars and images, which were left on estates to protect the fields; an idea cherished by many of the landholders, as well as the labourers. Augustine says: "Many have those abominations upon their estates. Shall we go about to destroy them? No. Let us make it our first business to extirpate the idols in their hearts. Then, they will either invite us to so good a work, or they will anticipate us in it. At present, we must pray for them, not exasperate them."

Petitions came from all quarters, begging that places of worship might be spared. Libanius, the orator, who remained faithful to the old religion, pleaded for the preservation of the temples, in an oration addressed to the emperor. He entreated that they might be saved from destruction, if not for religious purposes, at least as beautiful ornaments to the cities, and sources of revenue, if applied to other purposes. More sadly and earnestly pleaded the eloquent Symmachus, an upright and fearless magistrate, who was fully persuaded that the welfare of his country depended on the worship of the ancient deities. In a petition which he wrote to be offered by the senate, alluding to a severe famine the preceding year, as proof that the gods were offended, he asks: "Were our fathers ever compelled to suffer anything like this, when the ministers of religion had a public maintenance?" He represents Rome herself as expostulating thus: "Most excellent princes, fathers of your country, respect my years, and still permit me to practise the worship of my ancestors in which I have grown old. This religion subdued the world to my dominion. Grant me but the privilege of living according to my ancient usage. I ask only for peace to the gods of Rome; the tutelary deities of your country. Heaven is above all. We cannot all follow the same path. There are many ways to arrive at the great secret. We presume not to contend. We are humble suppliants."

Ambrose, the able Bishop of Milan, resisted the slightest approach to a compromise. In his answer to Symmachus, he says: "The emperor, who should be guilty of such concessions, would soon learn that the bishops would neither connive at, nor endure his sin. If he entered a church, he would find no priest, or one who would defy his authority. The church would indignantly reject the gifts of him who shared them with Gentile temples. The altar disdains the offerings of him who has made oblations to images. It is written, 'Man cannot serve two masters.' "

Rome remained the last stronghold of the old worship. The city contained three hundred temples, and innumerable altars and statues, which stood long after all was falling in other parts of the empire. The magnificence of the edifices, the pomp of festivals, were there, more than elsewhere, connected with all great and interesting epochs of their history. Romans clung to these reminiscences of past glory, with the tenacious grasp of men in a death-struggle. The emperors had not yet ventured to proclaim such severe edicts there. The laws passed by Theodosius in the East were not in force in Rome. The temples were still open, and a portion of the public revenue was appropriated to worship.

A favourable moment was seized for insurrection, and Eugenius, a votary of the gods, was placed on the throne. The temples were re-opened throughout Italy, the smoke of sacrifices ascended, the altar of Victory was restored to its place, and pictures of the gods again floated on the banners. Ambrose fled from Milan, for the victorious soldiers threatened to stable horses in the churches, and compel the clergy to serve in the army.

The tidings of this rebellion made Theodosius pass still more stringent laws in the East. All divination or magic was punishable with death, whatever might be its object. Whoever offered any sacrifice, or connived at its being offered, even in a private house, was fined twenty-five pounds of gold; nearly five thousand dollars of our money. Any house in which incense was burned was confiscated to the imperial treasury. Whoever made an altar of turf on his own grounds, or hung a garland on a tree, forfeited his estate thereby. Theodosius marched against Eugenius, who was slain. Rome gave up the struggle in despair.

Many of the noble families went over to the religion of the conqueror. The senate debated the claims of Jupiter and Christ. The Christian poet, Prudentius, says Jupiter was out-voted by a large majority. But Zozimus, the Greek, who belonged to the other party, has recorded, in his History of the Roman Empire, that the senate adhered firmly, though respectfully, to their ancient deities. The household gods were not interfered with; the temples remained standing, and no one was forbidden to worship within them, provided they did it without sacrificing. The civil rights of the conservatives were respected. The schools, the army, and the senate, were filled with believers in the old gods. Platonists freely wrote sarcastic strictures on the proceedings of Christians. There was a personal friendship between Theodosius and Libanius the orator, and he was never required to conceal his opinions. Thus far, the emperor made politic concessions to a party still powerful in that part of his empire; but he refused to allow any funds from the public revenue for support of the ancient worship. The order of Vestal Virgins was abolished, the sacred fire extinguished, and oracles hushed by imperial command. Priests and priestesses, deprived of their maintenance, were scattered. Some priesthoods were still handed down in regular descent, and some rites and festivals continued to be observed, either without sacrifice or with sacrifice by stealth. Many conformed outwardly to the paramount religion, who were not inwardly convinced. External signs of the old worship disappeared from cities. But in country places, the rustic population long continued to assemble in the shadow of groves, and keep their old festivals, with sacrifices of sheep and oxen, under the appearance of a mere social banquet. They even contrived to sing hymns in honour of the gods, in such a manner as to evade the laws. Landholders connived at such practices, influenced by the old belief that the fertility of the fields depended on them. A poet who wrote after the time of Theodosius describes the Cross as the emblem of a god worshipped only in cities. In consequence of this long lingering of the old faith in rural districts, it came to be called the Pagan religion; from the Latin word Paganus, signifying a villager, or peasant.

But there were also men of education, who retained a strong predilection for the old ideas, which they had spiritualized by an infusion of Platonism. The simple phraseology of Scripture was not acceptable to these men, who had formed a taste for highly rhetorical embellishments; and they judged religion not so much by a standard of faith, as by respectable morality. When imperial edicts manufactured Christians by thousands, there were of course great numbers whose lives did little credit to the religion they professed. When attempts were made to convert Platonists, they often replied: "Why would you persuade me to embrace this new religion? I have been cheated by Christians, but I never defrauded any man. A Christian has broken his oath to me, but I never violated my simple word to any man."

All the Christian sects, that differed from the emperor in opinion, were more severely proscribed than the polytheistic worshippers had been. Constantine had summoned a Council at Nice, to settle the equal dignity of the Son and the Father. Theodosius summoned one hundred and fifty bishops to assemble at Constantinople, to settle the equal dignity of the Son and the Holy Ghost. This was followed by severe edicts against all who did not subscribe to the decision of that council. Their religious meetings were forbidden, in public or private, city or country, and every building or ground used for such purpose was forfeited to the imperial treasury. Very early in his reign, he published the following edict: "It is our pleasure that all the nations governed by our clemency and moderation should stedfastly adhere to the religion which was taught by Saint Peter to the Romans, faithfully preserved by tradition, and now professed by the Pontiff Damasus, and by Peter, Bishop of Alexandria, a man of apostolic holiness. According to the discipline of the Apostles, and the doctrine of the Gospel, let us believe the sole Deity of the Father, the Son,

and the Holy Ghost; under an equal majesty, and a holy
Trinity. We authorize the followers of this doctrine to
assume the title of Catholic Christians; and as we judge
that all others are extravagant madmen, we brand them
with the infamous name of heretics, and declare that their
conventicles shall no longer usurp the respectable name of
churches. Besides the condemnation of Divine Justice,
they must expect to suffer the severe penalties, which our
authority, guided by Heavenly Wisdom, shall think proper
to inflict upon them."

On the accession of Theodosius, it is said that Arians
possessed all the churches in the East, except in Jerusalem.
But after the publication of this edict, the Arian prelate at
Constantinople was ordered to subscribe the Nicene Creed,
or relinquish his episcopal palace, the cathedral of Santa
Sophia, and all the churches in his diocese, to orthodox
believers. He preferred banishment, and went into exile.
A large majority of the inhabitants of Constantinople were
Arians; but they were obliged to give up their hundred
churches to a sect not numerous enough to fill them.
Gregory of Nazianzen was appointed bishop, but he entered the enraged city guarded by the emperor and a strong
military force, and it was necessary to garrison the cathedral with imperial troops. He confesses that it seemed to
him like a city taken by storm. The sky was cloudy when
they started, but just as the procession began to enter the
cathedral, the sun burst forth and made the swords and
armour of the soldiers glitter in its rays. This was hailed
with acclamations, as an auspicious omen. The next
week, Theodosius expelled all the clergy throughout his
dominions, who refused to sign the established creed. In
the course of fifteen years, he published fifteen decrees
against heretical sects. His severest penalties were directed
against those who rejected the Athanasian doctrine of the
Trinity. No such person was allowed to hold any honourable or lucrative employment. Arians were forbidden to
build any churches, in city or country, under penalty of
the confiscation of their funds. Apollinarians were for-

bidden to have any clergy, or hold any meetings, or to reside in cities. Anomæans were not allowed to dispose of their own estates by will, or to receive any property by testamentary gift. The same was enacted concerning those who turned back from Christianity to Paganism. Manicheans were punishable with death, and prohibited from making wills. The Quartodecimans, who continued to keep Easter on the day of the Jewish Passover, instead of the day prescribed by the church at Rome, were also punishable with death. Confiscation and exile were denounced against all who preached the doctrines, or practised the rites of any of the "accursed sects." Some went so far as to maintain that not only all heretics, but all who held any intercourse with them, must not only make a public acknowledgment of their error, but must be re-baptized before they could be allowed to partake of the communion.

Theodosius appointed an Inquisitor of the Faith, to inquire into opinions; an office hitherto unknown. Christians had often killed each other in turmoils, and the government had put men to death for sectarian riots and depredations; but in this reign, blood was for the first time shed, by authority of Christian law, merely and avowedly on account of theological opinions. Priscillian, a man of rank in Spain, and a bishop, entertained many of the Gnostic views in connection with Christianity. He believed that the souls of men were portions of the Deity, imprisoned in material bodies, as a punishment. Consequently he denied the resurrection of the body, and was shocked at the idea that the Son of God could be born of a woman. He received all the books of the Hebrew and Christian Scriptures, even the apocryphal ones; giving them a spiritual interpretation, which sustained his doctrines. He was the founder of a numerous sect, famous for austere morals, and mortification of the senses. They abstained from marriage, never tasted animal food, fasted often, watched and prayed almost continually. Their mode of worship was exceedingly simple and spiritual. They rejected baptism, the Lord's Supper, and all external ordinances. They would not call their teachers bishops or priests, but named them Secretaries, or Companions in Travel. Priscillian was twice banished, and finally put to death, in three hundred eighty four, by order of Maximus, colleague of Theodosius. Several of his adherents, among whom were some noble women, were tortured and executed.

The private character of Theodosius was very exemplary, but his temper was imperious and violent. He was a strict observer of all ceremonies prescribed by the church; but the prevailing idea of the efficacy of baptism to wash away all sin led him to delay that rite until a dangerous illness, during the first year of his reign, induced him to hasten the ceremony.

The power which the church obtained over this despotic soldier was exemplified in a very remarkable manner on one occasion. In Thessalonica the populace had some dispute about a favourite charioteer in the circus. A riot ensued, and some of the imperial officers were killed in their efforts to quell it. Theodosius received the tidings when he was at Milan. His fiery temper kindled at once, and he vowed vengeance on the whole city; for he permitted no violence to be done, except in obedience to his own commands. In vain the clergy exhorted him to moderate his wrath. An army of barbarians was sent to Thessalonica. Public games were given by the emperor in the circus, and all the inhabitants invited. When the building was entirely filled, the soldiers received a signal for indiscriminate massacre of men, women, and children. From seven to fourteen thousand were slain. Ambrose, Bishop of Milan, who was then ill in the country, wrote to the emperor: "Sin can be removed only by tears and repentance. No angel or archangel can forgive sin; and the Lord himself forgives only those who come to him with repentance. I dare not distribute the holy elements, if you intend to be present and receive them. Where the blood of so many innocent persons has been shed, shall I venture to do that which I should not presume to do, if but one innocent individual had been killed?" He exhorted him to repent, and promised to pray for him, but would not change his determination to exclude him from communion. When the imperial culprit went to the church, to offer his devotions as usual, the bishop met him at the threshold, and said, "Stand back, thou man of blood!" Theodosius humbly pleaded that King David also sinned, yet God accepted him. Ambrose replied: "As you have imitated him in sin, copy him also in repentance." The emperor confessed his guilt, and promised to submit to any penance imposed upon him. He was ordered not to appear in church again for eight months, and to go through a certain form of prayers and religious exercises every day at home. Meantime, the Christmas festival occurred, and when all the world were thronging to the churches, Theodosius sent a message, imploring to be admitted; urging that he had every day obeyed to the letter all that had been enjoined upon him. Ambrose replied: "The emperor has power to kill me, but he must pass over my body, before he can enter the sanctuary of the Lord." When the eight months had expired, the episcopal interdict was removed, on two conditions. The emperor was required to publish an edict, forbidding any execution to take place throughout the empire, until thirty days after the culprit had been convicted by due process of law. In the next place, as his sin had been public, it was required that his penance should be public also. Accordingly, he took off his royal robes, and insignia of office, covered himself with sackcloth, prostrated himself on the pavement of the church, in view of the whole congregation, beat his breast, tore his hair, threw ashes on his head, and with tears implored forgiveness of his great sin; repeating the words of King David, "My soul cleaveth to the dust, quicken thou me according to thy word." Having thus publicly humbled himself, he was again allowed to frequent the church, but he confessed to Ambrose that not a day of his life passed without his feeling a pang for that cruel transaction.

Theodosius lived but few months after his triumph over

Eugenius in Rome.   But so active and energetic had been his measures for the downfall of idolatry, that the religion thenceforth called Pagan, lingered in the empire only as a pale disembodied ghost.   What the inflexible will of Athanasius had begun, was so effectually aided by his strong arm, and the powerful character of Ambrose, that the church which he decreed should be Universal, and therefore named it Catholic, ruled all Europe for a thousand years, and the creed thus established is still received as an inheritance by a large majority of Christendom.

THE LATER CHRISTIAN FATHERS.

I will now revert to a few of the most prominent characters in the Christian church, while the events I have related in its external history were in progress.

LACTANTIUS.—Lactantius, who is supposed to have died about the year three hundred and thirty, was a philosopher and rhetorician, who became so famous, that Diocletian invited him to settle near the imperial court at Nicomedia, and practise his art.   There he became a convert to Christianity.   When quite an old man, he was summoned to Gaul, to superintend the education of Crispus, the unfortunate son of Constantine.   He wrote many books on religious subjects, some of which are still extant.   From the elegance of his style, he has been called the Christian Cicero.

ATHANASIUS.—It is said that Alexander, Bishop of Alexandria, on the occasion of a festival in honour of one of his martyred predecessors, observed a troop of boys at their play, imitating the rites of the church.   One of them enacted the part of bishop, and performed all the usual ceremonies of baptism.   Regarding this as a forerunner of what the child was to be, he caused him to be educated with express reference to an ecclesiastical profession.   This boy was the celebrated Athanasius, who soon became distinguished at school for the quickness of his intellect. In his youth, he was the private secretary of his patron. Being drawn toward monastic life, he went into the desert, and spent some time with the famous hermit, Anthony. When he returned, he was appointed archdeacon, and at the Council of Nice gained great reputation by the ability he displayed in the Arian controversy. Six months after, he succeeded his friend as Bishop of Alexandria. He is said to have been little cultivated in general literature, but deeply versed in biblical learning. To him, more than to any other person, the Christian world owes what was afterward generally received as orthodox doctrine concerning the Trinity; therefore he is often called "the father of theology." He lived at a stormy period, and was a spirit well calculated to ride on the storm. He was banished from his bishopric, recalled in triumph, banished and recalled, again and again; attacked with the utmost rancour of theological hatred; protected and defended with the utmost warmth of theological zeal; accused of many misdemeanours and crimes, and always satisfactorily vindicated; unyielding in his opinions, hot in controversy, but never convicted of dishonesty toward his opponents. He sustained all reverses with fortitude, and could neither be driven or tempted to swerve from the course which his own mind had established as the right one. When Constantine deposed him on account of charges brought against him, he appeared in the midst of a long train of ecclesiastics, as the emperor was riding through the streets, and demanded a hearing. Constantine tried to pass in silence; but the bold prelate exclaimed: "God will judge between you and me, since you thus take part with my slanderers. I only demand that they should be summoned, and my cause heard in the imperial presence." The emperor acknowledged the justice of his request, and summoned his accusers. Being informed that Athanasius boasted he could force him to his wishes, by cutting off the supplies of corn from Alexandria to Constantinople, he formed a strong dislike of him, banished him to the distant city of

Treves, and was ever after accustomed to designate him
as "proud, turbulent, obstinate, and intractable." Where-
ever he resided, the clergy were devoted to him, and so
were a majority of the people. His commanding character
and inflexible will had immense power over the minds of
men. When Constantius, from motives of policy, recalled
him to Alexandria, bishops flocked from all parts to wel-
come him, the city was illuminated, incense waved before
him in the streets, alms distributed liberally to the poor,
and prayers of thanksgiving offered in all the houses of his
numerous friends. When Constantius again deposed him,
on account of fresh charges against him, it was deemed
necessary to send a force of five thousand men, to carry
the order into effect. He was performing service in the
church at midnight, preparatory to the communion, when
the soldiers burst in. Amid the trampling of horses, and
the clashing of steel, he exhorted the people to continue
their worship; and the choristers chanted "O give thanks
unto the Lord," while the people responded, "For his
mercy endureth forever." The clergy around him finally
hurried him out of a private door, and compelled him to
escape. He retired into the desert, where he outdid all
the hermits in fasting and watching, penances and prayers.
In vain his enemies hunted for his life. All the monks of
the desert were his faithful adherents, and it was impossible to trace him. During several months, he was concealed
in his father's tomb. Twenty years of his life were passed
in banishment; but he finally died in peaceful possession
of his bishopric, and left a high reputation for piety, benevolence, and unblemished virtue. He had the advantage of belonging to the victorious party, and nearly all
that we know of him is recorded by his friends and ad-
mirers.

BASIL.—Basil, called the Great, was born of a noble
Christian family in Cappadocia, in the year three hundred
and twenty-nine. During the persecution under Diocletian, his grandfather retired to a mountain forest, in Pon-

tus. His grandmother was a very devout woman, who had often listened to the preaching of Gregory Thaumaturgus; and her character and precepts had a powerful influence on her descendants. His father was an eminent lawyer, and he was educated for the same profession. Having received all the instruction Cæsarea afforded, he went to Constantinople, where he studied rhetoric with the celebrated Libanius. He afterward went to Athens, where at that time many young men of talent congregated; among whom was Julian, afterward emperor. He returned to Cæsarea, where he became distinguished for eloquence as an advocate. But the religious impressions received in childhood, and the persuasions of his pious sister Macrina, induced him to quit the career of brilliant success which was opening before him. He became interested in monastic life, and practised such severe austerities, that he reduced his body almost to a skeleton. He retired to a neighbouring mountain, where he built a monastery intended as a general asylum for orphans. There he spent twelve years, with a large company of devotees, who lived very austerely, and divided their time between useful labour, study of the Scriptures, and prayer.

Basil took part in the controversy against Macedonius, concerning the equal dignity of the Son and the Holy Ghost, with almost as much zeal as Athanasius contended with Arians for the equal dignity of the Father and the Son; but he manifested more charity toward opponents, than was common with theological partisans. During a severe famine in Cappadocia he devoted the whole of his fortune to the relief of the sufferers. This increased the popularity he had already acquired by his piety, learning, and comparative mildness in controversy. At the age of forty-one, he was chosen Archbishop of Cæsarea; but he always wore his monastic dress, and retained his ascetic habits. His administration was distinguished by energy, vigilance, strictness in church discipline, and careful examination of candidates for the priesthood; but especially for benevolence to the poor, for whom he caused asylums to

be built in several cities. He was much celebrated for
pulpit eloquence, and his prayers were believed to have
miraculous power. There was a tradition concerning him,
universally believed, that the Holy Spirit, in the form of a
white dove, was frequently seen perched on his shoulders,
inspiring him while he preached.

When the emperor Valens was travelling through his
diocese, he sent a messenger to him, requiring that he
should perform the rites of the church in the Arian mode,
and admit Arians to the communion. Basil refused to
comply, and when reminded that the emperor had power
to confiscate all his property, to banish him, and even to
put him to death, he calmly replied: "He who owns nothing can lose nothing. All the possessions the emperor can
take from me are my cloak, and a few books. Banishment
can be no exile to me, since the whole earth is the Lord's.
As for torture, my feeble body would yield to the first
blows; and death would only bring me nearer to the Lord,
for whom my soul longs." The messenger, astonished by
his quiet firmness, told the emperor that threats and blandishments were alike useless with that man; and he recommended violent measures. But Valens, aware of his great
popularity, and commanding influence, deemed it impolitic
to proceed against him. Fearing that his refusal to admit
Arians might occasion some tumult, he resolved to appear
at church himself, but to manifest his disapprobation by
declining to partake of the communion. To his great surprise, Basil proceeded with the usual services of the day,
without taking any notice of the imperial presence. No
one offered him the communion, yet he found it impossible
to be angry. The dignified appearance of the archbishop,
his uncommon eloquence, and the general solemnity of the
service, impressed him so deeply, that he went up to the
altar and presented a gift. The attendant clergy looked at
the archbishop, as if uncertain whether the offering of a
heretic might be accepted. Basil, seeing that the emperor
was much agitated, condescended to advance and receive
his oblation. An interview afterward took place between

them. Valens remained unconvinced on doctrinal points, but he forbore to interfere with Basil's regulations, and gave him a liberal donation for the poor of his diocese.

Basil died at fifty years old, his health being ruined by the severe asceticism he had practised. When the people heard he was dying, they flocked round the house, sobbing aloud, and praying earnestly to God to spare their good bishop. Gregory of Nazianzen says there was none of them who would not have willingly given up a portion of life, if they could have prolonged his. The funeral was solemnized with every possible testimonial of love and reverence. It was attended by a vast concourse of Christians, as well as Jews and Pagans; for all good men honoured his memory. Many were pressed to death in the crowd, and followed him to the unseen world. He left many writings of a controversial and religious character; Commentaries on the Scriptures, Treatises on Baptism, Virginity, Monastic Rules, and Christian Morals.

GREGORY.—Gregory was born at Nazianzen, in the same year as Basil the Great. His father belonged to one of the Gnostic sects, but was drawn over to the orthodox faith, by the prayers and tears and gentle example of his pious wife, Nonna, and was subsequently ordained Bishop of Nazianzen. They were childless for many years, and their affectionate souls longed for offspring. When at last a son was given to them, they carried him to the altar of the church, soon after his birth, placed a volume of the Gospels in his little hands, and dedicated him to the service of the Lord. The child was accustomed to hear this spoken of, and early learned to compare himself with the infant Samuel, whose infancy was consecrated to the service of the temple, where God called him in dreams. The devotional habits and religious teaching of his parents continually strengthened his serious tendencies. While he was yet a boy, he had a dream, which led him to resolve on a life of celibacy and holiness. In his sleep, he beheld two celestial virgins, in white robes, with faces that shone like stars. They took him in their arms and kissed him. Surprised at their wondrous beauty, he asked them whence they came. One of them replied: "I am Charity, and this is my sister Temperance. We come to thee from Paradise, where we stand continually before the throne of Christ, and enjoy ineffable delights. Come to us, my son, and dwell with us for ever."

His father caused him to be educated at the best schools in the empire. For that purpose he was sent to Alexandria, Constantinople, and Athens, where he pursued his studies in company with Basil the Great. From his observation of the young prince Julian, who was at the same school, he predicted that he would depart from his outward conformity to Christianity. Gregory was baptized in his thirtieth year, and retired to monastic solitude with Basil, for whom he had formed a very intimate and tender friendship. They divided their time between manual labour and study of the Sacred Scriptures, and the writings of the early Fathers. Their favourite author was Origen, for whose character and writings they cherished profound veneration. Like his friend Basil, he injured his health by the austerities he practised. He lived on bread and salt, drank water only, and slept but little. He confesses that a life of celibacy was utterly repugnant to his nature; but he deemed a departure from it incompatible with any great attainments in holiness. He wished to withdraw his mind altogether from worldly affairs, but a desire to assist the declining years of his parents compelled him to pay some attention to financial regulations. When Basil became Archbishop of Cæsarea, he appointed him Bishop of Sasina, a small marshy town, where many roads met, and where there was a continual strife between travellers and custom-house officers. It was a post ill suited to a man of his quiet, contemplative habits, and he complained of his friend for placing him in such an uncongenial situation. He soon withdrew again to monastic seclusion, and mani fested extreme reluctance to accept of any ecclesiastical office, from a feeling that he was not pure enough to serve

God at the altar. But his timid conscience being alarmed by representations that he was fleeing from duty, he consented to be ordained presbyter, and assisted his father in the discharge of his clerical functions. After the death of the old man, he was chosen bishop of his native place, and was much admired and respected for his eloquence and excellent character. But his love of contemplation and repose again led him to retire from the world and live among the monks. He emerged from his solitude occasionally to build up the Athanasian cause. There being no church belonging to that party in Constantinople, he preached in the house of one of his kinsmen. His earnest eloquence attracted crowds. The Arians, provoked by his success, broke into the house, pelted him with stones, and dispersed the meeting. When Theodosius came to the throne, he summoned him to preside over the churches at Constantinople, in place of the deposed Arian bishop. It has been already stated that he was placed in the episcopal chair by a formidable array of military force; an immense majority of the inhabitants being Arians. Fortunately, he was less inclined to polemical controversy than most teachers of that period. He preached against the prevailing tendency to speculation, and combatted the idea fast gaining ground that soundness in doctrine was of more consequence than the practical performance of religious duties. He said knowledge of divine things was not an end to be attained in this present life; it was to be used merely as a means of becoming holy, in order to be capable of full reception of the truth in the world to come. He bore dislike with humility, and sometimes disarmed his most bitter opponents by meekness. Yet even he approved of the severe edicts of Theodosius against heretics.

The dissatisfaction excited by his appointment, and questions which arose concerning its validity, induced him to ask liberty to resign his responsible and onerous office, to men who cared more for earthly honours and advantages. He delivered a farewell discourse before an assembly of the clergy, in which "he dealt out many a hard

K*

truth against the worldly-minded bishops." Worn down
with perpetual feuds in the churches, he retired to the
quiet of private life, amid the brooks and trees of his
native town. He was then old and bald, his frame enfeebled, and his face furrowed by inward and outward
struggles, and by the severe austerities he practised. But
still the conflict with nature continued. The presence of
women troubled him, and alarmed his conscience. He
allowed no repose to his aged body. He slept on a hard
mat, with a sackcloth covering. He wore one thin tunic,
went barefoot, and allowed himself no fire. He fasted and
prayed, and devoted himself to the composition of poetry
in Greek, which, from its difficulty, he considered a penance. In these devotional poems, the praises of virginity
are rung through all manner of changes, and Christ is represented as giving it the highest place of honour at his
right hand. This sensitive and religious soul lingered in
the body ninety years. His writings give a melancholy
picture of the clerical temper of his times; especially as
manifested in councils.

JEROME.—Jerome was born in Dalmatia, now a southern
province of Austria. The precise date of his birth is unknown, but it was not far from three hundred and forty.
His parents, who were in prosperous worldly circumstances, sent him to Rome to complete his education,
where he pursued with avidity the study of Greek and
Latin literature and philosophy. The great capital abounded
with temptations, and according to his own account, he fell
into some habits of dissipation, from which, however, he
soon emerged. The tombs of the martyrs, and the catacombs where Christians were accustomed to meet for
worship, in their days of obscurity and peril, made a deep
impression on his mind. He became devout, and was
baptized. After he left Rome, he travelled on the borders
of the Rhine, where he became acquainted with many
Christian preachers, and transcribed some commentaries on
the Hebrew Scriptures, and other polemical works. He

visited several countries of Western Asia, and at Antioch studied with the learned Appollinaris. In that city, when about thirty-four years of age, he had a very dangerous illness, from which he recovered in a state of religious enthusiasm, which strongly inclined him to become a hermit. He retired to the Desert of Chalcis, between Antioch and the river Euphrates. There he passed four years in solitude, supporting himself by the labour of his own hands, reading, and meditating upon religious books, fasting, watching, and in various ways tormenting himself, to atone for youthful sins. In this state of mind, his conscience reproached him for the time he had bestowed on Pagan literature; in which, however, he still delighted. He says: "To subdue the flesh, I became scholar to a monk, who had been a Jew, to learn of him the Hebrew language. I, who had so diligently studied the copious flowing eloquence of Cicero, and the smoothness of Pliny, had now to inure myself to the hissing and broken-winded words of the Hebrew." If at times he yielded to the temptation of reading Cicero, he endeavoured to atone for it by rigid fasts. If Plato enticed him, he deprived himself of sleep, as a penance. He says: "When I called home my thoughts, and returned to the Hebrew Prophets, their style appeared to me rude and negligent. Blind that I was, I ventured to accuse the light!" During this conflict between conscience and his mental predilections, he states that he had a vision of Christ coming to judgment. An awful voice demanded, "Who art thou?" With trembling accents, Jerome replied: "I am a Christian." "It is false," rejoined the voice. "Thou art a Ciceronian, and no Christian. Where the treasure is there will the heart be also." He was then severely scourged by the attendant angels; and while suffering under their blows, he made a solemn vow never again to read a Pagan book. He was the first of the Fathers, after Origen, who considered it worth while to undertake the great labour of understanding Hebrew.

Monastic asceticism became the ruling passion of Jerome's life. Two of his friends, who went into the same desert, died of the tortures they inflicted on themselves, and he also was often on the brink of the grave. Theological disputations in the church at last drew him forth from his retreat. He went to Antioch, and consented to be ordained presbyter, with the express stipulation that he should not be required to perform regularly the duties of his office. He soon after visited Constantinople, where he formed an intimacy with Gregory of Nazianzen, and occupied himself with various translations in the service of the church. Thence he went to Rome, where his learning and zeal commended him to Damasus the archbishop, who employed him in many important affairs. At his urgent intreaty, he undertook a laborious revision and comparison of various manuscripts of the Hebrew Scriptures, and the Christian Gospels, which in the course of much copying, had fallen into a good deal of confusion. At the same time he devoted himself to preaching zealously in favour of a life of celibacy and contemplation. He became a kind of confessor and guide to noble Roman ladies, directed their religious studies, and supervised their conduct. Many rich widows gave all their wealth to the church, and some deserted young families to devote themselves to a life of celibacy and religious contemplation. Such influence over the wealthy and noble naturally excited the indignation of relatives, disappointed in their expectations of legacies, and of young patricians deprived of advantageous marriages with rich maidens. The boldness and severity of his preaching against the indolence and luxury of the clergy in Rome, likewise created many ecclesiastical enemies. He was the object of secret insinuations and open invectives, and was frequently insulted when he appeared in the street. For a good while, he firmly withstood the opposition by which he was surrounded; but after the death of his powerful patron Damasus, he deemed it prudent to withdraw from Rome to Antioch. There he was soon after joined by some of the most zealous of his Roman converts to celibacy, both men and women. With them he made a pilgrimage to Jerusalem, and took up his residence in a monastery at Bethlehem. From this retreat he fulminated anathemas against various heretical sects. He prided himself on orthodox adherence to the established church, and his style of defending it was acrimonious in the extreme. His virulent attacks on the Pelagians so exasperated them, that they surrounded his monastery with an armed force, and he was obliged to hide himself two years. Soon after his return, his health declined under the continual pressure of toil and excitement. He died at his monastery, in the year four hundred and twenty. He has always been venerated by ecclesiastics as one of the greatest lights of the ancient church.

AMBROSE.—Ambrose was son of the Governor of Gaul. He was sent to Rome in his boyhood, to receive the best education the city afforded. He began his career as a lawyer at Milan, where he soon acquired a brilliant reputation for forensic eloquence. He was afterward invested with consular power over the provinces of which Milan was the capital. When the Arian Bishop died, in three hundred and seventy-four, a violent dispute arose between Athanasians and Arians concerning the election of his successor. Ambrose, as magistrate, deemed it necessary to be present to prevent tumultuous proceedings. He addressed them in a speech intended to allay the excitement. In the midst of his remarks, a little child called out: "Ambrose, bishop!" Whether the child thought that every man who talked to a church full of people was a bishop, and felt a wayward impulse to proclaim that idea, or whether some one instructed him what to say, is uncertain; but the exclamation was hailed as an oracle from heaven, and Ambrose was chosen bishop by acclamation of the people, in which bishops of both parties joined. He tried to avoid the honour thus conferred upon him; pleading that, though a Christian, he had never been baptized. Finding this did not avail, he escaped from Milan; but after travelling all night, he found, to his great surprise, that he had been going round in a circuit, and with the morning light had arrived at the city gates again. At last, he was obliged to yield to the express commands of the emperor, and was accordingly baptized and ordained bishop, at thirty-four years of age. He began by distributing all his property to the church and the poor, and devoting himself to theological studies. He espoused the orthodox side, and maintained it with rather a high hand. When Justina, mother of the young prince Valentinian, appointed an Arian bishop at Sirmium, he appointed an Athanasian bishop in his stead. When she demanded, in the name of the young emperor, at least one of the churches in Milan for Arian worship, he refused; probably fearing that if one were granted, the demands would be increased. When it was urged that the emperor had power to determine all matters within the empire, and consequently the churches belonged to him, Ambrose replied: "A bishop can not alienate that which is dedicated to God." Justina attempted to take forcible possession of one of the churches; but the populace were in such an excited state, that the soldiers hesitated to make an onset. Ambrose was commanded to leave the city; but he refused to obey. He preached a sermon in which he said sneeringly: "The emperor demands a church. What has he to do with the church of the heretics?" He even ventured to compare the empress-mother with Jezebel. The people, impressed by his boldness, magnetized by his eloquence, and charmed with his noble and affable manners, were ready to sustain him in everything. They kept continual watch in the church day and night, to prevent the Arians from getting possession of it. To sustain their spirits, Ambrose introduced a custom long practised in the Eastern churches, of choirs answering each other in responsive verses. This inspiring addition to the worship excited great enthusiasm. The form of music he then introduced is still used in the churches of Milan, under the name of Ambrosian Chants, characterized by majestic simplicity and fulness of harmony.

Ambrose raised the sacerdotal character to a degree of dignity and importance previously unknown. His power over the violent and despotic Theodosius has been already mentioned. When the young emperor Valentinian was urged to have an interview with him, during the contest for the possession of one of the churches, he said to the officers who recommended it: "If I were to follow your advice, his eloquence would induce you to lay me bound hand and foot before his throne." He was the adviser and guide of several sovereigns, though he never sought to gain their favour, or avoid their displeasure. Difficult negotiations were entrusted to him, and during the frequent revolutions and disturbances which occurred, the vanquished and oppressed always found in him a powerful protector. His administration was marked by increasing grandeur in the forms of public worship, and by zealous efforts in favour of celibacy in both sexes. He wrote three books in praise of virginity, which he dedicated to his sister.

When he was fifty-seven years old, he had a violent attack of illness, during which Christ appeared to him in person, and addressed him with consoling words. The Bishop of Vercelli, who attended upon him, having gone to sleep, was waked by an angel, who said: "Arise quickly! for he is about to depart." He hastened to the bed, where he found Ambrose kneeling at prayer, and had but just time to administer the sacrament before he expired. Some who were present affirmed that they saw his soul ascend to heaven, borne in the arms of angels.

CHRYSOSTOM.—John Chrysostom was the son of a General in the Roman army, who died soon after his birth, in the year three hundred and forty-four. His young mother, Anthusa, who was a very devout Christian, withdrew from society, and devoted herself entirely to the memory of her husband, and the education of her son. In boyhood, he was remarkable for a serious earnestness of mind, and love of solitude. He studied eloquence with the famous orator Libanius, who said he should like to see him his succes-

in the school, if the Christians had not stolen him. At the age of twenty, he was already a celebrated pleader at the bar. But the corrupt practices then prevalent disgusted him, and the religious impressions of childhood deepened more and more, until his fame as a lawyer became hateful to him, and he resolved to be a hermit. His mother tried hard to dissuade him, saying: "Make me not a second time a widow, I intreat thee. Awaken not again my slumbering sorrows. Wait at least for my death. Perhaps I shall depart before long. When thou hast laid me in the earth, and united my bones with those of thy father, then travel wherever thou wilt; even beyond the sea. But as long as I live, endure to dwell in my house, and offend not God by afflicting thy mother, who, whatever may be her faults, is at least guiltless toward thee." Her tears so touched his heart, that he was turned aside from his purpose. During her life-time, he lived in private apartments of her house, where her watchful love supplied him with everything, that his mind might not be distracted from religious pursuits. He studied the Scriptures and the Fathers diligently, prepared himself for the ministry, and became a reader in the church. Before he was thirty years old, his mother being dead, he joined a company of monks, who dwelt on the mountains in the vicinity of Antioch. He was greatly charmed with their mode of life, and remained with them four years. In search of more complete seclusion, he retired to a solitary cave, where he committed all the Hebrew and Christian Scriptures to memory. For two years, he did not lie down. Wakefulness and other forms of severe penance, brought on a dangerous illness, which compelled him to return to Antioch. After his recovery, he was ordained presbyter, and at the moment of consecration it is said a white dove descended on his head, which was regarded as a sign of divine inspiration. His eloquent preaching converted many Jews, Pagans, and heretics. He became so celebrated, that in three hundred ninety-seven, he was elected Archbishop of Constantinople. But such was his popularity at Antioch, that the emperor

Arcadius, son of Theodosius, caused him to be secretly conveyed away, before the citizens had time to interfere. He gave orders that all the ecclesiastical and civil dignitaries should go out six miles to meet him, and escort him into the city. His predecessor had maintained a system of luxurious hospitality at the episcopal palace; but John Chrysostom preferred a plain style of living, that he might be enabled to found hospitals, and relieve the indigent. He was so liberal in his charities, that he was proverbially called John the Alms-giver. He devoted much of his time to personal attendance on the poor and suffering. He sent missionaries to the Goths and the Scythians, to Persia and Palestine. In him the oppressed always found a protector, the sinner a sympathizing friend. He was accustomed to say: "With the Devil alone we have nothing in common; with every man we have much that is in common." He was bold, and even reckless, in rebuking hypocrisy and injustice, especially in high places. If there was controversy between the powerful and the lowly, his generous sympathies were always on the poor man's side. He required very strict morality in his clergy, and deposed several bishops for misconduct. He had a strong conviction that men have free choice to become good or evil, to believe or disbelieve; that the grace of God is always bestowed in proportion as men wish to receive it. Therefore, though ready to accept repentance, he was not prone to palliate wrong. Hence, his preaching was of a very practical, searching character, and his denunciation of sin and sinners was sometimes very severe. In one of his sermons, he asked the people of Constantinople: "How many think you will be saved in this city? What I am going to say will terrify you; but yet I must speak it. Of so many thousands, there will hardly be one hundred saved; and I doubt even of those." He was always so much in earnest in what he said, and his style of eloquence was so lively and dramatic, that people deserted the theatres to hear him thunder from the pulpit of Santa Sophia. It had become very much the custom to applaud preachers, as

well as orators, and the vanity of many was gratified by
such demonstrations; but when he was interrupted by acclamations, he was accustomed to say, with serious indignation: "The place you sit in is no theatre; nor are you
gazing upon actors." He showed neither fear nor favour
in his rebukes. In his peculiarly bold, straight-forward
manner, he bore public testimony against the extravagance
of the empress Eudoxia, the profligacy of her court, and
the ambition of ecclesiastics. This made him very popular
among the people, but rendered him odious to the empress
and her courtiers, whose rapacious avarice was often defeated by his zealous efforts to protect the property of
widows and orphans. The worldly-minded among the
clergy disliked his strict regulations, his simple mode of
living, and his scorching rebukes to those who sought pre-
ferment in the church for the sake of honour or gain. From
these causes there grew up a party extremely hostile to
this truly noble and religious man; and they waited only
for some occasion that would serve as a pretext to injure
him. Certain monks, who had been excommunicated by
Theophilus, Bishop of Alexandria, on account of their
attachment to the tenets of Origen, fled to Constantinople.
Chrysostom, always ready to help the destitute, supplied
the strangers with a comfortable abode, and wrote to
Theophilus beseeching him to pardon them. Instead of
complying with his humane request, the haughty prelate
sent messengers to Constantinople to accuse them. The
monks begged the protection of the empress, who placed
great reliance on the blessings and prayers of such devotees. A tangled controversy grew out of it, in which
Chrysostom was involved. Theophilus, whose character
was in every respect opposite, became his bitter enemy.
By various artifices, he contrived to have a synod summoned at Chalcedon, to try Chrysostom. Because he took
part with the excommunicated monks, they accused him
of favouring the tenets of Origen, of acting contrary to
ecclesiastical rules in receiving those whom a brother
bishop had excommunicated, of being passionate in his

expressions, and meanly inhospitable in his style of living. What they called passionate expressions doubtless originated in the exceeding sincerity of the man. On all great occasions, he was calm and self-possessed, and he bore personal injuries with the utmost patience; but when he witnessed oppression or hypocrisy, his nature was such that he could not refrain from an honest outburst of vehement indignation. Being summoned to appear before the synod, he professed his readiness to have his conduct examined by them, or by any other assembly in the world; but he required that four of his personal enemies should be excluded from the number of his judges. This reasonable request was not granted; his non-appearance was construed into a confession of guilt, and he was formally deposed. Chrysostom at first resolved to remain with the flock whom he believed God had intrusted to his care; and they, on their part, surrounded his house and the church, to prevent his being carried away. Meanwhile, he addressed to them one of his impassioned discourses, which wrought up their zealous affection to the highest pitch. Finding there was danger of bloodshed in his cause, he stole privately away, gave himself up, and was conveyed into exile. His people received the tidings with a loud outburst of passionate lamentation. They wept bitterly; saying: "It is better that the sun should not shine, than that John Chrysostom should not preach to us." A few days after his departure, a violent shock of earthquake was felt at Constantinople; a circumstance then universally regarded as a token of God's displeasure. When the empress felt her bed rock under her, she started up with intense terror, and falling at the feet of the emperor besought him to avert the wrath of Heaven by recalling John Chrysostom. The startling event had been construed in the same way by the populace; and early the next morning they surrounded the palace, clamouring for the return of their good bishop. Accordingly, messengers were sent to bring him. The whole population, men, women, and children, went out miles to meet him, and escorted him home with waving torches and hymns of thanksgiving.

About two months after, a magnificent silver statue of the empress was erected in front of the palace, accompanied with festivities resembling the old Pagan ceremonies. The cathedral of Santa Sophia being near by, the meeting for worship was disturbed by the noise; and Chrysostom in his sermon inveighed against such heathenish practices. The empress, being informed of it, became exasperated, and again leagued with his enemies. In consequence of which, he began a discourse by saying: "Again is Herodias angry; again she demands the head of John." Thenceforth, she became his irreconcilable enemy. Being zealously assisted by the machinations of hostile bishops, and having unlimited influence over her husband, the emperor Arcadius, Chrysostom was again sentenced to banishment. Soldiers were sent to seize him, and found him in the cathedral, celebrating the solemnities of Good Friday. They forced their way up to the altar, but the people were determined to protect their bishop. Many of them were wounded, others trodden under foot. The baptismal font was stained with blood; the bread and wine of the eucharist were spilled on the ground, and the church vessels seized as plunder. Chrysostom, foreseeing the danger of popular insurrection, exonerated the emperor, and attributed the proceedings against him to the influence of hostile bishops. In the tumult, he found means to escape from his friends, surrendered himself to the officers, and was carried away in the night. At the moment of his departure, the church took fire and was burnt down. Some accused him of having kindled it, others suspected his adherents. The city continued in an uproar several days. Wherever the partisans of Chrysostom assembled, they were dispersed by soldiers. He was conveyed to Cucusus, a small desolate town, in a mountainous and savage district of Armenia, infested with robbers. There he had much to suffer from external causes, but his faith and courage never forsook him. He wrote letters full of consolation to his friends at Constantinople, and continued to

administer paternal advice to his beloved flock, who under
his guidance continued to support zealously his missions
in foreign lands. He was also the means of extensive
good in the district where he was placed. He bore his
wrongs with such cheerful resignation, and was so unwearied in his efforts to benefit others, that he was even
more admired in adversity, than he had ever been in prosperity. Many churches expressed sympathy for him, and
Innocent, Bishop of Rome, declared strongly in his favour.
His enemies began to fear that he would again be brought
back to Constantinople in triumph. To prevent it, they
resolved to place him where he could not communicate
with his friends. He was accordingly conveyed, in the
year four hundred and seven, to Pityus, in a barbarian
district, at the extreme verge of the Roman empire. The
officers who had charge of him compelled him to perform
the journey on foot, with his head uncovered, under a
burning sun. His body, enfeebled by previous suffering,
sunk under these hardships. They carried him to a chapel
on the road, where he put on white garments, and received
the communion. Immediately after, he uttered a brief
prayer, which he had always been accustomed to repeat in
seasons of trial: "Blessed be the Lord for all things."
And with those words on his lips, he expired at sixty-
three years of age.

His memory was cherished with a degree of reverence
and love seldom bestowed on mortals; and few have ever
deserved it as he did. For a long time, there existed a
party at Constantinople called Johannites. They would
never acknowledge the justice of the decree by which their
beloved pastor was deposed. They refused to receive the
communion at the hands of his successor, but held private
meetings, where the rites were performed by clergymen
who were friends to Chrysostom. Bishops and clergymen
in other places protested against the injustice that had been
done him. To prevent a wide-spread schism, his name
was introduced into the public prayers of the church, and
a general amnesty granted to all his adherents. Thirty

one years after his death, the Patriarch of Constantinople persuaded the emperor, Theodosius Second, to have his remains brought back and placed in the royal sepulchre. The emperor himself went as far as Chalcedon, to meet the procession, and bending over the coffin, implored Chrysostom in heaven to forgive the wrongs he had received from his royal parents, Arcadius and Eudoxia. The surviving Johannites, appeased by these public honours to the memory of their good bishop, at last consented to be again united with the ruling church.

The surname of Chrysostom, signifying the Mouth of Gold, was early conferred on this celebrated Father of the church, on account of his rare eloquence. His writings are very voluminous. In his commentaries, he rejected the allegorical mode of interpretation, then so prevalent, and investigated the meaning of texts grammatically.

AUGUSTINE.—Augustine was born in the year three hundred and fifty-four, of Roman parents, in Numidia, Africa. His mother, Monica, was a devout Christian at the time of his birth. Many years afterward, her husband, who was a passionate, arbitrary man, was converted, mainly by the uniform gentleness and meekness of her deportment. She tried to train her son very carefully; but he being naturally ardent and impetuous, did not easily submit to restraint. His parents sent him to Carthage to complete his education; but he disappointed their expectations, by want of application. His mind was quick, inquisitive, and acute; but he liked a rambling mode of reading, and was impatient of hard study. The intensity of his temperament also led him into irregularities, which became more and more attractive by indulgence. His father having economized closely to give him a liberal education, was so ambitious to have him become an eloquent lawyer, that dangers to morality were a subordinate consideration. His godly mother wept and prayed, and gave him good advice; but even she was unwilling to entertain the idea of an early marriage; "for she feared

lest a wife should prove a clog and hindrance to his hopes."
"At Carthage," he says, "there sang all round me in my
ears a cauldron of unholy loves." "Among such as these,
in that unsettled age of mine, I learned books of eloquence,
wherein I desired to be eminent, out of a damnable and
vain-glorious end, a joy in human vanity." Before he
was nineteen years old, Cicero's Hortensius, containing
exhortations to philosophy, came into his hand, and excited
in him a strong desire to control his impulses. He says:
"This book altered my affections, and turned my prayers
to thee, O Lord; and made me have other purposes and
desires. Every vain hope at once became worthless to me.
I longed with an incredibly burning desire for an immortality of wisdom, and began to arise that I might return
to thee. How did I burn then, O my God, how did I
burn to remount from earthly things to thee! For with
thee is wisdom. But the love of wisdom is in Greek called
philosophy, with which that book inflamed me. And as
Apostolic Scripture was then unknown to me, I was delighted with that exhortation; but only so far that I was
thereby strongly roused and kindled, and inflamed to love,
and seek, and obtain, and hold, and embrace, not this or
that sect, but wisdom itself, wherever it could be found.
Thus enkindled, this alone checked me, that the name of
Christ was not in the book. For, according to thy mercy,
O Lord, my tender heart devoutly drank in this name
with my mother's milk, and deeply treasured it; and whatsoever was without that name, though never so learned,
polished, or true, took not entire hold of me. I resolved
then to bend my mind to the Holy Scriptures, that I might
see what they were. But not as I now speak, did I feel
when I turned to those Scriptures. They seemed to me
unworthy to be compared with the stateliness of Cicero;
for my swelling pride shrunk from their lowliness, nor
could my sharp wit pierce the interior thereof. I disdained
to be a little one, and, swollen with pride, took myself to
be a great one."

In this craving, unsettled state of mind, he became acquainted with the Gnostic sect, called Manicheans. They alleged that Christians were terrified by various superstitions, while *they* appealed to reason only, and "required no one to believe, until the truth had been sifted and cleared." Allured by this promise, he was attracted to their meetings, which he zealously attended during nine years; his longing for truth was never satisfied, but he was always hoping "that something of great account, would be laid open." His father was dead, but his mother mourned bitterly over his heresy. He says: "My mother, thy faithful one, wept to thee for me, more than mothers weep for the bodily death of their children; and thou didst not despise her tears, O Lord, when streaming down they watered the ground under her eyes in every place where she prayed." He records a dream, which was a source of great comfort to her. In her sleep, she seemed to be standing on a wooden rule, and a radiant youth came cheerfully toward her, and inquired why she wept so much. She replied: "Because I bewail my son's perdition." The shining messenger smiled and answered: "Content thyself. Look! dost thou not see that where thou art, there he is also?" And when she looked, she saw Augustine standing by her, on the same rule. In telling this story, he adds: "Whence was this, O thou Omnipotent Good, but that thine ears were turned toward her heart?"

In her anxiety for him, she went to a learned bishop, and besought him to argue with her son, and bring him into the Catholic church. But he replied: "You tell me that the young man is puffed up with the novelty of that heresy, and perplexes unskilful persons with captious questions. Let him alone for a while. Only pray to God for him, and he will himself, by reading, find how great is the impiety of that error." When she continued to weep, and importune him still further, he became a little impatient, and said: "Go thy ways; and God bless thee! It is not possible that the son of so many tears can perish." These words she considered oracular, and received them "as if they had sounded from heaven." Both of them placed great reliance on dreams and visions. His mother sought to negotiate a marriage for him, and following her advice, he wooed and was promised to a girl, who was so young, that it was agreed to delay the wedding two years. His mother prayed earnestly to God to have some vision concerning this project. But she dreamed "only vain, fantastic things," such as were brought together by her own mind, occupied on the subject. Augustine says: "These she told me of, but slighted them. For she said she could discern between the revelations of God, and the dreams of her own soul, by a certain feeling, which she could not express in words."

For some time, he taught rhetoric in Carthage, as a means of living. But, hoping for better arranged classes, he stole away from his loving mother, who would fain have detained him near her, and went to Rome. There he was visited by severe illness, to which he afterwards looked back with horror, at the thought of dying unbaptized. He says: "I was going down to hell, carrying all the sins I had committed against thee, O Lord, against myself and others, many and grievous, over and above that bond of original sin, whereby we all die in Adam. For thou hadst not then forgiven me in Christ any of these things; nor had he abolished for me, by his cross, the enmity I had incurred with thee by my sins. Had I parted hence then, whither had I gone but into fire and torments?" After his recovery, he still continued to attend the Manichean meetings, and became one of their Elect. But a teacher of rhetoric being wanted in Milan, he went thither. He says: "I came to Ambrose the bishop, known to the whole world as among the best of men, thy devout servant, O Lord; whose eloquent discourse did then plentifully dispense unto thy people the flour of thy wheat, the gladness of thy oil, and the sober inebriation of thy wine. That man of God received me as a father. Thenceforth, I began to love him; not indeed at first as a teacher of truth, but as a person kind toward myself. I listened diligently to his preaching, trying his eloquence, whether it answered the fame thereof. But though I took no pains to learn *what* he spake, but only to hear *how* he spake, yet together with the words there entered into my mind thoughts which I could not refuse. While I opened my heart to admit how *eloquently* he spake, it also entered how *truly* he spake; but this was by degrees."

He gradually rejected the Manichean theories, but could not as yet receive the doctrines of the church. Some writings of the New Platonists came in his way, and made a strong impression on him. He says: "I therein read, not indeed in the very words, but to the very same purpose, that in the beginning was the Logos, and the Logos was with God, and the Logos was God, by whom all things were made." Elsewhere, he says he found God the Father and the Son in the theories of Platonists, but nothing concerning the Holy Spirit; confessing that he did not understand what they meant by their Third Principle, which they called The Soul of the World. His inquisitive mind, searching everywhere for truth, led him to seek the acquaintance of an aged Christian, named Simplician, who he thought was "likely to have acquired much experience in the ways of the Lord." When he told Simplician of the Platonic books, which had interested him so deeply, the pious old man congratulated him, that such books had fallen into his hands, instead of the writings of other philosophers; acknowledging that "the Platonists, in many ways, prepared the mind for a belief in God and his Logos." He then told him that the man who translated those books from the Greek was a friend of his, named Victorinus, who, after having been many years a celebrated Platonic teacher at Rome, became a Christian in his old age. Augustine gives the following account: "Victorinus was a learned man, skilled in liberal sciences, who had read and weighed many works of the philosophers. He was the instructor of many noble senators, who placed his statue in the Forum, as a public testimony to his excellent discharge of his office. In his old age, he studied the

Scriptures diligently, and was wont to say to Simplician, 'I am already a Christian.' But his friend always replied, 'That I will not believe, till I see you in the church of Christ;' to which the philosopher would answer, jestingly, 'Do walls then make a Christian?' At last, he said, 'Let us go to the church, I wish to be made a Christian.' The dignitaries of Rome gnashed their teeth." It was customary to make profession of faith from an elevated place in the church, in sight and hearing of all the congregation. The presbyter inquired whether he would like to make his in a more private manner. He replied: "I have taught rhetoric and philosophy publicly; how much more ought I to acknowledge Christianity publicly." All the people knew him; and as he walked into the church, "there ran a low murmur through all the mouths of the rejoicing multitude: 'Victorinus! Victorinus!' Sudden was the burst of rapture when they saw him; suddenly they were hushed, that they might hear him. He pronounced the true faith with an excellent boldness, and all wished to draw him into their very heart." When the emperor Julian forbade Christians to teach from the classics, this aged man gave up the school, of which he had so long been the ornament.

The account of his conversion excited Augustine to emulation. He began to study the writings of the Apostle Paul, and they had a powerful effect on him. A young Christian from Carthage told him wonderful stories of Anthony and other holy monks, in the deserts of Egypt; and he had a longing to become as sanctified as they were. But his affectionate and ardent nature resisted the suggestion. He could not easily relinquish the idea of marriage. Ambrose, and nearly all the church Fathers of that period, zealously preached celibacy, as essential to holiness; and they seemed to him to be sustained by the words of Paul: "He that is unmarried, thinketh of the things of the Lord, how he may please the Lord; but he that is married, careth for the things of this world, how he may please his wife." He describes himself as "soul-sick and tormented."

"My ancient mistresses still held me, and whispered softly, 'Dost thou cast us off? and from that moment, shall we be no more with thee for ever?' And I blushed exceedingly that I yet heard the muttering of those toys, and still hung in suspense."

He had at that time a very dear friend, named Alypius, who had pursued the same studies, been attracted by the same Gnostic theories, and shared his interest in the writings of Paul. To him Augustine generally poured forth all his thoughts and feelings; but one day, when the conflict was very sharp within him, he says: "Alypius, sitting close by my side, silently awaited the issue of my unwonted emotion; and that I might pour it forth wholly, I rose and retired so far, that even his presence could not be a burthen to me. I cast myself down under a fig-tree, and giving vent to my tears, I cried out: 'How long, O Lord, how long? Why not now? Why should not this very hour put an end to my uncleanness?' Thus was I speaking, and weeping in the bitter contrition of my heart, when I heard from a neighbouring house, a voice, as of a boy or girl, chanting, and oft repeating: 'Take up and read! Take up and read!' Instantly my countenance changed. I began to think intently whether children were accustomed to sing such words, in any kind of play; and I could not remember ever to have heard the like. So checking the torrent of my tears, I arose; for I interpreted it to be no other than a command from God to open the book, and read the first chapter I found. Eagerly I returned to the place where Alypius was sitting; for there had I laid the volume of the Apostle Paul, when I rose thence. I seized, and in silence read the first section on which my eyes fell: 'Not in rioting and drunkenness, not in chambering and wantonness, not in strife and envying; but put ye on the Lord Jesus Christ, and make not provision for the flesh.' Instantly a serene light was infused into my soul, and all the darkness of doubt vanished away. With a calm countenance I made it known to Alypius. He looked, and saw that the following words were: 'Him that is weak in the faith, receive.' This he applied to himself. We went to my mother, and told her in order how it had all taken place. She leaped for joy, and triumphed, and blessed God, who had given her more than she had begged of Him by her pitiful and most sorrowful groanings. For thou, O Lord, hadst converted me unto thyself, so that I sought neither wife, nor any hope in this world; standing on that rule of faith, where thou hadst shown me unto her in a vision, so many years before."

Augustine had lived fifteen years with a woman to whom he was strongly attached, and she had given birth to a son, whom he had named Adeodatus. When arrangements were made for his marriage, he had parted from this woman with mutual tears, and she took a vow of perpetual celibacy. The boy was left with him to be educated, and seems always to have been an object of the tenderest affection. When Augustine took the resolution to become a monk, he left his occupation as a teacher of rhetoric, and retired into the country with his friend Alypius, his son, and his mother. There they devoted themselves to prayer and study of the Scriptures, preparatory to baptism. When he was dangerously ill in boyhood, he had greatly desired to be baptized, and his mother had tried to accomplish it, but had been disappointed. Now it was a matter of rejoicing with them both that the rite, which would cleanse him from all his sins, had been so long delayed. Alypius and Adeodatus were to be baptized with him, and they spent their time together in reading and prayer. He calls his friend: " A most valiant tamer of the body; so as with unwonted venture, to wear the frozen ground of Italy with his bare feet." Of his son he says: "In age he is the youngest of us all; but his talents, if affection deceives me not, promise something great. He is truly chaste, waits on God, and keeps himself to Him only." His mother was a happy woman in those days. He says: "Of all of us did she so take care, as though she had been mother of us all; so served us, as though she had been child to us all." The liveliness of their faith is indicated by the following incident, which he recorded years afterward: "When shall I recall all that passed in those holy days? Thou didst then afflict me with pain in my teeth; and when it had come to such a height that I could not speak, it entered my heart to desire all my friends present to pray for me to thee, God of all manner of health. I wrote this on wax, and gave it to them to read. So soon as with humble devotion we had bowed our knees, the pain went away. How went it away? I was affrighted, O Lord, my God; for from infancy, I had never experienced the like."

It was decided that the baptism should be administered by Ambrose, Bishop of Milan; and thither they all went, accompanied by the godly mother. They arrived at an exciting time, when the empress had demanded a church for the Arians, and when the people watched in the cathedral, night and day, cheered by the newly introduced Ambrosian Chants. To Augustine, in his tender and devout frame of mind, the effect was overpowering. He exclaims: "How did I weep, touched to the quick by the voices of thy sweetly-attuned church!" He was then thirty-three years old, and had acquired reputation for talent. The ceremony was made as impressive as possible. On that occasion the hymn called Te Deum was arranged for the church service: Ambrose and Augustine repeating the verses alternately, as they proceeded to the altar. Soon after this solemn scene, Augustine sold his estate, and gave most of the proceeds to the poor; reserving only a very moderate income for himself and his good mother. On their way home, she was seized with a fever, and all knew that her end was approaching. She was calm and cheerful, and full of love toward her child, whom she praised that in all his life he had never spoken to her a harsh or unkind word. She said: "All my hopes in this world are now accomplished. I see thee the servant of God, despising all earthly happiness. Why should I wish to linger any longer here?" Augustine says: "When she breathed her last, the boy Adeodatus burst out into a loud lament; then, being checked by us all, he held his peace. I closed her eyes; and there flowed withal a mighty sorrow into my heart, which was overflowing into tears. But the childish feeling in me, which through my heart's youthful voice was finding vent in weeping, was checked and silenced. We thought it not fitting to solemnize that funeral with tearful lament and groanings; for she was not altogether dead; of that we were certain, on the grounds of her good conversation, and her faith unfeigned. What then did so grievously pain me within? It was the sudden wrench of that most sweet and dear custom of living together; that life rent asunder, as it were, which of hers and mine together had been made but one."

Not long after, he was called to part with his beloved son. He says of him: "Excellently hadst thou made him, O Lord, my God, Creator of all! He was not quite fifteen, yet in intellect he surpassed many grave and learned men. His talent struck awe into me. Him we joined with us, our cotemporary in grace, to be brought up in thy discipline; and we were baptized, and uneasiness concerning our past lives vanished from us. Soon didst thou take his life from the earth. I remember him without anxiety; fearing nothing for his childhood, or youth, or his whole self."

Not long after his baptism, Augustine was ordained Bishop of Hippo, a small town near Carthage. His administration was characterized by strict morality, hospitality, and benevolence to the poor. He often boldly remonstrated with the rich in behalf of their labourers and tenants. He would never receive any bequest to the church, if it injured the relatives of the donor; and he never used any means to urge a reluctant giver. A citizen of Hippo, who willed his estate to the church, afterward sought to buy back the papers with a sum of money. Augustine sent back both the papers and the money, saying the church accepted only such offerings as were cheerfully given. Several situations of higher rank and greater income were offered to him, as a tribute to his intellectual ability, and upright character; but he preferred to remain with the flock first intrusted to his care. When Hippo was besieged by the Vandals, thirty-five years after, he refused to leave his people in the midst of their dangers and afflictions. He died there during the siege, in his seventy-sixth year.

He judged severely all non-conformity to the established church, and was constantly engaged in zealous controversy. Augustine though a more cultured man than Tertullian, had the same fiery character and tendency to excess. He adopted the doctrine that all human souls sinned in Adam, and that the inherent stain was physically transmitted by birth; but he carried it out to an extreme result, which had not been previously suggested; for he declared that every infant who died without having Adam's sin washed away by the waters of baptism, must remain in hell to all eternity. His writings exercised a very powerful and lasting influence on the theology of Christianity. On account of his fervid temperament, and glowing piety, painters generally represent him with the symbol of a flaming heart.

OPINIONS AND CUSTOMS OF THE LATER FATHERS.

Some of the later Fathers retained the old idea, so much dwelt upon by Tertullian, that Angels fell in love with mortal women, and produced a family of imps. But Chrysostom, Cyril, and others, declared that instead of *angels* of God, as written in the Septuagint, it ought to have been translated: "The *sons* of God came in unto the daughters of men, and they bare children to them." By sons of God, they understood descendants of Seth by Enos; a family peculiarly favoured by Heaven, because they "first began to call upon the name of the Lord." The daughters of men were understood to be the descendants of Cain. The ideas concerning Pagan deities remained much the same as those entertained by the primitive church. Lactantius says: "Evil Spirits, being adjured by Christians in the name of God, retire from the bodies of men; and being lashed by their words, as by scourges, confess themselves to be demons. They even tell their names, acknowledging that they are the same Spirits worshipped in the temples; and this even in the presence of their own worshippers; yet casting no reproach on religion, but on their own honour. It is not in their power to lie to God, in whose name they are adjured, or to the pious by whose voice they are tortured; therefore, after many howlings, they frequently cry out that they are scourged and burned, and are going out instantly." When Vigilantius protested against the honours paid to the bones of martyrs, Jerome attacked him violently. He bade him go into the churches of the martyrs where so many miracles were daily wrought, and he would be cleansed from the Evil Spirit which possessed him, and feel himself burnt, not by the wax candles which so much offended him, but by invisible flames which would force the Demon that talked within him to confess himself the same that had personated Mercury or Bacchus, or some other of the false gods. When Martin, Bishop of Tours, was zealously employed demolishing temples, he declares that the Evil Spirits who had been worshipped in them, under such names as Jupiter and Apollo, often appeared to him, and tried to stop his operations; but they had no power when he spoke to them in the name of Christ. Chrysostom, Gregory Bishop of Nyssa, and other Fathers, speak of the miraculous expulsion of Devils as a thing of frequent occurrence. The possessed persons are described as falling on the ground, tearing their hair, groaning with an inarticulate voice, and foaming at the mouth. Their faces grew black, and their eyes distorted; for "the Devil did not desist from strangling them." It is evident that the process of curing them was sometimes slow; for they often resorted to the churches as a kind of hospital. There a class of church officers, called Exorcists, took charge of them; whose business it was to pray over them, to provide their food, to keep them employed in some innocent business for exercise, such as sweeping and dusting the church, to prevent the more violent agitations of Satan, lest he should be tempted by their idleness to renew his attacks upon them." When they were in a sober state, those of them who had been baptized were allowed to partake of the Lord's Supper, which was thought to be very efficacious in warding off the paroxysms.

Miraculous power was everywhere attributed to holy relics; a custom unknown to the Jews, but prevalent among Hindoos and Buddhists from very ancient times. Chrysostom was eloquent on this theme. He says: "Not only the bones of martyrs, but their urns and their tombs overflow with benedictions. Let us prostrate ourselves before their relics. Let us embrace their coffins. Since their bones possess such great power, these also may have some. Not only on the days of their festivals, but on all other days, let us fix ourselves to them, and intreat them to be our patrons." Elsewhere, he says: "We are not to suppose the bodies of martyrs are left without active force, like those of common men; since a greater power than a human soul is superadded to them; the power of the Holy Spirit, which, by working miracles in them, demonstrates the truth of the resurrection." "Gold never dispelled diseases, or warded off death; but the bones of martyrs have done both." Basil says: "All who are in distress or difficulty fly for relief to the tombs of the martyrs; and whosoever touches their relics acquires some share of their sanctity." Even the oil in the lamps, kept continually burning before their remains, was believed to possess a miraculous virtue. Jerome says many were cured of the bites of venomous animals by touching their wounds with it. Chrysostom testifies that he knew many cases where the application of it dispelled various diseases. Augustine says a virgin of the church in his own time was cured of a devil by it; and that a young man, who was dead, was restored to life by being anointed with it. When one of his presbyters was accused of a misdemeanor, and he had no evidence but the parties themselves, he sent them to the sepulchre of Felix the martyr, to have it decided by his miraculous interposition; as he says had been done to his knowledge in a case of theft at Milan.

Bones believed to be the remains of Andrew, Luke, and Timothy, were brought from Palestine, and deposited in the magnificent Church of the Apostles, built on the banks of the Bosphorus, by Constantine the Great. Fifty years after, the ashes of Samuel, the Hebrew Judge and Prophet, were brought from his native land in a golden urn covered with a mantle of rich silk. All along the road, it was delivered by one bishop into the hands of another, so that a procession continually escorted it. The emperor Arcadius went out from Constantinople, with a long train of illustrious clergy and senators, to receive the sacred deposit. The bones of Stephen, the first martyr, lay buried and unknown for nearly four hundred years. But Gamaliel, the learned Jewish Rabbi, by whom the Apostle Paul was instructed, appeared three times, in a dream, to a presbyter at Jerusalem, and told him where to find them. When they were dug up, the earth trembled all around, and a fragrance from them floated on the air, which cured, of various diseases, seventy-three of the spectators. A church was built on Mount Zion to receive the treasure thus miraculously discovered. Some of these relics were conveyed to Hippo. Augustine relates many miracles performed by them. People were cured of gout, stone, and fistulas; the blind were restored to sight; and five persons were raised from the dead. Two of them were carried dead to the relics, and brought back alive; two were restored by garments that had touched the relics; and the fifth by oil from the lamps. Augustine concludes the enumeration with an apology for telling so few miracles, out of the great number publicly known and recorded. He says that merely the certified cures, without any of the other miracles, would fill a great number of volumes. Chrysostom says, as soon as the coffin of the martyr Babylas was placed in the chapel provided for it, the oracle of Apollo in the temple near by was struck dumb at once; so that when the emperor Julian went to consult it, the only answer he could get from Apollo was that the dead man would not allow him to speak any longer. And when Julian commanded the bones to be carried back to Antioch, the temple and statue of Apollo were struck by lightning, and consumed at the request of Babylas.

In such a state of feeling, the possession of celebrated relics not only rendered a church attractive, but greatly increased its revenue. In Jerome's time, they were regarded as a necessary appendage to every place of worship. They became such an important article of commerce, that the graves were extensively robbed; and Theodosius the Great found it necessary to pass a law forbidding men to disturb the bones of saints. The people of Milan intreated Ambrose to procure some relics for their church; and he was very desirous to gratify them. With this thought dwelling on his mind, he went to pray in the church of the martyrs, Nabor and Felix; and as he knelt, a kind of trance, which was not exactly sleep, fell upon him. In a vision, he beheld two young men of incomparable beauty, clothed in white garments; and the Apostles Peter and Paul were with them. It was revealed to him that the two young men were martyrs, whose bodies lay near the spot where he was kneeling. He convoked his clergy, and ordered search to be made. As they approached the spot indicated, a man possessed by a devil was seized with a sudden paroxysm; the devil being conscious of the presence of holy remains. Two skeletons of gigantic size were found, with the heads separated from the necks. With them was buried a writing, which stated that they were twin brothers, named Gervasius and Protasius, who were beheaded for Christianity, in the reign of Nero. Some good man had buried their bodies in his garden, where they remained undiscovered till thus miraculously revealed to the Bishop of Milan. Three hundred years had passed since the persecution by Nero; but though they had been buried so long, there was a quantity of blood in the tomb. Ambrose ordered them to be placed under the altar in his church. Alluding to the Lord's Supper which was laid on the altar, and called a sacrifice, he said: "Let the victims be borne in triumph to the place where Christ is the sacrifice. *Upon* the altar is he who suffered for all; and *under* the altar let them repose, who were redeemed by his suffering." Accordingly, the day after the bodies were found, they were carried in solemn procession to the church. It is recorded that many who were afflicted with diseases, or possessed by devils, crowded round the bier, and if they could but touch the drapery that covered it, they were immediately cured, and the devils which were cast out reluctantly confessed the power to which they had been compelled to submit. Augustine says: "I was then at Milan, and I knew the miracles. Not only they who were vexed with unclean Spirits were cured, (the devils confessing themselves,) but a certain man who had for many years been blind, a well-known citizen, hearing the confused joy of the people, and learning the cause, sprang forth, desiring his guide to lead him thither. When he arrived, he begged to be allowed to touch the bier with his handkerchief; which, when he had done, and put the handkerchief to his eyes, they were forthwith opened. He made a vow that for his whole life he would serve in that church. We rejoiced that he had recovered his sight, and when we went from Milan, we left him serving." Ambrose, in a sermon before a large audience, spoke thus concerning the miracle: "The Arians deny that the blind man received sight; but he does not deny that he is cured. He says, I have ceased to be blind; and he proves it by facts. He is a well-known man, formerly employed in public services, a butcher by the name of Severus. He proclaims publicly that when he touched the hem of the garment, wherewith the sacred remains of the martyr are covered, his sight was restored; and he calls those, by whose benevolence he was formerly supported, to testify to the fact." In the crowded church, Ambrose devoutly returned thanks for the wonderful vision which had been sent to inform him concerning the grave of these holy martyrs. They were reverently placed under

the altar, and the church was consecrated under the name
of Gervasius and Protasius.

All these wonderful circumstances are recorded by Ambrose himself, by his secretary Paulinus, and by Augustine.
The Arians, among whom were the young emperor, Valentinian Second, and his mother Justina, were sceptical concerning both the vision and the miracle. They accused
Ambrose of having hired the blind man to perform a part.
But the people believed that a man so signally favoured
by Heaven as their bishop had been, must be divinely inspired to know the truth. This incident so much strengthened the party over which Ambrose presided, that the
imperial family thought it best to desist from any further
efforts to obtain toleration for Arians.

Grecians and Romans had copied the ancient and almost
universal custom of invoking the spirits of departed ancestors, in cases of emergency, or when about to commence a
voyage, or a journey, or any other great undertaking. This
custom was transferred to the spiritual ancestors of the
Christian church. Basil, while commemorating the Feast
of the Forty Martyrs, thus addressed their spirits: "O ye
common guardians of the human race, coöperators in our
prayers, most powerful messengers, stars of the world, and
flowers of churches, let us join our prayers with yours."
Ephrem of Edessa says: "I intreat you, O holy martyrs,
who have suffered so much for the Lord, that you would
intercede for us with Him, that he may bestow his grace
upon us." Jerome, speaking of the souls of martyrs, says:
"They always follow the Lamb wheresoever he goes; forasmuch, therefore, as the Lamb is present everywhere, we
ought to believe that they also, who are with the Lamb,
are present everywhere." In the latter part of the sixth
century, the custom of invoking martyrs became a formal
regulation of the church.

Magnificent churches were built to martyrs, and became
the general resort of the diseased and the afflicted. In the
temples of Æsculapius it had been customary for those
who sought aid from the god to lie prostrate in his temple,

waiting for dreams or visions to inform them how they could be cured; and Æsculapius was often supposed to appear and prescribe the suitable remedies. Those who received benefit hung up in his temple the image of a hand or foot that had been healed, accompanied by a tablet describing the cure. The same customs were transferred to the churches of the martyrs. Invalids waited there for dreams or visions, and many accounts are given concerning the visible appearance of the departed saints. Theodoret, a church historian and a Syrian bishop, in four hundred and twenty-three, says: "We frequently offer up hymns each day to the Lord in the churches of the martyrs. We pray their spirits to continue us in health; when sick, we beg them to cure us; when we undertake a journey, we beseech them to be our guides and protectors; and when we return safely, we go to their churches to return thanks to them. That those who pray to them, with faith and sincerity, obtain what they ask, is testified by the great number of offerings made to them in consequence of benefits received. Some offer the images of eyes, some of feet, some of hands, made of gold or silver, which the Lord accepts, though but of little value; measuring the gifts by the ability of the giver. These monuments proclaim the power of the dead to cure distempers; and this power demonstrates their God to be the true God."

There were some who protested against these doctrines and customs. Vigilantius of Gaul wrote against the exceeding reverence paid to martyrs and their relics, and he influenced many minds. He doubted the miracles said to be performed at their tombs, and rejected the idea of their intercession in heaven. The practice of keeping lamps burning before the shrines of martyrs he considered a copy of the custom in Pagan temples. This opposition greatly exasperated Jerome, who attacked him in his violent way, comparing him to all sorts of dragons, scorpions, and beasts of prey. He brings forward the sanction of great names as an invulnerable argument. He says: "Was the emperor Constantine sacrilegious, who transported the

relics of Andrew, Luke, and Timothy, to Constantinople?
At whose presence the devils howl and are confounded;
such devils as inhabit the wretched Vigilantius. Was the
emperor Arcadius impious, who removed the bones of the
holy Samuel to Thrace? Were all the bishops sacrilegious, who enshrined those precious remains in a vessel of
gold, covered with silk? Were all the people sacrilegious,
who went to meet it, and received it as if it were the living
prophet himself? Is the Bishop of Rome impious, who
offers sacrifice [the eucharist] on the altar, under which
are the venerable bones of Peter and Paul? Vigilantius
would call it their vile dust. Are bishops of all the cities
of the world impious, who reverence relics, around which
the souls of martyrs are constantly hovering, to hear the
prayers of the suppliant?" "Answer me, how comes it to
pass that in this vile dust and ashes of the martyrs there is
so great a manifestation of signs and wonders? Thou most
wretched of mortals! I see what thou art so grieved at, so
afraid of. The Evil Spirit within thee, which compels thee
to write thus, has often been tortured, and is now tortured,
by this vile dust." But though Jerome fully believed that
the souls of departed saints received the prayers of mortals,
he totally denied that they were worshipped by the church.
He says: "We do not adore martyrs, or angels, or cherubim, or seraphim; lest we should serve the creature more
than the Creator, who is blessed for evermore. But we
honour the relics of the martyrs, that our minds may be
raised to Him, whose martyrs they are." Augustine likewise indignantly repelled the same charge, brought by his
old friends the Manicheans. He says: "We offer sacrifice
to no martyr, nor to the soul of any saint, nor to any angel.
We worship God only." The practice of bringing bones
and ashes from the graves, and depositing them in places
of worship, was more shocking to Pagans than any other
peculiarity of the Christians; for in all the ancient religions, contact with dead bodies was considered polluting,
and priests purified themselves before they performed worship, if even their garments had touched a bone. Those

who became Christians conquered this feeling by their belief that the bodies of martyrs had been made sanctified temples of the Holy Ghost, and would become so again at the resurrection.

Hindoos, from very ancient times, were accustomed to make pilgrimages from far and near to their Holy City, Benares; also to the tombs of celebrated saints, who had become one with God during their lifetime in this world; and to temples where the relics of Crishna, and other incarnated gods, were deposited. Buddhists made similar pilgrimages to the Holy Mountain, where was the last footprint of Bouddha, when he ascended to the celestial world; to other Holy Mountains, consecrated by the prayers and miracles of his disciples; and to shrines containing relics of those sanctified men; of which the most celebrated was the one which possessed a tooth of Bouddha in a golden box set with gems by which many miracles were said to be performed. This custom from the East also passed into Christianity. Helena, and her son, Constantine the Great, accompanied the bishop Eusebius on a pilgrimage to Jerusalem, and caused churches and chapels to be erected wherever Christ and his Apostles were said to have trodden. The True Cross then dug up on Mount Calvary was preserved in a silver shrine, and attracted an immense multitude of pilgrims, to whom the Bishop of Jerusalem sold small portions of the cross set in gold and gems. These fragments obtained such celebrity for curing diseases, and protecting people from danger, that all the timber in the cathedral could not have supplied the demand. But the sacred wood was declared to have the miraculous power of perpetual growth; so that it never diminished. The empress Eudoxia, wife of Theodosius the Younger, made a pilgrimage to Jerusalem in great pomp, and brought back to Constantinople the right arm of Stephen the martyr, the chains of the Apostle Peter, and a portrait of the Virgin Mary, painted by Luke the Evangelist. Paula, a wealthy patrician widow in Rome, and her daughter Eustochium, were converted by the preaching of Jerome, and soon after,

with a train of devout maidens, they went to Antioch, to
join him and other devotees, on a pilgrimage to Jerusalem.
They afterward went to Egypt, to visit all the spots said
to be consecrated by the footsteps of Joseph and Mary.
Augustine says the whole world flocked to Bethlehem, to
see the place of Christ's nativity; and that pilgrimages to
Arabia were undertaken, to look at the dunghill on which
Job sat. From all these places relics were brought, and
became lucrative sources of revenue not only to churches,
but to cities, on account of the great concourse of strangers
they attracted.   The relics were generally deposited under
the altars, or aisles, of churches; and the fame of the miracles wrought by them brought crowds of suppliants, who
might be seen at all times kneeling before the altar, or
prostrate in the aisles, kissing the pavement, imploring relief from disease, or lameness, praying for children, for the
welfare of distant relatives, and for all manner of temporal
blessings. Those who received benefit, gave money to the
church, hung commemorative tablets on the walls, or presented a picture or image of the martyr, to whom they
wished to express gratitude; as Buddhists and Grecians
had from time immemorial been accustomed to consecrate
a statue or a painting to their temples, on similar occasions.

Jerusalem, above all other places, attracted a devout
multitude. Yet in the presence of perpetual worship and
miracles, the Holy City was distinguished for the grossest
licentiousness, robbery, theft, poisoning, and other forms
of murder.   Such is the testimony of Jerome, who for
several years resided in the neighbouring village of Bethlehem. Gregory, Bishop of Nyssa, who passed through
Jerusalem on a visit to the Arabian churches, in the year
three hundred eighty, was so shocked by the violence and
sensuality he witnessed, that he sent abroad a letter earnestly dissuading Christians from congregating there; and
especially exhorting women not to undertake a pilgrimage
which would expose them to much insult and scandal, and
render them liable to see and hear many obscene things.

The belief in the marvellous does not seem to have diminished with the lapse of centuries. Arnobius, who lived in the fourth century, tells us: "In these days, Christ sometimes appears to just and holy men; not in vain dreams, but in his pure and simple form. The mention of his name puts Evil Spirits to flight, strikes their oracles dumb, deprives their soothsayers of the power of answering, and frustrates the efforts of arrogant magicians. Not because they have an aversion to his name, as the heathen pretend, but by the efficacy of his superior power.". Many miracles are recorded of Ambrose, Bishop of Milan. It is said that a woman afflicted with paralysis was carried to him in her bed, and as soon as she touched his garments, she recovered her health. An obstinate heretic, who used to go and hear him merely for the sake of refuting his arguments, was converted by seeing an angel at his side, prompting the words he uttered. One day, when Ambrose went to the Governor's house, to beg mercy for a poor wretch condemned to die, he was refused admittance. He turned away, saying: "Thou thyself shalt fly to the church for refuge, and shall not be able to enter." A short time after, the Governor being pursued by enemies, did fly to the church for protection, and though the doors stood wide open, he could not find his way in, but wandered about, in strange bewilderment, till he was killed. Martin, Bishop of Tours, cotemporary with Ambrose, was the greatest of all the wonder-workers of his time. The mere touch of his garments cured the most inveterate diseases; and it is recorded that he restored three dead men to life. He obtained such extensive reputation for casting out devils, that he was appointed to the office of exorcist in the church. Epiphanius, who was Bishop of Constantia, in the latter part of the fourth century, says: "For the conviction of unbelievers, whole fountains, and even rivers, are at the present day turned into wine. At Cibyra, a town of Caria, there is a fountain, which annually undergoes this change, at the very hour when, at the bidding of Christ, the attendants at the marriage feast in Cana of Galilee drew wine from the water vessels, and presented it

to the president of the feast. Another fountain of the same
kind exists at Gerasa in Arabia. I have myself drank
from the fountain of Cibyra, and my brethren from that of
Gerasa." Augustine tells of a pious old cobbler, who
prayed for a new coat at the Chapel of the Twenty Martyrs. Some young fellows, who overheard him, made
much fun of him. He walked away without minding their
jeers, and presently he saw a large fish gasping on the
shore. He took it to the market, and with the proceeds
bought wool, which he intended to have woven into cloth.
When the cook cut the fish open, she found a gold ring in
it, which she carried to the cobbler, saying: "Here is the
coat the Twenty Martyrs have given you." The same
Father tells of a lad who was cured of palsy by being carried to an oratory containing some holy earth from Jerusalem. Hunneric, the Vandal General, being an Arian,
forbid the Catholics to hold meetings in the provinces he
conquered. Some of them having assembled after this
decree, their tongues were cut out by his orders; but they
still continued to speak, and praise the Lord. An account
of this miracle was published two years after the event, by
Victor, a bishop in Africa. He says: "If any one should
doubt the truth of what I state, let him repair to Constantinople, and listen to the clear and perfect language of
Restitutus, the sub-deacon, one of those glorious sufferers,
who is now lodged in the palace of the emperor Zeno, and
is respected by the devout empress." Æneus, a Platonic
philosopher converted to Christianity, speaks of this miracle
in his work on the Immortality of the Soul. He says:
"I saw the men myself. I heard them speak. I diligently inquired how such an articulate voice could be
formed without any organ. I used my eyes to examine
the report of my ears. I opened their mouths, and saw
that the tongues had been completely torn away by the
roots; an operation which physicians generally suppose to
be mortal." This miracle is referred to by several later
writers, and by the emperor Justinian, in one of his edicts.
In after times, it was said that one of the sufferers was a

boy who had been dumb from his birth, until his tongue was cut out.

It was a custom with the Druids to borrow money, for which they gave people notes payable in another world; and these writings were buried with the dead, that they might take with them the proof of their claims. I find one similar transaction recorded of a Christian priest. Synesius, the learned Bishop of Ptolemais, early in the fifth century, had a friend, Evagrius, who resisted his efforts at conversion; requiring to have proof that the Scripture was true, which declares: " He that giveth to the poor lendeth to the Lord, who will repay him." At last, his doubts were so far overcome, that he gave the bishop three hundred pieces of gold to be distributed among the poor, and received a written bond for the money, payable after death, in the name of the Lord. He kept the writing carefully, and on his death-bed instructed his family to put it secretly within his hand when they buried him. They did so; and three nights afterwards, he appeared in a dream to Synesius, who had not been informed of the transaction, and said: "Come to my grave, and take back your note. I have received full payment, and have written a discharge." The grave being opened, the note was found, with a receipt in full endorsed upon the back of it, in the handwriting of the deceased. This note was long afterwards preserved in the church at Cyrene, as a precious relic.

The belief that miracles could also be performed by unbelievers, through the evil agency of magic, continued to prevail generally. The degree of faith on this subject, is indicated by Lactantius. Speaking of some who declared that the soul died with the body, he says: "They would not dare to affirm this in the presence of a magician; for he would refute them on the spot, by calling up the souls of the dead, rendering them visible to human eyes, and making them foretell future events."

There are, however, indications that human reason began to put some weight into the other scale; enough at

least to make the balance waver. Though Chrysostom relates so many wonders wrought by relics of martyrs, consecrated oil, and the sign of the cross, yet in other parts of
his writings, he apologizes for the diminution of miracles in
his day. He says: "Paul's handkerchiefs could once do
greater miracles than all the Christians of our day can do,
with ten thousand prayers and tears. Because no miracles
are wrought now, we are not to consider it proof that none
were performed then; for then they were of use, but now
they are not. In the infancy of the church, extraordinary
gifts of the Spirit were bestowed, even on the unworthy;
because those early times stood in need of that help to facilitate the propagation of the Gospel. But now, they are
not given even to the worthy, because the present strength
of the Christian faith no longer needs them." "There are
some who ask: 'Why are there no persons now who raise
the dead, and cure diseases?' It is owing to want of faith,
and virtue, and piety in these times." In another place, he
speaks of miracles as proper only "to rouse the dull and
sluggish; frequently liable to sinister suspicions of being
mere phantasms and illusions." He adds: "It is a proof of
the greater generosity of this age, to take God's word without such pledges."

Though Augustine enumerates more than seventy miracles, within two years, within his own diocese, three of
which were resurrections from the dead, he also offers an
explanation of the decline of miracles. He says: "They
ask why are not those miracles performed now, which you
declare to have been wrought formerly? I could tell them
that they were then necessary, before the world believed,
for the very purpose that it might believe; but he who
requires a prodigy to make him a believer now, when the
world believes, is himself a greater prodigy." He also
makes a statement which implies a certain degree of indif-
ference, if not incredulity on the part of the public. He
says: "Though miracles are often wrought by the name of
Jesus, or by his sacraments, or by the relics of martyrs, yet
they do not acquire so much reputation as did those of the

Apostles. They are scarcely ever known to the whole city or place where they occur, but for the most part are known only to a very few; and if they are told abroad, they are not recommended with such authority, as to be received without difficulty and doubting, though told by true believers to true believers." Therefore, when he heard of any miracle, he caused the parties to be examined, and if facts seemed to sustain the report, an account of them was drawn up, and publicly read to the people. But he says: "Those who hear it, retain nothing of it a few days after, and seldom take the pains to repeat it to anybody else."

It was an oriental custom to wear religious symbols marked on the forehead. The devotees of different sects in Hindostan were distinguished by such marks. Allusions made by Chrysostom and Augustine imply that in their day Christians frequently had a cross impressed in some way upon their foreheads. The cross was at first merely a sign, made by motion of the hands; but after the time of Constantine, it began to be used as an image, made of wood, silver, or gold, and often adorned with precious stones. It was considered a talisman, to cure diseases and protect from all kinds of dangers; hence representations of it abounded everywhere, in public and private, as did the Cross of Hermes, among the Egyptians. Chrysostom affirms that in his own time it had sometimes been miraculously impressed upon the garments of people. He calls it "a defence against all evil, and a medicine against all sickness." He says: "This sign, both in the days of our forefathers and our own, has thrown open gates that were shut; destroyed the effects of poisonous drugs; dissolved the force of hemlock; and cured the bites of venomous beasts." "This sign of universal execration, of extremest punishment, has now become the object of universal longing and love. We see it everywhere triumphant. We find it in houses, on the roofs and the walls; in cities and in villages; on the great roads, and in the deserts; on mountains, and in valleys; on the market-place, and on

ships; on books, and on weapons; on the bodies of those
possessed with Evil Spirits; on diseased animals; on wearing apparel; on vessels of gold and of silver; on beds, and in
pictures; in the marriage chamber, and at banquets; in
the dances of those going to pleasure; and in the associations of those that mortify their bodies," [monks.]   Augustine says: "The sign of the cross on the forehead of
kings is now more precious than a jewel of his diadem."
He cautioned men against the mere mechanical custom,
and reminded them that it was not the outward image, or
the external sign described on the forehead, that was pleasing in the sight of God, but the imitation of Christ's humility in the soul.

Other religions were made tributary to the prevailing
tendency to invest Christianity with supernatural interest.
The simple fact that priests of Apollo considered it profanity to perform their rites in the presence of dead bodies,
was construed by Chrysostom into a miracle.   He said
Apollo confessed it was not in his power to utter any more
oracles, because the martyr Babylas had commanded him
to be silent.   The Fourth Eclogue of Virgil was continually quoted as a prophecy of Christ.   Eusebius, the historian, who manifests great credulity in many instances,
regarded as true prophecy the acrostic attributed to the
Erythræan Sibyl, forming the words Jesus Christ, Son of
God, Saviour.   He says: "Many people, though they admitted that the Erythræan Sybil was a prophetess, rejected
this acrostic, suspecting it to have been forged by the Christians.   But the truth is manifest.   Our people have been
so exact in computing the times, that there is no room left
to imagine the verses were made after Christ, and falsely
sent abroad as predictions of the Sibyl.   All agree that
Cicero had read this poem, which he translated into the
Latin tongue, and inserted in his works."   The simple fact
is, Cicero alluded to certain verses, which partisans of Julius Cæsar wrote to serve a political purpose, and attributed
them to the Erythræan Sybil.   He ridiculed the poetry,
and said the acrostic form implied labour and study, and

.therefore could not have been uttered by any of the Sybils, who always prophesied in states of ecstasy.

Eusebius likewise quotes the following story from Plutarch. In the reign of Tiberius, a vessel sailing from Asia to Italy, passed by certain Islands in the Ægean Sea, in the evening. A voice was heard from the shore calling out to Thamus, one of the mariners on board, telling him when they came to the Palades, to inform the people that the great Pan was dead. The commander, who doubtless had the common tendency to be impressed by any sudden or mysterious utterance, resolved to obey the injunction, if circumstances seemed to favour it. When the vessel arrived at the designated place, it was detained by contrary winds, and the message was proclaimed. Whereupon, there came upon the breeze a sound as of many voices, howling and wailing. As Jesus was crucified in the reign of Tiberius, Eusebius believed these woful sounds came from Evil Spirits, lamenting that Pan was overthrown, and the kingdom of Satan in general subverted by the sacrifice of the Son of God. Christian writers of the third and fourth centuries likewise relate that when the Roman Senate decreed divine honours to the emperor Augustus, he consulted the Sibyl Tiburtina whether he ought to allow himself to be worshipped. After some days of meditation the Sybil summoned him, and pointing to the sky, showed him an altar in the opening clouds, and above it a beautiful woman with an infant in her arms. At the same time, he heard a voice saying: "This is the altar of the Son of the living God." In consequence of this vision, it is said Augustus erected an altar on the Capitoline Hill, inscribed to the "First Born of God."

These stories were often founded on some real occurrence, exaggerated or changed in the course of repetition; as was the case with regard to the oracle of Apollo silenced by the bones of Babylas, and the thunder-shower which refreshed the army of Marcus Aurelius. Desiderius Herauldus remarks: "The Christians of that time strained to their advantage all the actions, words, and writings of the

Pagans, which they often interpreted contrary to the true meaning." The candid examiner is obliged to confess that there is too much foundation for this assertion.

It was a common opinion among the Fathers that the Garden of Eden still existed in all its primeval beauty, though inaccessible; being on the summit of a high mountain, reaching into the third region of the air, near the moon. This extreme elevation protected it from the waters of the deluge. Augustine did not urge it as an essential point of faith, but he thought it improper to reject it, inasmuch as Irenæus, and other primitive Fathers, declared it to have been a doctrine taught by the Apostles. Some supposed that Enoch and Elijah both existed in the body in that terrestrial Paradise waiting the appointed time to appear on earth again and contend with Antichrist, preparatory to the coming of the Lord.

On some moral questions there was a diversity of opinion among the Fathers. Some thought it wrong to take interest for money. Lactantius differed from the generality of Christians in regarding all war as a violation of the commandment: "Thou shalt not kill." He was the last of the Fathers who clung to the belief that Christ would come visibly and establish a kingdom on earth. There was an increasing tendency to give predictions on that subject a spiritual interpretation. But the doctrine still retained its hold on popular belief, and was a frequent theme for prophets. Jerome speaks of a millennium of wine, and wheat, and fruitful marriages, as "a Jewish fable, which ought to be rejected;" but he adds that he foresaw how many people would be angry with him.

Ideas concerning animals in Paradise which Jews derived from the Talmud, they transmitted to the Fathers. Basil, describing the garden of Eden, says: "Then the beasts of the field, and the fowls of the air were all tame and mild. They heard, and spoke so as to be understood without any difficulty. There was then nothing in the appearance of the serpent to excite horror. He did not crawl on his belly, but walked erect."

The mode of interpreting Scripture continued to be exceedingly arbitrary and undefined. Ambrose says when Jesus told his disciples, "Ye shall say unto this mountain, Remove hence to yonder place, and it shall remove," he meant the Devil by the word mountain. Hilary, Bishop of Poictiers, quotes the words: "Are not two sparrows sold for a farthing? And one of them shall not fall on the ground without your Father." He says by the two sparrows are meant sinners, who sell themselves to sin for mere trifles; thus becoming both as one; the soul thickening into a body, as it were, by means of sin. By the ninety-nine sheep that went not astray, he understood the angels; and by the one lost sheep, mankind; inasmuch, as all mankind were lost by partaking the sin of one man. The following exposition by Epiphanius, Bishop of Constantia, is as singular a specimen of natural history, as it is of Biblical interpretation: "There is no bird that manifests such love for its offspring, as the pelican. The female, while setting on her nest, cherishes her young with such tenderness, that she pierces their side with her kisses, and they die of the wounds. In three days, the male bird visits the nest, and is deeply affected at finding his young ones dead. Under the impulse of his grief, he strikes his own side, and opens wounds in it; and the blood which flows thence, infused into the wounds of the young birds, restores them to life. Thus our Lord Jesus had his side pierced by a spear, and immediately there came forth blood and water; and he dropped his blood upon his young ones; that is, upon Adam and Eve, and the prophets, and all the dead; and enlightened the world, and gave them life, by his three days' burial and his resurrection. It is on this account he said, by the prophet: 'I am a pelican in the wilderness.'"

The early Fathers applied to the person of Jesus the prophecy concerning the Messiah, which declares he would have no beauty that men should desire him. Some of the later Fathers, including human beauty in their general contempt for every thing connected with the body, adhered to the same opinion. Basil took this view of the subject;

and Cyril of Alexandria alludes to Christ's "ignoble appearance, faulty beyond all the sons of men." But this idea was generally rejected after their time. Jerome says: "Assuredly that splendour and majesty of the hidden Divinity, which shone even in his human countenance, could not but attract all beholders, at first sight." "Unless he had something celestial in features and expression, the Apostles would not have immediately followed him." Chrysostom says: "The Heavenly Father poured upon him in full streams that corporeal grace which is only distilled drop by drop on mortal men." Gregory of Nyssa applies to him all the glowing pictures of the bridegroom in the Song of Solomon. Augustine declares: "He was beautiful on his mother's bosom, beautiful in the arms of his parents; beautiful upon the cross, beautiful in the sepulchre."

The opinion that Mary lived with Joseph as his wife, after the birth of Jesus, was early ranked among the heresies. It was maintained that she was always a virgin from her birth to her death; and Joseph was represented as a very old man under whose protection she was placed, for the sake of appearances. In discussions on this subject, in all its branches, there is a strange mingling of sincerely devout feeling with the most material forms of thought and expression, which will by no means bear translation to modern ears. Eusebius and Epiphanius agree with Origen and Tertullian, in supposing that Joseph was a widower when Mary married him, and that the brothers and sisters of Jesus, spoken of by Matthew and Luke, were his children by a former wife. This opinion was violently assailed by Jerome and others. They regarded it as impious to suppose he had children by a previous marriage, and maintained that he also was perpetually chaste. It was said the word brethren was merely a general term to designate relatives. It was finally decided that Mary, the wife of Cleophas, was sister of the Virgin Mary; and that it was her son who was called "James, the Lord's brother."

A book called "The Gospel of the Infancy of Jesus,"

supposed to have been written by some of the Gnostics, was in general circulation in the third century, and portions of it are quoted by the Fathers as reliable traditions. In this Gospel the Virgin is called "the holy Mary," and represented as saying: "As there is not any child like to my son, so neither is there any woman like to his mother." Another book, called the Protevangelion, or First Gospel, supposed to have a similar origin, purporting to be written "by James the Lesser, Cousin and Brother of the Lord Jesus," is frequently alluded to by the Fathers. Joseph is therein represented as an aged man with children, who objects to marrying one so young as Mary, lest he should "appear ridiculous in Israel." But the High Priest overruled his scruples, by saying to him: "Thou art the person chosen to take the Virgin of the Lord, to keep her for him."

After the Arian Controversy, when Mary began to be called the Mother of God, the ardour of expression increased toward her, until it sounds like actual adoration. Athanasius, who lived early in the fourth century, addresses her thus: "Remember us, O most holy Virgin, and for the feeble eulogiums we give thee grant us great gifts from the treasures of thy grace, thou who art full of grace! Queen, and Mother of God, intercede for us!" Ephrem of Edessa, nearly a century later, says: "We fly to thy patronage, holy Mother of God! Protect and guard us under the wings of thy mercy and kindness! Most merciful God, through the intercession of the most blessed Virgin Mary, and of all the angels, and of all the saints, show pity to thy creature!" There was a sect called Maryanites, who believed that Mary was one of the persons of the Godhead. It is said some of them urged this opinion at the Council of Nice. The first mention of direct worship of the Virgin is by Epiphanius, who lived at the close of the fifth century. Enumerating eighty-four heresies which had sprung up, he mentions a small sect called Collyridians, which means offerers of small cakes. They emigrated from Thrace into Arabia, and seem to have brought with them the customary worship of Ceres. transferred to the Virgin

Vol. III.—13*

Mary, whose mother they supposed was also a virgin.
Women among them, who were appointed priestesses, presided at her festival, during which small cakes, made of
meal and honey, were placed in a chariot and carried
through the streets, followed by a procession. They were
then laid on an altar, and offered to the Virgin Mary with
invocations. Epiphanius rebuked this custom. He says:
"I own her body was holy, but she was no god. She continued a virgin, but she is not proposed for our adoration.
She herself adored him, who having descended from heaven,
from the bosom of his Father, was born of her flesh. She
stands before all the saints of God, on account of the
heavenly mystery accomplished in her. But we adore no
saint; and as worship is not given to Angels, much less
can it be allowed to the daughter of Ann. Let Mary
therefore be honoured, but the Father, Son, and Holy
Ghost alone adored. Let no one worship Mary." The
rapturous mode of expression concerning the Virgin, and
the tendency to deify her, led adherents of the old religion
to call her "The New Cybele, or Mother Goddess of the
Christians."

In the history of sects it has already been stated what
multifarious difficulties arose, and what hot controversies
were excited, before the doctrine of the Trinity was satisfactorily arranged by the frequent assembling of bishops.
Some of the arguments made use of, in the course of these
controversies, were very peculiar, and characteristic of the
times. Augustine considered the creation in six days a
proof of the Trinity; because "six is twice three." Ambrose says: "Jesus appeared to be the son of a carpenter,
to signify that Christ the Son was the Maker of all things."
In controversy whether the generation of the Son was
voluntary, or involuntary, Chrysostom speaks of eructation as a good thing, and compares it to the production of
the Logos from God; but he says it was an "eructation
from the heart, not from the stomach." Lactantius, to
guard against the idea that any Archangel could be equal
with the Son, speaks of Angels as the *breath* of God, and

of Christ as the *Word* of God. He says: "The breathings of men are dissoluble, but the breathings of God remain, and are immortal. His silent breathings from the nostrils become Angels. But his Word is a breath emitted from the mouth, with a sound; therefore there is a great difference between the Son of God and the Angels. For though he also is a Spirit, yet since he issues from the mouth of God, with a voice, like a word, for this reason he was to make use of his voice to the people; because he was to teach with authority the doctrine of God, and communicate heavenly secrets to men."

The early Fathers were frequently quoted during the Arian controversy, to prove that there was a time when the Son did not exist; but this idea was decided to be heresy. Gregory of Nyssa says: "If there had been no Son there could have been no Father; if no beam, no sun; if no image, no substance." The question arose, if Christ was co-eternal with God, and the same as God, how he came to say: "Of that hour knoweth no man; no not even the Son but only the Father." The Council at Chalcedon decided that in Christ existed two perfectly harmonized natures, the divine and the human. Therefore, some argued that as God, he knew all things; but as man, many things were hidden from him. But some of the Fathers did not admit that Christ really was ignorant on any subject. Cyril of Alexandria says: "If God affected ignorance where Adam was, and of what Cain had been doing, why should we wonder that the Son of God affected ignorance concerning the Day of Judgment. Christ also affected ignorance, when he asked how many loaves his disciples had."

Augustine says: "If all things were made by Christ, then Mary, of whom he was born, was made by him." Cassian says: "Mary produced one who was older than herself, even her own Maker; so that she was the parent of her parent."

Some curiously inquisitive minds asked, why God did not have more than one Son. This gave rise to many

remarks, seriously and honestly made, but unfit for quotation. Hilary, Bishop of Poictiers, says: "The doctrine of
the generation of the Son is much ridiculed; because they
say it implies the necessity of a wife to God."

Discussions concerning the Third Person of the Trinity
were also involved in difficulties. The question arose
whether the Holy Spirit proceeded from the Father, or
from the Son. Some said: "If the Spirit proceeded from
the Father, then he and the Logos are brothers. How
then can the Logos be called the only begotten Son of
God!" Others objected: "But if he proceeded from the
Son, then God is the Grandfather of the Holy Spirit."
The speculative tendency always very busy in some of the
Eastern churches, especially at Constantinople, queried
whether the Holy Ghost could also himself have had a
son. Athanasius says: "Both Macedonians and the orthodox agree in supposing that the Spirit could have
generated, as well as the Father, but that he did not choose
to do it, lest there should be a multiplicity of gods." Some
minds were troubled because the Angel Gabriel had announced to Mary: "The holy thing which shall be born
of thee is of the Holy Spirit." From this ground arose a
sect, who said that Christ was the Son of the Holy Ghost.
Ambrose decides the question thus: "The holy, undivided
Trinity never does anything separately. The Father, the
Son, and the Spirit created the body of Christ. The
Father, because it is said, 'God sent his Son, made of a
woman;' the Son, because it is said, 'Wisdom has builded
her a house;' the Spirit, because Mary was with child by
the Spirit." The personality of the Spirit being much
questioned, Epiphanius replied, that he assumed the form
of a dove, at the baptism of our Saviour on purpose to
show that he had a real person.

Unbelievers in the divinity of Christ continually asked
why the Prophets, the Apostles, and Christ himself, had
either not spoken at all on the subject of the Trinity, or
made allusions so vague, that a doctrine deemed so important was left to be settled with so much difficulty by

repeated Councils of Bishops. The Fathers replied, that the Prophets did not mention the Son of God clearly, on account of the material tendencies of the Jews, who would immediately have thought that he was generated with passion; and so they would have been guilty of profanity. Many of the Fathers say Christ was careful to conceal his divinity, because it was necessary to keep the Devil in ignorance of the fact; for if he had known him, he would not have ventured to encounter him, and so would not have been conquered by his death; and thus the great object of his mission would have failed. Lactantius says: "Our Saviour taught that there is but One God, who alone is to be worshipped; nor did he himself ever once say that he was God. He would not have been faithful to his trust, if, when he was sent to take away polytheism, and assert the unity of God, he had introduced another beside the One God. This had not been to preach the doctrine of One God, or to do the business of Him who sent him; but his own." Athanasius says: "I will venture to assert that not even the blessed disciples themselves were fully persuaded concerning his divinity, till the Holy Spirit came upon them at the day of Pentecost; for when they saw him after his resurrection, some worshipped, but others doubted, yet they were not on that account condemned." Basil of Seleucia says: "The Apostles themselves were as ignorant of his being God, as the rest of the Jews; some of whom said he was Elijah, others Jeremiah, or one of the Prophets." Theodoret, the learned Bishop of Cyrus, says that before the crucifixion all held him to be a man; "but after his resurrection and ascension, the descent of the Holy Spirit, and the various miracles performed by invoking his name, all the believers knew that he was God, and the only begotten Son of God." Chrysostom says: "It was necessary for Christ to conceal his high dignity from his disciples; because they would immediately have told everything, through excess of joy. When he was discoursing about the creation of the human race, he did not say *I* made them, but *He* that made them. He never clearly

G*

said that he made the world; but he signified it by the miracle of the fishes, the wine, and the loaves."

Similar reasons are given why the Apostles said so little that could be considered as evidence of the Trinity, and why even John alludes to it only in a few verses, and not very plainly. Chrysostom, speaking of the great mystery of the incarnation, says: "Mary herself, when she carried him in her womb, did not know the secret. The Devil himself did not know it. If he had not been at a loss to know whether Christ were God or not, he would not have repeated thrice, 'If thou art the ,Son of God.' On this account, Christ said to John, who was beginning to reveal him, 'Hold now ! It is not yet time to reveal the secret of the incarnation. I must yet deceive the Devil. Keep silence now; for thus it becometh us.'" The same Father adduces the incredulity of the Jews as another reason why the Apostles dwelt chiefly on the topic of his resurrection, and were so cautious in making allusions to his divinity. He says: "The Jews had been daily taught out of their Law, 'The Lord thy God is *one* Lord, and beside him there is no *other*.' Having seen Jesus nailed to a cross, having killed and buried him themselves, and not having seen him after he had risen, if they had been told that this person was God, equal to the Father, would they not have spurned at it?" He assigns the same reason why Paul, writing twenty or thirty years after the death of Christ, is still so guarded as to say, "God who spake by the prophets," instead of saying that Christ spake by them. For the same reason, Peter, when addressing the Jews, said, "Jesus of Nazareth, a *man* approved of God among you, by miracles, and wonders, and signs, which God did by him in the midst of you, as ye yourselves also know." Theodoret says caution was also necessary toward Gentile converts; lest, being accustomed to worship many deities, they might think Christians taught more Gods than one. Therefore, it was that Paul spoke to them of God as raising Christ from the dead; not that Christ was unable to raise himself, but because he condescended to his hearers, as if they were

little children. From the same cautious motives, he says
Paul made no mention of the Holy Spirit, but said to
them: "There is one God; and one mediator between God
and man; the man Christ Jesus." The same writer expresses the opinion, that Paul in the fifteenth chapter of
his Epistle to the Corinthians, speaks of the subjection of
the Son to the Father in terms more lowly than was necessary for the benefit of his hearers. When Macedonius and
his followers said that the Scriptures did not teach that the
Holy Ghost was one of the Trinity, Epiphanius replied
that the want of express testimony on that point, was owing
to the fact that the Holy Spirit himself dictated the Scriptures, and he was reluctant to dwell too much on his own
share in the transactions there recorded. Chrysostom,
alluding to the incarnation of the Son of God, says: "If
Joseph needed the vision of an Angel, in order to believe
the fact, how would the Jews have received it? On this
account, the Apostles did not at first speak of it, but rather
discoursed largely concerning his resurrection; for of this
there were examples in former times, though not in all respects the same; but they had never heard of a person
being born of a virgin. Nor did his mother dare to mention this; for observe how she says, 'Behold thy father
and I have sought thee.' If it had been suspected, he
would not have been thought to be a descendant of David;
and if that were not admitted, many mischiefs would have
arisen. On that account, the Angels mentioned it to Mary
and Joseph only; and not to the shepherds, though they
acquainted them with the fact of his being born." The
same reason is given why Matthew and Luke traced the
genealogy of Jesus up to Abraham and Adam.

All the Fathers, who wrote on this subject, agreed that
it was necessary for Mary to have a nominal husband, in
order to conceal the miraculous conception. Basil says:
"Mary was married to Joseph, that the Devil might not
suspect she was a virgin; for he knew that the Messiah,
who was to put an end to his power, was to be born of
one." Jerome suggests that one reason why Mary was

married to Joseph was that her son might appear to be of
the genealogy of David.   Another was that her character
might not be injured, or her life endangered, as it would
have been by the Law of Moses, if the miraculous circumstances had been made known.   He says: "Except Mary
herself, her husband, and a few others, who might have
been informed by them, all persons regarded Jesus as the
son of Joseph; and the Evangelists themselves, expressing the common opinion, called Joseph the father of our
Saviour."   Basil of Seleucia, says: "When the devils
called Christ the Son of God, they did not know that he
was God; for *all* uncommonly good men were called *sons*
of God; and Israel was called his first-born son."   Cyril
of Jerusalem says: "It was necessary that Christ should
suffer for us; but the Devil would not have gone near
him, if he had known that.   The body was the bait of
death, that the dragon, thinking to swallow it down, might
vomit up all that he had swallowed."   Rufinus also affirms
that the divinity of Christ was concealed, in order to catch
the Devil, as with a bait; and he supposes the words of
Ezekiel signify this, where he says: "I will draw thee out
with my hook."   When some objected that it was wrong
to conquer the Devil by such means, Gregory, Bishop of
Nyssa, replied: "It is fair enough to deceive the deceiver."
It was the general opinion that the body of Christ was
not subject to any human necessities, and that he ate and
drank merely because it was necessary to seem to do it, in
order to keep the secret of his divinity.   To one who
thought otherwise, Hilary exclaims: "Impious heretic!
You will not believe otherwise than that Christ *felt*, when
the nails pierced his hands."   Cyril says: "The holy and
divine body of Christ had no passions."   Ambrose, alluding to Christ's temptation in the wilderness, says: "See
the artifice of the Lord, whereby he c cumvented his
adversary!   After a prolonged fast, he pretended to be
hungry, that he might plague the Devil, whom he had
already overcome by fasting."

The Fathers agreed in thinking that the honour of par

tially disclosing the great secret was reserved for the beloved Apostle John, whose Gospel they supposed to have been written after all the other Apostles were dead. Epiphanius says: "John found men arguing concerning the humanity of Christ. The Ebionites were in an error about his earthly genealogy, deduced from Abraham, carried by Luke as high as Adam. The Cerinthians and Merinthians maintained that he was a mere man; also the Nazarenes, and many other heretics. Therefore, he, coming last, (for he was the fourth to write a Gospel) began to call back the wanderers; saying, The Logos, which was begotten by the Father from all eternity, was not from Mary only. He was not of the line of Joseph, or David, or Abraham, or Adam. But in the beginning was the Logos, and the Logos was with God, and the Logos was God." Jerome says: "John, the Apostle whom Jesus loved, wrote his Gospel the last of all, at the entreaty of the bishops of Asia, against Cerinthus and other heretics; especially against the doctrine of the Ebionites, then gaining ground, who said that Christ had no existence before he was born of Mary. Therefore, he was compelled to declare his divine origin." Eusebius says: "John began the doctrine of the divinity of Christ; that being reserved for him as the most worthy." Ambrose says: "The other Evangelists, who treat of the humanity of Christ, were like animals that walk on the earth; but John, contemplating the power of his divinity more sublimely, flies to heaven with the Lord, and with an open voice he proclaims that he was always with God, and that he is God." Chrysostom represents John soliloquizing with himself thus: "Why do I not write what Matthew, and Mark, and Luke, through a wise and praiseworthy fear, passed by in silence, according to the orders that were given them? How shall I speak what has been given me freely from above?" He goes on to represent John holding the pen "with a trembling hand, but rejoicing in spirit, considering how to begin the theology. Being in the body at Ephesus, but with a pure heart and holy spirit, he leaves the earth, and is carried upward, and fishing out of the Father's bosom the doctrine of the divinity, he, in his body on earth, wrote: 'In the beginning was the Logos, and the Logos was made flesh, and dwelt among men.'" He says: "John taught what the Angels themselves did not know, till he declared it." "John first lighted up the lamp of theology; and all the churches, even the most distant, running to it, lighted up their lamps of theology, and returned rejoicing, saying: 'In the beginning was the Logos.'"

There was a great tendency in the Fathers to deprecate the exercise of reason, and to substitute for it the authority of the church. It was settled that Scripture was the only guide, and that the right understanding of Scripture was a thing for bishops to decide. Athanasius, alluding to the doctrines of Paul of Samosata, says: "It grieves those who stand up for the holy faith, that the multitude, and especially persons of low understanding, should be infected with these blasphemies. Things sublime and difficult are to be apprehended only by faith; and ignorant people must fall, if they cannot be persuaded to rest in faith, and avoid curious questions." Basil called reasoning "the Devil's work." Cyril of Alexandria says: "In matters of faith, all curiosity must cease." Ambrose says: "When faith is in question, away with all argument." Rufinus says: "That God is the Father of his own Son, our Lord, is to be believed, and not to be discussed; for slaves must not dispute concerning the birth of their masters."

It was the universal opinion of the early Fathers, that the Logos had often appeared to Abraham and the Patriarchs. But Augustine advanced the idea that all such appearances were Angels, who took upon themselves fictitious bodies, and the Logos spoke in and by them.

The doctrine of inherent depravity in human nature, inherited from Adam's sin, early became a prevailing doctrine. Ambrose says: "We have all sinned in the first man. With the propagation of the *nature*, the propagation of the *guilt* also has passed from one to all. In him, human nature sinned." Augustine carried this doctrine to extreme results; for the character of his intellect was such that, whatever premises he adopted, he must needs carry them out to ultimate and consistent conclusions. But his writings on the subject varied at different periods of his theological growth. For nine years he belonged to the sect of Manicheans, who, in common with many other Gnostics, believed that the souls of some men emanated from Good Spirits, and whatever sins they committed, they must eventually return to their heavenly source; that the souls of other men emanated from Evil Spirits, and by an eternal law of the universe they must forever remain exiles from the spheres of light. After Augustine was converted to the Catholic church, he was engaged in zealous controversy with his old friends the Manicheans; and in opposition to their views, he maintained that no man was wicked by nature, but only by abuse of his free will. But afterward, when Pelagius taught that every man had power to perfect himself in holiness, by divine assistance, which was always granted to him who sought it, Augustine entered the lists against him also. The sum of the doctrines he maintained in this controversy may be briefly expressed in two extracts: "The whole essence of Christian faith consists in the opposition and contrariety of two men. One is he through whom we were brought into the bondage of sin, and the other is he by whom we are redeemed from sin. One ruined us in himself, in that he did his own will; the other redeemed us in himself, in that he fulfilled not his own will, but the will of Him who sent him." "Man is by nature corrupt. He is incapable of any good, and absolutely unable to do anything for his own renovation. He cannot even will that which is good; everything must be effected by the operation of grace upon the heart." From these premises, he came to the conclusion that God had, of his own will, elected from all eternity some souls to be saved, and had predestined others irrevocably to eternal misery. No one knew who among professed Christians were fore-ordained to be reprobates; but it was every one's duty to resign himself to the divine decrees, with all humility, and be willing to be damned, if it was for the glory of God. After Augustine's time, the doctrines of original sin, total depravity, election, and pre-destination, prevailed in the church.

Origen had proved the sincerity of his Christian faith by much self-sacrifice and suffering. In his own day, and for more than a century afterward, Christians were proud of him as a man of great learning and unblemished charac-ter; and his writings exerted a great influence. But the Arians often quoted his theory of the subordination of the Son to the Father, and this began to bring him into disre-pute. The severer class of theologians were offended by his doctrine that good would finally triumph over evil, and all things in the universe be restored to harmony and happiness. Jerome accused him of wishing to save all sinners, even the Devil himself. Despisers of human learning scoffed at his culture, and charged him with min-gling Pagan philosophy with Christianity. But many cultivated men, especially those of mystical tendencies, reverenced that spiritual-minded Father, and loved his writings. Gregory of Nazianzen, and Gregory of Nyssa, took similar views concerning the final victory of good over evil. They considered all punishment as a means of purification, ordained by divine love. They said God would not have permitted the existence of evil, if he had not foreseen that by the redemption, all rational beings would, in the end, attain to a blessed fellowship with him-self. Theodore also said: "God would not revive the wicked at the resurrection, if they must needs suffer only punishment, without reformation." The Persian idea of purification by fire, and the final restoration of all things, re-appeared in a Christian form, under various modifica-tions.

A very intimate friendship existed between Jerome and Rufinus, who, like himself, was a presbyter, and a distin-guished Christian writer. They kept up a very affection-ate correspondence, and always spoke of each other with the warmest praise. They both delighted in the writings of Origen; but after the Arians appealed to them as authority, Jerome, who watchfully guarded his reputation for orthodoxy, began to attack with violence the writings he had formerly admired; and at last boasted of it, as his work, that "the whole world was set in a blaze of hatred against Origen." Theophilus, Bishop of Alexandria, a great persecutor of Arians and other heretics, condemned the writings of Origen, and banished from Egypt certain monks who favoured them. Because the kind-hearted Chrysostom gave them shelter, he stigmatized him as "the prince of the sacrilegious; an enemy of mankind; a filthy devil." Jerome thus commends Theophilus for his zeal against heretics: "I write briefly to assure you that the zeal of your emissaries for the faith, their activity in exploring the districts of Palestine for heretics, their perseverance in hunting the creatures to their dens, and dispersing them, will give a triumph to the whole world, and fill it with the glory of your victories. The multitude will gaze with exultation at the standard of the cross lifted at Alexandria, and the brilliant trophies won from heresy. To speak candidly to your lordship, we used to lament that you were so patient. We were ignorant of the tactics of our leader, and eager for the destruction of these wretches. But I see you kept your hand aloft so long, and suspended the blow, only to strike more terribly." Rufinus wrote in defence of Origen, and quoted some of Jerome's former praises of that learned Father. A fierce altercation ensued, in the course of which they mutually accused each other. Jerome exhausted the bitter epithets of language; and when he heard of the death of his former friend, he composed the following epitaph: "The hydra-headed monster nas at length ceased to hiss, and the scorpion lies beneath the earth in Sicily."

Controversies concerning the tenets of Origen continued to disturb the peace of the church more or less for a century and a half longer. Finally, in the sixth century, when he had been dead three hundred years, the emperor Justinian, and the bishops of his time, condemned his

writings to the flames, and pronounced the opinion that
Origen himself could not be saved.

Augustine expressed the general sentiment of the Catholics of his time, when he said: "No one can attain salvation, who has not Christ for his head; and no one can have
Christ for his head, who does not belong to his body, which
is the church." In one of his epistles, approved by a synod
of bishops, he tells the Donatists: "Whoever is separated
from this Catholic church, however innocently he may
think he lives, yet being separated from the unity of
Christ, for that crime alone he will not have life, but the
anger of God remains upon him." When they complained
of the violent persecutions they suffered, he vindicated the
persecutors by quoting the example of Elijah, who slew the
prophets of Baal with his own hand. But when he was
reminded that the spirit of the New Testament differed
from that of the Old, he admitted the justice of the distinction. When it was proposed to obtain penal laws to force
the Donatists into the Catholic church, he and several of
the younger bishops argued that men must seek to conquer
by arguments only, unless they would have hypocritical
Catholics, instead of avowed heretics. Honorius, the son
and successor of Theodosius the Great, persecuted the Donatists with great severity. Three hundred bishops and
many thousands of the clergy in Africa, were stripped of
their possessions and exiled, and their people were punished and heavily fined, if they assembled together for worship. These coercive measures drove many of them into
the Catholic church. Augustine, forgetful of his own argument, that force merely induced hypocrisy, warmly approved of the emperor's proceedings, and sustained them by
reference to the parable concerning those who were forced
to come in to the supper from the highways and the hedges.
Large numbers of the Donatists still held out obstinately,
and filled the country with tumult and bloodshed. The
Vandals were at that time making war upon the Roman
empire, and Genseric, their leader, had been converted to
Christianity in the Arian form. He made common cause

with the Donatists, probably from motives of policy, and exerted himself to get the oppressive edicts against them repealed. They joined his army, helped him to conquer Africa, and fiercely retaliated the injuries they had received. All the Catholics whom they took prisoners were compelled to be baptized over again, and partake of the communion after their manner. If they refused, they were hung up with weights to their feet and cruelly scourged, or branded with red-hot iron, or had their hands, ears, noses, or tongues cut off. These cruel punishments were inflicted upon all ranks, and even upon respectable matrons and virgins of the church. Catholics complained loudly of the persecutions they themselves suffered; but they praised the Vandals for burning Manicheans at the stake; and they rejected with horror a proposition that Arians and Catholics should be mutually tolerated by Romans and Vandals. Soon after Nestorius was appointed Patriarch of Constantinople, he thus publicly addressed the emperor, Theodosius the Younger: "Purge the earth of heretics for me, sire, and I will in return bestow heaven upon you. Join me in extirpating the heretics, and we will join you in subduing the Persians." Whoever ventured to differ from his theological opinions, was whipped, or imprisoned. When some of the people complained that they had an emperor instead of a bishop, they were punished with lashes. Not long after, because he objected to calling Mary the Mother of God, he was himself forced to drain the bitter cup of persecution, which he had forced others to drink.

Now and then there were gleams of a better spirit, and wherever they appeared, even the fiercest sectarians acknowledged their divinity. Cyril of Alexandria was so violent and overbearing in his tone, that Nestorius relinquished all attempts at explanation, and refused to answer any more of his letters. Lampon, a presbyter at Alexandria, who was noted for his gentle and loving spirit, went to Constantinople, with the hope of healing the schism. He easily induced Nestorius to renew the correspondence with his haughty episcopal brother. In his letter to Cyril, he bears the following testimony: "Nothing surpasses the power of Christian gentleness. By that man's might I have been conquered. I confess I am seized with fear, when I perceive in any man the spirit of Christian love. It is as if God dwelt in him." Theodosius, the fierce despotic soldier, truly reverenced the meek and gentle character of Christ, though he would have deemed it mean and contemptible for him to imitate it. In the same way, the sternest polemical soldiers of the church militant acknowledged the heavenly nature of qualities they seldom attempted to copy. Athanasius could argue thus, when his *own* party was persecuted by the Arian emperor Constantius: "Because there is no truth in Satan, wherever he gains admittance, he pays away with hatchet and sword. But the Saviour is so gentle, he says, Will any one come after me? He only knocks at the door of the soul, and says, Open to me, my sister. But if any one is unwilling to open the door, he withdraws. The truth is not preached by sword and javelin, nor by armies, but by persuasion and admonition." Yet eighty Arian bishops signed a protest, in which they accused Athanasius of robbing their churches in Alexandria, "with violence and bloodshed," and of forcing people by torture to partake of the communion in his churches. Jerome seems to have been deeply touched by the Apostle John's oft repeated injunction: "My dear children, love one another." He says: "It was worthy of him, who rested on the bosom of God, and was trusted with its secrets." Yet he himself was accustomed to denounce, as "scorpions," "dragons," "wolves," and "devils," all men who could not see theological doctrines from his own point of view.

In that transition state of the world, when a new mode of worship was being formed from multifarious scattered elements of the older times, Christian teachers were unavoidably engaged in perpetual controversy; an atmosphere always unfavourable to the exercise of love, or candour. This allowance ought to be made for the exceeding bitter-

ness of their sectarian strife; and also for the untruthful-
ness in which it must needs be confessed they sometimes
indulged. In their anxiety to build up the church of
Christ, they occasionally resorted to means well calculated
to make Christianity appear disreputable to the conscientious and intelligent among Jews and Pagans. Mosheim,
author of the Ecclesiastical History, expresses his fears that
"those who search with attention into the writings of the
Fathers of the fourth century, will find them disposed to
deceive, when the interest of religion seemed to require it."
Dr. Cave, author of Primitive Christianity, speaking of the
much-quoted Sibylline Prophecies, inquires: "Who does
not see that they were forged, for the advancement of the
Christian faith?" Dr. Milman, in his History of Christianity, says: "That some of the Christian legends were
deliberate forgeries can scarcely be questioned. The principle of pious fraud appeared to justify this mode of working on the popular mind. It was admitted and avowed.
To deceive into Christianity was so valuable a service, as
to hallow deceit itself." Eusebius, Bishop of Cæsarea, in
his Ecclesiastical History, has a chapter with the following
heading: "How far it may be lawful and fitting to use
falsehood as a medicine, for the advantage of those who
require such a method." In explaining the line of limitation, he cites cases from the Hebrew Scriptures, where
Jehovah is described as jealous or angry; which he says
was done "for the advantage of those who required such a
method." The fact of making such an inquiry indicates
the prevailing ideas of his time. Chrysostom, in his book
on the Priesthood, distinctly declares that falsehood may be
meritorious, if used for the benefit of the church. Jerome
relates that Christians in Jerusalem showed certain red
stones found among the ruins of the temple, and told people they were stained with the blood of Zacharias, who was
slain between the temple and the altar. He adds: "But I
find no fault with an error, which springs from hatred to
the Jews, and a pious zeal for the Christian faith." In a
letter to his patrician proselyte Eustochium, he tries to dis-

suade her from reading Pagan literature; and to enforce
the lesson, he gives an account, quoted in the preceding
sketch of his life, of seeing Christ come to judge the world,
and of being so severely beaten by angels, for reading
Cicero, that he made a solemn vow never to look into a
Pagan book again.   He writes to her thus: "Think not
that this was any of those drowsy fancies, or vain dreams,
which sometimes deceive us.   For the truth hereof, I call
to witness that tribunal before which I then lay, and that
judgment I was then in dread of. So may I never fall
into the like danger, as this is true!   I do assure you I
found my shoulders all over black and blue, with the stripes
I then received, and which I felt, after I awoke.   Ever since
that, I have had greater affection for reading Divine Books,
than I previously had for the study of human learning."
Long afterward, when he and his former friend Rufinus
were engaged in bitter disputation, Rufinus accused him
of breaking his vow to Christ never again to read Pagan
books; and as evidence of his assertion, adduces the fact
that the writings of Jerome still continued to abound with
accurate quotations from the classics.   Jerome at first replied, that he made all such extracts from memory.   Afterward, he wrote: "Thus much I would say, if I had really
promised anything in my waking moments.   But with rare
impudence, he objects against me a dream of mine.   Let
him who criminates a *dream*, listen to the voice of the Prophets, that no confidence is to be placed in dreams."   The
same Father, in reply to the charge of artifice in his mode
of conducting theological controversies, seeks to excuse
himself by quoting precedents.   He says: "Origen, Me-
thodius, Eusebius, Apollinaris, have written many thousands of lines against Celsus and Porphyry.   Consider with
what arguments, and what slippery problems, they baffle
what was contrived against them by the spirit of the Devil;
and because they are sometimes forced to speak, they speak
not what they think, but what is necessary against those
who are called Gentiles.   I do not mention the Latin writers, Tertullian, Cyprian, Minucius, Victorinus, Lactantius,

Hilarius, lest I be thought not so much to be defending myself, as accusing others."

The priesthood of all nations had always acted upon the system that it was necessary to deceive the mass of the people, for their own good; that it was not possible to guide them by the plain open truth. Similar motives induced philosophers to veil their doctrines, and evade direct inferences. The same idea of managing the people, for their spiritual benefit, prevailed among the Christian Fathers. Even Origen, who seems to have been an unusually conscientious man, thought it might sometimes prove useful to partially conceal the truth. He assigned the highest place in heaven to those who lived single, for the sake of religion; and the second place, to those who married but once; but he did not agree with some teachers, who maintained that the twice-married must be damned. He says: "It is, however, better for people to be deceived into the belief that the twice-married cannot be saved; and through that deception be enabled to live in purity, than to know the truth, and thereby be degraded into the rank of the twice-married; though it would indeed be better to live unmarried, or in widowhood, *without* being deceived, and with a knowledge of the fact that the twice-married may partake of a degree of salvation." The Fathers also occasionally resorted to evasions, and subtle distinctions, which resembled diplomacy. Among other objections to Christianity, it was common for Pagans to declare that no state could maintain its existence, if such precepts of non-resistance to evil were carried into practice. Augustine replied, that those peaceful maxims referred rather to the disposition of the *heart*, than to outward *actions;* that the *heart* ought always to cherish patience and good will; but *actions* might vary according to the best interest of those whose good we wished to promote.

The fear of trusting truth to find its own way, and to rest simply on its own merits, produced lamentable results, in various ways. Many spurious productions were published under the names of men whose writings were habitually referred to with deference; such as Peter, Paul, Barnabas, Clement of Rome, Ignatius, Polycarp, and others. And books really written by the Apostolic Fathers were altered and interpolated in the copying, to suit the theological views of those who transcribed them. The learned and candid Neander says: "The writings of the so-called Apostolic Fathers have, for the most part, come down to us in a condition very little worthy of confidence; partly because under the names of those men, so highly venerated in the church, writings were early forged, for the purpose of giving authority to particular opinions or principles; and partly because their own writings, which were extant, had become interpolated." Jews made similar charges concerning their history by Josephus, who was represented as speaking almost like a Christian in some cases; though it is evident, from the general character of his works, that his Jewish opinions remained unchanged. Different copies of his manuscripts do not agree in chronology, and in other particulars. Origen and Jerome allude to passages not now to be found. That manuscripts were mutilated, either by accident or design, is very evident; for scarcely any two copies could be found which were exactly alike. The celebrated passage, where he expresses a doubt whether Jesus were a mere man, exists in very few copies; and the same is said concerning his mention of James the Just, "the Lord's brother." These statements were not quoted, or referred to, by any Christian writers before the fourth century. This circumstance, combined with the fact that they are not found in many copies, and that they are obviously incongruous with the opinions of Josephus, always excited suspicions of their authenticity, in reflecting minds. At the present time, they are generally regarded by the learned as interpolations by some zealous Christian of the third century. The absence of printing at that period rendered such impositions comparatively safe from detection, especially where few had the wish to expose them.

The discipline of the church retained its early character of strictness; but as the line of demarcation between the orthodox and all manner of heretics was more closely defined, errors of faith began to be regarded as of equal, if not of greater importance than moral delinquencies, unless of a very gross character. Those who violated their baptismal vows were not allowed to partake of the communion, and were excluded from fellowship with the church, until it was decided that they had shown satisfactory marks of repentance. They were divided into four classes, according to the degree of their sin. The first class were obliged to remain outside of the church, prostrating themselves on the earth and imploring with tears that those who were passing in would pray for them. The next class were allowed to listen to the service with the unbaptized, in the area of the church. The third class were those for whom public prayers were offered; they kneeling meanwhile. The fourth class were allowed to be present at all the ceremonies of the church, but were not permitted to partake of the Lord's Supper, or to place an offering on the altar. The communion was never refused to any dying person, however great his crime, if he had shown signs of repentance. The tendency to asceticism had increased since the time of the early Fathers. Basil maintained that clothing should be for two purposes only; for warmth and modesty. He says: "In Paradise, innocence was the only robe. Sin brought into the world the fig-leaved coat; and what should more induce us to be humble in our apparel is that clothes are monitors of our apostacy." Some objected to the use of musical instruments in churches. The introduction of women's voices into the church service was also regarded as a dangerous innovation. It was one of the charges against Paul of Samosata, that by introducing this custom he had rendered the music of the church effeminate, and seductive in its sweetness. The Gnostics, and other heretical sects, had made very effective use of fervid and ecstatic hymns; and the prejudice excited against these led many of the orthodox to require that nothing but the words of Scripture should be used in church music. Others again objected to have sacred words conveyed in melodies, which had been used by Pagans. Athanasius required that the singing in churches should be with the slightest possible inflections of voice, that the beauty of tones might not withdraw attention from the words. Jerome says: "Not with the voice, but with the heart, must we make melody to the Lord. We are not to smooth the throat with sweet drinks, like comedians, in order that the church may hear theatrical songs and melodies. Knowledge of the Scriptures, piety, and the fear of God should inspire our songs; so that not the voice of the singer, but the divine matter expressed, may be the point of attraction; that the Evil Spirit which entered into the heart of a Saul may be expelled from those who are in like manner possessed, rather than invited by those who would turn the house of God into a theatre." The sensitive conscience of Augustine was alarmed when the Ambrosian Chants in the church at Milan brought tears into his eyes. Whatsoever was of the senses he deemed sinful; and he feared that he was moved by the sensuous luxury of sweet sounds, rather than by the devotional spirit of the Psalms.

If the Fathers in the second century found occasion to rebuke some converts for luxury in furniture and dress, it may well be supposed that it would be far more necessary when Christianity was patronized and pampered by emperors, and when it of course became a matter of custom, rather than conviction, with multitudes of professors. Wealthy converts painted their faces, and followed the fashion of colouring the hair with a golden tint. Garments richly embroidered with silk and gold were then much in vogue; the patterns representing flowers, landscapes, or hunting scenes. Christian matrons copied the fashion, but sought to manifest their piety by wearing dresses embroidered with the miracles of Christ; such as the marriage at Cana, the paralytic carried in his bed, or the blind man receiving his sight. The preachers were continually reproving such vanities. Jerome exclaims: "What business has paint on a Christian cheek? Who can weep for her sins, when tears wash her face bare, and make furrows on her skin? With what confidence can faces be lifted up toward heaven, which the Maker cannot recognize as his own workmanship?"

But it was the same in those times, as it has been in all others. Women were quite as conspicuous for devotional tendencies, and unqualified self-sacrifice, as they were for manifestations of personal vanity. They always formed so large a proportion of the converts, that the most common sarcasm of the Pagans was that Christian assemblies were filled with women and slaves. The emperor Julian, and those who sympathized with his views, constantly reproached the men for permitting their wives to give so much to the "Galilean churches." Very many were proselyted by their wives, mothers, or sisters; and the Christian character of others was greatly influenced by such relations. Nonna, the mother of Gregory of Nazianzen, won her husband from Gnosticism, and did much to form the kindly and devout character of her son. He tells us that she was never satisfied with helping the destitute; that he often heard her say she would willingly sell herself and her children, if it were lawful, that she might bestow the price upon those who were suffering for food and clothing. Her whole life was divided between charity and devotion; and her spirit passed from the body while she was kneeling before the altar. He praises his sister Gorgonia for the extreme plainness of her apparel; and says: "The only colour that pleased her in her complexion was blushing from modesty. The only whiteness she esteemed was the pallor that came through fasting and abstinence." It was mainly through the influence of his sister Macrina, that Basil the Great was induced to relinquish his brilliant prospects as a lawyer, and devote himself to an ascetic life. Anthusa, mother of Chrysostom, devoted her life to the formation of his religious character. Monica, the mother of Augustine, converted her passionate husband by her gentleness and piety, and was a powerful agent in reclaiming her wayward son. Wealthy ladies in Rome, converted by Jerome's preaching, renounced costly clothing, sold their jewels, and devoted their revenues to the suffering and the indigent. He says: "Ladies who could not endure to step on the filthy streets, who were fatigued to ascend a hill, who were carried by the hands of eunuchs, who considered the sunshine a conflagration, and were oppressed by the weight of a silken robe, now wear squalid and mourning garments of their own making." "They trim lamps, kindle the fire, sweep the pavement, boil vegetables, set the table, hand the cups, and run hither and thither." A patrician lady, named Fabiola, sold her estates, and with her ample revenues built and endowed the first asylum that was ever established for poor invalids. She gathered all the lame and diseased from the streets, and personally attended upon them in the hospital; preparing their food, washing their wounds, and performing for them the most disagreeable offices. When she died, all Rome mourned, as for the loss of a mother. A long procession of old and young preceded her bier, singing hymns in her praise. The streets, the windows, and the tops of the houses were crowded with spectators; and as the funeral passed along, a chorus of voices in all the churches sang, "Hallelujah!" The empress Placilla, wife of Theodosius the Younger, was constantly in the habit of visiting the poor at their own houses, and in the hospitals; washing their cups, handing them their broth, and arranging their pillows, with her own imperial hands.

The early Fathers generally spoke favourably of marriage, and though they denounced the amusements of social life, they said nothing in praise of withdrawing from its active duties. But as time passed on, the oriental element became more and more obviously mingled with Christianity. The later Fathers, almost without exception, lived and died unmarried; and nearly all of them wrote and preached earnestly in favour of celibacy. It was the leading theme of Jerome's exhortations, and he was eminently successful in gaining converts.

It was a prevailing belief among ancient nations, and was adopted by Plato, that spirits of the dead hovered round their burial-place for some time, and afterward frequently revisited it. Therefore, they were in the habit of resorting to their tombs, to offer sacrifices, oblations, and prayers for their benefit, and also to invoke their assistance in time of need. These opinions were engrafted upon Christianity. An ordinance of the church, which continued for many centuries, prohibited having lights in graveyards, or making merriment there at night,.lest the souls that came thither should be disturbed. At the celebration of the Lord's Supper, which it has already been stated was regarded in the light of a sacrifice, each time offered anew for mankind, it was customary to intercede for the souls of the dead. Husbands, wives, parents, and children, placed a gift on the altar at each anniversary of the death of their loved ones. And in return, the prayers of the church were offered for those who had fallen asleep, and for those who celebrated their memory. Individuals who had made donations to the church were publicly recommended to the Lord, by name.

Ephrem of Edessa, in his last will, requested his friends to offer constant oblations for him after his decease. He says: "When the thirtieth day shall be completed, then remember me; for the dead are helped by the offerings of the living." He seems to have supposed that Moses blessed the departed *spirit* of Reuben, though apparently he intended to bless his posterity, the *tribe* of Reuben; for he asks: "If the dead are not aided, why was Reuben blessed, after the third generation? Why does Paul say, 'If the dead rise not at all, what shall they do who are baptized for the dead? *Why* are they then baptized for the dead?'" Chrysostom says: "Not without reason was it ordained by the Apostles that in celebrating the Sacred Mysteries, the dead should be remembered; for they well knew what advantages would thence be derived to them." Cyril of Jerusalem says: "When the emperor condemns one to banishment, he may be induced to show him favour, if his kinsmen present a chaplet in his behalf. So we present to God the Christ who was offered for our sins, in behalf of those who are asleep, though they were sinners." "We pray for the holy Fathers, and the Bishops that are dead, and for all those who have departed this life in our communion; believing that the souls of those for whom our prayers are offered receive very great relief, while this holy and tremendous victim lies upon the altar," [alluding to the bread and wine of the eucharist].

It had been a very ancient Hindoo idea that immersion in rivers, with religious ceremonies by the priests, purified the soul from sin, "as water cleansed the body from mud." It has been already stated that Christians imbibed the same idea concerning baptism. This belief in the efficacy of an external rite produced an increasing tendency to defer it till the approach of death; for it naturally seemed to many minds an agreeable and easy process to enjoy the pleasures of life to the utmost, and then to have all stains washed away in a few moments, preparatory to entering upon another existence. Preachers were continually combatting this inevitable tendency, by holding up warning examples of death too sudden to admit the performance of the essential rite. But their own descriptions of the mysterious efficacy of baptism had such a counteracting influence, that people generally ventured to run the risk, until frightened by an earthquake, or war, or pestilence; and then they rushed to baptism in such multitudes, that it was often difficult to find priests enough to perform the ceremonies. Cyril of Jerusalem, addressing a candidate for baptism, said: "If thou believest, thou wilt not only obtain forgiveness of sins, but as much of grace as thou canst hold." Gregory of Nazianzen says: "Baptism for adults is forgiveness of sins, and restoration of the image degraded and lost by transgression." In the case of infants, he supposed it secured their human nature in the germ from moral evil. He calls baptism "a more divine, exalted creation, than the original formation of nature." To those who found it difficult to conceive how children could be benefitted by a rite, of which they had no consciousness, Augustine replied: "The faith of the church which consecrates infants to God, takes the place of their own faith; and although they possess as yet no faith of their own, yet there is nothing in their thoughts to hinder the divine efficacy." From the time that Cyprian had decided that children ought to be baptized as soon as they were born, because they brought with them into the world "the infection of the old death" from Adam, the doctrine had been gradually gaining ground that all unbaptized infants must be damned. The Pelagians expressed horror at this idea. They believed that the highest state of perfection and happiness in heaven could be attained only by the baptized; but they said those who died in childhood without having been thus purified, would remain in an intermediate state, where they would be exempt from suffering. Gregory of Nazianzen, and some others, believed the same concerning all those who remained unbaptized through no fault of their own. Augustine rejected this idea. Believing Tertullian's theory that the sin of Adam was physically transmitted, he declared: "There is no innocence in childhood." He said only two states could be conceived of; that of blessedness in the presence of God, and of misery expelled from Him; that unbaptized infants could not be received into the presence of God, and must therefore be irrevocably damned; though their sufferings would doubtless be lighter than those inflicted on actual sinners. Some theological writers carried out the theory so consistently, that they applied the same doctrine to babes that died unborn. It had always been a common idea among Christians that devils had possession of Pagans and heretics. In the third century, it began to be customary to repeat over them a form of words, called an exorcism, to compel the Evil Spirits to depart, preparatory to baptism. After the doctrine of original sin became a portion of the established creed, the church used the ceremony at the baptism of infants also. A council held at Carthage, in the year four hundred and eighteen, condemned the doctrine of an intermediate state for unbaptized children, on the ground that nothing could be conceived of as permanently existing between the kingdom of heaven and perdition. The eternal damnation of all who died unbaptized was expressly affirmed. But notwithstanding the terrors of such preaching, some parents were very reluctant to have the ceremony performed on babes; for it seemed to them almost a waste of the precious remedy to bestow it on those who had committed no actual sin, and who, if they lived, would of course commit sins subsequent to baptism. To a mother in that state of mind, Gregory of Nazianzen said: "Let sin gain no advantage in thy child. Let it be sanctified from the swaddling clothes, consecrated to the Holy Ghost. You fear for the divine seal, because of the weakness of nature. What a feeble and faint-hearted mother you must be. Hannah consecrated her Samuel to God even before he was born. Immediately after his birth, she made him a priest. Instead of fearing the frailty of man, she trusted in God."

People of all religions were accustomed to the idea of sacrifice offered as an expiation for sin. Jews who became converts to Christianity, accepted the idea that Christ was a Lamb slain for atonement, instead of the Paschal Lamb annually offered by their High Priest, from time immemorial. Gentile converts accepted the same idea in lieu of the sacrifices with which they had been accustomed to avert the anger of their gods. The habit of frequently offering sacrifice was supplanted by frequent participation of the Lord's Supper, supposed to be the body and blood of Christ, each time offered anew for the expiation of sin. In consecrating the bread and wine, it was deemed very essential that the exact words in the Gospel should be used; for it was the universal impression that when the priest uttered the words, "This is my body; this is my blood;" the elements became miraculously changed into the actual body of Christ, by means of some inherent power in the holy words. When the bishop was about to finish the consecration, the curtain, which hung before the altar, was drawn up, and he raised the bread and wine, to be adored as the body and blood of Christ. Those who partook of it were supposed to receive a supernatural infusion of the

Logos into their own souls and bodies, which imparted to them a principle of imperishable life. Gregory of Nyssa says: "This bread is instantly changed into the body of Christ; agreeably to what he said, 'This is my body.' Therefore does the Divine Word commix itself with the weak nature of man, that by partaking of the Divinity, our humanity may be exalted." He explains it by saying that as bread and wine nourished and helped to form the body of the Logos while he was on earth, so after his departure the same elements were changed into his flesh and blood by an immediate miracle. Gregory of Nazianzen calls the eucharist, "A sacrifice by which we enter into fellowship with the sufferings and with the divine nature of Christ; the holy transaction which exalts us to heaven." Chrysostom, maintaining that the Holy Supper was the full accomplishment of the typical Passover, says: "This blood, even in the type, washed away sin. If it had so great power in the *type*, if death were so affrighted by the *shadow*, how he must be frightened by the verity itself!" He contemplates this institution as "the greatest proof of love Christ gave to dying men, that he should thus unite himself to them in the most intimate manner, and cause his own flesh and blood to pass into their entire nature; that he gave himself not only to be seen and touched, but to be eaten by those who desire him." He says: "As many of you as partake of this body, as many of you as taste this blood, should think of it as nothing different from that which sits above, and is adored by angels." Cyril of Jerusalem says: "After the Holy Spirit has been invoked, the eucharistic bread is no longer common bread, but is the body of Christ. He himself declared, 'This is my body,' and who shall dare to doubt it?" "Christ changed water into wine, by his will only; and shall we think him less worthy of credit, when he changes wine into blood?" Jerome says: "Our Lord Jesus invites us to the feast, and is himself our meat. He eats with us, and we eat him." Augustine says: "Because he walked here in the flesh, he gave us this same flesh to eat, for our salvation. No one eateth this flesh without having first adored it. We not only commit no sin by adoring it, but we should sin by *not* adoring it." Eusebius of Cæsarea, whose mind had been much influenced by the writings of Origen, takes a more spiritual view of the subject. He represents Christ as saying: "Think not I bid you drink my bodily blood; but know that the words I have spoken to you are spirit and life; so that my *words* and *doctrines* are my flesh and blood. He who appropriates to himself *these*, becomes nourished with bread from heaven, and will be made a partaker of eternal life." It was the opinion of the Fathers, that the eucharist was as essential to the salvation of infants, as was the rite of baptism. Therefore it was always administered to baptized children, till after the sixth century.

In all religions, great account was made of Mysteries. Among the Jews, none but the High Priest ever went behind the veil of the Holy of Holies. If any other person had ventured to do it, the people would have expected to see him drop down dead. When Grecians celebrated the Eleusinian Mysteries, a herald proclaimed: "Go hence, all ye profane!" a form which dismissed all but the initiated. Christianity, while seeking to establish itself, naturally adopted new forms of whatever ideas or customs were strongly rooted in the minds of men. The celebration of the Lord's Supper was represented as a Sacred Mystery. Before the veil was withdrawn from the altar, a deacon proclaimed: "Holy things to holy men. Depart all ye catechumens!" a form which dismissed all but the baptized. The doctrine of the Trinity likewise was not discussed or explained in their presence. There was a public and a private doctrine, according to the general custom of philosophers. Cyril of Jerusalem says: "We do not declare the Mysteries concerning the Father, Son, and Holy Ghost, to the Gentiles; nor do we speak plainly to the catechumens about those Mysteries. But we may say many things in an occult way, that the faithful, who know them, may understand, while those who do not understand them can not be hurt thereby." Augustine says: "If we asked a catechumen, 'Dost thou eat the flesh, and drink the blood of the Son of Man?' he would not know what we mean; for Christ has not committed himself to them. They do not know what Christians receive." Chrysostom, alluding to the eucharist in the light of a sacrifice offered, says: "Truly tremendous are the Mysteries of the church! Truly tremendous are the altars!" Some of the Fathers style it "the awful solemnity;" "sublime in the eyes of angels." Jerome says: "The very chalices, and coverings of the mystic table, are not to be considered like things inanimate and void of sanctity; but they ought to be reverenced as much as his body and his blood." It was customary to allude to the subject in a very blind way, in the presence of the uninitiated. Augustine says: "Christ was held in his own hands. *How* was he held in his own hands? Because when he gave his own body and blood, he took into his hands—what the faithful know." Epiphanius says: "We see that our Lord took something in his hands; that he rose from table, and having given thanks, he said: 'This is my somewhat.'" After alluding to the Trinity or the Eucharist, in this mysterious manner, it was common to add: "Those who are initiated know what has been said." The Fathers assign as one reason for pursuing this course, that young Christians were thereby stirred up to greater eagerness to be admitted into the mysteries of baptism and the Lord's Supper. Another motive was to preserve the sacredness and dignity of religion. Basil says: "A thing cannot be properly called a Mystery when it is once exposed to every common ear."

Numerous miracles were ascribed to the eucharist. Ambrose tells of an intimate friend of his, a pious Christian, but one who had not yet been admitted to the more perfect Mysteries. Being wrecked on a voyage to Africa, he begged some of the initiated, who were on board, to give him a portion of their consecrated bread; without the presence of which no voyage, or journey, was considered safe. Having received a piece, he fastened it in a hand-kerchief, tied it about his neck, and plunged into the sea, without troubling himself to look for a plank. "For he wanted nothing more than the armour of his faith. Nor did his hopes deceive him; for he was the first of the ship's company, who got safely to the shore." Augustine tells of a country-house near Hippo which was haunted. But when a priest went and "offered the sacrifice of Christ's body on the spot," praying fervently that the vexation might be removed, it instantly ceased.

It is obvious that some of the opinions and customs of the church cannot be traced either to the Jewish or the Christian Scriptures. All such were sustained upon the authority of tradition from the early Fathers. Epiphanius says: "We must look also to tradition; for all things cannot be learned from the Scriptures." Basil says: "In my opinion, it is apostolical to adhere to unwritten traditions." "The Apostles and Fathers, who prescribed from the beginning certain rites to the church, knew how to preserve the dignity of the Mysteries, by the secrecy and silence in which they enveloped them. What is open to the eye and the ear is no longer mysterious. For this reason, several things have been handed down to us without writing; lest the vulgar, by becoming too familiar with our dogmas, should pass from being accustomed to them to contempt for them." Chrysostom says: "The Apostles did not deliver all things by means of epistles. They made many communications without writing. Both are equally entitled to belief. It is a tradition. Inquire no further."

The later Fathers were as devotional in their habits, as their predecessors had been. They always washed their hands before entering a church; and required kings to lay down their armour and their crowns at the door, and leave their guards behind them. They fasted often, and prayed three times a day. They prayed and sang Psalms before and after eating, and never drank without making a sign of the cross over the cup. Chrysostom says: "The Devil is never so ready to ensnare us, as at meals; either by intemperance, indolence, or immoderate mirth; therefore, both before and after eating, we should fortify ourselves with Psalms."

The bond between Christians was exceedingly strong. They were always ready to assist each other in poverty, sickness, and trouble. The Pagans were continually surprised to see men of totally different education and habits, sympathizing with each other, and relying upon each other, like brothers of the same family. If fierce denunciations and bitter persecution of all who differed from them in theological doctrines excited the remark, "How these Christians hate each other," their unstinted kindness and truly fraternal feeling toward all within the fold excited the general remark how Christians loved each other. And their benevolence flowed copiously, not only to their own communities, near and distant, but also to poor and suffering strangers. To them the Roman empire owed its first asylums for widows and orphans, the sick and the indigent. Even the Emperor Julian set them up as an example in these respects, worthy of all imitation. It was a common custom to appoint fasts when any of the sister churches needed assistance, and the money saved from food enabled even the poorest to contribute something toward their relief. In times of sickness, their courageous kindness is said to have furnished a striking contrast to their Pagan neighbours, who had no such central bond of union. Dionysius, Bishop of Alexandria, describing a pestilence in that city, says: "It was true of most of our brethren, that in the fulness of their brotherly love, they spared not themselves. Their only anxiety was a mutual one for each other. And as they waited on the sick without thinking of themselves, ministering to their wants for Christ's sake, so they cheerfully gave up their lives for them. Many who took the bodies of Christian brethren into their arms, and to their bosoms, composed their features, and buried them with all possible care, afterward followed them in death. Some of the best among our brethren, presbyters, deacons, and distinguished men of the laity, thus ended their lives; so that

the manner of their death being the fruit of such eminent
piety and mighty faith, seemed not to fall short of martyrdom. With the Pagans it was quite otherwise. They
drove from them those who showed the first symptoms of
disease; and fled from their dearest friends. They cast the
half dead into the streets, and left the dead unburied;
making it their chief care to avoid contagion." Chrysostom records that in his time the church at Antioch, which
consisted of about one hundred thousand persons, daily
maintained three thousand widows and orphans, besides
supporting the clergy, and the hospitals, assisting strangers
in distress, and ransoming many Christian slaves. Basil
the Great established in all the principal towns of his diocese institutions for the reception of indigent strangers, and
the care of the sick. Physicians and nurses were in attendance, and every arrangement made for the comfort of the
inmates. Workshops were provided for all the labourers
and artisans that were needed; so that each establishment
was described as having the appearance of a small town.
When the brother of Basil died, he left this brief testament:
"I will that all my estate be given to the poor." Paulinus,
Bishop of Treves, in the fourth century, was very wealthy;
but when he became a Christian, he sold all his vast estates,
and distributed the proceeds among the poor. Theodoret,
Bishop of Cyros, at about the same period, though he had
a poor diocese, saved enough to construct a canal from the
Euphrates to the town, which had previously suffered for
want of water; to repair and improve the public baths; to
erect two porticoes for the use of the city; and to build
two large bridges. Ambrose sold the ornaments, and even
sacred vessels of the churches to redeem Christians, who
had been taken in war, and sold into slavery. He says:
"The church possesses gold, not to treasure it up, but to
distribute it for the welfare and happiness of men. We are
ransoming souls from eternal perdition. It is not merely
the lives of men and the honour of women, that are endangered by captivity, but also the faith of their children.
The blood of redemption, which has glowed in those golden

cups, has sanctified them not merely for that service, but for the redemption of men."

The Bishop of Nola expended his whole estate to redeem as many as he could. At last, a poor widow went to him and intreated him to rescue her only son, who had been sold to a prince of the Vandals. He told her he had not a single penny left, but he would freely give himself as a ransom. The poor woman thought he was jesting with her anxiety; but he assured her that he was in earnest. Accordingly, he accompanied her to Africa and begged the prince to release the young man, because he was the only son of a widow; offering to labour freely in his stead. The prince accepted his proposition, and employed him to work in his garden. His industry and faithfulness gained the favour of his master, who, after some time, discovered that he had been a bishop. Impressed by the greatness of such an example, the prince gave him his liberty, and promised to grant whatsoever he wished. The good man asked no favour for himself, but begged the release of all his countrymen in bondage. They were accordingly all sent home in ships laden with provisions.

Christians had the same feeling as the Israelites of old concerning allowing their own brethren to be in slavery; and a similar degree of exclusiveness led them generally not to include Pagan bondmen within the circle of their sympathies. It early began to be the feeling that one Christian ought not to hold another as a slave; the relation, even under the best circumstances, seeming inconsistent with Christian brotherhood. Many converts emancipated all their slaves as soon as they joined the church, being impelled by their own consciences, though no ecclesiastical law required it. When slaves were converted, it was common for Christian masters to emancipate them; so that baptism came to be considered a sign of freedom. Among the crowds of nominal professors, after Christianity became the established religion, there were of course many who were entirely uninfluenced by its spirit. The Archbishop of Ravenna, in the fifth century, complains of such, who could scarcely be distinguished from the hardest masters among the Pagans, in their treatment of slaves. But as a general thing, the difference between the old and the new religion was very striking on this point. Lactantius says: "We may be asked, are there not among you rich and poor, masters and slaves, distinctions of rank between individuals? Not at all. No reason can be assigned why we call one another brethren, except that we consider ourselves equals. We measure human beings by their souls, not by their bodies. There is diversity in the condition of bodies; but to us none are slaves. We address all as brothers in the Spirit, and regard all as fellow-servants, in a religious sense." Chrysostom says: "In the bosom of the Christian church, there are no slaves, in the old sense of the word. The name exists, but the thing has ceased." "The slave glorifies Jesus Christ as his master, and the master acknowledges himself a slave of Jesus Christ. Both are subjects, both are free in this common obedience; they are equals, both as freemen and as slaves." In another place, he exhorts Christians to "buy up slaves, instruct them in the arts, and give them the means of livelihood." Chromacius, Præfect of Rome, who was converted during the reign of Diocletian, was baptized with fourteen hundred of his slaves, to whom he gave freedom, saying: "These, who are the children of God, ought to be no longer the slaves of men." He crowned this act of justice and humanity by taking paternal care concerning their means of livelihood.

EXTRACTS FROM THE FATHERS.

Nearly all the writings of the Fathers consisted of sectarian controversy, Biblical interpretation employed in its service, and fervent exhortations to celibacy; but some precious gems of morality, scattered about, indicate that the world was rising to a higher level of humanity than it ever attained under the pure and elevated, but unsympathizing teaching of the Platonic school. The following brief extracts will serve as specimens:

"God, who creates and inspires men, willed that they should be 'equal. He made them all capable of wisdom, imposed the same laws on all, and promised immortality to all. No one is excluded from his heavenly gifts. He makes the sun to shine equally on all, and the fountains to issue freely for all. As he furnishes food for all, and gives the sweet repose of sleep unto all, so does he give virtue and equality to all. With Him, no one is a slave, and no one master. He is the Father of all, and we are all, by equal right, his children. In his sight, no man is poor, but him who is wanting in goodness; and no man is rich, but him who abounds in virtues."—*Lactantius.*

"The poor shake with cold beneath their miserable rags, while we envelope ourselves in long floating robes of the finest silk. The poor can scarcely find a refuse morsel wherewith to appease the cravings of hunger; while we luxuriate in the choicest delicacies. We lavish the most delicate odours, as if our courage were not already sufficiently enervated. Our tables bend beneath dishes, for which all the elements have been laid under contribution; and all this is done to satisfy the avidity of an ungrateful stomach, an insatiable brute, which will soon be destroyed, together with the perishable viands that are accumulated to nourish it. The poor would think themselves happy to get water enough to quench their thirst; and we drink wine to excess, even while we feel our senses disordered by its potency. My brethren, these diseases of the soul, which infect the rich, are more grievous than the bodily infirmities that afflict the poor. Theirs are not of their own seeking; ours are what we bring upon ourselves. Death will deliver them from theirs; ours will go with us to the grave, and rise with us."—*Gregory of Nazianzen.*

"Since you alone are amenable for your own vices, or follies, what good does it do to talk of your forefathers, and rake up the ashes of the dead? One man may draw forth nothing but discordant sounds from a golden harp; another will give birth to ravishing melodies on a simple reed. Such is your history, my friend. You descended from an

illustrious race, which is to you as the harp of gold. But
if you have no merit in yourself, upon what can you build
your pride? What real subject of exaltation can you find
for yourself in ancestors long since dead? What is all that
to us? It is with yourself alone we have to do. Are you
good, or are you bad? Every thing is reduced to that simple question."—*Gregory of Nazianzen.*

"What was I before I was born? What am I now?
What shall I be to-morrow? I asked the learned to guide
me, but I found no one who knew any more than myself.
I exist. What does that word mean? Already, whilst I
speak, a portion of my existence has escaped me. I am
no longer what I was. Should I still exist, what shall I
be to-morrow? In no one thing permanent, I resemble
the water of a stream, perpetually flowing on, which nothing stops. Like the brook, in another moment I shall no
longer be the same I was a moment before. I ought to be
called by some other name. You seize me, now you hold
me, yet I escape. Fugitive wave! never again will you
traverse the space over which you have already flowed.
The same man, whom you have once reflected in your waters, will never be reflected by them again, exactly as he
looked in them before."—*Gregory of Nazianzen.*

"Why is it that you are rich, and your neighbour poor?
Is it not that you may sanctify your abundance by your
benevolence, while he may sanctify poverty by patience
and resignation? Do not deceive yourself with respect to
the ways of Providence. The bread that you keep shut
up belongs to the hungry. The shoes which you hoard
belong to the barefoot. To withhold assistance from those
who are in need, when you have the means of relieving
them, is not only cruel, it is unjust."—*Basil the Great.*

"Has any one made use of injurious expressions concerning you? Reply to them by blessings. Does he treat
you ill? Be patient. Does he reproach you? Condemn
yourself, if the reproach be just; if not, it is a mere breath
of air. Flattery cannot impart to you a merit, if you have
it not, nor can calumny give you faults you do not really

possess. Are you accused of ignorance? You justify the charge by showing yourself angry. Are you persecuted? Think of Jesus Christ. Can you ever suffer as he suffered?"—*Basil the Great.*

"The slanderer does injury to three persons at once. To him *of* whom he speaks ill; to him *to* whom he says it; and most of all to himself *in* saying it."—*Basil the Great.*

"Is it a misfortune to pass from infancy to youth? Still less can it be a misfortune to go from this miserable life to that true life into which we are introduced by death. Our first changes are connected with the progressive developement of life. The new change, which death effects, is only the passage to a more desirable perfection. To complain of the necessity of dying, is to accuse Nature of not having condemned us to perpetual infancy."—*Gregory of Nyssa.*

"'I possessed myself of servants and maids.' Possessed, do you say? Who can be the possessor of human beings, save God? By what right can any other claim possession of them? Those men that you say belong to you, did not God create them free? Command the brute creation; it is well and good. But do not degrade the image of God! Bend the beasts of the field beneath your yoke. But are your fellow men to be bought and sold, like herds of cattle? Who can pay the value of a being created in the image of God? The whole world itself bears no proportion to the value of a soul, on which the Most High has set the seal of his likeness. This world will perish; but the soul of man is immortal. Show me then your titles of possession. Whence have you received this strange privilege? Is not your own nature the same with that of those whom you call your slaves? Have they not the same origin with yourself? Are they not born to the same destinies?"—*Gregory of Nyssa.*

"All the immense space by which we are surrounded is peopled with angels, whose eyes are continually turned toward us. The most hardened in wickedness still shrinks from observation. The thought that he is watched checks

the criminal in the fury of his passion.   Can the Christian
then, who knows that celestial Spirits not only behold his
every action, but also read his most secret thoughts, can he
ever, in mere levity and thoughtlessness, deliver himself
up to evil?"—*Hilary of Poictiers.*

"There is always something of injustice and inhumanity
in the possession of immense wealth, however legitimate
the possession of it may be in point of law, and however
honest in the sight of man may be the means by which it
was acquired."—*Ambrose of Milan.*

"There are certain persons, not altogether asleep in ignorance, nor yet fully awake in the light of reason, who
hold that right is nothing but that which is commonly received.   Since laws and customs differ, they conclude that
there is nothing binding in its own nature; but that whatsoever a man is persuaded of in his own mind, the same
must be right and good.   These people have not yet
looked far enough into the world to discover that all
nations under heaven accept, as a standard, the maxim,
'Do unto others, as ye would they should do unto you.'"—
Augustine.

"Blessed is he who loveth God; and his friend *in* God;
and his enemy *for* God."—*Augustine.*

"Your very existence is not your own.   How is it then
that your riches are?   They belong rather to those for
whom God has given them into your keeping.   Wealth is
a common property, like the light of the sun, the air, or
the productions of the earth.   Riches are to society what
food is to the body.   Should any one of the members
absorb the nutriment which is intended for the support of
the whole, the body would perish utterly; for it is held
together only by the requisite distribution of nourishment
to the divers parts.   In the same manner, the general harmony of society is maintained only by the interchange of
services between the rich and the poor."—*John Chrysostom.*

"Nobility consists not in illustrious ancestry, but in the
virtues of the soul.   I call the slave a patrician, though
bound in chains, if I know his soul to be noble; and I

deem the patrician a slave, though invested with outward
dignity, if he has an ignoble mind." "How many drunken
patricians lie stupified on their couches, while their sober
servants stand by. Which of these ought to be called a
slave? Should the term be applied to him who has been
made captive by man, or to him who is the slave of his
passions? One is enslaved by external circumstances;
the other carries about his slavery within him." "Let
there be no wall of separation between freemen and slaves.
It is better that they should serve one another; for mutual
service is preferable to an exclusive and solitary liberty.
Suppose a master to own a hundred slaves, who all serve
him with repugnance; and then suppose a hundred souls,
who help each other from affection. On which side will
there be most happiness? On which will life be the most
lovely? On the first, is misery and fear; everything being
effected by force, and done from necessity. On the other,
vengeance is banished, and all comes from free-will, benevolence, and gratitude. Such is the order of God. He
himself washed the feet of his disciples, and said: 'Let him
who would be your master, be your servant.'"

FESTIVALS AND FASTS.

SUNDAY AND THE SABBATH.—As the separation from
Judaism increased, the custom of observing both their Sabbath and Sunday gradually changed. But even as late as
the year three hundred and sixty, a Council at Laodicea
deemed it necessary to forbid Christians to abstain from
labour on the Sabbath, [Saturday.] In connection with
this decree, they remark: "Christians ought not to Judaize
and cease from labour on the Sabbath. They ought to
work on that day. As Christians, they should prefer to
rest from labour, if they can, on the Lord's Day," [Sunday.]
Laws stricter than those of Constantine were passed by his
successors. Civil transactions of every kind were forbidden
on Sunday, as sacrilegious. In four hundred and twenty-
five, Jews and Pagans were required to abstain from thea-

tres and festivals on that day, because the noise in the
streets disturbed the devotions of those assembled in the
churches. Neander, the learned inquirer into Ecclesiastical History, says: "The celebration of Sunday, like that
of every festival, was a human institution. Far was it from
the Apostles to treat it as a divine command; far from
them, and from the first apostolic church, to transfer the
laws of the Sabbath to Sunday."

AGAPE.—It has been already mentioned that the Feast
called Agape gradually changed its character, as the number of worldly Christians increased. The fraternal kiss,
with which it had been customary to separate in the good
old times of affectionate simplicity, probably led to some
abuses among those who were not pure of heart. At all
events, many scandalous stories concerning these meetings
were circulated by Pagan opponents, and by Gnostic ascetics. To prevent this, the church ordained that men
should confine the customary salutation to the brethren
only, and women to the sisters. At that period of the
world, it was the common practice to eat in a half reclining
posture; but the church ordered them to dispense with
couches at the Agape. Notwithstanding these, and other
restraining laws, intemperance and excess became so noto-
rious, that the Council at Carthage, in three hundred ninety
seven, forbade these feasts to be held in churches; considering them a desecration of the holy place. The Fathers
everywhere preached against them, and they were finally
laid aside

FESTIVAL OF THE MARTYRS.—The great annual Festival
among the Pagans for the Souls of all their Ancestors, had
been adopted by Gregory Thaumaturgus, as a matter of
policy, and appropriated to the honour of All the Martyrs.
Gregory of Nyssa, in his life of that proselyting bishop,
says: "The Pagans were delighted with the festivals of
their gods, and unwilling to part with those delights.
Therefore, Gregory, to facilitate their conversion, instituted

annual festivals to saints and martyrs." On these occasions, a great banquet was provided, and dances and pantomimes introduced, as had been the custom in the Pagan Parentalia. The gathering-place was usually at, or near the tomb, or chapel, of some celebrated martyr, where prayers were offered, and hymns sung in honour of the dead. The roads, for many miles round, were crowded with pilgrims, who went to implore the martyrs to send them good weather, abundant crops, smooth seas, and healthy children; to protect them from diseases or accidents during the year, and if they died, to bear their souls into the bosom of Christ, and intercede for them at the last day. On account of the great concourse of people, it was customary to have markets, or fairs, established near by, for the sale of provisions, and other conveniences, consequently a large proportion of the assembly was brought together merely for purposes of merriment or traffic. Some of the less strict among the bishops sanctioned the scene by their presence, after the religious portion of the ceremonies was completed; but their influence was not sufficient to restrain excesses. The health of the martyrs was often drunk to complete intoxication. Gregory of Nazianzen and Chrysostom severely denounced the luxury with which this festival was celebrated at Antioch. Many of the clergy strongly disapproved of the practice; but it was exceedingly difficult to wean the people from the old customs, which had become universally engrafted on the new faith. Basil preached against such scenes as altogether unsuitable to the solemnity of the subject, and of the places where they assembled. He reminded the people that they ought to remember how Christ whipped out buyers and sellers from the House of Prayer. As the rich, on these occasions, furnished provisions, of which the poor partook freely, the feast was often called by the old name of Agape; which was thus brought into still greater disrepute among opponents of the church. The Council of Laodicea formally condemned these festivals; but it was a long time before they were suppressed. The Manicheans, who were very

abstemious in their habits, and extremely simple in their
mode of worship, frequently taunted Catholic Christians
with their festivals, and multiplication of ceremonies.
They said: "You have but substituted your Agape for
the Pagan sacrifices. In the place of their idols, you have
set up your martyrs, whom you worship with the same
ceremonies they did their gods. Like them, you appease
the souls of the dead with wine and with meat offerings."

LENT AND EASTER.—In addition to the weekly fasts on
Wednesday and Friday, Christians held an annual fast
preceding the first full moon after the vernal equinox. It
was variously observed in different times and places.
Some fasted several days, others abstained from animal
food during several weeks. It was immediately followed
by the joyful festivities of Easter, the most ancient Christian festival on record; being a continuation of the Passover, to which the Apostles, and Jewish converts, had
always been accustomed. In the East, the members of
churches assembled in grave-yards, on the Friday preceding the joyful Sunday, to commemorate the crucifixion.
During the Festival of Easter, Constantine the Great released all prisoners, except those who had committed very
great crimes; and he always distributed large donations
among the poor. Theodosius the Great ordained that no
lawsuits should be commenced, no accusations should be
brought, and no punishments inflicted, during the continu-
ance of the holy season. After the time of Constantine,
this festival was observed with great pomp. On the evening preceding Easter Sunday, all the churches and the
principal houses were brilliantly illuminated; people
poured through the streets with torches, and vigils were
kept in the churches till the morning dawned. The next
day, all the churches resounded with Hallelujahs, and
friends and relatives feasted at each other's houses. The
holy season began on Palm Sunday, a week before Easter,
and continued till the Sunday after Easter; including
fourteen days. Not only the Jews, but all the ancient

nations, kept a festival near the vernal equinox, to wel-
come in the budding spring-time with thank-offerings to
their gods. The Saxon word Oster means rising; and the
German word Osten means the east, in allusion to the sun's
rising. The Saxons had a season of thanksgiving in the
spring, which they named Ostern, in honour of the old
Teutonic Goddess of Nature, called Ostera. This is supposed to be the origin of the English name Easter, applied
to the Christian festival in honour of Christ's rising. The
French call it Pâques, and Italians Pasqua; in allusion to
the Paschal Lamb slain at the Passover. It was early
customary for the Bishops of Rome to distribute the remains of the tapers consecrated on Easter Eve. The people
burned them at home, as a preservation against all manner
of misfortunes.

WHITSUNDAY.—The Jewish Pentecost was likewise retained by Christians, but kept by them in commemoration
of the descent of the Holy Ghost upon the disciples. As
the Holy Spirit was supposed to be imparted by baptism,
the day was peculiarly appropriated to the performance of
that ceremony. The numerous candidates who assembled,
being clothed in white robes, made a conspicuous show on
the margin of rivers and ponds. Hence the festival came
to be called White Sunday, or Whitsunday.

EPIPHANY.—Egyptians observed the sixth of January,
as a joyful festival in honour of Osiris found; probably in
allusion to the sun returning from the winter solstice.
Christians in some countries adopted this festival. They
at first kept it in commemoration of the Star which guided
the Wise Men of the East; and presents were interchanged
on that day, said to be in allusion to the offerings of the
Magi; though in fact that custom, as well as the festival
itself, was of much more ancient date than the birth of
Christ. The Ebionite "Gospel according to the Hebrews"
commenced at the baptism of Christ; and declared that
when Jesus entered the water, "straightway a great light

shone round the place." Justin Martyr, who probably
derived the idea from that source, says that "a fire was
kindled in the Jordan." Hence, the Eastern churches
often called baptism Illumination. After a time, the sixth
of January, instead of being observed by Christians in
honour of the miraculous star, was supposed to be the very
day on which Christ was baptized; when "all the persons
of the Trinity were present. The Father in a voice from
heaven; the Son in the person of Jesus; and the Holy
Spirit in the visible shape of a dove." In some places,
many torches and fires were lighted during the celebration,
to commemorate the star that guided the Magi to Bethlehem, the light that shone round the shepherds, and the fire
"kindled in the Jordan." At Constantinople, it was originally called the Feast of Lights. It afterward received
the name of Epiphany, from Greek words signifying The
Appearance, or the Manifestation; because the Holy Ghost
appeared at the baptism, and Christ was for the first time
manifested as the Messiah. Chrysostom relates that during
this festival people were accustomed to draw water at
midnight, and preserve it carefully, believing it to possess
certain miraculous powers; because Christ, by going into
the Jordan, "sanctified water to the mystical washing away
of sin." He affirms that water drawn at that holy season
would keep pure a whole year; sometimes two or three
years.

CHRISTMAS.—Most of the ancient nations observed seasons of rejoicing when the sun began to return from the
winter solstice. Egyptians had two festivals of this kind;
one on the twenty-fifth day of December, to commemorate
the birth-day of the infant Horus, and the other on the
sixth of January, to rejoice over the lost Osiris found.
Persians kept a festival on the twenty-fifth of December,
in honour of Mithras, the attendant Spirit of the Sun. At
Rome, there was a series of festivals in the latter part of
December. There was the Saturnalia, in commemoration
of the Golden Age of Saturn, when all distinctions of rank

were abolished and the earth was filled with abundance. On this occasion, relatives and friends feasted each other, and interchanged presents. There was the Festival for Children, during which it was customary to give children little images. The twenty-fifth day of December was celebrated under the name of Dies Natalis Invicti Solis, The Birth Day of the Invincible Sun. It is not known at what season of the year Christ was born, and the custom of keeping his nativity is not mentioned till the second century, when it was observed by the Eastern churches on the sixth of January. In the Western part of the empire, the Roman Birth Day of the Sun, the twenty-fifth of December, began, in the middle of the fourth century, to be observed in honour of the nativity of Christ. The Eastern churches continued their old custom for some time after; but in the fifth century, the twenty-fifth of December was established, by decree of the church, as a festival to be universally observed. The Roman people had been attached to this holiday, from very ancient times; and it was deemed peculiarly appropriate to transfer it to the honour of Christ, who was called "the sun of righteousness," and often compared to the natural sun, illuminating a world in darkness. The Gospel of Luke represents Christ as born in the night; it was therefore customary to have the churches lighted up, and public worship performed the midnight preceding. The prayers and ceremonies, accompanying the eucharist were called Mass; hence the festival came to be denominated Christmas. Manicheans and other heretical sects, reproached the Catholics for observing the Birth Day of the Sun, with the Pagans. Leo the Great, Patriarch of Rome, in the middle of the fifth century, complains that in his time many Christians retained the Pagan custom of paying obeisance to the rising sun, from some lofty eminence; also in the morning, when they were ascending the steps of St. Peter's church. Theodosius the Younger prohibited games at Easter, Whitsunday, Christmas, and Epiphany; and ordered all the theatres to be closed, not only for Christians, but for Jews and Pagans.

BISHOPS.

The preceding pages have shown how the simple church government in the days of the Apostles had changed, when Cyprian maintained that bishops were supreme arbiters of theological truth.   Early in the second century it began to be the custom for country churches to unite themselves to some church in a neighbouring city, which was thus constituted their head.   Sometimes several churches in the same city united themselves under the guidance of one, and formed what was called a Metropolitan church.   The Metropolitan Bishop presided over inferior bishops and clergy, when they came from the country to attend a council in the city where he resided; and all the clergy of his province were required to refer to him for advice, in any cases of difficulty; hence he came to be called Archbishop, or Chief Bishop.   From the beginning of the fifth century, the Archbishops of Rome, Constantinople, Alexandria, Antioch, and Jerusalem, began to take the title of Patriarchs; and to them was conceded the power of supervision over all the other bishops and archbishops within their jurisdiction.   In almost every difficulty that occurred, Rome, the representative of the West, took one side, and Constantinople, the representative of the East, took the other.   The supremacy of Rome was strongly urged, on the ground that the first church there was established by Peter, to whom Christ had said: "On this rock will I found my church."   By the middle of the fifth century, it was decided by decrees of councils, and of the emperor, that the Patriarch of Rome was the last tribunal of appeal; and that the Patriarch of Constantinople was to take the second rank in Christendom.   The increasing power of Rome was of course watched with jealousy by her old rival.   The Eastern churches frequently rebelled against the decisions of the Primate; and even in the West, where alone his edicts had the force of law, they often met with strenuous opposition, till as late as the eighth century.   As early as the time of Cyprian, it began to be customary to call all bishops Papas, a title of respect, from a Greek word signifying Father. This was the origin of the English word Pope; which was not exclusively applied to the Roman Pontiff till the eleventh century. After the fourth century, bishops were often nominated by the emperor, instead of being elected by the people, as they had previously been.

Deaconesses, before entering upon their office, were originally ordained, like others of the clergy; but as the clerical order increased in dignity, the priesthood began to declare against this custom. Synods in the fourth and fifth centuries forbade the ordination of women; and those who had been previously ordained were required to receive the bishops' blessing in company with the laity, not with the clergy.

The belief that the Holy Spirit was transmitted by the imposition of hands at ordination led many to attach little importance to any preparation for the priesthood. This idea, combined with the tendency to consider mere external rites sufficient for salvation, produced an increasing contempt for intellectual culture. To have received the Holy Ghost, and to be able to perform ceremonies, was deemed sufficient for a priest. The more eminent teachers of the church, such as Basil and the two Gregories, sought to counteract this tendency, by representing human learning as a valuable servant to divine truth; but they were exceptions to the general rule.

In the first centuries of Christianity, the clergy married, if they chose; considering themselves sustained by the opinions of the early Fathers, and the example of the Apostles. Gregory of Nazianzen was born after his father was a bishop. Gregory, Bishop of Nyssa, and Hilary, Bishop of Poictiers were married. Eusebius, the historian, mentions numerous instances of married bishops and presbyters. Augustine also speaks of Catholic clergymen in his time, who had wives. For the first three hundred years, there was no ecclesiastical law or regulation to enforce celibacy of the priesthood. But a large proportion

of the most eminent of the later Fathers, sustained celibacy
by eloquent writings and their own example; and monks
were so venerated by the populace, for their superior sanctity, that it seemed to a make a similar degree of holiness
desirable, if not necessary, to all the clergy. The feeling
first showed itself in opposition to second marriages. Any
one in holy orders, even a clerk or a deacon, was immediately ejected from office, if he married a widow. At the
Council of Nice, it was a disputed point whether those
who had been married previous to their consecration, should
be required to put away their wives. Paphnutius, the
aged Bishop of Upper Thebais, himself unmarried, maintained that it was sufficient for the clergy to be required
not to marry after their consecration; and his advice prevailed. Eustathius and his followers refused to receive
the sacrament from any but an unmarried clergyman. On
the other hand, Jovinian and Vigilantius disapproved of
these oriental ideas concerning the sinfulness of marriage,
which they said were not sustained by the teaching of
Christ, or the example of his Apostles, and in their practical effect were unfavourable to morality. Some, even
among the bishops, thought such rigid rules likely to produce secret vice, and, therefore, they refused to ordain
unmarried deacons. But the Bishop of Rome, at the close
of the fourth century, issued a letter positively forbidding
any clergymen of the higher orders to live with their
wives. A man of thirty years old, who had not married
a widow, and who had had but one wife, might be a sub-
deacon. If he lived ten years in strict continence, he
might become a priest. If he lived ten years more in the
same way, he might be promoted to the rank of bishop.
This injunction was repeated by several councils; but met
with more or less opposition from some of the clergy.
Early in the sixth century, the emperor Justinian declared
all children of clergymen illegitimate, and incapable of
any hereditary succession or inheritance.

The lavish donations of Constantine, and the law authorizing his subjects to seek salvation for their own souls

by bequeathing estates to the church, to the detriment
of their natural heirs, rendered the church exceedingly
wealthy. The religious reverence and theological fears of
the people, induced profuse liberality to monks and priests,
which successive emperors sought to check by restraining
laws. The ecclesiastical revenue was divided into four
parts. One for the poor, one for the expenses of public
worship, one for the inferior clergy, and one for the bishops.
In the early times, salaries were merely sufficient for a
moderate competence; but they were gradually enlarged,
until the bishops in cities lived much more like princes,
than like Paul the tent-maker. They dwelt in splendid
palaces, gave sumptuous dinners, made lavish presents,
and conferred important benefits, as a means of obtaining
political influence, and popular favour, to be used for the
aggrandizement of the church. Jerome thus loudly complains of the state in which he found the clergy of Rome,
toward the close of the fourth century: "I am ashamed
to say it, but there are men, who seek the priesthood, and
become deacons, only that they may see women with less
restraint. Dress is all their care. Their hair is curled
with tongs; their fingers blaze with diamond rings; they
will scarcely touch the ground with their feet, so afraid are
they of a little dampness or dirt." He charges all the
ecclesiastics of Rome with hunting for legacies, with
making use of the sacred name of the church to extort
money for their own emolument, from the fears of the
dying, or the devotion of the living. The law of Valentinian, prohibiting the clergy and monks from receiving
bequests, he acknowledges was just. He says: "I complain not of the law, but that we have deserved such a
law." Ambrose and Augustine likewise admit that ecclesiastical avarice made such restraining edicts necessary.
The church at Rome especially had become very wealthy
and powerful. The bishop was the confidential adviser
of illustrious ladies, the distinguished guest of patricians
and princes. Such a position was of course a prize to
excite the avarice and ambition of men. In the year

three hundred and eighty-four, Ursinus and Damasus violently contended for it. Their adherents fought, and one hundred and thirty-seven dead bodies remained in the church; the price which Damasus paid for his victory. The candid Pagan, Ammianus, who was their cotemporary, thus alludes to these factions, in his History of Rome: "I am not astonished that so valuable a prize should inflame the desires of ambitious men. The successful candidate is sure that he will be enriched by the offerings of matrons; that as soon as his dress is arranged with becoming care and elegance, he may proceed in his chariot through the streets of Rome; and that the sumptuousness of the imperial table will not equal the profuse and delicate entertainments provided by the taste and at the expense of the Roman Pontiff. How much more rationally would those Pontiffs consult their true happiness, if they would imitate the exemplary life of some provincial bishops, whose temperance and sobriety, plainness of apparel, and humble deportment, recommend their pure, unpretending virtue to the Deity, and to all his true worshippers."

Hosius, Bishop of Cordova, in Spain, complained at the Council of Sardica, that bishops went to court so frequently with demands having no connection with their calling; merely to secure places of honour and profit for individuals they wished to patronize, or to manage for them some worldly concerns. Theophilus, Bishop of Alexandria, was so ambitious to erect splendid edifices, that he paid comparatively little attention to the spiritual welfare of his flock. He was so grasping of funds, that a wealthy widow, who wished to have a thousand gold pieces employed in clothing the poor women of that city, entrusted them to a benevolent presbyter, charging him to keep the transaction secret from the avaricious bishop. He discovered it, however, and persecuted the good presbyter to such a degree, that he fled into the desert. Even there the anger of Theophilus pursued him and the monks that sheltered him; and a prolonged quarrel in the church was the consequence.

Gregory of Nazianzen was so disgusted with the clerical competition he witnessed, that he exclaimed: "Would to heaven there were no primacy, no eminence of place, no tyrannical precedence of rank, and that we might be distinguished only by eminence in virtue! But, as things now are, the distinction of a seat at the right hand or the left, or in the middle; at a higher or lower place; of going before, or aside of each other, has given rise to many disorders among us, to no salutary purpose whatever, and has plunged multitudes into ruin." When Chrysostom visited the Asiatic churches, he deposed thirteen bishops for misconduct. He declared that licentiousness, and the habit of selling ecclesiastical preferments, had more or less contaminated the whole order; and he expressed a conviction that the number of bishops who would be saved was fewer than those who would be damned. Paul of Samosata, Bishop of Antioch, in the third century, was conspicuous for his luxurious style of living. He held a civil office, upon which he prided himself, and was accustomed to ride through the streets accompanied by guards, and followed by a multitude of attendants; and he sat upon a splendid throne when he presided at ecclesiastical assemblies. He exacted large contributions from the opulent, much of which he was accused of spending for his own gratification. He dressed with elaborate elegance, kept a luxurious table; and theological opponents, who attacked his heretical views concerning the Logos, said that two beautiful women were his companions in the episcopal palace.

A singular instance of compromise with regard to theological opinions occurred in the case of Synesius of Cyrene, said to have been a descendant of Hercules. He was a Platonist, or rather an eclectic philosopher, distinguished for his elegant style of writing, and knowledge of classical literature. At the close of the fourth century, he became a convert to Christianity, though not according to the prescribed pattern. But his character for eloquence, learning, and integrity, stood so high, that Theophilus, Archbishop of Alexandria, was desirous to rank him among the bishops.

I*

He was reluctant to assume the clerical office, for many reasons. He said that he loved classic literature and philosophy, and would by no means consent to relinquish them: that he was much addicted to field-sports, and should continue to be so; that he did not believe in the resurrection of the body, and had no sympathy whatever with the prevailing views concerning celibacy. Being still urged, notwithstanding this candid avowal of his opinions and habits, he consented to become Bishop of Ptolemais, in Egypt. With admirable frankness, he said to those who were to ordain him: "God, and the law of the land, and the holy hand of Theophilus the bishop, have bestowed on me my wife. I therefore solemnly declare, and call you to witness, that I will not be plucked from her; nor will I consent to live with her in secret. But I hope and pray that we may have a large family of virtuous children." In consideration of his distinguished talent and learning, and his well-known probity, a compromise was agreed upon, and he was permitted to enjoy his own habits and opinions unmolested. For twenty years he presided over his diocese with great energy and dignity, and with a scrupulous regard for the welfare of his people. He continued to devote his leisure to literary pursuits, and his writings have been much admired both by ancient and modern scholars. Dr. Milman thus describes them: "They blend, with a very scanty Christianity, the mystic theology of the later Platonism; but it is rather philosophy adopting Christian language, than Christianity moulding philosophy to its own uses."

The proceedings of Constantine at the Council of Nice had greatly increased the tendency to clerical pride. He had voluntarily taken a seat lower than the bishops, professing that it was not for him to assume authority, in ecclesiastical matters, over the successors of the Apostles, whom God had appointed his vicegerents on earth. The vantage-ground thus accorded to the clergy, they ever after claimed as an inalienable right. The son and successor of Constantine was denounced as a heretic, and excluded from councils, on the ground that no layman, even though he were an emperor, had any right to be present at the discussions of bishops. The administration of the sacrament was refused to the Arian emperor, Valens; and even the orthodox Theodosius was obliged to acknowledge himself inferior in ecclesiastical concerns. It had been customary for the emperor, when at church, to sit within the railing, which separated the congregation from the officiating priests and their attendants. But when Theodosius attempted to enter within the sacred enclosure of the church at Milan, Ambrose, with a gesture of dignified politeness, pointed to a lower seat reserved for the emperor, at the head óf the laity. The imperious Theodosius yielded to this assumption of clerical superiority, and the people applauded an arrangement which placed the lowest of the deacons above their monarch in spiritual rank. When messengers from the Arian empress Justina and her son accused Ambrose of tyranny, in not allowing the imperial family one church in Milan for their own mode of worship, he proudly replied: "In ancient times priests *bestowed* empire, they did not condescend to *assume* it. Kings have desired to be priests, rather than priests to be kings." Martin, the pious but illiterate soldier, who afterward became Bishop of Tours, was invited to dine with the emperor Maximin. When wine was brought, the monarch passed the goblet to the bishop, expecting and wishing to receive it from his holy hand after he had drank of it. But Martin passed it to his presbyter, not deeming it proper that even an imperial layman should take precedence of a priest; and Maximin, though of a haughty and ferocious temper, was not offended. The empress, to do all possible honour to the holy man, tended the table herself. She afterwards picked up the crumbs he dropped, and preserved them as sacred relics. Princes were continually reminded that the civil power was merely earthly and transitory, while the authority of bishops was derived from God himself, and extended beyond this world into the next; that priests were as much superior to kings, as the soul was to the body. The people, of course, paid homage to a power acknowledged to be above royalty, and claiming to be derived from heaven. When Athanasius returned from exile, the people of Alexandria waved incense before him as he passed through the streets. Jerome calls Epiphanius "a shining star among bishops, a pattern of ancient holiness, to whom the people flocked in crowds, offering their little children to his benediction, kissing his feet, and catching the hem of his garment." Chrysostom says when the Bishop of Antioch came to Constantinople, the multitudes went out to meet him, and as many as could come near him kissed his hands and his feet. Jerome says the populace sometimes sang hosannas to their bishop, as they had done to Christ. Paul of Samosata was displeased when he entered a church, if the audience did not receive him with applause; and the hosannas introduced as an occasional salutation to the bishops, became a prominent part of the ceremonial of his church. Ambrose says that kings and princes did not disdain to bow their necks to the knees of the priests and kiss their hands, and it is recorded that this was the customary respect paid to himself.

The universal adulation and homage to bishops, though grounded in religious reverence, was not unmingled with selfish policy, and fear of their great authority in spiritual and temporal concerns. Of all the power lodged in their hands, none was more dreaded than that of excommunication. In the early days, a person guilty of misconduct was expelled from the church by vote of the community to which he belonged. But this power gradually passed from the people into the hands of bishops; and as time went on, the forms increased in severity. The ancient Druids practised terrible forms of excommunication, by which every person was forbidden to furnish the culprit with food, or fire, or to minister to his necessities in any way, whatever might be his sufferings. The awful anathema often included whole families, and even nations. This custom, which gave the priesthood great power, was imitated by the Christian church. Athanasius excommunicated one of the clergy in Egypt, and transmitted orders to the churches to refuse him the use of either fire or water. Synesius excommunicated a magistrate who grievously oppressed the people of Libya, and who could not be persuaded to alter his despotic course, by any remonstrances or exhortations. Synesius at last expelled him from the church, and issued orders to all other Christian churches, on pain of being considered guilty of schism, not to allow him to partake of the sacrament, to hear prayers, to attend worship, or even to be buried with any Christian ceremonies. Private citizens were required to exclude him from their tables and their houses, on pain of being themselves excluded from religious privileges. His accomplices were included in the sentence, and even their wives and children, who had no participation in their crimes. This sentence was very terrible, because men believed that it shut them out from heaven; involving as it did the necessity of dying without Christian sacraments, which they regarded as absolutely necessary to expiate the sins of the soul. The guilty magistrate quailed before this dreadful prospect. He submitted to the bishop, acknowledged the justice of his sentence, and amended his ways.

In the days of primitive Christianity, those who committed any misdemeanour confessed their fault before the whole congregation, and were publicly prayed for. But in the fifth century, the Bishop of Rome substituted the custom of private confession to the clergy, who prescribed what penance they thought proper. This practice greatly increased the power of the priesthood.

With the increasing wealth and power of the church, subdivisions of rank gradually multiplied. Instead of the deacons and presbyters of the ancient time, elected by the congregation, and claiming no preëminence among their brethren, there were now patriarchs, archbishops, bishops, priests, deacons, subdeacons, exorcists, readers, and door-keepers. But with all this pomp of retinue, and the luxury and worldly-mindedness so conspicuous in many of the clergy, there were many bishops and priests, especially in the country towns, who were real blessings to mankind. Men of true piety, and unostentatious benevolence, such as the candid historian Ammianus describes. Men who lived plainly themselves, and appropriated their revenues to the building of hospitals, alms-houses, bridges, and fountains; who patiently instructed the ignorant, and sympathized with the suffering; to whom the dying could intrust their widows and orphans, secure that their rights would be courageously defended against the machinations of the cunning and the powerful; to whom the indigent and the oppressed could go in their troubles, and find such friends as the good Bishop of Nola, who sold himself to redeem the widow's only son. And even the high-handed assumption of power, which would be intolerable in our day, sometimes exerted a salutary restraining influence in those rude, superstitious times. We cannot otherwise than reverence and bless Ambrose for using his authority to fetter the tyrannical temper of Theodosius, and secure the people from outbursts of his despotic violence. In the records of those stormy times, when the rights of the common people were so entirely overlooked, there are some beautiful instances of the mediation of bishops, turning the hearts of kings when no other earthly influence could have prevailed. At the close of the fourth century, the citizens of Antioch rose in open rebellion, on account of oppressive taxation. Flavianus, the bishop, was old, and at that time very ill; but knowing the passionate temperament of the emperor Theodosius, and anxious to avert his vengeance from the people, he hastened with all speed to Constantinople. As soon as he entered into the emperor's presence, he said: "I have come as the deputy of our common Master, to address this word to your heart: 'If ye forgive men their trespasses, then will your Heavenly Father also forgive your trespasses.'" The festival of Easter was then approaching, and he alluded to it as a peculiarly fitting season to show clemency. The haughty and violent soldier was as susceptible as a woman to religious impressions.

The exhortation of the aged prelate melted him at once. He replied: "How can it be a great thing for me, who am but a man, to remit my anger toward men, when the Lord of the world himself, who for our sakes took the form of a servant, and who was crucified by those to whom he was doing good, interceded with his Father, in behalf of his crucifiers, saying: 'Forgive them, since they know not what they do.'" He promised to forget the offences committed against his government, and to institute inquiries into the real causes of grievance. Flavianus hastened back to his anxious people, and arrived in season to proclaim the joyful tidings before Easter.

When Priscillian and his followers were condemned to death for heretical opinions, by influence of Spanish bishops, Ambrose and Martin, and most of the bishops of Italy and Gaul exclaimed against it as an act of cruelty and a dangerous precedent. When Meletius, Bishop of Antioch, was exiled by the Arian emperor Constantius, his people, who were devotedly attached to him, resisted the execution of the decree. They assembled in great numbers on the road and threw stones at the magistrate who was conveying him out of town. But Meletius exhorted them to patience, and spreading out his mantle, protected the Præfect with his own body.

COUNCILS.

Synods were early held at Jerusalem, Ephesus, and Rome, to settle the dispute between Eastern and Western churches, concerning the day on which Easter should be observed. Toward the end of the second century, Provincial Synods were adopted; and it soon came to be an established custom for the bishops of all the towns to meet, every spring and autumn, in the capital of the province where they resided, to settle the disputed questions continually arising. To these were added occasional councils, as emergencies required. Heresies within the church occupied most of their attention, though Jews and Pagans re-

ceived a full share. Seven councils were held at Carthage
to decide whether those who had been frightened into any
concession or evasion in times of persecution should be re-
admitted to communion with the faithful; and whether it
was necessary to re-baptize heretics, who wished to return
to the bosom of the church. After Christianity became
established as the state religion, the emperors occasionally
summoned General Councils, to which bishops from all
parts of the empire were invited. These assemblies were
generally very discordant, and one council frequently reversed what the preceding had established. Nevertheless
the idea began to prevail in the fourth century, and soon
became an established opinion, that the deliberations of
assembled bishops were under the especial direction of the
Holy Ghost; that their decisions were therefore infallible;
and consequently the salvation of the soul depended on unquestioning belief in whatever they decreed. The famous
Simon Stylites, speaking of the fourth General Council, says:
"In my declared attachment to the faith of the six hundred and thirty holy fathers assembled at Chalcedon, I take
my stand upon an actual revelation of the Holy Spirit. If
the Saviour is present among two or three gathered together
in his name, is it conceivable that among holy fathers so
numerous and eminent, the Holy Spirit should not be present throughout?" Gregory the Great, Patriarch of Rome
in the sixth century, alluding to the Council of Nice, which
settled the equality of the Son with the Father, to the
Council of Constantinople which settled the equality of the
Holy Ghost with both, and to the Councils of Ephesus and
Chalcedon which settled the dispute concerning the divine
and human natures in Christ, says: "I believe as fully
and fervently in the Four Councils, as I do in the Four
Gospels."

Yet the spirit manifested in these councils often seemed
the reverse of holy, and there were few indications of the
clearness and certainty to be expected from men supernatu
rally guided. According to Socrates, the Christian historian, the bishops assembled at the Council of Nice presented

the emperor with numerous letters of accusation against each other; many of them founded on personal animosity. Constantine, in his zeal to protect Christianity from ridicule or reproach, burned these slanderous documents, and advised mutual forbearance and concession. The same historian, describing the discussions in that council, whether the Son of God was created or begotten, compares it to a battle in the night, where men are unable to discern on which side they are fighting. At the Council of Ephesus, Cyril, Patriarch of Alexandria, violently hurried through the decisions before all the bishops had arrived, though a magistrate sent by the emperor Theodosius Second, demanded delay. Nestorius, patriarch of Constantinople, who refused to call Mary the Mother of God, was deposed and condemned as a second Judas. One of the bishops declared that, "having presumed to falsify the doctrines of orthodoxy, he deserved every punishment, both from God and man, as did he who counterfeited the imperial coin." John, Patriarch of Antioch, arriving after the sentence was passed, convened a synod of thirty bishops, who deposed Cyril, and described him as a monster born for the ruin of the church. The adherents of the two parties fought with words and blows. The cathedral was stained with blood, and the streets were kept in a perpetual tumult. Nestorian bishops were obliged to ask for a guard from the emperor, either to remain at Ephesus in safety, or return to their churches without peril. The magistrate finally interfered, dispersed this riotous council by force, and placed the deposed bishops in safe custody. A second Council was called at Ephesus, about eighteen years later, to decide concerning the heresy of Eutyches, who taught that Christ had but one nature. A great concourse of monks assembled, and silenced opposition by violent threats and clamorous outcries, which drowned the voice of any speaker they did not approve. The presence of soldiers, sent by the emperor, likewise served to intimidate the minority. Blank papers were placed before the bishops, which the monks and soldiers compelled them to sign, to

be afterward filled up with whatever the ruling party
thought proper. The contest was so rude, that Dioscurus,
Patriarch of Alexandria, is said to have buffeted and kicked
Flavian, Patriarch of Constantinople, to such a degree that
he afterward died of the wounds and bruises he had received. This council took the ground that Christ had but
one nature. They sought to maintain by Scripture, that
heresy was a sin against God, and far greater than any
possible sin against men. When one of the bishops attempted, in a conciliatory way, to explain in what sense he
understood the doctrine of two natures in Christ, many
voices vociferated: "Burn him alive! Let him be cut
asunder, as he has sundered Christ!" A Council at Chalcedon, two years later, reversed the decrees of the second
Council at Ephesus, which was thenceforth styled "The
Synod of Robbers." At the Council of Chalcedon, ten
Egyptian bishops, of venerable age, begged that they might
not be required to sign an anathema against Eutyches, till
they could ascertain what was the opinion of the new Patriarch of Alexandria, about to be elected; for so despotic
was his authority, that if they declared opinions independent of him, they could not be certain of their lives, when
they returned to their own country.

That such scenes of fierce altercation were painful and
humiliating to good men might be readily supposed, even
if there were no record of it. Some of moderate temper
continued to take part in councils, hoping to regulate the
spirit of contention, and believing that the humanizing
influences of Christianity could not be extended, unless
the church could be established in unity of doctrine.
Others became thoroughly disheartened and disgusted, and
avoided all such assemblies. Gregory, Bishop of Nazianzen, who had much experience of councils, says: "I am
so constituted, that, to speak the truth, I dread every assembly of bishops; for I have never yet seen a good end
of any one. I have never been present at a synod which
did more to suppress evils, than to increase them. An
indescribable thirst for contention and rule prevails in

them. I am weary of struggling with holy bishops, whose jealousies render harmony impossible, and who make light of the interests of the faith, in pursuit of their own quarrels." Again he says: "They fight, and run into schism, and divide the whole world for the sake of thrones. The Trinity is a mere pretext for their wrangling; the true cause being an incredible spirit of hatred." Constantine had commanded that the public establishment of post-horses should gratuitously afford every facility for the journeys of bishops, and that during their sessions they should be sumptuously maintained at the public expense. This became a heavy charge; for it required many and prolonged meetings to settle questions, which every curious mind could ask, but which no finite understanding could possibly explain or comprehend. The historian Ammianus says: "The highways are covered with troops of bishops, galloping from every side to the assemblies which they call synods. And while they labour to reduce the whole sect to their own particular opinions, the public establishment of post-horses is almost ruined by their frequent and hurried journeys." Hilary, Bishop of Poictiers, thus laments the perpetual discord: "It is a thing equally deplorable and dangerous that there are as many creeds as opinions among men, as many doctrines as inclinations, and as many sources of blasphemy as there are faults among us; because we make creeds arbitrarily and explain them as arbitrarily. The Homoousian is rejected, and received, and explained away, by successive synods. The partial or complete resemblance of the Father and the Son is a subject of dispute for these unhappy times. Every year, nay, every moon, we make new creeds to describe invisible mysteries. We repent of what we have done; we defend those who repent; we anathematize those whom we have defended. We either condemn the doctrine of others in ourselves, or our own doctrine in that of others. Thus reciprocally tearing each other in pieces, we have been the cause of each other's ruin." Again he says: "The East and the West are in a perpetual state of restlessness and disturbance. Deserting our spiritual charges, abandoning the people of God, neglecting the preaching of the Gospel, we are hurried about from place to place, often to a great distance, some of us infirm with age, or feeble with ill health, sometimes obliged to leave our sick brethren on the road. The whole administration of the empire, the emperor himself, the tribunes and the commanders, at this fearful crisis, are occupied with the lives and condition of the bishops. The people are by no means unconcerned. The whole brotherhood watches in anxious suspense the result of these troubles. The public post-horses are worn out with our journeyings."

These sectarian controversies were often intertwisted with personal quarrels, growing out of mutual jealousy, and competition for power. The Patriarchs of Rome and Constantinople were always rivals, and prone to sustain opposite sides in every dispute. A similar state of feeling grew up between Alexandria and Constantinople; for as the church of Alexandria was said to be founded by Mark the Evangelist, the Patriarch thought it gave him a claim to be the acknowledged head of the Eastern churches. Councils summoned under such circumstances, and in such a temper, settled the theological doctrines of the Christian world. Men were required to believe their decisions infallible; and it was customary to conclude their decrees with this declaration: "Whosoever teaches any other doctrine than this, let him be accursed." This remained the state of things for centuries; but as the central power of the church at Rome grew stronger, the decisions of councils were pronounced not to be infallible, till they had received the sanction of the Pope.

HERMITS AND MONKS.

The first volume of this book proves that monastic associations existed at a very early period of the world in the forests of Hindostan. It also shows that their old theological doctrine, which attributed all evil to the existence of Matter, led the ancient anchorites of that country to hate their bodies, and to inflict upon them all manner of tortures for the good of the soul. Ancient Egypt, whose religious theories so much resembled those of Hindostan, probably had some modification of the same institution; though I am not aware of any proof that it was so, except the mention of associations called Gymnosophists and Therapeutæ.

Jews, who entertained different views concerning the origin of evil, never manifested such abhorrence of the body. There were individual ascetics among them, such as the Nazarites, devoted to the Lord by a special vow; and it is recorded that some of the prophets went without clothing, wounded themselves with sharp instruments, or remained for a long time in one position. But these things appear to have been done merely as symbolical of some event they prophesied; while Hindoo devotees resorted to similar practices, as means of atoning for sins, or of laying up a store of extra merit, to procure additional rewards in Paradise. The Essenes resembled Pythagorean communities, and both had many features in common with the old Hindoo associations. Perhaps both found their model in ancient Egypt; for there is evidence, derived from various sources, that two classes of ascetics existed in that country before the introduction of Christianity. The Gymnosophists, or naked philosophers, who lived in communities on the banks of the Nile, appear to have been regarded by Apollonius as similar to the associations of devotees in India. The Therapeutæ, described in the chapter on the Jews, in many of their customs and regulations bore a striking resemblance to the Pythagorean communities, and the Braminical schools. Eusebius the historian, thinks they were converts of the Apostle Mark, who is supposed to have founded the first church at Alexandria. But in all that is recorded of them, there is no trace whatever of Christianity. Moreover, Philo, who probably died before there was a church gathered at Alexandria, gives a detailed account of the Therapeutæ, whom he describes as already an ancient sect in his time.

A good deal of curiosity concerning "the wise men of India" was manifested by various writers in the first centuries of Christianity. Apollonius visited them. Plotinus was on his way thither, attracted by their fame. Origen evidently had some knowledge of them. Bardesanes the Gnostic, and Porphyry the New Platonist, describe them in a way implying some information concerning the Buddhists also. That some Christian converts began to imitate the East India Fakeers, as early as the time of Irenæus, seems to be indicated by his allusion to men who lived alone on the mountains, without clothing, subsisting on herbs like wild beasts. These idle ascetics appear to have reproached pious Christians who manufactured articles, which were purchased by their Pagan neighbours; but Irenæus speaks of them and their advice with disapprobation; and says such men had no correct idea what Christian life ought to be. There was certainly nothing in the teaching of Christ, or the example of the Apostles, to favour such customs. The utmost Paul said concerning a life of celibacy was, that those who chose to devote themselves to it would have more freedom from worldly cares. The early Fathers, even the stern Tertullian, commended marriage. But the Gnostics who spread so widely in all parts of the Christian world, were thoroughly imbued with Hindoo theories, derived from some source or other. The superior strictness of many of those sects was often brought into comparison with orthodox Christianity, and their example and arguments doubtless had a good deal of influence in favour of celibacy. From the earliest periods, some individuals chose to impose such a vow upon themselves as a means of devoting themselves to religion with more uninterrupted freedom. What Christ said to the rich man was very generally understood to imply that renunciation of property was essential to Christian perfection. Therefore, if such devotees had estates, they sold them, and distributed the proceeds among the destitute; and whatsoever they earned, over their very simple wants, was given to the poor. But in the early days of the church, this class of members bore no resemblance to the self-torturing Fakeers of India. They lived in Christian families, were cheerful and diligent, and sold the proceeds of their industry to whomsoever wished to purchase.

PAUL.—The first Christian hermit, of whom there is any record, was a youth named Paul, born of a noble family in Thebes. He was not impelled by a desire to devote himself to monastic life; but during the reign of Decius, persecution raged with such terrible violence in that part of the world, that he hid himself in the desert, to escape from death, or from continual temptations to abjure his faith. He found a cavern, near which were some palm trees and a fountain. He fed on the dates and drank from the stream; and when his clothes dropped off, he substituted a garment of braided palm leaves. He became so much attached to that mode of life, that when the Christian churches were safe from outward dangers, he had no wish to return to the world. He is said to have lived ninety-eight years in the desert, seen by human beings at very rare intervals, and spending his time in meditation and prayer. He does not appear to have made any attempts to proselyte others to his mode of life, and there is no account that any were attracted to reside in his neighbourhood.

ANTHONY.—Anthony is considered the father of Christian monasticism. He belonged to an old and rather wealthy Egyptian family, near the Thebaid. They spoke the Coptic language, the ancient vernacular tongue of Egypt. The Coptic families generally neglected education, because it involved the necessity of acquiring the Greek and Latin languages, in which all the literature of that period was written. Anthony was brought up piously, but without intellectual culture. It even seems doubtful whether he knew how to read. In boyhood he was of a serious and meditative cast of mind, little inclined to worldly learning. He attended church constantly, and all

he heard there was deeply impressed upon his memory.
His parents died before he was twenty years old, and the
care of a younger sister devolved upon him.   Like all the
people of those old times, he was prone to look for supernatural guidance in sudden exclamations, or whatever passage of a book was first opened.   One day, as he walked
toward the church, his thoughts were occupied with the
days of primitive Christianity, when the disciples held all
things in common.   He entered just as the preacher was
reading: "Go sell all that thou hast, and give to the poor."
Believing that these words were particularly addressed to
him, he gave away all his lands to the inhabitants of his
native village, on condition that they would never trouble
him or his sisters about taxes, or any other worldly matters.   His other property he sold, and divided the proceeds
among the poor, reserving only a small income for the
support of his sister.   Soon after that, his mind was again
impressed, while in church, by hearing the words: "Take
no thought for to-morrow."   Regarding this as a direct
admonition from the Lord, he gave away the little property he had reserved for the maintenance of his sister,
and placed her under the protection of some pious virgins
of the church.   Being now free from all earthly cares, he
sought out a venerable old hermit in the neighbourhood
and took up his residence near him.   The mountains and
deserts of the Thebaid abounded with caves and grottoes,
well adapted for anchorites.   Anthony found many devotees inhabiting these solitudes.   Whether any of them
belonged to the Therapeutæ, or had belonged to them, is
not stated.   But it is recorded that whenever he heard of
any remarkable ascetic, he travelled to see him, staid with
him some time, learned from him all that he could, and
returned to his own cell to imitate whatever he deemed
admirable in his penances and devotions.   He supported
himself by the labour of his own hands, and gave the over-
plus of his earnings to the poor.   His fervent piety and
rigid austerity excited great reverence, though he was so
young.   But inwardly he had many conflicts with what

he considered Evil Spirits. His heart yearned for his sister, the beloved playmate of his childhood. Sometimes he thought of the comfortable food and clothing, and the pleasant relatives he used to enjoy, and the devils tempted him to ask whether he had done wisely to sacrifice all these, for such a dreary life of perpetual self-denial. He struggled hard against these promptings of nature. He fasted almost to starvation, and prayed in agony of spirit, till great drops of sweat stood on his forehead. The devils finding whisperings were vain, attacked him with visible temptations. They raised up visions of tables laden with delicate viands, and of beautiful women, who poured out sparkling wine, and sought to allure him by smiles and blandishments. He resolved to flee from all human beings, and subject himself to still more rigid penances. He betook himself to a distant grotto in the rocks, which had been used for a tomb. He slept but little, and that on the bare earth, and often went without food for two or three days in succession. In this state of exhausted nature and excited nerves, he had terrible visions. "The Devil fearing the whole desert would soon be filled with holy hermits, came upon him one night, with a whole troop of demons, and beat him so unmercifully, that he lay on the ground like a dead man." One of the hermits he had left behind was accustomed to carry him bread. When he arrived, the day after this disaster, he found Anthony stretched on the sands of the desert, apparently dead. He summoned assistance, and carried him to his native village, where his relatives and friends assembled to watch over the body. Anthony waked in the night, and seeing the company asleep, he roused the hermit, and insisted upon being carried back to his tomb in the desert. The hermit obeyed his orders, and left him alone. Anthony shouted to the Devil: "Ha! thou tempter! Didst thou think I had fled? Here I am again. I have strength to fight thee still." He remained in this sepulchre a long time, avoiding the sight of human beings, fasting and praying, and practising the most rigid austerities. He after-

ward retired to a distant mountain, where he spent twenty
years in an old ruined castle. The fame of his great holiness attracted visitors, and a band of hermits wished to
have him for their spiritual guide. He finally consented
to their intreaties. Many joined themselves to him, and
new comers continually solicited to be trained by him in
the monastic life. The desert swarmed with hermits, who
lived in separate cells, and met together for devotional
exercises. Those who served a novitiate with Anthony
had their faith and patience tried in various ways. Sometimes he ordered them to draw water out of a well for the
whole day, and pour it on the ground: sometimes to weave
a basket and pull it to pieces continually; sometimes to
rip a garment, sew it, and rip it again. If these tasks were
performed without questions, and without signs of weari-
ness, it was a sign of their growth in grace. Often he
related to them his own experiences, by way of encouragement. Upon one occasion he said to the younger monks:
"For your instruction, I will speak what I have seen concerning the devices of devils. As often as they blessed
me, I cursed them, in the name of the Lord. Sometimes
they would come like an army of horsemen, fully equipped,
threatening me; but when I made the sign of the cross
they vanished. Sometimes, they would fill the house with
wild beasts and with serpents: then I sang Psalms. Sometimes they came in the dark, with a shining appearance,
and said: 'Anthony, we have come to give you light;' but
I shut my eyes and prayed, and the light of the wicked
was extinguished in a moment. Sometimes they came
reciting Scripture: but I stopped my ears and would not
hear them. Sometimes they came clapping, whistling, and
dancing: but when I prayed, or sang Psalms, they began
to whimper and cry, as if unnerved. Many a time, a tall
devil displayed before me the appearance of gold in the
desert, that I might touch it; but when I sang Psalms, it
melted away. Oftentimes they lashed me with whips: but
when I said: 'Nothing shall separate me from the love of
Christ,' they turned and scourged each other."

He fasted almost continually, and wore a coarse hair
shirt, which he never took off. In cold weather, he added
the skin of an animal for a mantle. He never washed
himself, not even his feet. He was ashamed of the necessities of the body, and disliked to have any one see him eat
or sleep. Multitudes came from all countries to see the
celebrated saint. Those who were in trouble went to him
for consolation. Those who had disputes, agreed to settle
them according to his decision. The diseased were brought
to him to be cured, and those who were afflicted with fits,
had the devils cast out of them by his prayers. "A great
many of the afflicted were healed by merely sitting outside
of his door, believing and praying there." Those whom
he could not cure, he taught to cultivate a patient submission to the divine will. Those who were at enmity, he
exhorted to imitate the forgiving spirit of Christ. He
checked the monks in their tendency to place excessive
value on miraculous gifts. He was accustomed to repeat
to them: "Let us not rejoice that Spirits are subject to us,
but rather rejoice that our names are written in heaven;
for that is a witness of our virtue; but to expel Evil Spirits
is a grace, which Christ has bestowed upon us."

The continual throng of people so disturbed his medita-
tions and prayers, that he escaped to a distant mountain
near the Red Sea. Some wild palm trees, and a spring
of water furnished him with nourishment; and the wandering Arabs, awe-struck by his appearance, reverently
brought him bread. The monks, whom he had left, discovered his retreat, after a while, and would have furnished
him with food; but he preferred to save them the labour of
sending it. He procured tools, and sowed some of the
neighbouring land with grain and vegetables, which served
for his own support, and for the refreshment of strangers,
who again began to resort to him. He also wove baskets,
and gave them in exchange for articles of nourishment.
He exhorted those who came to him to remember that it
was not he, but Christ, who wrought the cures. To a military officer, who besought him to heal a diseased daughter,

he said: "I also am a man, like thyself. If thou believest
in the Christ, whom I serve, only depart and pray to God
in faith, and it will be done." Wild beasts that came to
drink at the spring, injured his crops of grain; but he ex-
orcised them in the name of the Lord, and they were so
over-awed, that they never ventured near the place again.
He was then old, and alone, and the monks begged to
come once a month to bring him olives and oil. Those
who went to carry him food, often heard many voices, and
as it were the clashing of arms. Sometimes, they saw him
on the mountain at night, surrounded by wild beasts, or
praying, or fighting with apparitions. "The Devil let
loose upon him nearly all the hyenas of the desert. They
came out of their holes, and surrounded him, grinning,
and threatening to bite. Anthony said to them: 'If ye
have received power against me, come on ! I am ready to
be devoured. But if the Devil has put this into your
heads, begone this moment ! I am the servant of Christ.'
And they hurried away, as if driven by the whip of his
word." After his death, a story was circulated, that when
he was ninety years old, a vision informed him there was
a hermit in the desert more ancient and more holy than
himself. Whereupon, he took staff in hand, and went
forth to find Paul, the first Christian anchorite. Many
miracles are recorded concerning his journey, and the interview between the two aged saints. Among other things,
it is related that Anthony, passing through a deep narrow
valley, encountered a Satyr, with a horned head, and
goats' feet, who bowed reverently before him, and said: " I
am one of those creatures, which haunt the woods, whom
the blind Pagans worship as gods. But we are mortals,
as thou knowest; and I come to beseech thee that thou
wouldst pray for us to thy God, who is my God, and
the God of all." When Anthony heard these words, tears
trickled down his venerable face, and stretching his aged
arm toward Thebes, he exclaimed: "Such are your gods, O
ye Pagans ! Woe unto you, when even such as these confess the name of Christ, whom ye, blind and perverse

generation, deny." Jerome tells this story, and adds, "though some may consider such an apparition improbable, yet all the world knows that a Satyr was brought to Alexandria, by the emperor Constantine, and his body preserved for the edification of the curious." The Satyr was doubtless an Ourang Outang.

Anthony went to Alexandria but few times in his life, and only on extraordinary occasions. When he was nigh sixty years old, being informed that the emperor Maximin was cruelly persecuting the Christians, he immediately proceeded to Alexandria, visited those who were in prison, offered them religious consolation, and exhorted them to remain stedfast unto death. His influence so stimulated the zeal and courage of Christians, that the governor commanded all monks to leave the city. Others escaped, or concealed themselves; but Anthony boldly pursued his course; and such was the renown of his sanctity, that no one ventured to touch him.

In three hundred fifty two, when he was a hundred years old, Athanasius and other bishops sought to avail themselves of his powerful influence to arrest the spread of Arianism. At their urgent request, he left his mountain and travelled four hundred miles, to Alexandria, where he preached zealously against Arianism, as the *last* heresy, the immediate forerunner of Antichrist. "Believe me," said he, "the whole creation is angry with them, for putting the Creator and Lord of all things, the Eternal Word and Wisdom of the Father, in the number of creatures." His appearance in that excitable city produced a great sensation. His long thin hair and flowing beard, of silvery whiteness, his mild serene aspect, his kindly manners, and his uncouth raiment, were well calculated to make a deep impression. The populace, of all religions, thronged about him, trying to touch his staff, or his garments, that they might be cured of diseases. Even Pagan priests and philosophers went to church, for the sake of seeing and hearing the wonderful hermit. More were converted to Christianity during the few days he staid

there, than during a whole year at other times. He cured
many of diseases and insanity, and cast out many devils.
When he was passing out of the city gate, to return to his
solitary mountain, a woman ran after him, calling out:
"Stop! stop! thou man of God! My daughter is wofully
afflicted with devils. Stop, I pray thee!" When the
woman came near him, her daughter was suddenly jerked
down on the ground by the demon; but Anthony prayed
over her, and she rose up well.

Constantine the Great, and his sons, wrote to Anthony,
as to their spiritual father. Being unused to courtly customs, and not knowing how to answer an imperial letter,
he was at first reluctant to receive it; but being reminded
how much they had done for Christianity, he listened to
the letter, and dictated an answer, in which he exhorted
them to make just and humane laws, to be charitable to
the poor, and to remember that Christ was the only true
eternal king. He knew all the Scriptures by heart, though
it seems doubtful whether he could read them, even in the
Coptic translation. A learned Pagan, who visited him, inquired how he could endure to live without books. He
replied: "Which was first, letter or spirit?" Being answered, he rejoined: "The healthy spirit needs no letters.
My book is the whole creation; the Word of God, which
always lies open before me. I can read it whenever I
please." To some, who ridiculed Christians for excess of
faith, he said: "What *we* know by faith, *you* seek to prove
by arguments; and often you cannot even *express* that
which we behold clearly in spirit." To an abbot, who
asked what he ought to do, he replied: "Trust not in your
own righteousness, and regret nothing which is already
past." To Didymus, a learned Christian teacher in Alexandria, who had been blind from his youth, he said: "Be
not troubled that you are in want of such eyes as enable
even flies and gnats to see, but rejoice rather that you have
the eyes by which angels see, by which God is beheld, and
his light received." Synesius, the learned philosopher,
while he was yet a Pagan, expressed great reverence for

Anthony. He compared him to Hermes and Zoroaster; and spoke of him as one of those rare men, the flashes of whose spirit enabled them to dispense with culture.

When he had lived one hundred and five years, he felt that his soul was about to be released from his emaciated frame. He retained his mental faculties, and talked of his departure with cheerful faith. The ancient custom of embalming bodies was still retained by many of the Egyptians, especially when the deceased had been venerated as a saint. These mummies, being carefully enveloped and sealed up, were placed on couches and preserved in some recess of the house. Anthony, wishing to guard against undue reverence for his remains, earnestly besought his friends the monks to bury him secretly, and reveal to no man the spot where he was laid; saying it would ill become him to be more highly honoured than the patriarchs of old, and Christ himself, who were all buried. A few of his disciples retired with him to a solitary place, grieving deeply that they should soon look upon his venerable face no more. They kissed his feet, and bathed them with tears, exclaiming: " O Anthony, father, instructor, friend, how can we live on earth without thee?" But he comforted them with the prospect of eternal reunion, and while they were praying around him, his spirit passed gently away from the body it had so much abused.

Athanasius, who greatly revered his memory, wrote his biography, from which the preceding account is abridged. In the preface he says: " I have inserted nothing but what I knew to be true, from my own acquaintance with the saint, whom I often saw, or from what I gathered from one who long ministered to him, and poured water on his hands." He makes no allusion to the miraculous interview with the hermit Paul, which was probably not spoken of in his day.

PAUL THE SIMPLE.—The earliest and oldest of Anthony's disciples is said to have been a hard-working, ignorant peasant, who retired into the desert at sixty years old, on account of his wife's misconduct. Anthony was at first unwilling to receive him, thinking monastic life would not prove suitable for him. To prove him, he prescribed tasks more severe and difficult than usual. He never allowed him to eat or drink until evening, and then merely sufficient to sustain life. Once, when a visitor brought a pot of honey, he ordered Paul to pour it on the sand, and gather it up carefully in a shell, without mixing any dirt with it. The honest peasant obeyed these, and many other similar commands, without asking any questions, or betraying the slightest impatience. Finding that nothing could tempt him to disobedience or anger, Anthony received him as a brother monk, and was accustomed to hold him up as a pattern to younger disciples. Sometimes he had occasion to blush for his extreme ignorance. Once, when some learned monks were conversing with Anthony concerning Christ and the prophets, Paul inquired which of them was born first. Anthony made a customary sign to him, which signified that he was to hold his tongue. Paul retired to his cell, and when any one spoke to him, he returned no answer. Anthony perceiving that he persevered in this for a long time, asked him one day why he did not speak. He meekly replied: "Because you, my father, ordered me to hold my tongue." Anthony, turning to his disciples, said: "Verily he rebukes us all; for often we do not attend to the voice of God himself, while he obeys my slightest word." On account of the ignorance and child-like innocence of the man, the other hermits called him Paul the Simple, and believed that his soul was very near to God.

One day they brought to Anthony a young man who was possessed by a remarkably furious devil. He tried to rend all who approached him, and uttered the most shocking blasphemies. Anthony said: "This man is possessed by one of the most powerful order of demons, whom I have not received grace to command; but Paul the Simple has the necessary grace." So saying, he went with them to the hermit's cell, and said: "Paul, you must drive the demon out of this man, and heal him, so that he may return home, and glorify the Lord." "But do you drive him out, my father," replied Paul. "I have not leisure," said Anthony; "I have other matters to attend to." So he left the possessed young man, and returned to his cell. Then Paul addressed an ardent prayer to God, and in all simplicity said to the demon: "Father Anthony commands you to go out of this man, that when he is well he may glorify the Lord." But the Devil answered: "I will not go out, you poor beggar-man." Then Paul laid his sheepskin mantle on the shoulders of the demoniac, and said: "Now go out, will you? Father Anthony commands you." But the Devil replied by abusing Father Anthony. "You *shall* go out," said Paul, "or I will go and tell Jesus Christ, and I give you my word that he will treat you as you deserve." But the Devil blasphemed Christ also, and declared he would not go out. Then Paul went out of his cell, and ascended a rock on the mountain, and there he stood at noon-day, like a pillar of stone, under the scorching sun of Egypt. Weary with his unavailing efforts, in the extreme simplicity of his heart he prayed thus: "Jesus Christ, you who were crucified under Pontius Pilate, I declare to you that I will not eat nor drink this day; I will stand here on this rock and starve, if you do not listen to me, and drive the Devil out of that man, that he may be delivered from torment." "Immediately, as if God were afraid of vexing a man whom he tenderly loved, the demon was heard crying from the cell, where the young man had been left, 'I am going! I am going! I am going! I am going! Paul's humility and simplicity compel me to fly; and I know not where to go.' He departed that instant, and took the form of a dragon, more than a hundred feet long, crawling toward the Red Sea."

Rufinus, the friend of Jerome, has recorded that this same Paul the Simple could tell the disposition and thoughts of people, by merely looking at them; and that he could also see their attendant angels. One day, as he stood at the door of a church, seeing the brethren pass in

to celebrate the Lord's Supper, he saw, with his spiritual
eyes, that their angels had bright joyful countenances, as
if well pleased with the state of their hearts. But one man
went in, whose countenance was dusky; demons pulled
him by the nose, and his guardian angel followed sadly at
a distance. At that sight, Paul threw himself on the
ground and wept bitterly. In vain the brethren tried to
persuade him to go in with them to partake the sacrament. He refused to be comforted, and remained outside
weeping and praying for the wretched man. When the
people came out of church, he watched to see if any change
had taken place; and lo! the man came out with a bright
and happy face; the demons had left him, and his angel
was rejoicing. When Paul told him what he had seen,
the man confessed that he had been a fornicator, but that
his heart had been deeply touched by passages of Scripture read in the church, that he had prayed earnestly to
Christ, and promised to sin no more.

Rufinus, and Sozomen, the Christian historian, give accounts of Paul the Simple.

HILARION.—Hilarion, one of the most celebrated of the
old saints, was born in Palestine, and sent to the Alexandrian schools. He had been educated in the old Roman
religion, but the fame of Anthony, which was then spreading through Egypt, kindled his young imagination. He
went out to the desert to see him, and remained with him
some months. After the death of his parents, he returned
to his native place, with several monks, divided all his
share of the property with his brothers and the poor, and
at fifteen years old retired into the solitude of a neighbouring desert, where he commenced a mode of life in imitation
of Anthony. Finding that the Devil tried to tempt him
with visions of beautiful women, and luxurious feasts, he
subdued his body by protracted fasts, and when he ate, he
confined himself to a few dried figs and the juice of herbs.
He laboured incessantly digging the ground, singing
Psalms meanwhile, to keep away evil thoughts. He be-

came so attenuated that his bones could hardly hang together. This severe discipline had the same effect on his nerves, that is recorded of the ancient devotees in Hindostan. "On a certain night, he heard the crying of children, the wailing of women, the bleating of sheep, the lowing of kine, the roaring of lions, and the tramp of an army. He knew the tricks of demons, so he fell on his knees, and made the sign of the cross on his forehead. All of a sudden, a coach with glowing wheels came rushing toward him; but he called aloud on the name of Jesus, and the earth opened and swallowed it up. Then he began to sing: 'The horse and his rider hath he cast into the sea.'"

Jerome, who wrote the life of Hilarion, from which this account is taken, has recorded many miracles performed by him. He had been twenty-two years in the desert, many monks had joined him, and his fame had spread throughout Palestine, when a woman who had been blind ten years was brought to him. She told him she had spent all her money on physicians, and begged him to cure her. He replied: "If you had given to the poor, what you have squandered on doctors, Jesus, the true physician, would have healed you." But when she continued to beg for mercy, he spit on her eyes, and immediately she received her sight.

"A Christian kept horses to run in the chariot races at the circus, against his rival, a chief magistrate of Gaza, and a worshipper of idols. Now this rival employed a magician, who, by certain incantations, made his horses run very swiftly, while he checked the speed of the Christian's horses. The latter went to Hilarion to ask assistance. The venerable saint thought it a silly business to waste his prayers about; he therefore said: 'Why not sell your horses and give the money to the poor, for the salvation of your soul?' The man answered that it was an ancient custom to observe the chariot races; that he did not do it from choice, but was bound as a magistrate to take part in them; that he came rather as a servant of God for aid against those who insulted the church of Christ. There-

fore, at the request of the brethren who were present,
Hilarion filled with water the earthen cup out of which he
was accustomed to drink, and gave it to the petitioner. He
took it and sprinkled his stable, horses, chariot, and charioteer; also the bars of the starting place in the circus.
His competitor ridiculed the action, but he was confident
of victory; nor were his hopes disappointed. His horses
flew like the wind, while those of his rival were impeded.
The wheels of his chariot glowed, and the other party
could scarcely keep sight of them. The populace exclaimed
that their god had been conquered by Christ. The defeated party were furious, and demanded that Hilarion
should be punished as a Christian enchanter. The victory
being manifest, however, both in these games, and in many
afterwards, caused great numbers to embrace Christianity."

Men and animals possessed with devils were constantly
brought to Hilarion, and he cured them all. Among the
rest, a mad Bactrian camel was dragged to him by thirty
men. "The beast's eyes were bloodshot, he foamed at the
mouth, his lolling tongue was swollen, and his roaring was
terrible. When the old man told them to let him loose,
they all ran away. But he walked up to the animal, and
standing with outstretched hands, said: 'You are not going
to frighten me, you Devil, big as you are! It is all the
same to me whether you take the body of a small fox, or a
huge camel.' The furious beast came up as if he would
devour him; but instantly fell down, and lay with his
head to the ground. All wondered to see such tameness
follow such ferocity. But the old man told them the
Devil often took possession of beasts, because he had such
burning hatred against men, that he desired to destroy not
only them but their property. He said no one ought to be
disturbed because two thousand swine had been killed by
demons, at the Lord's command; because that was the
only way by which spectators could be convinced that
such a multitude of demons had gone out of a man."

"One day, as he returned from the garden, he saw a
man lying before his door, whose whole body was para-

lyzed. He wept, and stretching out his hand over him, said: 'In the name of the Lord Jesus, I say unto thee rise up and walk.' With wonderful quickness, while the old man was yet speaking, the members of the paralytic re ceived such strength, that he began to rise."

When he was in Epidaurus, there was a terrible earth- quake, which caused the sea to break over its bounds, and threaten a second deluge. The inhabitants, fearing the town would be completely overwhelmed, led Hilarion to the beach, and placed him there as a bulwark against the encroaching waters. " He drew the figures of three crosses in the sand, and stretched forth his hand against the waves. It is incredible to what a height the swelling sea rose and stood before him. After raging for a considerable time, as if indignant at the obstacle, it retired by degrees to its proper boundaries. This fact is affirmed, in all that region, to this day; and mothers teach it to their children, that they may transmit it to their posterity."

He was unable to stay long in any one place, because the fame of his miracles drew such multitudes round him, that he was oppressed by their constant demands upon him. When it was rumoured that he was about to leave Palestine, ten thousand people, men, women, and children, assembled and implored him to stay. Jerome says: "Others may admire his miracles, his incredible absti- nence, his knowledge, and his humility; but for my part, nothing so astonishes me as his ability to tread all that glory and honour under his feet. There flocked to him bishops, priests, companies of clergymen and monks, of Christian women, too, (a great temptation), and from all sides a multitude of the common people, besides mighty men and judges, that they might get some bread, or some oil, on which he had pronounced a blessing. But he thought only of solitude."

He died at eighty years old, requesting to be buried in his garden, in the hair shirt and rustic cloak, which he had worn for many years without having them changed, or even washed. However, his remains were too valuable to

be left in an obscure place. They were secretly taken,
carried to a monastery, and buried with great solemnity.

MARTIN.—But none of the old saints wrought so many
and such great miracles as Martin; who was first a valiant
soldier in the army of Constantius, then a rigid monk, and
finally the zealous, uncompromising, orthodox Bishop of
Tours, in thĕ year three hundred and seventy. In all
these capacities, from youth to death, he was characterized
by great sobriety, purity, serenity of temper, and unbounded benevolence. One of his young disciples, not yet
baptized, chanced to die in his absence. When Martin returned, after three days, he found him a corpse, laid out
for the funeral. "Feeling himself filled with the Holy
Spirit, he commanded all the brethren to leave the cell
where the body lay. He then prostrated himself on the
corpse, and prayed. After a while, he rose a little, looked
steadfastly on the countenance of the deceased, and prayed.
In about two hours, the youth began to open his eyes.
Then Martin lifted up his voice to the Lord, and made the
cell resound with thanksgiving." The brethren rushed in,
astonished to find him alive, whom they had left dead.
He was baptized immediately, and lived many years afterward. He was accustomed to relate, that when he left the
body he was brought before the Judge, "who sentenced
him to dark places, among the common herd of departed
spirits." [This was because he had died unbaptized.]
"Then two angels suggested that this was he for whom
Martin was praying; whereupon, they were ordered to
convey him back to life again."

There are several other instances of raising the dead,
recorded by the biographer of Martin. He says also that,
"at Paris, while he was entering the gate of the city, to
the horror of all, he kissed a leper, and gave him his blessing, though the man's face was deformed by the disease.
The leper was instantly cleansed; and the next day he
came to the church with a clear skin, to give thanks for
his cure." Diseased people were cured by having a letter

from Martin laid upon the breast. The blind received sight, when he touched their eyes with his cloak. "It is known that angels often visited his cell and held conversations with him. He kept the Devil, too, so closely and distinctly under his eye, that the fiend, whether he retained his proper shape, or assumed various disguises, could never hide himself from the view of Martin. Many a time he tried mischievous tricks upon the holy man. One while, he would personate Jupiter; more frequently Mercury; often he presented himself with the countenance of Venus, or Minerva. But Martin always met him with an undaunted spirit, and protected himself with the sign of the cross and the weapon of prayer."

Sulpicius Severus, an ecclesiastical historian, who wrote toward the close of the fourth century, was a personal friend of Martin, and wrote a biography of him, which is still in existence. Among other marvellous things, he relates that the Devil one day appeared to Martin, "shedding round himself a purple splendour, clothed also in a royal robe, crowned with a diadem of gold and jewels, wearing golden slippers, with a serious aspect and a smiling face, so as to appear like anything rather than the Devil. Martin, who was at prayer in his cell, was dazzled at first, and both kept silence for some time. The Devil began by saying: 'I am Christ. Being about to descend upon the earth, I have resolved first to manifest myself to you.' Receiving no answer to this declaration, he had the audacity to repeat: 'Martin, why do you hesitate to believe? I am Christ!' Then the Spirit revealed to Martin that it was the Devil, not God. And he said: 'The Lord Jesus did not foretell that he would come clothed in purple, and with a glittering crown. I will not believe that Christ has come in any other dress than that in which he suffered; and bearing the marks of his cross.' At that word, the Evil Spirit vanished like smoke, and filled the cell with such a stench, as to afford indubitable evidence that he was the Devil. Lest any one should think this story fabulous, I aver that I heard from

Martin's own mouth the circumstances as I have related them."

He informs us Martin's popularity was so great, that an incredible multitude assembled out of the city and all the neighbouring towns to give their suffrages to elect him bishop. "But some of the bishops who were summoned to consecrate him, resisted his election; alleging that he was a contemptible person, of mean countenance, dirty clothing, and shaggy hair; unworthy of the bishop's office. By people of sound mind this madness of theirs was derided." After he became bishop, he continued to be a monk, lived in a small cell, and wore the same mean apparel. His admiring biographer says: "I declare truly, that if old Homer himself were to rise from the dead, he could not do justice to this subject; so much above the power of language are the merits of Saint Martin. Not an hour, nor even a minute passed, in which he was not engaged in prayer; for however employed, he never suffered his mind to relax from its devotional frame. Happy man, in whom there was no guile! Judging nobody, condemning nobody, never rendering evil for evil! For he had attained to such a degree of patience under injuries, that although he was the chief priest in his diocese, yet he might be injured with impunity by the lowest of the clergy; nor did he ever, on that account, remove them from their places, nor cease to treat them with all possible kindness. No one ever saw him angry, or disturbed, or sorrowful, or laughing. He was always the same; bearing in his countenance a sort of heavenly cheerfulness. He seemed to have risen above the weaknesses of human nature. There was nothing in his mouth but Christ; nothing in his heart but piety, peace, and compassion. There were some who envied his miracles and his purity of life, and hated in him what they were conscious of not possessing. But he had few persecutors; very few indeed, except the bishops." The biographer concludes by saying: "If any one reads this work without believing it, he will sin. I am conscious that I have, under the influence of love to Christ, faithfully related well-known facts, and have adhered to the truth in all my statements."

For centuries after the death of Martin, the most astounding miracles continued to be performed at his tomb, which became a place of resort for people of all nations, of whom multitudes were converted to the Christian faith by the marvels they witnessed.

MONASTERIES.—It is recorded of the Therapeutæ in Egypt that their reverence for Mosaic ceremonies gradually diminished, and that great numbers of them became converts to Christianity. It seems most likely these were the hermits, whom Anthony found in the deserts, whom he was accustomed to visit, and to take for examples. Therefore, when he drew around him a band of devotees, whom he guided, the customs introduced bore a strong resemblance to those anciently observed in the forests of Hindostan, whence Egypt had derived the model of such institutions. Anthony's disciples lived in separate huts, or caves, and only met together at stated hours, for devotional purposes. Such isolated devotees were called Anchorites, from Greek words signifying those who live alone. Their collection of hermitages was called a Laura, which means an open space.

Long before Anthony died, an Egyptian monk, named Pachomius, believed he heard the voice of an angel, saying it was not the will of God that he should devote himself entirely to his own spiritual perfection, but rather that he should seek to be an instrument of good to his brethren. Accordingly, he assembled a band of anchorites, who agreed to occupy separate cells enclosed in one large building. The regulations and ceremonies introduced were said to have been revealed by an angel; but they were exactly like those of the ancient Therapeutæ, and so were the titles bestowed on the various officers of the institution. It will be sufficiently obvious to every observing reader that there was also a striking resemblance to Buddhist Lamaseries, as described in the chapter on Thibet. As the monks of

Pachomius ate at one common table, they were called
Cœnobites, meaning those who live together. He, as head
of the establishment, was called Abbot, from a Hebrew and
Syriac word signifying Father. The association was divided
into classes, according to their degrees of spiritual progress.
Each class had its own presiding officer, and its allotted
tasks. Pachomius was opposed to a life of idle contemplation, and the inmates of his establishment were as diligent
as the occupants of Buddhist Lamaseries. They were agri-
culturists, basket-makers, weavers, tailors, carpenters, tan-
ners, and whatsoever other trade was needed. They raised
and manufactured all that was wanted among themselves,
and sent a great deal to the markets. Each department
had its own steward, and all gave in their accounts to a
general steward, who had oversight of the income and ex-
penditure of the whole association. All that remained of
their funds, after their own necessities were supplied, was
distributed in the prisons, or sent to the poor, the aged, and
the diseased. Very strict inquiry was made into the character of every one who wished to be admitted. He was required to make solemn asseveration that he was legally
entitled to act for himself, that he had committed no crime,
from the consequences of which he wished to seek refuge,
that he could submit to perpetual chastity, be strictly obedient to superiors, cheerfully renounce his property, and
consent never to call anything his own. If he answered
all these questions satisfactorily, he was still required to
serve a season of probation, to test his qualities. When he
entered, he shaved his head, and changed his name.

This first Christian Monastery was erected on the island
of Tabenna, in the Nile. Pachomius died in three hundred forty-eight, and during his life-time, it numbered
three thousand inmates. It increased so rapidly, that in
the first half of the fifth century, less than a hundred years
from its commencement, there were fifty thousand monks
included within its rules. Beggars and travellers always
received gratuitous food and shelter; as had been the case
with the ancient anchorites and the Braminical associations

in Hindostan, and with the Lamaseries of the Buddhists. The well-ordered industry of these Monasteries not only supplied the wants of all the poor in their own vicinity, but ships were built at their expense, and whole cargoes of grain and vegetables were sent to the destitute in foreign lands. The monks wore long linen tunics, fastened with a girdle, to which they added a sheep-skin cloak in winter. They usually went barefoot, but sometimes wore wooden sandals, to protect them from the extreme heat or cold. They lived on bread and water, to which, on festal occasions, was sometimes added the luxury of a little oil, or salt, an olive, or a fig. They ate in companies of tens, and in perfect silence. They were bound to obey their superiors without remonstrance, or question. Each had his separate cell, with a mat on the floor, and a roll of palm leaves, which served for a seat by day, and a pillow by night. Every morning, evening, and night, the sound of a horn summoned them to prayer. At each meeting one of the brethren rose up, and standing in the midst chanted a Psalm. On stated occasions, portions of Scripture were read. No one spoke, or sneezed, or sighed, or yawned, or even looked up. If affecting passages were read, they wept in silence, unless some over-charged heart relieved itself by an involuntary sob. If the happiness of heaven was described, a very gentle murmur sometimes intimated the satisfaction of the audience. No one was allowed to have more than enough for daily subsistence; and so strict was the vow of poverty, that no man was allowed to say my tunic, or my sandal. Such expressions were punished with six lashes. Every one was obliged to do his share of the work. It was a proverb with them that a labouring monk was tempted by only one devil, but a lazy one with a legion.

These early Egyptian monks were generally true to their professions. They had no lands, or revenues, and would accept of none. It being discovered after the death of one of their number, that he had laid up a hundred shillings from the proceeds of his labour, they buried the money with him, repeating over his grave: "Thy money perish with thee." The discipline was exceedingly strict. The slightest deviation from the rules was punished by penance of some kind, and more serious offences by incarceration and scourging. Unquestioning obedience to superiors was inculcated as the highest virtue, and was sometimes tested by extravagant trials; such as being ordered to walk through a heated furnace, or to plant a staff in the ground, and water it till it blossomed. Complete suppression of all the natural affections was required. Cassian tells the story of a man named Mucius, who begged to be admitted to a monastery. He had with him a son of eight years old. They were placed in separate cells, lest the sight of the child should inspire a sinful degree of tenderness in his father's heart. The boy was dressed in rags, and left so filthy as to be a disgusting object even to parental love. He was frequently beaten, to ascertain whether any remains of "carnal affection" would force tears from his father's eyes. The historian says: "Nevertheless, for the love of Christ, and from the virtue of obedience, the heart of the father remained hard and unmoved." As a final test of his implicit submission, he was ordered to throw the child into the river. He proceeded to obey, as cheerfully as if it were the command of God; exalted and strengthened in his mind by the idea that he was imitating the example of Abraham. But the brethren interposed, and "as it were rescued the child from the waters." Cassian relates this as if it were the highest effort of Christian heroism; and Mucius attained such holiness by this process of heart-stifling, that he became a bishop.

Basil the Great travelled in Syria, Palestine, and Egypt, to make himself thoroughly acquainted with monastic rules. He returned to establish a monastery in the forests of Pontus, on a plan very similar to that of Pachomius. Basil agreed with him in disapproving of idle meditation. Prayer and psalm-singing had their stated seasons, but were not allowed to encroach on the hours appropriated to labour. The money obtained by the diligent pursuit of various trades, after defraying the expenses of their own very abstemious mode of life, was appropriated to the maintenance and education of orphans, of all classes and religions. Other children were received, if parents gave their consent, certified by witnesses; but none of these young pupils were compelled to take vows of celibacy. In all these institutions the ties of kindred were regarded as entirely subordinate to spiritual relationship. Basil pronounced him "a slave to carnal nature," who loved a brother in blood more than a brother in the religious community. He lived twelve years in the monastery endowed with his wealth, and strictly conformed to its rules of poverty and abstinence. After he was chosen Archbishop of Cæsarea, he made frequent journeys to visit such associations, and wrote them many letters of advice and encouragement.

The later Fathers expressed unbounded admiration for these institutions, where many of them passed more or less of their time. The following extract from the writings of Gregory of Nazianzen sounds very much like the praises of holy anchorites, which abound in the ancient Sacred Books of Hindostan: "How dearly do I love to represent to myself a pious hermit, who has subjugated his senses to the dominion of reason; who, though still confined to earth, yet stands on its outmost boundary; and who from day to day emancipates himself from the ties by which he may yet be linked to human beings. Elevated above external objects, breathing a life altogether spiritual, he has relinquished commerce with men, except what may be required by the duties of charity, or the actual necessities of life. He communes with his own thoughts; he occupies himself with God; he has neither voice nor language for anything, but to converse with Him, to bless and glorify Him. Solely bent on the discovery and contemplation of eternal truth, he catches it at intervals, in characters of radiant light; and the sublime and lofty ideas he conceives of its perfections remain imprinted on his mind, free from all the fugitive deceptive phantoms and shadows, with which they would be obscured by earthly things. Thus the interior of his soul becomes a mirror, in which God is pleased to reflect the rays of his divinity, and to manifest the splendours of his glory. Joined to blessed Spirits in this region of light and peace, he maintains celestial intercourse with them, and feeds upon his grand and solid hopes of a future life."

Basil says: "Let us suppose a solitude like the desert, in which I now am; where the pious exercises of a religious life, uninterrupted by outward things, afford continual nourishment to the soul. Can you imagine felicity more desirable than that of imitating on earth the life that angels lead in heaven? To commence the day with prayers and sacred hymns, to mingle with our labour the holy songs which make it still more pleasant, and diffuse perpetual serenity. We become purified by this majestic equilibrium in the movements of our souls; by not permitting the tongue to indulge in idle conversation; the eyes to dwell on the vain glory of outward things; the ears to introduce to the soul anything effeminate or frivolous, like mere earthly music, or the heartless jests of trifling minds. The soul, secured by these precautions from outward distractions, and the temptations of the senses, elevates itself to contemplation of the Deity. Enlightened by the rays, which shine forth from his Divine Essence, it rises above its own weakness; freed from temporal cares, corporeal necessities, and the affections of earth, it devotes all its powers to the search after immortal good."

Chrysostom says: "The stars in the firmament are not so numerous as the solitaries in Egypt. With them, contemplation is not idleness. Not contented with renouncing earthly things, with being crucified to the world, they exercise their bodies with laborious occupations, the produce of which, distributed by the hands of charity, contributes to the support of the poor. In the night, they watch, and sing praises to the Lord. During the day, they pray and labour with their hands, copying the example of the great Apostle. If St. Paul, occupied as he was with the government of all the churches, could yet find time for manual labour, how much more are men removed from the tumult and distraction of cities called upon to occupy their leisure with everything that may be useful to others, as well as to themselves. Thus do these virtuous solitaries argue. Before the day has dawned, anticipating the orb of light, they are already on their feet, singing praises to the Creator. More fortunate than Adam himself in his terrestrial Paradise, and comparable to the angels alone, they sing with them, 'Glory to God in the highest, and on earth peace and good-will toward men.'"

The "majestic equilibrium," which Basil praised so highly, and which was preserved in the monasteries under his guidance, did not long continue a characteristic of monastic life. Ancient Egypt shared the temperament, as well as the theology, of Hindostan. To the high, bright tone of aspiration there always echoed a minor third of sadness. There was something of exuberance in their whole character; a tendency to excess, in festivity and in penitence. In both countries the climate produced such results, as it did lotus blossoms and deadly serpents. The hot sunshine of Africa poured fire into the temperaments, and thence into the theology, of Tertullian and Augustine. When Christianity was introduced into that part of the world, it took a character of extravagant zeal, and rigid asceticism. No other Christians fasted so often and so long, as those of the North African churches. There the Donatists and Montanists wrought themselves up to a frenzy of devotion and a furor of intolerance. In that region, above all others, it was natural that monasticism should first unite itself with Christianity. It was also natural that the same asceticism, which introduced the institution, should soon manifest itself in excesses similar to those practised by the devotees of Hindostan. An Alexandrian named Heron, who joined a company of hermits in the Desert of Nitria, often lived there months on nothing but wild herbs and the bread of the eucharist. He frequently travelled thirty miles into the desert, under a

scorching sun, without food or drink, constantly repeating
passages of Scripture. Perpetual contemplation of his own
state of mind induced a belief that he had arrived at spiritual perfection, and could not possibly commit sin. From
this there was an extreme reaction. The string of the bow
snapped from extremity of tension. He was seized with
an uncontrollable restlessness. He returned to Alexandria, and plunged into all sorts of amusement and sensuality. Excessive dissipation brought on severe illness;
and after terrible struggles, mental and physical, he at last
attained to a calm and cheerful state of mind. Arsenius,
a learned man, who had been tutor to the emperor Arcadius, became disgusted with the world, and retired into
the desert. He contrived to invent a method of discomfort
from the quiet and useful employment of mat-weaving.
The water in which the leaves were soaked he changed
but once a year; considering the fœtid smell a suitable
penance for the perfumes he had enjoyed when he was a
courtier. On Saturday evening, it was his custom to lie
down at the setting of the sun, and continue in fervent
prayer till the rising sun shone full upon his face. Onofrio
lived in a deep cave in the deserts around Thebes. For
sixty years, he never saw a human being, or uttered a
single word, except in prayer. He wore no covering, except a few twisted leaves. His hair and beard grew uncut,
till he resembled a wild beast. In this state, a hermit,
who was travelling, discovered him crawling on the
ground, and was doubtful what sort of animal it might be.
When he discovered that it was a human being, and
learned the privations and sufferings he had endured for
more than half a century, he was filled with wonder and
reverence, and fell at his feet to receive a blessing. John
of Lucopolis formed a small cell for himself on the summit
of a lofty mountain in Thebais. There he lived fifty years,
without opening his door, without seeing the face of a
woman, and without tasting any food prepared by cooking.
Five days of the week he spent in silent meditation and
secret prayer. On Saturdays and Sundays, he opened a

small window, and gave audience to the crowd of suppliants, who came to him from all quarters, to have devils expelled, diseases cured, and the future predicted. He answered their questions, and drew up with a string the fruit and vegetables supplied by their charity. Theodosius the Great sent a messenger to him to inquire what would be the result of his projected war with Eugenius. He respectfully proposed the question, and received assurance of a certain though bloody victory. This greatly excited the emperor, and stimulated the courage of his troops to verify the prediction. The prosperous result greatly increased John's fame as a prophet.

Hermits generally lived in low, narrow, wooden huts, with a palm-leaf mat on the ground, and a bundle of leaves for a pillow. Some constructed cells in such a way that they were compelled to sit doubled up in a most uncomfortable manner. Some exposed themselves to the fury of storms and sunshine, unsheltered, on the tops of mountains. Some lived in deep caves, where not a ray of light could penetrate; some in the clefts of steep, inaccessible rocks; some in the most retired chambers of ancient tombs; some in the dens of wild beasts; and some in iron cages, with weights hung to their arms or feet. Some retired to districts where no rain fell, and where they could obtain no drink but the dew, which they lapped up from the rocks. Some never cut their nails, or combed their hair or beard. Some wore a coarse garment unwashed, until it dropped off in rags; others were partially screened by a few plaited leaves; others were entirely uncovered, except by their long flowing hair, which they never cut. Sleep, being a refreshment to the body, was regarded as sinful. One hour of unbroken slumber was deemed sufficient. They were wakened by each other often in the night to attend prayers and watch; the precise time being determined by the position of the stars. They lived on berries, roots, and vegetables, drank water only, and even from this abstemious diet fasted often; sometimes for days in succession. If, by any accident, they happened to look upon a woman, they inflicted upon themselves severe penance for the crime. One of them allowed his sister to visit him, at her urgent entreaty; but he shut his eyes during the whole interview. The natural instincts which they tried so zealously to repress acquired exaggerated importance in their imaginations. This is manifested in the sorrowful struggles recorded by the gentle Gregory of Nazianzen; in the general testimony of monks and anchorites that the devils had a peculiar proneness to appear to them in the forms of women; and in the following passionate outburst of confession from Jerome: "Oh, how often in the desert, in that vast solitude, parched by the sultry sun, did I fancy myself in the midst of luxurious Rome! Plunged in an abyss of bitterness, I have thrown myself on the floor of my solitary cell. My limbs were rough with the friction of coarse hair-cloth; my skin, dried and blackened in the sun, was like that of an Ethiopian, and my complexion was livid as a corpse. I groaned and wept throughout the day; and if, in spite of my resistance, drowsiness overcame me at night, my bones, which scarcely held together, clashed on the naked earth. I say nothing of my food. In the deserts, even those who are ill never permit themselves to drink anything but water. If they took anything that required the aid of fire in its preparation, they would accuse themselves of sensuality. Yet even I, who, from fear of hell, had condemned myself to this dungeon, with no other companions than scorpions and wild beasts, often imagined myself in the midst of dancing girls. Fires boiled up in this body prematurely dead. Criminal remembrances, desires, and regrets, overwhelmed me. I shrunk from my very cell, seeming to dread its walls as the accomplices of my thoughts. I penetrated to the inmost recesses of the desert, or wandered on the summits of mountains, or hid myself in the cavities of rocks. I went and came, not knowing where to seek refuge from myself, until at last I threw myself at the foot of the cross, bathing it with my tears, that flowed in rivers, and which I wiped with my hair. I strove to subdue my rebellious nature by fasting a whole week. I frequently passed entire nights uttering loud cries, until the Lord himself dispersed the tempest that raged within me, and restored peace to my soul."

The tendency to asceticism, which had strongly manifested itself in the Syrian sects of Gnostics, produced the extremest results when monasticism prevailed in that country. In Syria and Mesopotamia were bands of hermits called Graziers, because they fed only on grass and herbs. They lived unsheltered in the forests, or on the sides of mountains, continually praying and singing psalms. When the stated hour for eating arrived, each one took a knife and cut as many herbs as he wanted; and this was the only care they took for temporal concerns.

SIMEON STYLITES.—A Syrian shepherd named Simeon devoted himself to the austere life of a hermit when he was only thirteen years old. It is recorded that he once caused himself to be locked up in a cell, to fulfil a vow he had made to fast forty days. He persisted in his resolution, though a friend took the precaution to place bread and water within his reach. He was found senseless, but survived. For twenty-eight years he went without food one hundred days in the course of each year. During his protracted fasts, he stood till he could stand no longer, then sat, but at last fell down half dead. Finally, he took up his residence on the top of a column, nine feet high, and seven in circumference. There he stood for nine years, like an image on its pedestal. As the pillar admitted of no other posture than standing, he tied himself to a beam fastened to it, to prevent falling when he underwent very severe fasts. He afterward ascended a column sixty feet high, and only three in diameter at top. It was about thirty miles from the city of Antioch. There he stood twenty-eight years, enduring the scorching sunshine of the climate, and the cold of winter. He was called Stylites, from a Greek word meaning a column. He made but one meal in a week, and that a very light one. When

he slept, he leaned against a sort of balustrade. He spent
the day in prayer till three o'clock in the afternoon, then
preached to the audiences collected round the foot of his
column, and answered the various requests that were
brought to him. By practice, he had learned to assume
various attitudes while engaged in prayer. On solemn
festivals of the church, he stood with his hands stretched
out, so as to resemble a cross, from the setting of the sun
to its rising, without a wink of sleep. While praying, he
continually bowed so low as to touch his toes with his
head. These performances excited the wonder and admiration of spectators. One of them counted his bowings,
till he came to twelve hundred and forty-four, and then he
gave up the task. His pillar was constantly surrounded
by crowds of invalids, who besought his prayers and went
away miraculously cured. Devotees from all parts of the
world, even from India and Arabia, came to obtain his
blessing. Churches often sent delegates to ask his advice,
which he gave in the form of letters. Theodosius the
Younger frequently consulted him, both in political and
theological emergencies. Theodoret, bishop of Cyrus, the
pious historian of that period, says: "The holy Simeon,
being placed in a middle region, as it were, between heaven and earth, conversed with God, and glorified him
with the angels; offering up supplications from man to
God, and drawing down blessings from heaven for men."
He testifies to many miracles performed by Simeon, of
which he says he was himself a witness. He heard him
foretell a famine, a pestilence, and a destructive irruption
of locusts: all of which took place. He likewise correctly
foretold the death of one of Theodoret's enemies a fortnight
before it happened. A man who made a vow to God, in
the presence of Simeon, never to eat animal food, was afterward tempted to eat a chicken; but when he tried to taste
it, the flesh turned to stone. Theodoret says there were
many eye-witnesses of this miracle, who handled the fowl,
and found the breast to be a compound of bone and stone.
This celebrated devotee expired on his column, about the

year four hundred and sixty. During the thirty-seven years he passed in this manner, he was seldom left in solitude. In addition to the innumerable people cured by his prayers, it is recorded that some were cured by his touch. His miracles converted many to Christianity, and the celebrity he acquired induced many anchorites to imitate his mode of penance. The highest dignitaries of church and state formed a procession to convey his body to Antioch; and the possession of it was considered a greater safeguard to the city than walls or armies.

Of course, these unnatural modes of life tended to irritate the nerves and bewilder the mind. Effects similar to those produced on the ancient anchorites of Hindostan are recorded concerning Christian ascetics. Considering every pleasant reminiscence, and natural impulse, as a temptation of the Devil, they lived in a perpetual state of vigilant anxiety, or mournful contrition. Feeble in body, and excited in mind, they doubtless saw fiery visions, which they supposed to be Evil Spirits, and heard mysterious noises, which they mistook for the howling and hissing of Demons. The places they chose for their residence also contributed to render their imaginations more impressible. Night settling down over the vast solitude of the desert; mighty mountains, shrouded in dark clouds, revealed by fitful flashes of lightning; shrieks of the stormy winds; howlings of wild beasts; the fantastic shadows of moonlight; to hear and see all these, and be alone with them, for ever alone, required great strength both of body and mind. And even without external sources of solemnity and awe, the firm belief that fiends were always lurking near them, to tempt their unwary souls to hell, was of itself enough to drive men mad, when made a subject of perpetual contemplation. Some grew sceptical about the existence of a God, or of themselves. They regarded all things as phantoms, and creation as a self-moving show. Some rushed into furious licentiousness, from the idea that where the soul was holy, the body could commit no sin. Insanity manifested itself in so many forms, that in the sixth century it became necessary to establish a hospital at Jerusalem for lunatic devotees. But indefinite degrees of insanity often passed for inspiration; and multitudes continued to be attracted toward a mode of life, which gave them such influence over their fellow men. The degree of veneration paid to Christian hermits and monks appears to have been fully equal to what was accorded to the ancient anchorites of Hindostan, when the world was many centuries younger. The holiest of these devotees were believed to be invested with miraculous power, which in many cases was imparted to the garments they had worn, the staffs with which they walked, and the vessels they had handled. It was supposed that they could cast out devils by their prayers; cure diseases by a touch, a word, or even a distant message; perceive the secret thoughts of men; foretell future events; cause iron to swim, and dead trees to blossom; pass safely through fire; handle serpents uninjured; and compel devils and wild beasts to obey their commands. All these things are recorded as of frequent occurrence in the lives of remarkable saints. The bishop Theodoret, a man of learning, benevolence, and sincere piety, was in the constant habit of visiting celebrated hermits in their caves, and monks in their cells. He thus made a great collection of their maxims and miracles, which he recorded in his Ecclesiastical History. He affirms that both himself and his father were often cured of distempers, by applying a piece of the girdle of a holy monk named Peter, "whose garments wrought wonders, like those of the Apostle Paul." He tells of a noble and wealthy lady at Antioch, who became delirious, could not recognize the members of her own family, and obstinately refused to eat or drink. It was generally believed that she was possessed by a devil; but physicians said she had a disease on the brain. All medical aid having proved vain, her husband applied to a celebrated monk, named Macedonius. When the holy man entered the room, he addressed a fervent prayer to God, and ordered some cold water to be brought. As the physicians had forbidden her to drink water, he requested every one to leave the apartment; he then made the sign of the cross over a goblet of water, and himself gave it to the lady to drink. As soon as she had swallowed it, her senses began to return. She recognized the Holy Father, reverently kissed his hand, and soon recovered her health completely. Whatever these renowned devotees said concerning theological doctrine, or modes of worship, was supposed to be expressly revealed to them by the Holy Spirit, and was therefore obeyed as reverently as had been the oracles of Ammon, and of Urim and Thummim. Emperors visited them in their cells, to consult them on affairs of state; their benediction was esteemed an important prelude to every great undertaking; and they were frequently summoned from seclusion to preside in episcopal palaces. It would have been altogether inconsistent with the constitution of human nature, if such extreme adulation and profound deference had not excited spiritual pride. Symptoms of it do in fact abound. Simeon Stylites had a vision of a flaming chariot from heaven, guided by an angel toward his column. The angel urged him to ascend the chariot, saying the Heavenly Spirits were longing to receive him. Simeon had already placed his right foot on the step, when it was suggested to him to take the precaution of making the sign of the cross. He did so, and immediately the chariot vanished; being a mere phantom sent by Satan to deceive him. His right foot was sprained, and he said it was done in his attempt to mount the visionary vehicle. Some monks, whose minds were better balanced, regretted the excessive tendencies of many of their brethren, and occasionally cautioned them against the results. Nilus thus addressed one of the imitators of Simeon: "Whoever exalts himself shall be abased. You have done nothing worthy of commendation, in having stationed yourself on a lofty pillar; yet you covet the greatest praise. Look to it, lest you be extravagantly lauded by mortals, and hereafter be obliged to appear wretched before the eternal God, because you were intoxicated here by the undeserved praise of men."

Extravagances of asceticism were generally more conspicuous among anchorites of the deserts and mountains, than in the monasteries. Such institutions were often under the guidance of wise and prudent men, and in the beginning, visionary tendencies were much checked by the salutary influence of useful occupation. But the industrial character of the early establishments soon changed. An idea began to prevail that buying and selling was detrimental to holiness, by occupying the mind too much with external affairs, and bringing saints into contact with worldly men. Martin, who was afterward bishop, established a monastery in a very secluded spot, about two miles from Tours. It was enclosed between a river and precipitous mountains. There was but one way of access to it, and that was extremely narrow. He began with eighty disciples, most of whom lived in holes they had scooped out among the steep rocks. Himself, and some others, constructed very small wooden cells for their habitations. They raised barely enough for their own scanty subsistence. There was no buying or selling, to create a fund for charity, as in other monasteries. The elder members of the community did nothing but read the Scriptures and pray, and the juniors copied the Scriptures, and the Lives of Saints. They all wore coarse garments of camel's hair, fasted often, and rarely left their cells, except to assemble for prayer. The biographer of Martin says: "What made this more wonderful, was that many of them belonged to noble families, and had been far differently educated. Most of them subsequently became bishops; for what city or church could do otherwise than desire to have pastors from the monastery of Martin?" There gradually grew up classes of monks who gave especial prominence to the Hindoo doctrine of a divine intuitive science, obtained by those who had completely subjugated the senses. They thought they had attained to a state of spiritual perfection, which no longer needed the Scripture,

or any other external aid: that they were a sufficient law
unto themselves, being constantly guided by immediate
revelations of the Holy Spirit. They considered labour a
degradation to the soul, and lived by alms only. These
were the origin of what were afterward called Mendicant
Friars. What might at first have originated in sincere
fanaticism, before long degenerated into shameless impos-
ture. Tribes of importunate beggars roamed about the
country in monkish costume, committing all manner of
licentiousness and deception, and often robbing the charitable who sheltered them. This was carried to such an
extent, that in some places monks came to be regarded as a
nuisance. When a band of them came from Jerusalem to
Carthage, about the middle of the fifth century, the populace ridiculed and cursed them, as they passed through the
streets. So loud was the remonstrance against the abuses
of monasticism, that Chrysostom was obliged to write several books in defence of the system. But through evil report and through good report, these associations continued
to spread, till they covered the whole face of the Christian
world. Jerome estimated the number of monks and anchorites in Egypt only, at seventy-six thousand in his time.
There were at that period five thousand monks in the
Deserts of Nitria, near Alexandria, who could be immediately rallied by sound of trumpet to attack Jews, Pagans,
or heretics. They often committed terrible devastations
under the covering of zeal for religion. The abstraction
of such large and ever-increasing numbers of men from the
various trades and occupations also became a serious evil.
The emperor Valens published an edict, in which he styled
the monks "those followers of idleness," and commanded
that they should serve in the army.

The idea that the perfection of human nature consisted
in complete estrangement from the senses was oriental
in its origin, and thoroughly oriental in its character.
It did not find its way into Europe, till introduced with
Christianity. Some tendency that way was indeed indicated by the general celibacy and extreme temperance

L*

of philosophers. But this element, which they brought from Egypt, was tempered by the active and joyous spirit of Greece, and by the restraining sense of Roman dignity. The grove in which Plato taught was full of beautiful statues, and he always wore stainless garments of fine and soft material. His followers the New Platonists, though tending more and more to oriental doctrines, were always gentlemen in dress and manners. The majestic and the beautiful was the pervading character of Grecian and Roman temples, and their houses were adorned with images of joy and grace, such as dancing nymphs, frolicsome Cupids and laughing Bacchantes. Among people descended from such ancestry, monasticism could not fail to meet with some repulsion. A monk was never seen in Rome, till Athanasius introduced a few of the companions of Anthony the Hermit, in the year three hundred and forty. Their emaciated bodies, dirty dress, and matted hair, excited horror and disgust, which was very slowly conquered by stories of their superior sanctity and supernatural power. When Jerome went there, a little more than forty years afterward, he found that the very few who had been converted to the monastic practices taught by Athanasius, were regarded by the Roman people as "ignominious and vile." But his fervent exhortations soon kindled wonderful enthusiasm on the subject. Roman Senators, wealthy matrons, and beautiful young maidens of patrician rank, were seized with longing to leave their luxurious palaces, and purchase eternal happiness and glory, by renouncing all the pleasures of the world in some narrow cell of a monastery. The zeal thus kindled caused a great deal of domestic disappointment and unhappiness. There had always been more converts to Christianity among women, than among men. It often happened that noble Romans retained their attachment to the old worship, while their wives and daughters were Christians. Young men, influenced by their mothers and sisters, suddenly resolved to become monks, when their fathers had opened for them a brilliant career as lawyers, magistrates,

or military officers; and the pride of patrician friends was
mortified to see them exchange their elegant and perfumed
robes for the squalid dress of monks, and in lieu of dignified offices occupy themselves with weaving mats and baskets. Beautiful young girls, for whom wealthy marriages
had been arranged, took upon themselves vows of perpetual celibacy, and no persuasion or threats could change
their purpose; the vexation of ambitious relatives, and the
grief of affectionate parents, were extreme. All who did
not share the enthusiasm detested monks in general, and
Jerome in particular. It was much the same in other
cities. In Constantinople, parents appealed to the government to have some legal measures taken to prevent their
children from being persuaded to desert their homes. But
Chrysostom preached from the pulpit of Santa Sophia that
all who thus wished to expose their offspring to the temptations of the world must expect misery here, and eternal
perdition hereafter. The number and wealth of the monasteries increased continually; for in Christian countries, as
it had always been in Hindostan, alms given to a monk
was considered as so much paid toward the salvation of the
donor's soul. They gradually monopolized the practice of
medicine, as had been done among Hindoos and Buddhists.
They cured diseases by their prayers and exorcisms, and
they cultivated a knowledge of herbs to assist their miraculous power.

There were Christians who strongly remonstrated against
these doctrines and customs. Jovinian of Rome, though
himself a monk, disapproved the exaggerated importance
awarded to celibacy. He urged that it was by no means
peculiarly Christian, since the priests of Isis and of Cybele
always took upon themselves a similar vow. He said the
union of Christ and his church would never have been
typified by marriage, if there were anything wrong in the
relation. He exhorted those who chose to lead a single
life, for the sake of freedom from worldly cares, to be careful not to pride themselves upon it, as a great merit and
distinction; since the married could be truly religious also.

Jovinian appears to have been one of those men, whose good sense restrains them from extremes. Jerome could not accuse him of selfish reasons for depreciating the value of celibacy; for he scrupulously observed his own monastic vow. But he reproached him with wearing clean linen garments, and making frequent use of the bath; as if cleanliness were incompatible with religion. Vigilantius, who so greatly exasperated Jerome by protesting against invocations to martyrs, and the burning of lamps before their relics, likewise provoked his wrath by writing against the doctrine that celibacy was essential to holiness. He maintained that there was no authority for it in the teaching of Christ, or the Apostles. He urged that Paul had merely required bishops and deacons to have but one wife, and that he sanctioned the election of a bishop who had a wife and children. He protested against monastic life, as a desertion of social and domestic duties, and as a warfare with nature, well calculated to produce secret immorality. He denied that virgins had any higher merit than widows, or married women, unless they excelled them in good works; and he maintained that it would be far more acceptable to God to spend money judiciously for the industrious poor at home, than to send alms to indolent monks at Jerusalem. These views gained favour with many minds. They were approved by some even among the clergy, who candidly admitted that excess of rigour did produce secret licentiousness. But this opposition served to stimulate zeal on the other side, and failed to arrest the progress of monasticism.

NUNS.

It has been stated that in very early times there were individuals, both among men and women, who voluntarily devoted themselves to a single life, for the sake of more leisure for religious pursuits. These "virgins of the church," as they were called, generally lived in Christian families, and assisted in the care of the household. Cyprian calls these celibates, "the flower of the ecclesiastical tree;

the most illustrious portion of Christ's flock;" and tells
them that the best mansion in the Heavenly Father's
house is reserved for them. It was early the custom for
women thus dedicated to live in the houses of clergymen,
whether married or unmarried. Many of them were poor,
and were glad to obtain a comfortable home by the management of household affairs; and to the sincerely devout
among them the opportunities for religious instruction,
which such situations afforded, would doubtless be very
precious. The title of "spiritual sister," usually bestowed
upon them, would naturally be attractive, from the spiritual equality it expressed. Such a mutually helpful relation might have been generally pure and salutary in the
primitive days, when there were no Christians except those
who became so through conscientious conviction. But
after a time, it became customary for these virgins to receive pecuniary assistance from the church, and this would
naturally induce many to join, who had no higher motive
than selfishness. That some of them were not very seriously impressed is implied by Cyprian's finding it necessary to preach to them against painting their faces, and
colouring their hair of the fashionable tint. He asks if
they are not afraid their Maker will not know them for his
own work, when their bodies rise from the dead. Under
such circumstances, their residence in the houses of unmarried clergymen would naturally give rise to suspicion.
Cyprian says: "The church often complains of her virgins,
and groans at the scandalous stories told of them. Their
glory and dignity are profaned." He gave orders that
those who were living in the houses of unmarried clergymen should immediately depart. Several of the Fathers
allude to the custom with disapprobation. Jerome, who
never sacrificed strength to delicacy, describes it in coarse,
sarcastic terms. Basil wrote to an old presbyter of his
diocese to dismiss his "spiritual sister," though he was
seventy years old, lest his example should prove a stum-
bling-block to younger ecclesiastics. The Council of Nice
formally condemned the practice, and forbade clergymen

to have any woman reside in the same house with them,
except a mother, sister, or aunt. But the evil had become so extensive and deeply rooted, that the emperor was
obliged to pass very strict laws on the subject.

When Pachomius established the first monastery, he
likewise founded a separate institution for women vowed
to celibacy. They received the name of nuns, from a
Coptic word signifying mother; a term of respect, applied
to them, as holy father was to the monks. As women had
few profitable employments, Pachomius made it a rule
that the expenses of the nunneries should be defrayed by
the monasteries. Women were as emulous of this kind of
sanctity as men. Jerome says there were nearly twenty-
eight thousand nuns in Egypt in his day. When Athanasius introduced monks at Rome, they proselyted a lady
named Marcella, who with a few other devout women retired into seclusion, and devoted herself to celibacy and
prayer. But that mode of life had not then become
fashionable at Rome, and her example was not praised or
followed. When Basil the Great established his monastery
in Pontus, he built a nunnery on the other side of the
river, where his mother and his sister Macrina presided
over a community of pious women. The three sisters of
Theodosius the Great made a vow of perpetual celibacy,
which was inscribed on a golden tablet set with gems, and
presented by them to the cathedral at Constantinople.
They lived in religious community with a company of devout maidens, who had taken the same vow. They were
exceedingly abstemious, fasted often, and spent their time
praying and singing Psalms. Their example was eulogized
as the perfection of human virtue. The enthusiasm for
monastic life, which Jerome's preaching excited at Rome,
was peculiarly conspicuous among women. His argument,
that "as the Lord had angels to attend upon him in heaven,
he ought also to have angels devoted to him on earth,"
proved very attractive to young maidens, who felt a degree of spiritual dignity in resolving to become "the
spouse of Christ." Jerome was fond of applying to this

subject all the glowing descriptions of the bridegroom in the Song of Solomon; and if he had been painting earthly love with a free pen, some of his pictures could scarcely have been more impassioned. This mingling of earth and heaven in his eloquence had a powerful influence over the devout and susceptible nature of women. Under its influence, the young, the beautiful, and the wealthy, renounced the world and its pleasures, assumed coarse garments, and devoted themselves to poverty, chastity, and obedience. Ambrose had similar success in his diocese. Many parents tried to keep their daughters out of hearing of his eloquence, lest he should induce them all to become nuns. The most distinguished among Jerome's converts at Rome were the widow Paula, and her daughter Eustochium, descendants of the Scipios and the Gracchi. Paula impoverished her own family, to bestow her great wealth on the church. The enemies of Jerome attributed his influence over them to human love. He admitted that both the ladies were attached to him, but solemnly denied that he ever made any base or selfish use of his influence. They left kindred, friends, and country, and accompanied by a number of women, who were excited by a similar religious enthusiasm, they joined Jerome and a band of monks in a pilgrimage to Bethlehem. There Paula built and endowed a monastery and two nunneries. Jerome presided over the first, and herself and Eustochium over the others. When she left Rome, a younger daughter and a little son watched her departure with looks of sorrowful intreaty. But without turning to take a farewell glance, she raised her tearless eyes to heaven, and went forth to the Holy Land. Jerome eulogizes this as the sublimest height of self-denying piety. Paula died in her nunnery, and he boasted that she did not leave a farthing to her daughter, but many debts.

The Fathers were lavish in their praises of women who thus dedicated themselves to the Lord. Jerome calls monks and nuns "the precious gems and flowers of the church." He says: "Marriage replenishes the earth, but

virginity peoples heaven." "There must be vessels of
wood and of earthen, as well as of gold and of silver."
Chrysostom says: "Transport yourself in imagination into
Egypt. You will there see a new Paradise, more beautiful than the richest gardens; innumerable troops of angels
in human forms; entire nations of martyrs and virgins.
There the weaker sex rival the most fervent solitaries in
their virtues. A holy phalanx of pious Amazons, not
armed, as of old, with bucklers and javelins, keep themselves continually on their guard against an enemy the
most subtle and dangerous of any." Elsewhere, he says:
"It is a life worthy of heaven, and not inferior to that of
angels."

It was the same with Christianity as it always has been
with all sects. In the beginning all the members of it
were in earnest; all were deeply impressed by the new aspects of truths presented to their minds; in a word, all
were religious. But after Christianity was patronized by
the state, multitudes received it as an inheritance, or merely
adopted it as a custom. It was easy to do so, because the
church itself laid so much stress on external ceremonies,
such as baptism, the Lord's Supper, and the sign of the
cross. To these was added the old Hindoo idea that donations to priests, and alms to monks, were so much paid
toward the expiation of sins and the increase of future rewards. The more Christianity set itself up in opposition
to nature, and demanded entire suppression of the instincts
and affections, the more the separation widened between
the worldly class and the religious. Hindoo rationalists
and moralists had asked, centuries before, how the business
of the world was to get on if all devoted themselves to celibacy and contemplation. The same theory introduced
into Christianity gave rise to similar reflections. The result was, that men engaged in active pursuits came to
regard religion as incompatible with the necessary business of life; as an affair belonging to priests and monks
only. They supposed their own duties adequately per
formed if they paid the consecrated class for the perform-

mance of ceremonies, which they declared to be essential to salvation. If such men were exhorted to become sober and devout, it was common for them to reply: "I have worldly duties to perform; I am neither priest nor monk." Augustine, alluding to this line of separation, says: "As the Pagan who would be a Christian hears rude words from the Pagans, so he among the Christians who is striving to lead a better and more conscientious life must expect to hear himself mocked by Christians themselves, who will say: 'You are really a very righteous man; a second Elijah or Peter; you must have descended from heaven.'" Elsewhere he says: "As soon as a man begins to despise the world, to refrain from revenging injuries, and from the accumulation of riches, to walk faithfully in the ways of Christ, and think of nothing but God, we must expect Christians themselves to remark: 'What is the man about? What can have entered into his head?'"

GENTILES.

It has been already stated that Justin Martyr, Clement of Alexandria, Origen, and others of the early Fathers, had such reverence for Plato, that they thought he must have been inspired by a degree of the Logos, which inspired the Hebrew Scriptures. Some of the later Fathers retained a portion of this feeling. Eusebius says: "Plato alone, of all the Greeks, reached to the vestibule of truth, and stood upon its threshold." Lactantius calls him "the wisest of all philosophers." Augustine declares that any Platonist might become a Christian by merely changing a few words and sentences. But this very similarity, combined with the eclectic tendency of the new Platonists, induced an increasing hostility to philosophy, and to classic literature in general, as a polished and insidious enemy, likely to destroy the individuality of Christianity by fusing all systems together. Jerome says: "The vain words of philosophy, in the doctrines of Plato, kill the infants of the church, and are turned to divine vengeance and blood to them." He has himself told us that he was so in love with the rich, harmonious Greek, and the majestic Latin, that he tried to do penance for his besetting sin, with "the hisses of Hebrew;" and that angels were obliged to come to his assistance and scourge it out of him. Yet some of the old leaven seems to have remained after that castigation; for he always continued to quote the classics. Rufinus, seeking to heap accusations on him, brings it against him, as a very serious charge, that he employed monks on the Mount of Olives to copy portions of Cicero. He says: "I have held the sheets in my own hands. I have read them. He cannot deny that when he came from Bethlehem, he brought one of Cicero's Dialogues with him; and that, in his Greek Paganism, he gave me a volume of Plato."

Lactantius complains that Pagans pertinaciously defended their religion, because they derived it from their ancestors; deeming it impiety to question what had been handed down from very ancient times; that they reproached Christianity with being a new worship, unlike anything that had ever been approved by kings, lawgivers, or philosophers. To meet this objection, Christians claimed the revelations made to Hebrews as the fountain of their religion, and affirmed that they were not only as old as the world, but were also the only revelations of divine truth that had ever been given to mankind, before the advent of Christ. Eusebius, in his efforts to give antiquity to Christianity, affords a curious example how words may be pressed into the service of theological theories. He asserts that the Hebrew patriarchs had the same faith and the same worship as the Christians, and even the same name. To prove this position, he quotes: "The Lord said, Touch not mine anointed." As the word Christ signifies anointed, he thence derives the inference that God called them Christs, or Christians. Augustine says: "What is true and good in the writings of Pagans should be used for the service of Christianity; since it was not created by themselves, but, like their gold and silver, was dug out from stores everywhere provided by Divine Providence." He also says: "That which is now called the Christian religion existed among the ancients; nor was it wanting from the beginning of the human race till Christ came in the flesh; from which time the true religion, which had always existed, began to be called Christian."

Jewish converts of course retained the fixed idea of their nation, that God never inspired any but his chosen people of Israel. They adopted the opinion of Aristobulus, Philo, and Josephus, that any fragments of truth found in the writings of Plato and other philosophers must have been borrowed from Hebrew sources, while all that was false in their teaching came from the Evil Spirits whom they worshipped as Gods. They succeeded in firmly fixing this idea in the minds of the Christian Fathers. Some said Plato had conversed with the prophet Jeremiah in Egypt. Others said he went to Egypt for the express purpose of studying the Hebrew Law and the Prophets; and that he became acquainted with them through the medium of the Greek translation called the Septuagint. They did not explain how it happened, that Plato, having taken all that trouble, never made the slightest allusion to the Hebrews or their books, though he continually referred to the learning of the Egyptians. The total dissimilarity between his writings and those attributed to Moses was explained by the assertion that all of truth in Plato could be found in Moses by allegorical interpretation. Augustine for a time maintained this Jewish theory concerning Plato, but he subsequently retracted it; being convinced that Plato was born near a hundred years after Jeremiah was in Egypt, and that the Hebrew Scriptures were not translated into Greek till sixty years after Plato's death. Lactantius and Jerome likewise acknowledged that chronology would not sustain such a theory. Then a conjecture arose that the Grecian philosopher, during his stay in Egypt, must have conversed with some learned interpreter of Moses. This opinion, which satisfied Jewish exclusiveness, generally prevailed among Christians. That Hebrew patriarchs and prophets were directly inspired by the Logos—that is, by

Christ himself—was universally maintained; but the old idea that the best philosophers might have been thus inspired, though in a lesser degree, was rejected by all the later Fathers. The learned among them acknowledged that the doctrine of One God was very anciently taught in Egypt. Lactantius says: "Thoth, or Hermes, a most ancient philosopher, instructed in all kinds of learning, and therefore called Trismegistus, [thrice greatest,] wrote many books concerning the knowledge of divine things; wherein he asserts the majesty of One Supreme God, calling Him, as we do, God and Father. Lest any one should inquire his name, he said that he was without any name; that is, ineffable and incomprehensible."

To rightly estimate the opposition to Christianity manifested by many good and sincere men among the Pagans, it is necessary not only to make allowance for the strong attachment men naturally feel for the ancient faith of their nation, but it is also just to remember that Christianity did not then present itself to reflecting minds with the same aspect it now does in the most enlightened parts of Christendom. The alleged efficacy of mere external rites naturally excited distrust, when so many manifested a lax morality, and selfish policy, after being baptized. Spurious Gospels, abounding with marvellous and childish tales, were then in general circulation; and prophecies by Sibyls, which learned Pagans knew to be forged, were constantly appealed to in confirmation of Christianity. Allegorical interpretations of Homer seemed to the Fathers like foolish conceits; but the symbolical interpretations which they gave to the Scriptures, Old and New, seemed quite as forced and unmeaning to Grecian and Roman minds. They had been accustomed to regard Jews in very much the same light that we regard Hindoos; as a people of small intellectual culture, and strongly wedded to strange, unsocial customs. Not being educated to consider Moses inspired, they did not look at his laws through the glorifying medium of reverence, but judged them with the same freedom that we judge the laws of Menu, Minos, or Numa.

The bold and sublime, but rough style of the Hebrew Prophets was offensive to ears accustomed to flowery rhetoric, and the harmonious versification of Grecian and Roman poets. Moreover the allusions and metaphors were so Jewish, that much of their significance was lost upon other nations. Therefore, notwithstanding the strong inducements to accept a religion on which successive emperors lavished funds and honours, there still remained a considerable class of educated minds strongly, though silently attached to old religious ideas, clothed in the robes of refined philosophy. And though the indigent and the helpless were sure of shelter and nourishment in the arms of the mother church, there were still many peasants, who believed that their flocks would not multiply, if they ceased to offer oblations to Pan, and that their harvests would be unblest, without an altar to Ceres in the fields.

As the new religion grew more powerful, it became less merciful toward the old. It was the general belief that all Pagans, who lived before the world had heard of Christ, could not possibly be happy in another world; not even the wise and virtuous Socrates, and the excellent Phocion. And no Christian entertained a doubt that every Pagan must be eternally damned, whatever might be his degree of moral worth, if he worshipped the ancient gods, after the religion of Christ had been offered to him. At the beginning of the fifth century, when the persecuting Cyril was Archbishop of Alexandria, a learned and beautiful woman, named Hypatia, was head of the school of New Platonists in that city. She gave lectures on philosophy, and her uncommon eloquence and graceful manners attracted very large audiences. She is said to have been free from pedantry, strictly virtuous in character, and eminently modest in her manners. She was under the protection of her father, who was also a philosopher, and their house became the resort of all the learned and distinguished. Orestes, Governor of Alexandria, was frequently their guest, and she was supposed to have great influence over him. A jealousy arose that this influence was exerted unfavourably to Cyril. He and his monks began to utter calumnies concerning her friendship with Orestes; though it does not appear that she was guilty of any other offence than that of exerting extraordinary talent and learning to render the old religion attractive in its mystic veil of Platonism. The monks of the neighbouring deserts, who prided themselves on contempt for human learning, were much displeased by the applause her eloquence excited; and their enmity increased to hatred. As Hypatia was returning home from one of her lectures, she was seized by a mob of these violent devotees, who dragged her through the streets into one of the churches, murdered her, stripped off all her clothing, tore her limb from limb, and burned the mangled remains to ashes. Theodosius the Younger, who was then emperor, either did not dare to punish this terrible outrage, or he had no will to do it.

The decrees of the church and the laws of the state. manifested the same hostility toward the vanquished religion. Whoever allowed his daughter to marry a Pagan priest was expelled from the Christian church, and not permitted to receive the sacrament even in the hour of death. When Justinian became emperor, in the year five hundred and twenty-seven, he appointed a bishop to hunt out all who were suspected of secret attachment to the old worship. Their silence was not sufficient. They were ordered to make ready for baptism or death. Seventy thousand were discovered; mostly in the Asiatic provinces. They were immediately converted into as good Christians, as outward ordinances could make them. Photius, a man of patrician rank, stabbed himself rather than submit to the enforced ceremony. The emperor caused his corpse to be ignominiously exposed.

JEWS.

It is not recorded that any dispute ever arose between the Apostles and their countrymen whether Christ was the Logos; or concerning the question of his divinity, in any form. The only complaints which Jews brought against the disciples of Jesus were, that they ate forbidden articles of food with foreigners; that they profaned the temple by bringing Greeks into it; and that they admitted the uncircumcised to associate with them, even in their worship. The Psalmist says: "By the word of the Lord were the heavens made;" and similar expressions abound in the Old Testament. But Jews never entertained the idea that this Messiah was to be an impersonation of the Word; and the idea that God could have a son was very shocking to their established mode of thought. Eusebius says: "If any Jew be asked whether God has a Logos, he will say, 'Certainly.' Every Jew will say that He has one or more of them. But if asked whether God has a Son, he will deny it." Elsewhere he says: "If any one suppose that the Son is a mere *word;* quiescent in the Father when He is quiescent, but active when He made the world; resembling the word of man, which is quiescent when we are silent, but active when we speak, it is evident that he interprets according to human reason, as the Jews do, and that he denies the true Son of God." The Rabbi Jonathan says: "The Messiah and Moses will appear at the end of the world, one in the desert, the other at Rome; and the Logos will march between them."

As soon as the doctrine of the Messiah's divinity was made known to the Jews, they controverted it most strenuously, as an idea totally at variance with their strict belief in the unity of God. Basnage, in his History of the Jews, says: "Christians and Jews separated at the second step in religion. Having adored together one God, absolutely perfect, immediately afterward, they find the abyss of the Trinity, which separates them entirely. The Jew considers three persons as three Gods; and this shocks him." This obstruction in the path was probably the principal reason why so much fewer Jews than Pagans were converted. The following remarks, by Herbanus, a learned Jew, in the fifth century, in controversy with a Christian bishop, express the substance of what they always said on the subject: "The prophet Moses pronounces

a dreadful curse upon the children of Israel, if we should
ever receive any other God beside the God of our fathers.
God himself strictly orders us, by the prophets, saying:
'There shall be no other God in thee, nor shalt thou worship a strange God.' Why, then, should you make any
words on the subject?" "It is grievous to me to desert
the God of the Law, whom you also acknowledge to be the
true God, and to worship a younger god, not knowing
whence he sprung." "Whence do you derive your faith
in the Father, Son, and Spirit, and introduce three strange
gods?" "Where did any prophet foretell that the Messiah
was to be a God-man, as you say?" "Why did not God
order Moses and the prophets to believe in the Father,
Son, and Holy Spirit, but yourselves only, who have lately
discovered it, as you pretend?" Another of their writers
says: "Moses commands to worship only one God. He
makes no second like him, or unlike him, as you have
done. If you can produce a single expression in Moses to
this purpose, do it. That saying of his, 'A prophet shall
the Lord your God raise up unto you, of your brethren, like
unto me, hear him,' is not said of the son of Mary. But
even if this be granted to you, Moses says the prophet
shall be like himself, not like God; a man, not a deity."
What Isaiah prophesied concerning Emanüel, which means
God with us, they interpreted by their own ancient custom
of giving significant names to children. Eusebius says:
"The Jews teach, I know not how, that all those things
were said of a common child." Those who adopted the
Cabalistic idea that Adam Kadman created the world, that
he appeared as the earthly Adam, and would again appear
as the Messiah, seem to have been a small minority,
both among Jews and the Christianized Jews called
Ebionites.

To meet the objections started by their opponents, the
Christian Fathers said God spoke to his Logos, when he
said: "Let us make man after our own image." But Jews
replied that God then addressed his conclave of ministering
angels. In answer to their demand for proofs from the

Old Testament, the Fathers said that the Godhead of the Messiah was predicted, but purposely veiled. Eusebius says: "The prophets, who foretold concerning Christ, concealed their treasure in obscure words." Epiphanius says: "Adam, being a prophet, knew the Father, Son, and Spirit, and knew that the Father spake to the Son, when he said, 'Let *us* make man.'" Chrysostom says: "When Moses said the world was made by God, not by Christ, he accommodated himself to the stupidity of his hearers; and justly, because it would not have been proper to give those meat, who had need to be fed with milk." It was generally maintained that the doctrine of the Trinity was hidden from the Jews, on account of the danger of their relapsing into their old tendencies to worship other gods than Jehovah. The Fathers said it was for this reason that Christ and his Apostles purposely concealed it. Eusebius says: "The multitude of the Jews were kept in ignorance of this hidden mystery, when they were taught to believe in one God only, on account of their being frequently drawn into idolatry. They did not know that God was the Father of the only begotten Son. This mystery was reserved for the Gentile church, out of special favour to them."

The virginity of Mary was likewise opposed to Jewish habits of thought and feeling. Their theories concerning the creation of man did not recognize an eternal principle of Matter, the origin of evil. Consequently, they did not hold the human body in contempt. The mother of the largest family was the woman most honoured among them; and there are indications that the idea of giving birth to the long-expected Messiah was a cherished hope among Hebrew women. Learned Rabbis denied that Isaiah predicted the Messiah would be born of a virgin. They said the Hebrew word thus translated in the Septuagint simply signified a young woman. They ridiculed what some of the Christian Fathers said concerning the miraculous birth of Christ, differing from all other births. They asked: "If this were so, why was Mary represented as going to the temple to make offerings for purification?"

If the warfare had been confined to words, it would have been better and more creditable to both parties. But unfortunately many causes were at work to increase the hostility always felt by a long-established church toward a non-conforming sect. After the introduction of Christianity, Jews began to attract more attention from other nations than they had previously done. This was partly owing to the fact that they had grown with the growth of the world. They formed a large, wealthy, and enterprising class in all the principal cities of the Roman empire, and there were many men among them who commanded respect by their learning and their virtues. In the early times, Jews had little zeal for making converts. But intercourse with foreigners, and the rapid spread of Christianity, roused in them a spirit of proselytism; and at a time when the Pagan religion was undermined by general scepticism, some devout minds were solemnly impressed with sublime passages from the Hebrew Scriptures, and with the worship of one God, of whom no image was allowed to be made. In large cities considerable numbers of the populace were converted by Jewish magicians, called Gœtæ, whose wonderful skill they believed to be miraculous. The later Jewish writers were accustomed to trace the miracles of Christ to magic. They said he had power over Evil Spirits, because he had learned the secret and ineffable name of God, expressed only by a mysterious sign, and had dared to utter it.

After our era, Jews were brought into notice in one way peculiarly annoying to themselves. They were constantly identified with the seceders, whom they so much abhorred; for when Christianity began to be a troublesome element in Roman affairs, magistrates regarded the sect as merely a peculiarly refractory portion of the Jews. This induced a habit of mutually vilifying each other, to repel the charges brought by Romans. The breach widened continually, and when Christianity became the paramount influence of the state, Jews were deprived of the protection and toleration they had enjoyed under emperors of the old religion. Constantine, in his edict concerning the observ- ance of Easter, declares that it was unsuited to the dignity of the church to follow "that most hateful of all people, the Jews," in their celebration of the Passover. He enacted that if the Jews should stone a Christian convert, or other-wise endanger his life, all concerned in it should be burned alive. He prohibited all Christians from becoming Jews, under pain of arbitrary punishment. He forbade Jews to hold Christian slaves; assigning as a reason that those who had been made free by the blood of Christ ought not to be slaves to the murderers of the prophets, and of the Son of God. They were constrained to take upon them-selves certain public offices, which were burdensome and avoided by others. Some degree of justice was, however, observed. The right of Roman citizenship was not taken from them, they chose their own officers to regulate their markets, and their Patriarchs and Rabbins were exempted from military duty and civil offices, the same as the Chris-tian Archbishops and their clergy.

In Spain it was customary for landholders and peasants to keep a joyous festival in the spring time, and at the gathering of the harvest. Many of them were Jews; and according to the devout custom of their nation, before they partook of the banquet, they prayed to God that even in the land of the stranger he would send sunshine and dews to produce abundant crops. A Council held at Illiberis forbade Jews to assemble with Christians on such occa-sions, lest the blessings pronounced by them should render unavailing the powerful benedictions of the church.

Constantius passed laws still more severe than those of his father. The Jews were very heavily taxed and bur-thened in every way. They were forbidden, under pain of death, to hold Christian slaves, or marry Christian wo-men. The old edict of Adrian, forbidding them to approach Jerusalem, was renewed. A painful pilgrimage it must have been, had it been allowed; for their Holy Mountain lay desolate, while the glittering cross, surmounting the splendid church on Mount Calvary, might be seen from afar. Under the short administration of Julian all these oppressive enactments were abolished, and he proposed to rebuild their temple, as has been already stated; but Jovian restored the old state of things.

These persecutions of course excited bitter animosity in the objects of them. When disturbances occurred, the Jewish population, especially in reckless Alexandria, rushed to the aid of Pagans, or Arians, and often committed frightful excesses. Christians availed themselves of every pretext to insult, harrass, and plunder the Jews; and Jews lost no opportunity to retaliate.

After the time of Jovian, several of the emperors were inclined to restrain the animosity of the bishops toward the Jews, who were everywhere a numerous and useful class of citizens. Maximus commanded the Christians to rebuild at their own expense a synagogue which they had wantonly destroyed at Rome. Theodosius the Great gave the same orders concerning a synagogue demolished at Callinicum. The outrage occurred at a great distance from the jurisdiction of Ambrose, but he felt called upon to remonstrate with the emperor concerning the intended restitution. He expressed disapprobation of such acts as setting fire to synagogues, but asserted that no bishop could conscientiously contribute anything toward building a place of worship for Jews. He also said, somewhat inconsistently: "I myself would willingly assume the guilt, and say, I have set this synagogue in flames; at least in so far that I have urged on all; that there might be no place left in which Christ is denied." From the pulpit, he preached in the same strain he had written. The emperor, who was at Milan, yielded his sense of justice to the zeal of the bishop, and the Jews were left without a synagogue. But he recognized the right of their Patriarchs to judge and punish members of their own community, according to their own laws, and Roman magistrates were forbidden to interfere in such cases. When near the close of his life, and away from the influence of Ambrose, he issued an edict of toleration to the Jews, and ordered that all who pillaged or destroyed their synagogues should be punished according to the discretion of the magistrate.

Where two classes of people were so hostile to each other, occasions were never wanting for a quarrel. Brawls in the streets were continually occurring between Jews and Christians, upon the slightest provocation; and Jews, being the party out of power, were not very likely to obtain a candid hearing. At a place not far from Antioch, some Jews in a state of intoxication manifested their rancorous animosity in a manner they would not have ventured to do while sober. They mocked at Christ in the public streets, and erected a cross, on which they fastened a Christian boy, whom they scourged till he died. They were rigorously punished; but the transaction deepened popular hatred of the Israelites. Some years afterward, a mob of Christians plundered a synagogue at Antioch. The Roman Governor represented the case to the emperor, Theodosius the Younger, who commanded the clergy to make restitution; but they appealed to Simeon Stylites, who remonstrated with the emperor. Theodosius could not resist the intercession of such a celebrated saint. He granted his request, and wrote him a letter soliciting his prayers, addressed to the "Holy Martyr in the Air." The magistrate, who had exerted himself to preserve justice from being warped by intolerance, was removed from office.

In the excitable city of Alexandria, where Jews were always numerous, commotions were more frequent than elsewhere. At the theatre, a quarrel arose between some of the Hebrew population and one of the partisans of Cyril the archbishop. Cyril threatened to make all the Jews responsible, if such scenes were not prevented. This threat excited the Hebrew populace, who well knew that he always availed himself of every pretext for persecution. They raised a false alarm that the church was on fire in the night, and when the Christians rushed out, they fell upon them and killed many. The next morning, the archbishop, without waiting for any examination into the affair, or any warrant from the civil authorities, led on an army of monks to attack the Jewish citizens, who were unarmed, and not aware of danger. Synagogues were demolished, houses pillaged, many Jews slaughtered, and all the rest driven out of the city. There were forty thousand Jews in Alexandria, and a large proportion of them were wealthy. Orestes, the Governor, as a matter of policy, wished that such a large and valuable class of citizens should feel security in the possession of their property. He accordingly represented to the emperor that compensation ought to be made for the extensive robberies committed, and the buildings destroyed. Five hundred monks attacked him, as he was riding through the street. In vain he protested that he was a Catholic Christian. One of the great stones they hurled at him, made the blood gush from his head, and nearly cost him his life. He was generally popular, and the citizens rose in his defence. The monks were driven back to their deserts, and the man who had thrown the stone was put to death. But Cyril caused his body to be taken up, and accorded to him all the honours of a martyr, who had fallen in defence of the church.

Justinian, who was a great persecutor of Jews and heretics, passed laws more severe than any of his predecessors. He forbade the reading of the Talmud, and compelled Jews to keep their Passover on the same day that Christians observed Easter.

A similar state of feeling existed between Christians and Samaritans. On Easter Sunday the Samaritans, for some unexplained reason, broke into the church in their city of Sichem, killed a great many people, and cut off several fingers from the hands of the bishop, who held fast to the consecrated bread, he was just about to administer in the sacrament. It was wrenched from him, and treated with the utmost fury and contempt. The bishop fled, and sought redress from the emperor Zeno, showing his mangled hands, and quoting the prophecy of Jesus to the woman of Samaria: "The time shall come when ye shall worship God, neither on this mountain, nor yet at Jerusalem." The Samaritans had built no temple on Mount Gerizim; but the ancient veneration for the holy place continued, and on its summit they offered their devotions. At the request of the bishop, the emperor not only severely punished the Samaritans for the outrages they had committed, but ordered them to be expelled from Mount Gerizim, and caused a chapel to the Virgin Mary to be erected on its summit. It was necessary to build a strong wall round it, and place an armed guard to watch it. A small party of Samaritans clambered up the precipitous side of the mountain and slew the guard.

Justinian passed very severe laws against the Samaritans. They were deprived of all dignities, and not allowed to hold any office whatsoever, civil or military; "lest they might have opportunity of judging and punishing Christians; even bishops." These stringent measures produced furious insurrections, in which many Christians were killed, and their churches destroyed. The Samaritans were finally expelled from Sichem, their capital city, and forbidden to enter it again. In litigation, where one or both parties were Christians, the testimony of a Jew or a Samaritan was inadmissible. Those who adhered to their religion were not allowed to inherit property. To provide for cases where the wife became a convert to Christianity, while the husband remained a Jew, or a Samaritan, it was enacted that the true religion should rule. The unbelieving father was bound to maintain his children, but the believing mother was invested with authority to regulate their education and marriages. These laws had the intended effect of causing many of the Samaritans to submit to baptism.

When there was great competition among conflicting sects to increase their number of proselytes, when converts were rewarded with worldly advantages, and driven by legal disabilities, frequent deceptions were the inevitable result. Those among the Jews, who had no sincere reverence for any religion, made a traffic of being baptized in several places, managing to receive banquets and presents for their trouble. This was carried to such an extent, that it became necessary to pass laws that no Jew should be

baptized without previous inquiry into his character, and
serving a period of probation.   An instance is recorded of
the detection of one of these hypocrites by miracle. When
he would have entered the pool, the water recoiled from
him, as if conscious that he had often made traffic of the
ceremony.

The Jewish population always sided with the Arians in
times of disturbance, and when Arians were in power,
they always protected the Jews.   This probably arose
from mutual sympathy, growing out of the fact that both
were persecuted by the dominant church. How much evil
might have been averted, if Christians had obeyed the
gentle precepts of their founder, is proved by the fact that
both Jews and Pagans were prompt to manifest gratitude
toward those who treated them with justice and moderation. The published letters of Sidonius Apollinaris, Bishop
of Clermont, contain several epistles from eminent Jews,
full of friendly feeling. Basil the Great aimed at impartial
justice in the administration of his episcopal office, and in
debate with theological opponents, he was always courteous. Hilary, Bishop of Poictiers, also manifested a candid
and kindly disposition.   At the funeral of both these prelates there was a great concourse of Pagans and Jews, and
Israelites mingled their voices with Christians in Psalms
of lamentation.

· HERETICS.

The spirit manifested toward Christians, who departed
in any respect from the Catholic standard, was hardly less
bitter than that exhibited toward Pagans and Jews.   Various disputes, which germinated in the Nestorian controversy, long continued to divide and subdivide the church.
The Asiatic and Egyptian clergy were generally followers
of Eutyches, called Monophysites; while the Western
clergy were strenuous advocates for the decree of the
Council at Chalcedon, which condemned Eutyches.   In
four hundred eighty-two, five hundred assembled bishops
decided that the decrees of the Synod of Chalcedon might

be supported by bloodshed, if necessary. There were a multitude of monks in Jerusalem, who espoused the Monophysite cause, and pillaged and murdered their opponents. The sepulchre of Christ was stained with blood shed by furious combatants; one side maintaining that he had two natures completely united in one *nature*, the other that he had two natures completely united in one *person*. The Bishop of Alexandria was constantly guarded by two thousand soldiers; and for two years he contended with the people of that city, who were violently opposed to the decree at Chalcedon. At last, they besieged him in his cathedral, murdered him, burnt his corpse, and scattered the ashes to the winds, to prevent his relics from being honoured. Many thousands were slain in consequence of this theological splitting of a hair. Such a state of excitement existed, that the smallest spark was sufficient to kindle a devouring flame. The Apocalypse of John represents angels and cherubim continually singing before the throne of God, "Holy, holy, holy, Lord God Almighty!" As this was supposed to express the Trinity, it became customary, in the fifth century, to sing this in the churches, under the name of the Trisagion, Thrice Holy. A Monophysite bishop, in his zeal to represent the one nature of Christ as God, added the words, "who was crucified for us." This practice was copied at Constantinople and some other places. The opposite party regarded it as a blasphemous and dangerous heresy to represent God as crucified. The emperor Anastasius took one side, and the Patriarch of Constantinople took the other. Two adverse choirs in the cathedral sang the Trisagion; one without the additional phrase, the other with it. They strove to drown each other's voices, and when their lungs were fatigued, they attacked each other with clubs and stones. A mob of men, women, and children, led on by an army of monks, went about the streets, shouting and fighting. The statues of the emperor were broken, he hid himself to save his life, and was finally compelled to abdicate. Sixty-five thousand Christians were slaugh-

M*

tered before the insurrection was quelled. This was the first war between Christians on account of theological differences.

In the first half of the sixth century, a complete separation took place between the Catholic Church and the Monophysites. They formed independent churches in Egypt, Syria, and Mesopotamia, and appointed their own patriarchs. They soon divided into sects. Controversies arose among them whether the body of Christ was created or uncreated; whether it was corruptible or incorruptible. Some of them arrived at the conclusion that the three persons of the Trinity were three gods. This sect, called Tritheists, were rejected as heretics by the Monophysites, as well as by their opponents.

In connection with the discussion concerning two *natures*, arose the query whether Christ had two *wills*. Believers in one will were called Monothelites, from Greek words having that meaning. Many of the Eastern clergy favoured that view, but considered controversy on the subject unnecessary and injudicious. The clergy at Rome were displeased with this advice, and pronounced the doctrine of the Monothelites heretical. Bishops were summoned to assemble in that city. They signed a sentence of condemnation on St. Peter's tomb, and rendered it more emphatic by mingling sacramental wine with the ink. After prolonged controversy, it was finally settled that two wills, divine and human, were perfectly harmonized in Christ.

The controversy with Macedonius likewise left a wake behind it. The equality of the Holy Spirit with the two other persons of the Trinity was settled by decree of council; but new discussions arose concerning what was called "the procession of the Holy Ghost." Scripture declared that the Spirit was sent by Christ; which led some to infer that he proceeded from the Son, as well as from the Father. Others rejected this as involving the idea of double parentage, and maintained that he proceeded from the Father only. In five hundred eighty-six, the Council of Toledo added three words to the creed established by

the Council of Constantinople, and made it declare "the
Holy Ghost proceeded from the Father, *and the Son.*" This
gave great offence to the churches in the East. Rome decided that "the Holy Spirit is eternally from the Father
and the Son; and he proceeds from them both eternally,
as from a single principle, and by one single procession."
The churches in Constantinople persevered in maintaining
a different opinion on this subtle question, and the contest
ended in complete separation from the Catholic church.

GREGORY THE GREAT.

It was in this state of things, that Gregory the First,
commonly called the Great, became Patriarch of Rome in
the year five hundred ninety. His father was a Roman
senator, and his mother was a woman of uncommon endowments. She was a devout Christian, and watched
most . carefully over his youthful education. Her pious
tendencies are indicated by the fact that while he was yet
a babe, she dreamed the holy hermit Anthony appeared to
her, and foretold that her son would be a bishop.

Gregory commenced his career as a lawyer with distinguished success. He became a member of the senate, and
was employed in various other services of honour and
trust. He was Prefect, or Governor of Rome, and resigned
the office after having fulfilled its duties with great ability
and integrity, for twelve years. Satiated with worldly success, his spirit craved something more satisfactory and
abiding; and he longed for religious seclusion. On the
death of his father, he inherited a large fortune, which he
immediately devoted to pious and charitable purposes.
His paternal mansion, on the Celian Hill, was converted
into a monastery, and hospital for the poor, dedicated to
the Apostle Andrew. A small cell was reserved for himself, and thither he retired from the world, taking upon
himself the usual vows of poverty, chastity, and obedience.
His time was divided between prayer, devotional studies,
and attention to the poor. When a terrible pestilence

raged at Rome, he devoted himself most assiduously to the
care of the needy and the suffering. The Pope, Pelagius
Second, employed him as his secretary; and when he died,
the popular voice immediately named Gregory as his successor. He wrote to the emperor, intreating him not to
ratify the choice of the people; it being his earnest wish
to devote himself to the quietude of religious seclusion.
Finding that his election was confirmed, he fled from the
city, and hid himself in a cave. Tradition says those who
were sent to search for him were guided to the place of his
concealment by a celestial light. He was brought back
and solemnly installed in the high dignity of the Roman
Pontiff, with far more power and splendour than had ever
belonged to the old Pagan office of Pontifex Maximus.

Gregory was the first Pope who assumed the title "Servant of the servants of God." He discharged the duties
of his elevated station with an unusual degree of humanity
and wisdom, if we judge him by the standard of that age.
When the Jews in Sardinia appealed to him, in consequence of some outrages they had suffered, he commanded
that the synagogues, which had been taken from them and
converted into churches, should be immediately restored.
He forbade any interference with the worship of the Jews,
and severely rebuked those whose zeal led them to place
in the synagogues images of the Virgin Mary and of the
crucified Christ. At the same time, he sought to proselyte
them by a process more kindly and considerate, though it
appealed to selfish motives; he offered remission of taxes
to all converted Jews. He exerted himself to the utmost
to prevent the "cruel and impious" traffic in Christian
slaves, and to redeem from bondage to Jews or Pagans all
who were Christians, or who professed a wish to become
Christians. He advised bishops to sell the church plate,
if necessary, for this purpose, as a service well-pleasing in
the sight of God. Before he was Pope, his compassion had
been greatly excited by some young English captives offered for sale in Rome. He formed the design of going as
a missionary to England, and had in fact started on his

journey; but his services were so much needed at home, and he was so much beloved by the people, that they induced the Patriarch of Rome to send after him, and forbid his departure. He returned accordingly; but the sight of those beautiful youths, so desolate and sad in the markets of a foreign land, made an impression on his soul which he never forgot. It was one of the earliest acts of his administration to send missionaries to England. His zeal for the general dissemination of Christianity was very great. He not only sent missionaries to neighbouring nations, but to Huns, Bactrians, Persians, Medes, East Indians, and Chinese. He displayed similar zeal for the conversion of Jews and heretics, and for the advancement of monasticism. He rigidly enforced the celibacy of the clergy; a regulation which still continued to meet with a good deal of opposition. Its tendency was to guard the wealth of the church; for married bishops and priests would have been likely to use the ecclesiastical revenues for the benefit of their own families; and the effect would have been, in those times, to establish an hereditary priesthood. Gregory not only protected the wealth of the church, but greatly increased it. The distinctness and prominence which he gave to the doctrine concerning Purgatory, proved a valuable source of revenue. The idea that the soul, after death, went to some place where it was purified by fire, was a feature common to the oriental religions, and the Gnostic systems, and was also introduced into Platonism. Origen, and Clement of Alexandria, thought it was proved by the Christian Scriptures. Most of the Fathers so construed the third chapter of Paul's first Epistle to the Corinthians. That prayers, oblations, and penances of the living could affect the condition of the dead, was another idea which pervaded the oriental religions; particularly the Braminical and the Buddhist. The early Christian Fathers also inculcated it as a duty to offer prayers and oblations for the deceased; on the ground that such ceremonies were a benefit to their souls. This conviction was strengthened by the feeling that though original sin was washed away by baptism, penance was required for sins committed after baptism. Gregory the Great defined these doctrines with more precision; and from that time henceforth they were invested with accessories both terrifying and attractive to the imagination. Purgatory was represented as a region on the borders of hell, where souls not good enough to enter heaven were detained, for a longer or shorter time, to be purified by suffering. One spark of its fire was said to cause more agony than any bodily pain that could be endured, or conceived of, in this world. Prayers offered for the dead, and donations given to churches and monasteries in their behalf, would lessen the intensity and shorten the term of this probationary suffering. Priests were paid for reciting these prayers; and as tenderness for the departed, whether founded in affection, remorse, or pride of family, is one of the strongest feelings in the human heart, masses repeated for the dead became a source of great emolument. Gregory's administration was marked by increasing splendour in the decoration of churches, the richness of ecclesiastical costume, and the pomp of ceremonies and festivals. He revised the ritual of worship, and arranged the liturgy as it has ever since been preserved. He introduced chants sung by male voices in unison, and himself trained choristers to perform them. The voices of the whole congregation had heretofore joined in the music of the church, but it was thenceforth intrusted to trained bands of singers. These Gregorian chants, supposed to have been formed on the model of the old Greek chorus, with more complex modulation, remained for centuries the orthodox standard for all church music, from which it was considered a sort of heresy to deviate. The pomp and ceremony thus introduced, and the ecclesiastical authority established over the minutest forms, had a great effect to dazzle and overawe the ignorant; especially barbarian converts, to whom the Pope did indeed appear like God's vicegerent upon earth, and his attendant bishops, priests, deacons, and choristers, like so many ministering angels. This increase of Roman greatness was by no means pleasing to many of the Eastern churches. In fact, the splendid pontificate of Gregory was a constant struggle for power with his competitor, John, Patriarch of Constantinople.

But if his ambition was great, his benevolence was perhaps even greater. He was truly a kind shepherd to the poor of his flock. When told that a beggar had died of hunger in the streets of Rome, he seemed to consider himself personally responsible. He imposed penance on himself, and for several days refrained from the administration of his priestly office, as one unworthy to appear before the Lord. It is related of him that when he was only a monk, a beggar presented himself at the gate of the monastery. Being relieved, he came again and again. At last, Gregory had nothing to give him but a silver porringer, in which his mother had sent some nourishment to sustain him during his penances. He gave that also to the beggar. After he became Pope, it was his daily custom to invite twelve poor men to sup with him. One night, he observed that thirteen were at the table. When the steward was asked the reason of this, he replied that there were but twelve. Gregory inquired no further; but after supper, he privately asked the unbidden guest who he was. He answered: "I am the beggar, whom thou didst formerly relieve so often at the monastery. I am now called The Wonderful; and whatsoever thou shalt ask of God, through me, thou shalt obtain." Then the charitable Pope knew that he had entertained Christ.

Innumerable miracles are recorded of him. His Secretary declared that while he was writing, he had often seen the Holy Ghost perched on his shoulder in the form of a dove. Once, when a man was present in the church, who doubted that the bread and wine were really changed into the body and blood of Christ, Gregory prayed that he might be convinced; whereupon, Jesus himself descended upon the altar, with his cross and crown of thorns.

Gregory died at sixty-four years of age, fourteen years

after he was chosen Pope. He suffered much from physical infirmities, said to have been induced by severe fasts and vigils, while he was a monk. He left numerous writings, which have been frequently published. A book of Dialogues, written at the end of the sixth century, has been ascribed to him; but many suppose the sanction of his name was assumed without authority. These Dialogues describe·monks in Italy as curing all manner of diseases; walking on the water as freely as on dry land; turning rivers out of their course; suspending the arm of an executioner in mid air, so that he was unable to lower it to behead a Christian; replenishing vessels of wine and oil miraculously; and having pieces of gold, fresh as if just from the mint, dropped into their laps from heaven.

SLAVERY.

Slaves in the Roman empire were those who had been taken captive in war, or poor men sold for debt. Being subject to the arbitrary will of their masters, their condition was dreadful in the extreme. Even Nero compassionated their situation so far as to forbid masters to expose their slaves to be torn by wild beasts. Adrian decreed that the master who killed a slave, except for a lawful cause, should be put to death. Antoninus Pius ordained that whoever punished a slave unreasonably should be compelled to part with him. The altars and statues of the gods, and many of the temples, were places of refuge for abused slaves, from which they could not be forced by their masters, till their complaint had been inquired into; and if they had been cruelly dealt by, they could demand to be sold to another master.

Constantine the Great passed a law that masters should not punish their slaves "except with moderation." Justinian also passed several laws restricting the power of masters. But the efforts of Christian emperors, and of the bishops, were mainly directed against Christians being held in bondage by Jews or Pagans. Constantine prohibited

Jews from holding Christian slaves, under pain of confiscation of property. This law apparently fell into disuse; for laws were subsequently passed forbidding Jews to attempt to convert their Christian slaves. A Council at Orleans in five hundred and forty, enacted that if a Christian slave was required to perform any service incompatible with his religion, and the master proceeded to punish him for disobedience, he might find an asylum in any church; that the clergy of that church were on no account to give him up, but to pay his value to the master. Another council the next year enacted that if a Christian slave, under the same circumstances, should seek the protection of any Christian whatsoever, he was bound to shelter him, and to redeem him at a fair price. Any Jew, who proselyted a Christian slave by promises of freedom, forfeited all his slaves. The slave, who had agreed to such a condition, was pronounced unworthy of freedom, and the contract with him was rendered null and void.

Jews, being more engaged in merchandize than any other class of people, became the principal traders in slaves, which were exchanged for other commodities. Gregory the Great was much troubled by the fact that Christians often came into the possession of Jews by this process. He ordained that no Jew or Pagan who wished to embrace Christianity should be held in bondage by any but a Christian. If a slave expressed such a wish within three months after he was bought, the purchaser was obliged to accept the market price offered by any Christian. If he was kept longer than three months, he was free without being paid for; it being evident that the Jewish slave-merchant kept him for his own service, not for sale. The Council of Macon, in five hundred eighty-one, forbade Jews to hold Christian slaves at all, or to sell Christian slaves to any but Christians. Notwithstanding the remonstrances of bishops and the decrees of councils, the cruel traffic continued to prevail extensively. Different provinces were under different jurisdictions; many of the clergy could not read the decisions of councils; and those who were acquainted with such decrees, sometimes cared more for pecuniary profit, than for humanity to Christian brethren. In a Council held at Toledo, in six hundred fifty-five, complaint was made that "even the clergy, in defiance of the law, sold captives to Jews and Pagans."

It has already been stated how great sympathy was expressed in the churches for Christians carried into captivity, and how general was the custom of raising contributions, and even of selling the church-plate, for their relief. But the Jews of old would sell any into foreign bondage except those of their own faith; and Christian humanity was limited by a similar theological boundary. No decrees were passed prohibiting either Jews or Christians from holding in bondage those who were *not* Christians, or to prevent Christians from owning each other. The Council at Chalcedon, in the middle of the fifth century, forbade convents to receive slaves without the consent of their masters; and threatened excommunication for the offence. The reason assigned was "that the name of God may not be blasphemed;" that is, that the church should not be accused of exciting insubordination. Basil the Great made it a rule that slaves, who sought refuge in the monasteries he founded, should be sent back with an admonition, unless their masters had ordered them to do something contrary to the law of God.

After the Pagan temples and statues were destroyed, slaves, who had been accustomed to fly to them for safety in emergencies, began to take refuge in churches. During the reign of Theodosius Second, several slaves in Constantinople sought shelter in the sanctuary of the principal church, to escape from the wrath of a cruel master. There, for several days in succession, worship was disturbed by attempts to regain them. When, at last, resort was had to force, the slaves, in their desperation, killed one of the ecclesiastics, wounded another, and then put an end to their own lives. This and similar occurrences led to the enactment of a law to protect the inviolability of church asylums; passed in four hundred thirty-one. It was then enacted that not only the altar, but whatever formed any part of the church buildings, should be an inviolable place of refuge. It was forbidden on pain of death to remove forcibly those who fled thither unarmed. When a slave sought shelter there, the clergy were ordered not to delay longer than a day to give information of it; but the master was required to grant full forgiveness, and promise to receive him back without inflicting any punishment. Whoever violated such a promise was expelled from communion. Excommunication from all the churches was likewise the punishment decreed by several councils, for the crime of killing a slave.

Though Christian emperors and bishops enacted no laws which indicate the recognition of the institution itself as a crime, indications abound that such a conviction pressed on the individual consciences of Christians. Manumissions at baptism were very frequent; still more frequent at the approach of death. A latent consciousness of wrong is betrayed by the following form in common use on such occasions: "Almighty God having blessed us in our day with health of body, we ought, for the salvation of the soul, to turn our thoughts somewhat to the cutting off from the number of our sins. Therefore, in the name of God, for the good of my soul, and redemption from my sins, I have set at liberty my slave," etc. How boldly some of the Fathers rebuked the iniquitous system has been already shown by extracts from their writings. A similar spirit was manifested by the best of the monks. Nilus, who in the fifth century retired from a dignified station in Constantinople to a monastery on Mount Sinai, in his writings especially inculcates compassion for slaves, "whom a mastership of violence, destroying the fellowship of nature, has converted into tools." A monk named Eloi, called "the Glory of his Age," was in the habit of attending all the slave-sales he could hear of, buying up large numbers of them and setting them free. He then offered them the choice of entering a monastery, or of returning to the countries whence they had been brought. The Abbot Isidore of Pelusium, writing to a master in behalf of a slave who had begged for his intercession, says: "I did not suppose that a man who loves Christ, who knows the grace which has made all men free, could still hold a slave." The celebrated Benedict, a truly religious man, established the following rule for his monasteries: "The Abbot shall not prefer one to another, except for obedience and faithfulness. He shall not rank one born free above one who was a slave before his conversion; for whether bond or free, we are all one in Christ Jesus. With God there is no respect of persons." The Abbot Theodore, in his will, left this injunction to his monastery: "Never make a slave of man, who is made in the image of God; either for your private service, or for the monastery, or for the cultivation of the fields." A great many slaves became monks, and many were chosen bishops. It was requisite that they should be previously emancipated; but in general this was easily accomplished; for it was deemed a sort of impiety to place any obstacles in the way of a slave, who wished to devote himself to a religious life. Perhaps this class of people were found to be a useful check upon the pride of nobles. At all events, there was in many portions of the empire an increasing predilection for ordaining bishops who had been slaves. The Archbishop of Treves, in the ninth century, declares that a large proportion of the bishops were of servile extraction, and commonly took sides against the nobility. Some remonstrated with the bishops for habitually giving such candidates a preference, and felt obliged to quote, in favour of the free-born, the declaration that "God is no respecter of persons."

CHURCHES, IMAGES, AND SAINTS.

The churches were not only asylums for slaves, but for debtors, who could thus gain time for the bishops to interfere in their behalf, or raise money for their relief. In times of invasion, or civil war, the conquered took refuge there. Ambrose protected multitudes from the sword, during the frequent revolutions in the Western part of the empire. The noble-hearted Chrysostom, always ready to shelter the unfortunate, extended the powerful arm of the church over every victim of arbitrary violence, whether patrician or peasant. When Alaric the Goth captured Rome, the churches of Peter and Paul, and the chapels, were places of universal refuge. Amid the general uproar, not a single Gothic soldier touched those consecrated spots; on the contrary, they themselves conveyed thither many women, children, and aged people, whose helplessness excited their compassion. This was the more commendable, because the Goths were Arians, and the churches in Rome were Athanasian.

The privilege of asylum was of course abused, as the increasing number of churches rendered sanctuaries easy of access for criminals of all sorts; and the clergy must have been more than human, if they had not made the great power, which this custom conferred upon them, sometimes subservient to purposes of ambition or avarice. The Pagans had made great complaints of justice defeated, or evaded, by criminals taking refuge in their temples. In process of time, similar complaints were made concerning the abuse of sanctuary in the churches; but in the latter case, the evil was more extensive; for a single city in Italy contained more asylums for criminals and debtors, than there had formerly been in the whole of Greece.

The earliest Christians met in each other's houses for devotional exercises. When Gentile converts became numerous, they had, in some places, the use of domestic chapels, belonging to wealthy proselytes, who had previously devoted them to the worship of Pagan deities. Sometimes they assembled in the woods, or at the burial-place of martyrs, whose tombs, covered with red cloth, in memory of their blood, served as altars on which to place the bread and wine of the eucharist. If there were no such tombs in the vicinity, moveable boxes, covered with cloth, were often used for the same purpose. When persecution raged, the faithful met together at night in caves, or in the

large subterranean burial-places called catacombs. Under
the emperors who tolerated Christianity, churches began
to be built, but in very simple style. The father of
Gregory of Nazianzen, though bishop of only a small diocese, built one at his own expense. They generally faced
the east, as was the custom with the temples of all nations.
Jewish converts retained their national dislike for sculpture
and painting, always closely associated in their minds with
the idea of idolatry; and the early Christian Fathers imbibed a similar feeling, in the course of their efforts to overthrow a system of worship abounding with pictures and
statues. Epiphanius, who was a bishop in the middle of
the fourth century, was of Jewish extraction. When he
visited Palestine, he was surprised to find a curtain hanging over the door of the church, whereon was painted a
likeness of Christ. He says: " When I saw the image of
a man hanging up in the church, contrary to the authority
of the Holy Scriptures, I immediately tore it, and advised them to use it as a winding-sheet for some poor
man's burial." The congregation being somewhat troubled
by this summary proceeding, he sent them another curtain,
but without painting. Eusebius, Bishop of Cæsarea, declared strongly against images. He says he once saw in a
woman's possession two figures, wearing the philosopher's
robe, which she said were Christ and Paul. But he made
her give them up; lest it might seem that Christians, like
idolaters, carried about an image of their God. Tertullian
mentions pictures of Christ upon communion cups, as
though it were the custom in his day. These cups were
of various materials, according to the wealth of the church;
of wood, crystal, onyx, silver, and in some cases gold.
The most common representations on them were the Crucified Jesus, and the Good Shepherd, carrying a lamb on
his shoulders. On the walls of an ancient cemetery near
Rome, is an ill-drawn figure, with short robe and sandals,
his arms outstretched, in the act of prayer. There is a
glory round his head, and above it the inscription, Paulus
Apostolos, the Apostle Paul. It is supposed to be as old

as the second or third century. The glory, or halo, with which it became customary to represent holy personages, was copied from the Pagan artists, who represented their deities crowned with rays, or the head surrounded by a luminous circle, to indicate that they dwelt in fulness of light. It is supposed that it began to be customary to paint the interior of churches with emblems, as early as the close of the third century. A cross was the most common emblem; sometimes a lamb with a cross; or a lamb standing on a mound, whence four rivers flowed, to represent the four Gospels; an anchor represented faith; the old Hindoo emblem of a triangle with an eye in the centre, was a symbol of the Trinity. At the commencement of the fourth century, a Council at Elvira forbade objects of worship to be painted on the walls. After the time of Constantine, the churches rapidly increased in number and magnificence. The columns and the pavements were of the most beautiful and highly polished marble. They contained shrines of martyrs set with precious stones, and their relics covered with rich embroidery, or cloth of gold, before which lamps of gold or silver were continually burning. The smoke of frankincense, which for ages had filled the temples of Hindostan, Egypt, Jerusalem, Greece, and Rome, now floated round the Christian altars. Marble basins filled with holy water, stood in the porch of Christian churches, to sprinkle those who entered; as was formerly the case in the vestibule of Pagan temples. Early in the fourth century, wealthy men who founded churches, introduced the custom of presenting images and pictures, in memory of some martyr or saint; as it had formerly been the custom to consecrate a statue, or a painting, to some temple, as a thank-offering for benefits received from the gods. Churches dedicated to martyrs were enriched by such gifts, more than others; on account of the cures supposed to be performed by them. Like the ancient temples of Apollo and Æsculapius, they were hung with tablets inscribed with golden letters, with pictures representing cures, and with eyes, hands, and feet, made of silver or gold. One of the earliest descriptions of Christian painting is that of the church at Nola, in Italy, built in honour of Felix, the Martyr. On the colonnades were painted passages from the history of Moses and Joshua, Ruth and Naomi, and other characters in Scripture. As little children receive ideas from pictures before they can read, so those paintings afforded some degree of instruction to the crowds of illiterate pilgrims who annually flocked to the shrine of St. Felix; for, however rude the impressions they received, they were at least a degree above the mere sensual pleasures of the banquet provided on such occasions. Gregory of Nyssa, brother of Basil the Great, describing a church where the relics of Theodorus the Martyr were deposited, says: "The artist has here shown his skill in the figures of animals, and the airy sculpture of the stone; while the painter's hand is most conspicuous in delineating the high achievements of the martyrs. The figure of Christ is also beheld looking down upon the scene." It early became a custom to have the ground plan of churches in the form of a cross. They went on increasing in magnificence and beauty, until finally a church was built over the tomb said to be St. Peter's, at Rome, the cost of which has been estimated at over forty-three millions of dollars.

The ancient Hindoos and Egyptians were accustomed to carry about with them little images and symbols of their deities, which they considered as amulets to protect them from evil. Among these symbols, the Cross of Hermes was conspicuous. Greeks and Romans never travelled by land or sea, without tying about their necks small images of the Goddess of Fortune, or of the household gods, called Lares, which represented the spirits of their good ancestors. After the time of Constantine, it became customary for Christians to wear a cross as a protection from evil. Those made of the wood of the true cross found in Mount Calvary, were, of course, believed to possess superior efficacy. The wood was cased in gold, often set with pearls or diamonds. Sometimes there was a ruby or carbuncle at each

extremity and in the centre, to denote the five bloody
wounds. In the sixth century, it became customary to
have an image of Christ embossed on the cross, which was
thus converted into a crucifix. Small images of Christ, of
his Mother, the Apostles, and the Martyrs, were also worn
about the neck, as amulets.

Not only ancient ceremonies were adopted with merely
a change of object, but in some cases the images and emblems themselves were retained, with simply a change of
name. The statue of a river-god was named the Jordan;
Orpheus with his lyre was called Christ; and the image of
Apollo was made to personate the Good Shepherd. In
the oldest pictures of the Virgin Mary, the face was covered
with a blue veil; from which it might be inferred that
they were representations of Isis, taken from Egyptian
temples, and produced under a new name. Ancient pictures of the Virgin and her Child are so much like the representations of Isis with her infant Horus, that one might
easily be mistaken for the other. It was the universal
custom to represent Pagan deities accompanied by some
emblem sacred to them, as Jupiter with his eagle, and
Minerva with her owl. In very ancient nations, as in
Egypt and Chaldea, the emblem was sometimes joined to
the deity. Thus Osiris is often represented with the head
of a hawk, and Isis with a cow's head; the hawk and the
cow being symbols consecrated to them. Among the curi-
osities dug up at Nineveh, winged animals abound, as they
did in the sculptures of Egypt; and so do human figures
with wings and with the heads of animals. Similar things
are found in the earliest specimens of Christian Art. The
prophet Ezekiel describes a vision of four living creatures
which he saw. One had the face of a man, one of a lion,
one of an ox, and one of an eagle. The Jewish Rabbins
considered them typical of the prophets Isaiah, Jeremiah,
Ezekiel, and Daniel; but Christians applied them to the
four Evangelists. In the recess over the altar, in the most
ancient Christian churches, it was common to represent a
man's head and shoulders, with wings, to indicate Matthew;

a lion's head on a man's shoulders, with wings, for Mark; the head of an ox, with wings, for Luke; and an eagle, with a glory round its head, for John. These winged animals are generally represented as holding a volume of the Gospels. In some places, John is represented with the body of a man, and the head and clawed feet of an eagle. Sometimes the four stand in a row, with human bodies, each holding a gospel in his hands; Mark with a lion's head, Luke with the head of an ox, and John with the head of an eagle. The resemblance to the Egyptian deities is very striking. In later times, artists separated the emblem from the figure, and represented Mark accompanied by a lion, Luke by an ox, and John by an eagle. In some very ancient churches, and on some of the old Christian tombs at Rome, may still be seen effigies of Peter and Paul; also on old glass lamps in the Vatican. In some cases, Christ is represented as a lamb with a glory round his head, and six sheep in a row on each side of him, to signify the twelve apostles. Sometimes he stands in the midst of the sheep, as the Good Shepherd, with a lamb in his arms. In an old Roman church, built in the sixth century, he is represented standing on the clouds, with the Book of Life in his hand, and the river Jordan flowing at his feet.

Augustine states that the form and person of Christ were entirely unknown, and painted with every variety of expression; also that there were no authentic portraits of his mother, or of the apostles. Eusebius of Cæsarea says that Abgarus, King of Edessa, in Mesopotamia, wrote to Jesus, inviting him to come and cure him of a disease; and that Jesus replied, promising to send one of his disciples to him after his ascension. For the authenticity of this correspondence, Eusebius refers to public registries in the city of Edessa, which he had himself read. The letters were regarded as genuine in his time; and it was afterward said, that with his answer Jesus sent to Abgarus a perfect likeness of his face, miraculously impressed upon a napkin. It was concealed in a niche of a wall, whence it was brought out by a bishop, early in the sixth century. It was regarded as a divine protection to the city. Some very old pictures of Christ have been found in ancient cemeteries; but they merely embody the ideas formed of his character. The hair is parted in the middle of the head, and falls in long masses over the shoulders. The expression of the face is mild, serious, and plaintive.

Lucian, the Pagan, mockingly describes Paul, as " the bald-headed Galilean with a hook-nose." Ancient traditions of the Fathers also describe him as a small thin man, with bald head, aquiline nose, high forehead, sparkling eyes, and long flowing beard. They describe Peter as a robust old man, with broad forehead, large features, fearless expression, thick gray hair, and short curly beard. The oldest pictures extant are according to these traditions.

After the Council of Ephesus had anathematized Nestorius, theological zeal multiplied images and pictures of the Virgin, bearing the inscription " Mother of God." There is no evidence that the church recognized them as sacred before the beginning of the sixth century. Their general diffusion and popularity throughout the Western churches dates from the time of Gregory the Great. On a tablet in the church of St. Dominick, at Rome, is the following inscription : " Here, at the high altar, is preserved that image of the most blessed Mary, which, being delineated by St. Luke, the Evangelist, received its colours and forms divinely. This is that image with which St. Gregory the Great, as a suppliant, purified Rome; and the pestilence being dispelled, the angel messenger of peace, from the summit of the Castle of Adrian, restored health to the city, and the Queen of Heaven rejoiced." Pictures and images of Christ and the Virgin abounded everywhere before the end of the sixth century. The picture of the Virgin, said to be painted by Luke, brought by the empress Eudoxia from the Holy Land, was considered a celestial safeguard to the city of Constantinople. When the emperor led his army to battle, it was carried on a superb

ear, in the midst of the troops. Houses were supposed to
be protected by the presence of such pictures and images;
and soldiers fought with more confidence under their
guardianship. Incense was waved, and lamps kept burning before them, in the churches. Their aid was implored
in emergencies, and many were the miracles believed to be
wrought by them. Images and pictures of saints and
martyrs were supposed to possess similar efficacy, though
less in degree.

Many people objected to these customs; and in the eighth
century the opposition was embodied in a numerous sect
called Iconoclasts, which means image-breakers. Leo
Third, emperor in the East, favoured their views, and gave
orders that the images in churches should be demolished,
and the pictures covered with plaster. A council at Constantinople decreed that all visible symbols of Christ, except
in the Eucharist, were blasphemous, and that the kissing
of images, and burning lights before them, was a renewal
of Paganism. The emperor ordered a statue of Christ
above the gate of his palace to be destroyed. But a crowd
of zealots, principally women, shook the ladder so violently,
that the men fell on the pavement and were killed. The
Pope, Gregory Second, applauded the women for their
piety, and defended the images. He maintained that the
Pagan statues were fanciful representations of Demons, at
a time when God had not visibly manifested himself;
while the likenesses of Christ, his mother, and the saints,
were proved to be genuine by a thousand miracles, and by
their antiquity also, having been in use ever since the
apostolic age. The cities of Italy swore to defend the
Pope and the images. The emperor Leo was excommunicated. Successive emperors supported the Iconoclasts, and
for more than a hundred years the East and the West were
in conflict. Several battles were fought, and many people
put to death. Councils in the East condemned images,
while Councils in the West inflicted punishment upon all
who maintained that religious honours should be paid to
God alone. At last, the Pope was victorious, and an an-

nual festival was observed in commemoration of the triumph of the images.

The martyrs took the place of the old tutelary deities.
Every nation, every city, every trade, every household,
and every individual, was under the protection of some
particular saint, whose images or pictures they especially
venerated. Some of the oldest pictures of the Virgin had
Lucas inscribed upon them. It was probably the name
of some obscure artist; but it was supposed to signify
Luke the Evangelist, who, on that account, became the
tutelary saint of painters. A martyr named Agnes was
the protector of flocks; probably because her name signified a lamb. A martyr named Phocas was the guardian
of sailors. During a voyage, the crew always set a plate
for him, believing that he was invisibly present at their
meals. Each day, they took turns in purchasing the plate;
and when the vessel arrived safely in port, the money thus
collected was distributed among the poor, in token of gratitude to their tutelary saint. The old autumn festivals in
honour of Ceres, were transferred to the Virgin Mary;
and in many places the peasants laid the first flowers and
the last fruits upon her altar, as they had been accustomed
to do for the Pagan goddess.

CANONIZATION.

The number of saints multiplied so fast, and so many
old customs were transferred to the worship of fictitious
personages, that a Council at Frankfort, in the eighth century, deemed it necessary to prohibit the invocation of any
new saints. At last the Pope decided that only those
should be regarded as true saints, whom the church authen-
ticated by certain public ceremonies, called canonization.
This custom has been thought to resemble the Roman
apotheosis, by which emperors and great men were placed
among the gods. But ceremonies of apotheosis were sometimes performed for the living, while saints were never
canonized till after their death. Nearly all the Fathers

and the celebrated monks were canonized, and, of course, received the title of Saint. The zealous Tertullian was not canonized, because he became a Montanist. The good and great Origen met with the same fate, because the Arians found a defence for their doctrines in his theory of ema‑ nations; while, by a singular chance, George, Bishop of Alexandria, was sainted, although he was an Arian. He became wealthy by furnishing the army with bacon; and after he was forced upon the people as a bishop, he made himself odious to all classes by his greediness for gain, his tyrannical temper, and his persecuting spirit. But as the populace murdered him during the reign of Julian, he was considered a martyr to Pagan animosity, was canonized, and became the renowned St. George, the guardian saint of England. The emperor Constantine had double honours. His Pagan subjects, by ceremonies of apotheosis, placed him among the gods, whose worship he had abjured, and Christians afterward placed him among the saints, by pro‑ cess of canonization. In the Eastern parts of the empire, it was common to stamp medals with a monogram, signify‑ ing Jesus, Mary, and Constantine.

ROSARIES.—The anchorites of ancient Hindostan were accustomed to say their prayers on strings of Lotus seeds, or cords with knots tied at intervals. The Buddhists used strings of berries, or beads, for the same purpose. In the sixth century, the Benedictine monks are said to have re‑ peated their prayers according to a series of beads on a string. This custom afterward became universal in the Catholic church. The poor used the stones of olives, and other hard seeds; but the wealthy wore the rosary as a rich ornament, formed of gold, pearl, agate, and other pre‑ cious stones.

AUTHORITY OF TRADITION.—The traditions of the Fa‑ thers were decided to be of equal authority with Scripture; and such doctrines or customs as derived no support from Scripture were sustained by appeals to tradition, on the ground that they had been orally transmitted from the Apostles. But the authority of the Fathers was not acknowledged, if in any of their views they departed from the standard of the church. Thus the writings of Tertullian, after he became a Montanist, were not accepted as authority, and the writings of Origen were condemned and burned.

CHRISTIAN SACRED BOOKS.

THE OLD TESTAMENT.—For some time after the death of Christ, his followers had no other Sacred Books than those of the Old Testament. Hebrew being a language unknown to scholars until after the establishment of Christianity, the Fathers depended entirely on the Greek translation of the Old Testament, called the Septuagint. It has been stated, in the chapter on the Jews, that the Alexandrian Jews added to that version several books, which they regarded as sacred, though not as strictly canonical. These books are what we now call the Apocrypha of the Old Testament. The Septuagint being held in very great reverence by the Hellenistic Jews, and by the early Christians, there grew up a tendency to consider all the books it contained as equally sacred. Origen accepted the book of Baruch, which, in the Alexandrian version, was appended to the prophecies of Jeremiah. He also quoted from the story of Susanna, as genuine Scripture. To some who expressed doubts on that point, he replied: "Consider whether it is not well to think of those words, 'Remove not the ancient landmark, which thy fathers have set.'" The learned De Wette says: "There can be no doubt that the most celebrated teachers of the second and third centuries made frequent and public use of the writings we call apocryphal. They pronounce them inspired and divine, quote them as authorities, and regard them with the same esteem as the canonical writings. The Wisdom of Solomon, and of Sirach, the Books of Macabees, Tobit, and Judith, are most frequently appealed to."

Several of the Fathers believed that Ezra restored the

mutilated Pentateuch, and other books of the Old Testament. They doubtless received this idea from Alexandrian
Jews, who drew that inference from the fourteenth chapter
of the second book, purporting to be written by Esdras
[Ezra]. In that chapter, Ezra is represented as saying to
the Lord: "The world is set in darkness, and they that
dwell therein are without light. For thy Law is burnt;
therefore no man knoweth the things that are done of thee,
or the works that shall begin. But if I have found grace
before thee, send the Holy Spirit into me, and I shall write
all that hath been done in the world since the beginning,
which was written in thy Law; that men may find thy
path, and that those in the latter days may live. And the
next day, behold a voice called me, saying, Esdras, open
thy mouth and drink! Then I opened my mouth, and he
reached me a cup, full as it were with water, but the colour of it was like fire. And I took it and drank; and
when I had drunk of it, my heart uttered understanding,
and wisdom grew in my breast; for my spirit strengthened my memory." In the Book of Esdras, it is stated
that it was written by Ezra, who was captive in Babylon.
But the most learned critics generally agree that it was
written by some Jewish convert to Christianity, well acquainted with Rabbinical traditions. The Book of Wisdom, ascribed to Solomon, is supposed by Biblical critics
to have been written by some Alexandrian Jew, about a
century before Christ. It contains internal evidence that
the writer was imbued with the ideas of Plato.

The habit of sustaining doctrines by quotations from the
apocryphal books led to a great deal of trouble in controversies with Jews of Palestine, who had always disliked
the Septuagint, and regarded with aversion the new books
it contained. The Septuagint varied in some respects from
the Hebrew original, and different copies of the Septuagint
did not agree together. Origen complains that many errors had crept in, "from the negligence of some transcribers, and the boldness of others." To obviate difficulties
arising from this state of things, he undertook the immense

labour of revising the copies of the Septuagint, and the translations from it, comparing them with the Hebrew, and giving the different readings in five distinct columns. Prideaux says: "The copies which went about in Origen's time, for use among Hellenistic Jews and Christians, were very much corrupted, through the mistakes and negligence of transcribers, whose hands, by often transcription, it had now long gone through. By comparing many different copies and editions, he endeavoured to clear it from errors of transcribers; and also, by comparing the Septuagint with the Hebrew original, to clear it from the mistakes of the first composers also; for many such he found in it, not only by omissions and additions, but also by wrong interpretations made in it by the first authors of that version. The Law, which was the most exactly translated of all, had many of these, but other parts a great many more." Printing was then unknown; and as Origen's learned work consisted of many volumes, it was seldom copied, not only on account of its bulk, but from the difficulty of finding Christians who understood Hebrew. It was, however, exceedingly valuable for reference in later times.

In Jerome's time, copies of the Septuagint had become yet more changed by transcribers. A Latin translation had been made from the Greek before the middle of the second century; and as Latin was the vernacular language of the Roman world, such versions naturally multiplied rapidly. Augustine says: "The number of those who have translated the Scriptures from Hebrew to Greek may be counted; but those who have translated the Greek into Latin cannot be counted." These various versions had fallen into lamentable confusion. Passages had been put in, and others taken out, or altered by transcribers, to sustain some doctrine they favoured, or overthrow some doctrine which they deemed heretical. Scarcely any two copies could be found exactly alike, and the discrepancies were often of a serious character. All sincere believers were alarmed by such a state of things. Damasus, Patriarch of Rome, entreated the learned Jerome to try to re-

N*

medy the evil. Accordingly, in the latter part of the
fourth century, he carefully compared the Greek and Latin
translations of the Old Testament with Hebrew originals;
and Latin copies of the New Testament with the most approved manuscripts in Greek. "His object being to retain
existing expressions, as far as possible, and not to introduce new ones, except where the true sense had entirely
disappeared." He encountered innumerable difficulties,
not only on account of the inextricable confusion of Latin
copies, but because the Greek also had been much altered,
by carelessness or design. He complains that he found
the copies very unlike in different places. Jews, in the
course of their controversies, continually accused the Christian Fathers of falsifying texts, to suit their own polemical
purposes; and the Fathers retorted the charge upon
them. These mutual accusations doubtless grew in part
out of the fact that the Septuagint version differed from
the Hebrew Scriptures in some particulars, and also contained several books which the Fathers were accustomed
to quote as authority, but which were never regarded as
either canonical or sacred by Palestine Jews.

A learned Jew, who had been converted to Christianity,
was employed by Jerome to instruct him in Hebrew. He
says: "I sweat in learning a foreign tongue, only for this
reason, that the Jews might no longer insult the churches,
by charging them with the falsity of their copies of the
Scriptures." The task was an arduous one. The Hebrew
language, on account of the exclusive habits of the nation,
and their discouragement of literature, was concise, meagre,
and limited. A sentence in Hebrew required twice as
many words to express it in Latin. Punctuation was not
in use in those days. The Hebrews omitted vowels in
their writing, as did the Egyptians in their hieroglyphics.
Of course, the translator, when he inserted them, was
obliged to rely solely upon the sense of the context. If
an English writer should express a word by p t, it would be
left for a translator to judge whether he meant pat, or pet, or
pit, or pot, or put. Prideaux says: "It must be confessed

that there are in Hebrew several combinations of the same consonants, susceptible of different punctuations, and thereby make different words, of different significations; and therefore, when put alone, have an uncertain reading. But it is quite otherwise, when they are joined in context with other words." In "The Englishman's Hebrew and Chaldea Concordance to the Bible," it is stated that the same Hebrew word has four different English meanings in four different places. In Genesis 2: 7, it is translated *nostrils;* in Genesis 3: 19, it is translated *face;* in Genesis 27: 45, it is translated *anger;* in Exodus 34: 6, it is translated *suffering.* It was for the judgment of the translator to decide whether the last-mentioned verse should be translated: "The Lord thy God, merciful and gracious, long-*nostrilled*, long-*faced*, long-*angered*, or long-*suffering*." Other similar instances are adduced to show the extreme difficulty of translating Hebrew correctly. The habits of many Jewish copyists created other obstacles. Notwithstanding their great reverence for the words of Scripture, they were prone to sacrifice correctness to the neat appearance of their manuscripts. If they made a slight mistake, they left it unerased, for fear of a blot; and if they wrote part of a word at the end of a line, they often began the word again on the next line, in order to make the lines appear even.

Jerome was remarkably well-fitted for the task, by his great learning, his laborious diligence, and especially by his long residence in Palestine, and consequent familiarity with the language, traditions, and localities of the country. His version has always been highly commended by scholars. De Wette calls it "perhaps the best work antiquity can boast." But he incurred much obloquy at the time. Converts from the Hellenistic Jews had deeply impressed upon Christians their own great reverence for the Septuagint. The early Fathers agreed with them in believing that every single word of the translation had been miraculously inspired by the same Holy Spirit, who inspired the original Hebrew authors. Palestine Jews had been greatly shocked at the impiety of their Alexandrian brethren, when they translated their Scriptures into Greek; and a majority of Christians were equally shocked at Jerome, for supposing that the Greek translation could have any imperfections. Rufinus indignantly asked how such impiety could be expiated, that perverted the very Law itself into something different from what the Apostles handed down. He complains that "the whole history of Susanna, which formerly afforded an example of chastity to the churches, is cut out by this fellow, cast away, and neglected."

Neander remarks: "This appeared to many, even to those who did not belong to the class of ignorant persons, a great piece of impiety—to pretend to understand the Old Testament better than the seventy inspired interpreters! better than the Apostles, who had followed this translation, and who would have given another, if they had considered it necessary! To allow one's self to be so misled by Jews, as for their accommodation to falsify the writings of the Old Testament!"

A bishop of one of the churches in Africa tried to introduce the corrected version of the Scriptures, but was forced to lay it aside, for fear all his people would desert him. One of the translator's cotemporaries published a letter in Jerome's own name, in which he was represented as feeling great remorse for what he had done. But Jerome immediately disclaimed any such feeling concerning a task, which he had conscientiously undertaken, at the earnest intreaty of the Patriarch of Rome. He translated the Apocryphal Books into Latin, and spoke very favourably of Tobit in the Preface. He says the church permitted no one under thirty years of age to read the beginning of Genesis, or the Song of Solomon, or the beginning and end of Ezekiel; that the mind might be in its greatest vigour to attain a perfect knowledge of the mystical sense of those portions of Scripture. Spiritual-minded Hindoos were accustomed to consider all descriptions of sexual love, in their Sacred Books, as typical of the complete absorption of the human soul into the Supreme Soul of the universe. The voluptuous imagery of the Song of Solomon was allegorically interpreted by Christians, to signify the perfect union of Christ with his bride the church.

Though Jerome's version found many advocates among the learned, it was not received into general use for two centuries. Gregory the Great acknowledged that he used the best old version, and the new likewise, for evidence; and the new version was thenceforth considered sanctioned. As the use of two versions caused confusion, one was made from both, forming the Latin Bible used by the Catholic church, well known under the title of The Vulgate, which signifies the common edition; for originally the word vulgar was merely used to designate what was common. The Vulgate contains all the Books we call Apocryphal, except the Books of Esdras. Jerome, and some other theologians of his time, did not consider those Books canonical. But the church generally received them, as it did other portions of the Old Testament, as an inspired guide.

THE NEW TESTAMENT.—The Christian Scriptures, called the New Testament, are composed of separate writings, very different from each other. First, there are four biographies of Christ, obviously fragmentary; some containing incidents and discourses which are omitted in the others. Second, there is a journal of the trials of Christianity when it first began to spread abroad from Palestine. Third, there is a series of letters written by the first Christian missionaries to the churches they had founded, containing such advice, encouragement, or reproof, as their situation required. Lastly, mysterious visions, regarded as prophetic, and supposed to have been written by the Apostle John, in his old age.

The first of the biographies, by Matthew, one of the Twelve Apostles, is supposed to have been written in Palestine, and the only one written in Hebrew, [Aramæan, or Syro-Chaldaic.] It more abounds with references to the peculiar customs of the Jews, than any of the other biographies; and seems to aim particularly at conciliating and converting that people. It contains a genealogy of Jesus

through David, up to Abraham; the line in which the
Messiah was expected by the Jews. It relates his birth in
Bethlehem, and refers to an ancient Hebrew prophecy
concerning that city of David. It describes his being carried into Egypt, and adduces his return as a verification of
Hosea's words: "When Israel was a child, I called my
son out of Egypt." This seems like the Rabbinical mode
of interpretation; for Hosea obviously alludes to the bringing of the *tribes* of Israel out of Egypt, in the childhood of
that people. In the book of Matthew, Christ is represented as charging his Apostles not to go "into the way of
the Gentiles, or enter into any city of Samaria;" an injunction exceedingly Jewish in its character, and not mentioned
in the other Gospels. Jerome noticed that Matthew quoted
passages out of the Old Testament differently from the
other Evangelists; that he did not appear to use the Septuagint, but to translate from the ancient Hebrew to the
modern Hebrew, or Syro-Chaldaic, which was spoken in
the time of Christ. Learned commentators in modern
times have made the same observation. In fact, the whole
Gospel bears marks of having been written before Christianity began to spread among the Gentiles. It cannot be
precisely ascertained at what period Matthew wrote his
recollections of the sayings and doings of Jesus. Dr.
Henry Owen, in his Observations on the Four Gospels,
thinks there is evidence that it was written A. D. 38;
which would be two years after the crucifixion, according
to the general supposition that Christ was thirty-six years
old when he died. Jones, in his Canonical Authority of
the New Testament, supposes it to have been written A. D.
41. Dr. Lardner in his Credibility of the Gospel History,
dates it A. D. 64. The writings of Paul make no allusions
to its existence. The Apostles were doubtless in the habit
of describing orally the example and maxims of their holy
Teacher; and this would excite a desire to have them
recorded. Matthew would naturally be selected for that
purpose; for having been a publican, or tax-gatherer, he
would necessarily be familiar with writing; an accomplish

ment very uncommon among the class to which the other Apostles belonged. That there was an ancient copy of a Gospel believed to have been by Matthew, and written in the modern Hebrew dialect, called Aramæan, is affirmed by Irenæus, Tatian, Origen, Jerome, and many other of the Fathers. There was a current tradition, from very early times, that Barnabas carried everywhere with him a Gospel written in Hebrew, by the hand of Matthew; and that when any were diseased, or possessed with devils, he laid it on their bosoms, and they were healed. Eusebius states that Pantænus, a Christian writer of the second century, found in India a Gospel according to Matthew, which had been left there by Bartholomew, one of the Twelve Apostles; and that it was written in Hebrew. To this statement, Jerome adds that Pantænus brought the Gospel back with him to Alexandria, and that it was written in Hebrew letters. The learned Neander thinks there is satisfactory evidence that Bartholomew carried a Hebrew Gospel with him; and he adds: "It was probably that compilation of our Lord's discourses, by Matthew, which lies at the basis of our present Gospel according to Matthew."

In the very earliest days of the church, the Judaizing Christians, already described under the name of Ebionites, had but one Gospel, and that was in Aramæan Hebrew. They believed it to be an authentic account of the sayings and doings of Jesus, as related by the Twelve Apostles, and recorded by Matthew. Epiphanius, who was originally a Jew, says it did not contain the two first chapters. Of course, the miraculous conception, the visit of the wise men, the flight into Egypt, and the slaughter of the children at Bethlehem, were omitted. It began with the baptism of Jesus; on which occasion, it declared that a great light shone all over the place, and fire burst forth from the Jordan. The copy used by the sect called Nazarenes appears to have differed in some respects from the Gospel used by the other Ebionites; for Jerome, who saw the manuscript, alludes to it as containing the two first chapters, and makes some quotations from them. The Ebionites considered Christ a mere man, with no peculiar circumstances preceding or attending his birth. But the Gospel used by the Nazarenes appears to have adopted the Cabalistic notion that the Wisdom of God was a feminine Spirit, the mother of Adam Kadman, or The Primal Heavenly Man, who appeared as the earthly Adam, and was to reappear as the New Adam, the Messiah. For this Gospel declared that the Holy Spirit was the *mother* of Christ. She is represented as descending upon him at baptism, and thus saluting him: "My Son, in all the prophets I expected thee, that thou shouldst come, and I might find in thee a place of rest; for thou art my resting place; thou art my first-born son, who reignest forever." Christ also is represented as saying: "My mother, the Holy Spirit took me by one of my hairs, and conveyed me to the holy mountain Tabor." In Gnostic theories, the Divine Wisdom, under the name of Sophia, figures very conspicuously, as the mother of Christ. This idea of a Mother of Spirits might have been derived from the writings of Philo, or the Cabalists, or from this Nazarene Gospel.

It seems likely that the Ebionite Gospel was in use in Justin Martyr's time; for he makes the following quotation from the Gospel of Matthew with which he was acquainted: "When Jesus came to the river Jordan, where John was baptizing, as he descended into the water, a fire was kindled in Jordan." When Jerome undertook the revision of both the Hebrew and Christian Scriptures, at the close of the fourth century, he examined the Nazarene copy of Matthew. He says: "Matthew was the first who composed a Gospel of Christ; and, for the sake of those among the Jews who believed in Christianity, he wrote it in the Hebrew language and letters; but it is uncertain who translated it into Greek. Moreover, the Hebrew copy itself is to this time preserved in the library of Cæsarea. The Nazarenes, who live in Berea, a city of Syria, granted me the favour of writing it out." Again he says: "The Gospel which the Nazarenes and Ebionites use, which I lately translated out of Hebrew into Greek, is by most esteemed the authentic Gospel of Matthew." Epiphanius says the Nazarene Gospel was more entire than the Ebionite. Iræneus, Eusebius, and Epiphanius say that the Gospel received by the Nazarenes and Ebionites was the Gospel of Matthew, altered in some things, according to their different sentiments. Ebionites broke off all communication with other Christians, in the time of Adrian, as already described. Being disliked by both Jews and Christians, they dwindled away, and in the fifth century, no traces of them were left. Christians would be likely to take little interest in the Hebrew copy of their Gospel, which few could read; and it was either destroyed or lost.

There appears to have been a Greek translation of Matthew very early in existence; for Clement of Rome, Polycarp, Ignatius, and Justin Martyr are represented as quoting from it. There has been much controversy concerning the two first chapters, as they have been handed down to us. The reasons given for doubting their authenticity may be briefly stated as follows: They are acknowledged to have existed in the Greek copies only. Though much has been written concerning Herod, by both Jewish and Gentile historians, none of them allude to such a monstrous act of cruelty, as the slaughter of all the children in the neighbourhood of Bethlehem. Several of the old Greek manuscripts, now in existence, begin at the eighteenth verse of the first chapter. In the British Museum, is an ancient Greek copy written in capitals. It is supposed to be twelve hundred years old, and is known as the Harleian Manuscript. The genealogy of Christ is separated from the Gospel, in the following manner:

" Thus far the Genealogy."

" Here begins the Gospel according to Matthew."

The same separation is made in a manuscript used by the ancient Britons, now in the Cottonian Library, in England; also in Latin copies, written in red ink, in Anglo-Norman characters, about the beginning of the eleventh century. Eusebius, speaking of Symmachus, an Ebionite, who was learned in Greek and Hebrew, says: "Symmachus was of the Ebionites, who suppose Christ to be a mere man, born of Joseph and Mary. There are now Commentaries of his, in which it is said that, disputing about the Gospel of Matthew, he eagerly defends that heresy." This Ebionite Commentary, probably disputing the account of the miraculous conception, in the first chapter of Matthew, was destroyed or lost, as was the case with all writings deemed heretical; therefore posterity has had no opportunity to judge impartially concerning their merits. Those who maintain the authenticity of the two first chapters of Matthew, urge that they exist in the Syriac translation, the most ancient manuscript now extant; also that Irenæus alludes to the flight into Egypt, and that he, Clement of Alexandria, and Tertullian, all speak of the genealogy as a portion of Matthew's Gospel. Many suppose that Matthew left a Hebrew Gospel with the Jews, and, after he travelled abroad, wrote a Greek translation of it, to which he appended the two first chapters, for the use of the Gentiles; and this opinion is sanctioned by high authority in antiquity.

The second biography of Jesus was written by Mark, the nephew of Barnabas. He was not one of the Apostles, and it is not recorded that he was ever with Jesus, or that he was among the disciples when the Holy Ghost descended upon them. Peter, in his first Epistle, calls him his son, and it has thence been inferred that he was converted to Christianity by his preaching. He is supposed to have been the son of the pious woman mentioned in the twelfth chapter of the Acts, at whose house the early disciples had met to pray, when they were surprised by the sudden appearance of Peter, whom an angel had conducted out of prison. Mark accompanied the Apostles in their missionary travels. Paul speaks of him as "profitable in the ministry," and alludes to him as being his companion in Rome. Nothing more is related of him in the Scriptures. But there was a tradition among the Fathers

that he afterward went into Asia, where he met Peter, and
returned with him to Rome. It is supposed that he there
wrote his Gospel, under the direction of Peter. No one
knows at what time it was written; but as Peter was believed to be in Rome during the reign of Nero, it is supposed that the Gospel was written sometime between A. D.
63 and 67. This account rests on the authority of early
tradition, and of writings attributed to Clement, Bishop of
Rome, said to have been ordained by Peter. These writings state that Peter's hearers at Rome were very desirous
to have written down what he related to them about
Christ; and that they did not desist from intreating Mark
to do it. At last they prevailed upon him; and Peter
gave it his sanction, as an authentic record, that might be
read in the churches. A considerable portion of this Gospel is word for word like Matthew; but, being intended for
Gentile converts, it passes over much that was adduced by
Matthew to prove Jesus was the Messiah. It gives no account of his birth or childhood, but begins with his baptism.
Quotations from Hebrew prophets, and allusions to Jewish
customs are avoided, and words and phrases not likely to
be understood by Gentile Christians are explained.

The third biography of Jesus was written by Luke, who
accompanied Paul in many of his missionary labours.
Eusebius states that he was a native of Antioch; but the
intimate knowledge of Jewish doctrines, customs, and
ceremonies, displayed in his writings, has led to the conclusion that he was either a Jew, or of Hebrew parentage. It
is not known when, or by whom, he was converted to
Christianity. He is described as a man of education, and
the style of his Greek is said to corroborate the statement.
Paul calls him "the beloved physician." He does not appear in connection with Christianity for many years after
the death of Christ, and it is not recorded that he was personally acquainted with any of the Twelve Apostles. Biblical critics suppose that he wrote his Gospel not far from
A. D. 63, which was nearly thirty years after the crucifixion.
In his introduction, he apparently alludes to spurious

Gospels, which probably had begun to be written by that time; for they were very numerous in the second century. He says: "Forasmuch as *many* have taken in hand to set forth in order a declaration of those things which are most surely believed among us, even as they delivered them unto us, who from the beginning were eye-witnesses, and ministers of the word, it seemed good to me also, having had perfect understanding of all things from the very first, to write unto thee, in order that thou mightest know the certainty of those things wherein thou hast been instructed."

This Gospel bears very evident marks of being written for Gentile converts. Matthew traces the genealogy of Jesus up to Abraham, whom the Jews considered the progenitor of their nation; but Luke traces it up to Adam. The two genealogies are very unlike, both in names and the number of generations. Between David and Jesus scarcely any of the names are similar; and Matthew gives only twenty-six generations, while Luke gives forty-one. Matthew dates the birth of Christ in the reign of Herod, king of Judea, but Luke dates from Augustus the Roman emperor. Luke mentions a census taken by the Roman government, as a reason why Jesus was born at Bethlehem, when his parents were on their way to Jerusalem to be taxed. After the forty days necessary for the purification of his mother were completed, according to the Law of Moses, he says they returned "into Galilee, to their own city Nazareth." Matthew makes no mention of Nazareth, until after Christ had begun his public ministry; and he says that Herod's command to slaughter all the young children was confined to the coasts of Bethlehem. That village was five miles south of Jerusalem; but Nazareth was fifty miles north of it. Of course, there would be no necessity of flying into Egypt from Nazareth. Luke makes no mention of the visit of the Three Magi, guided by a miraculous star, of the slaughter of the infants, or the flight into Egypt. But he relates several things not mentioned by the other Evangelists. Among them are the miraculous circumstances attending the birth of John the Baptist; the appearance of the angel Gabriel to Mary; the visit of Mary to Elizabeth; the vision of the shepherds; the prophesies of Simeon and Anna when the infant Jesus was carried into the temple to be circumcised; his disputation with the learned doctors of the Law when he was twelve years old; the story of the penitent thief on the cross; and of Christ's walking to Emmaus with his disciples after his resurrection.

The fourth Gospel is less biographical, and more doctrinal and spiritual than the others. It is attributed to John, the beloved Apostle, and confidential friend of Jesus; and is supposed to have been written at Ephesus, in his old age, after Jerusalem was destroyed, the Jews scattered abroad, and all the other Apostles dead. It was written for a foreign people, in a foreign land, and a foreign tongue. Irenæus declares that John was urged to do it by the bishops of Asia Minor, in their anxiety to refute Cerinthus, the Gnostic, who adopted the old Hindoo idea concerning the illusive nature of incarnations, and said that Christ only *appeared* to have a human body. John is the only one of the Evangelists who describes blood and water flowing from the side of Jesus when he was pierced by the Roman soldier; a circumstance which could not have happened, if he had been merely a spiritual phantom, as Cerinthus taught. John likewise expressly says: "The Logos was God, and was made *flesh*, and dwelt among men." Some of the later Fathers, who lived after the Arian controversy, said John wrote his Gospel to refute the Ebionites, who maintained that Jesus was born of human parents, like other mortals. The account of the woman, to whom Jesus said, "Go thy way, and sin no more," is omitted in most of the oldest manuscripts, and in the Syriac translation. Tertullian strongly objected to the story, as seeming to favour licentiousness. Chrysostom, when he wrote a Commentary on the whole Gospel of John, left it out. Jerome and Augustine state that in their time the Greek Christians did not insert it in their copies.

The verse in the fourth chapter, concerning an angel's troubling the pool of water, is wanting in some manuscripts.

The Book of Acts takes its name from the Latin word Acta, meaning Records. It is a very clear and circumstantial journal of the progress of Christianity during the first thirty years of missionary labour; supposed to be written A. D. 63 or 64. The Fathers unanimously attributed it to Luke the Evangelist; and this opinion is sustained by internal evidence. The Apostles Matthew and John make no mention of the ascension of Christ. Mark and Luke, who were converted after that event, allude to it indefinitely in their Gospels; but in the Acts of the Apostles, it is stated, that while he was talking with his disciples, after the resurrection, he visibly ascended into the clouds. "And while they looked stedfastly toward heaven, as he went up, behold two men stood by them in white apparel, and said, Ye men of Galilee, why stand ye gazing up into heaven? This same Jesus, who is taken up from you into heaven, shall so come in like manner as ye have seen him go into heaven."

The Apocalypse is a series of visions, or Revelations, from Heaven, to the Apostle John, either at Ephesus, or in the island of Patmos; supposed to have been written A. D. 95 or 96. It has given rise to more theories, and excited more controversy, than any other book in the Christian Scriptures. In the first ages, it was not unanimously accepted. Irenæus, Clement of Alexandria, and Tertullian, speak of it as received among the inspired writings. Athanasius is of opinion that the Egyptian churches so received it. But before the sixth century, only a portion of the Eastern churches received it as canonical. Jerome says it was rejected by the Greek churches in his time. Gregory, Bishop of Nyssa, classed it among spurious books. Eusebius says: "Some reject the Apocalypse of John, but others class it with the acknowledged books." One of the arguments brought against its being written by the Apostle John was, that one of the churches it addressed was the church at Thyatira, which was not in existence till after the death of John. Epiphanius met that objection by saying that John doubtless wrote prophetically; foreseeing that there *would* be a church at Thyatira. A Council at Laodicea, in three hundred and sixty, did not include it in the canon; though Laodicea was one of the churches to which it was addressed.

Concerning some of the Epistles, there was also much division of opinion among the Fathers of the church. Clement of Alexandria believed the Epistle to the Hebrews was from the hand of Paul; but Irenæus and Tertullian did not. De Wette says: "Origen had doubts, more or less strong, concerning the Epistle to the Hebrews; the Epistle of James; the Second Epistle of Peter; the second and third Epistles of John; and the Epistle of Jude." Origen says: "Peter left one acknowledged Epistle; that he wrote a second is doubted." "The thoughts of the Epistle to the Hebrews are admirable, and not inferior to any of the writings acknowledged to be apostolical; but the style and arrangement belong to some one who remembered the thoughts of the Apostle, and wrote commentaries on the words of his teacher. If any church receive this as the epistle of Paul, let it be commended therefore; since the men of old time did deliver it to us as Paul's, not without cause. But who it was that wrote the epistle, of a truth God only knows. Before our time, it was the opinion of some that Clement, Bishop of Rome, wrote that epistle; of others, that it was written by Luke, who wrote also the Gospel and the Acts." Didymus says: "It is not to be concealed that the Second Epistle of Peter is forged; and although it is published, yet it is not in the canon." Clement of Alexandria says: "Let it be understood that the Epistle of James is spurious." Jerome says: "The Epistle was published in James's name, by some other person; and in progress of time it obtained authority." The following verse in John's first Epistle is believed by very many to have been interpolated, either by design of some transcriber, or by the accidental insertion of some marginal note into the body of the text: "There are three that bear record in heaven, the Father, the Word, and the Holy Ghost; and these three are one." This passage is said to be wanting in the most ancient Greek manuscripts, in more than forty of the Latin translations, and in all the translations made before Jerome's time, in Syriac, Arabic, Coptic, and Persian; also in the ancient Armenian versions. It was not quoted by any of the Fathers preceding Jerome. The learned Neander says: "It is undoubtedly spurious; and in its ungenuine shape testifies to the fact how foreign such a collocation is from the style of the New Testament." The Rev. George Campbell, a distinguished Scotch divine, in the Preface to his Translation of the Gospels, says: "Many interpolations crept in by remissness of transcribers. Some few, however, appear to have been the result of design. After the Arian heresy enlisted the passions of belligerents, there appears to be some ground for ascribing to the pride and jealousy of polemics a design to foist into the text some words favourable to their distinguishing tenets. Some of these were soon detected; others have continued for many generations."

Eusebius of Cæsarea, who lived in the third century, before any councils of the church had established what books belonged to the canon, attempted to answer the oft-repeated question, "Which of the writings that pretend to belong to the New Testament, really do belong to it?" In making his catalogue he followed "the tradition of the church," by which he meant the prevailing opinion of all the Christian communities, both oral and written, as far as he could ascertain it. He divides the Christian Sacred Writings into three classes. First, those *universally* received; as the Four Gospels, the Acts of the Apostles, thirteen Epistles from Paul, one Epistle from Peter, and one from John. In the second class, he places those which were doubted of by *some;* as the Epistle to the Hebrews, and the Apocalypse of John. In the third class, he places those doubted of by *many;* as the Epistle of James, the Second Epistle of Peter, the Second and Third Epistles of John, and the Epistle of Jude. He says the Four

Gospels were pronounced canonical by the Apostle John.

Polycarp quotes from several books of the New Testament, especially from Paul's Epistles, and the First Epistle of Peter; which shows how very early those writings were in circulation. The early Fathers all testify that all the churches in their time agreed in accepting, as undoubtedly authentic and inspired, the Four Gospels, the Acts of the Apostles, thirteen Epistles from Paul, [exclusive of the Epistle to the Hebrews,] the First Epistle from Peter, and the First Epistle from John. Irenæus calls them "The Divine Scriptures"—"The Oracles of God"—"The Lord's Scriptures." Clement calls them "The God-inspired Scriptures." The four biographies of Christ very early received the name of Evangels, from Greek words meaning Good Tidings. In later times, they were called Gospels, from Saxon words having the same signification.

Nearly a hundred years elapsed, after the death of Christ, before there was any entire collection made of the Christian Sacred Writings. The Canon had been nearly or quite settled, by general usage, and the authority of learned Fathers of the church, before Councils made any decisions upon the question. The rule assumed by the Fathers was to limit their choice to such books as were written either by Apostles, or disciples of the Apostles; but this was not invariable—for the writings of Luke were included within the Canon, and those of Clement at Rome were excluded, though both were believed to have been companions of Paul. The testimony of the oldest ecclesiastical writers, and the authority of the church, formed the basis on which faith in the genuineness of the books rested. Origen says: "Among the Jews, many pretended to prophesy, and were false prophets. So likewise in the New Testament, many have attempted to write Gospels, but all are not received. You must know that not only four, but many Gospels have been written; from which those that we have are selected, and handed down by the churches. The church receives Four Gospels." We approve nothing but what the church approves." Augustine, who wrote

nearly two centuries later, says: "The church follows this
rule with respect to the canonical Scriptures. It prefers
those which have been received by *all* the Catholic churches,
to those which some do not receive. And respecting those
not received by all, it prefers those received by the *greatest
number* of churches, and churches of the greatest *authority*, to
those admitted by fewer churches, and of less authority."

Questions concerning the authenticity of books were occasionally brought before councils. A Council at Laodicea,
in three hundred sixty, forbade the reading of uncanonical
books, and gave a list of those which were canonical; from
which the Apocalypse of John, and the books of the Old
Testament, which we call Apocryphal, were excluded.
But a Council convened at Hippo, in three hundred ninety-
three, accepted Ecclesiastes, The Wisdom of Solomon,
Tobit, Judith, and the two books of Maccabees, as canonical.

As the New Testament was written in Greek, there was
little difficulty in transmitting it perfectly to posterity.
The structure of the language did not render it so liable
to mistakes, as was the Hebrew; and its phraseology
could be easily explained by comparison with cotemporary
literature. The errors which have crept in do not in the
least affect the spirit and moral teaching of the Gospel;
and, therefore, are of little consequence. Scholars who
have examined critically, find that they arise principally
from inserting into the text explanatory notes, originally
written on the margin, by transcribers.

The Bible was divided into the Old and New Testament,
because that word means Covenant. The old books were
regarded as God's covenant with the Jews, and the new as
his covenant with the human race. Both were received
by Christians as of equal authority. Origen says: "That
the Logos wishes us to be wise may be shown from the
ancient and Jewish writings, which we use, and which are
believed by the church to be no less divine than those
written after the time of Jesus." This joining of the old
with the new was inevitable, according to the laws of
human nature; but if it had some good effects, it was also

productive of evil. The Old Testament contained much that was vastly superior to anything the barbarian nations had been accustomed to receive in the form of religion; such as the thoughtful kindness to the poor everywhere enjoined, and the omnipresent guardianship of One Invisible God, in whose sight the heavens themselves were not pure. But on the other hand, the equal acceptance of the Old Testament, *as a rule of life*, and combining them both together in the instruction of the people, greatly impeded the humanizing influence of the New Testament. Moses commanded men to put out eyes, and knock out teeth, in retaliation for similar injuries; but Christ said: "Bless them that curse you, do good to them that hate you." Thus the two furnished equal authority for the good and the evil in man's nature. Intolerance, vengeance, and cruelty, rebuked by the New Testament, found plausible examples and excuses in the Old. This incongruity was felt by some, even in the first centuries, as is very plainly manifested by Gnostic writers. A Gothic Bishop, when he translated the Old Testament, omitted the Books of Kings, saying he feared they would increase the love of fighting, to which the Goths were already too much addicted.

If we strive to divest ourselves of the habitual predilection for Christianity, which education imparts to us, and endeavour to approach the Gospels in the same spirit that we should examine the Sacred Books of Hindostan or Persia, it appears to me that even in that state of mind, we cannot fail to be struck with their great superiority over all the other religious teaching, which God, by his various messengers, has given to mankind. There are variations in the statements, because they were formed of recollections which had been often and reverently repeated by the Apostles to mixed audiences, long before they were recorded. Some would naturally give more prominence to particular reminiscences than to others; especially as they were written at different times, in different places, and intentionally adapted to the class of people for whom they were prepared. But the character of Jesus is shown in the same heavenly light by all; gentle, benevolent, self-denying, forgiving, not satisfied with forms, but seeking for the spirit within them, indignant only toward hypocrisy and oppression, full of reverence for God, and love for man. We feel, in reading the record of his words and actions, that he was indeed a son of God; and that the picture must be a photograph portrait of a living original, made by the sunlight of truth; since the imagination of man has never risen to so high a conception of holiness and love.

If we turn from internal evidence to the external, we find it in the remarkable simplicity of these books. There is no attempt to conceal disparaging circumstances. It is frankly told that the family and townspeople of Jesus did not believe in his divine mission; that when a voice from heaven "glorified his name," the people, who stood by, "said it thundered;" that some of his disciples were ambitious to have high offices of honour in his earthly kingdom; that one of them betrayed him unto death, for a reward in money; that they all deserted him in his hour of danger; that Peter, in care for his own safety, thrice repeated a falsehood, swore to it, and then wept bitterly for what he had done; that after the resurrection of Jesus, when his disciples saw him, "they worshipped him, but some doubted." There is an artlessness in all this, which appeals strongly to the candid mind. Judging of these biographies merely as we would judge of any other human testimony, it would lead us to conclude that the writers were aiming to record things honestly, just as they appeared to their own minds.

As I have given samples of the best and of the most objectionable in the Sacred Books of other religions, I will also insert brief specimens from the Christian Scriptures:

"Thou shalt love the Lord thy God with all thy heart, and with all thy soul, and with all thy mind.

"This is the first and great commandment.

"And the second is like unto it, Thou shalt love thy neighbour as thyself.

"On these two commandments hang all the law and the prophets."

"Blessed are the poor in spirit: for their's is the kingdom of heaven.

"Blessed are they that mourn: for they shall be comforted.

"Blessed are the meek: for they shall inherit the earth.

"Blessed are they which do hunger and thirst after righteousness: for they shall be filled.

"Blessed are the merciful: for they shall obtain mercy.

"Blessed are the pure in heart: for they shall see God.

"Blessed are the peacemakers: for they shall be called the children of God.

"Blessed are they which are persecuted for righteousness' sake: for their's is the kingdom of heaven.

"Blessed are ye, when men shall revile you, and persecute you, and shall say all manner of evil against you falsely, for my sake.

"Rejoice, and be exceeding glad: for great is your reward in heaven: for so persecuted they the prophets which were before you."—*Gospel by Matthew.*

"And they brought young children to him, that he should touch them: and his disciples rebuked those that brought them.

"But when Jesus saw it, he was much displeased, and said unto them, Suffer little children to come unto me, and forbid them not; for of such is the kingdom of God.

"Verily I say unto you, Whosoever shall not receive the kingdom of God as a little child, he shall not enter therein.

"And he took them up in his arms, put his hands upon them, and blessed them."—*Gospel by Mark.*

"I say unto you there is joy in the presence of the angels of God over one sinner that repenteth.

"A certain man had two sons:

"And the younger of them said to his father, Father, give me the portion of goods that falleth to me. And he divided unto them his living.

"And not many days after, the younger son gathered all together, and took his journey into a far country, and there wasted his substance with riotous living.

"And when he had spent all, there arose a mighty famine in that land; and he began to be in want.

"And he went and joined himself to a citizen of that country; and he sent him into his fields to feed swine.

"And he would fain have filled his belly with the husks that the swine did eat: and no man gave unto him.

"And when he came to himself, he said, How many hired servants of my father's have bread enough and to spare, and I perish with hunger!

"I will arise, and go to my father, and will say unto him, Father, I have sinned against heaven, and before thee,

"And am no more worthy to be called thy son: make me as one of thy hired servants.

"And he arose, and came to his father: But when he was yet a great way off, his father saw him, and had compassion, and ran, and fell on his neck, and kissed him.

"And the son said unto him, Father, I have sinned against heaven, and in thy sight, and am no more worthy to be called thy son.

"But the father said to his servants, Bring forth the best robe, and put it on him; and put a ring on his hand, and shoes on his feet.

"And bring hither the fatted calf, and kill it; and let us eat and be merry:

"For this my son was dead, and is alive again; he was lost, and is found. And they began to be merry.

"Now his elder son was in the field: and as he came and drew nigh to the house, he heard music and dancing:

"And he called one of the servants, and asked what these things meant.

"And he said unto him, Thy brother is come; and thy father hath killed the fatted calf, because he hath received him safe and sound.

"And he was angry, and would not go in: therefore came his father out, and entreated him.

"And he, answering, said to his father, Lo, these many years do I serve thee, neither transgressed I at any time thy commandment: and yet thou never gavest me a kid, that I might make merry with my friends:

"But as soon as this thy son was come, which hath devoured thy living with harlots, thou hast killed for him the fatted calf.

"And he said unto him, Son, thou art ever with me, and all that I have is thine.

"It was meet that we should make merry, and be glad: for this thy brother was dead, and is alive again; and was lost, and is found."—*Gospel by Luke.*"

"Though I speak with the tongues of men and of angels, and have not charity, I am become as sounding brass, or a tinkling cymbal.

"And though I have the gift of prophecy, and understand all mysteries, and all knowledge; and though I have all faith, so that I could remove mountains, and have not charity, I am nothing.

"And though I bestow all my goods to feed the poor, and though I give my body to be burned, and have not charity, it profiteth me nothing.

"Charity suffereth long, and is kind; charity envieth not; charity vaunteth not itself, is not puffed up.

"Doth not behave itself unseemly, seeketh not her own, is not easily provoked, thinketh no evil;

"Rejoiceth not in iniquity, but rejoiceth in the truth;

"Beareth all things, believeth all things, hopeth all things, endureth all things.

"Charity never faileth."—*Paul to the Corinthians.*

"And I saw heaven opened, and behold, a white horse; and he that sat upon him was called Faithful and True, and in righteousness he doth judge and make war.

"His eyes were as a flame of fire, and on his head were many crowns; and he had a name written, that no man knew but he himself.

"And he was clothed with a vesture dipped in blood: and his name is called The Word of God.

"And the armies which were in heaven followed him upon white horses, clothed in fine linen, white and clean.

"And out of his mouth goeth a sharp sword, that with it he should smite the nations: and he shall rule them with a rod of iron; and he treadeth the wine-press of the fierceness and wrath of Almighty God.

"And he hath on his vesture and on his thigh a name written, KING OF KINGS, AND LORD OF LORDS.

"And I saw an angel standing in the sun; and he cried with a loud voice, saying to all the fowls that fly in the midst of heaven, Come and gather yourselves together unto the supper of the great God;

"That ye may eat the flesh of kings, and the flesh of captains, and the flesh of mighty men, and the flesh of horses, and of them that sit on them, and the flesh of all men, both free and bond, both small and great.

"And I saw the beast, and the kings of the earth, and their armies, gathered together to make war against him that sat on the horse, and against his army.

"And the beast was taken, and with him the false prophet that wrought miracles before him, with which he deceived them that had received the mark of the beast, and them that worshipped his image. These both were cast alive into a lake of fire burning with brimstone.

"And the remnant were slain with the sword of him that sat upon the horse, which sword proceeded out of his mouth, and all the fowls were filled with their flesh."—
Revelation of St. John the Divine.

The reverence paid to the Bible, after the church had

decided of what books it ought to be composed, partook of the same external character as other tendencies of the time. While the most palpable violations of its prevailing *spirit* were sanctioned, it was heresy to doubt that every book, nay every single *word*, was directly inspired by the Holy Spirit, and was therefore a rule for life, and a standard in matters of science, as well as of faith. Hebrews and Buddhists were accustomed to wear scraps of their Sacred Books for amulets; and it was common for the Christian populace to wear portions of the Gospels about their necks, supposing they would have efficacy, similar to the cross and the eucharist, to protect them from Evil Spirits, from diseases, and all manner of disasters.

Very few copies of the Bible, made before printing was invented, are now in existence. Butler, a learned and candid writer, belonging to the Catholic church, wrote a work in the nineteenth century, called Horæ Biblicæ, [BIBLE HOURS.] He therein says: "The New Testament was probably all written in Greek, except the Gospel of Matthew, and Paul's Epistle to the Hebrews." "There are not known to be in existence, at present, any original manuscript in the autographs of the authors; and there is no evidence that any of those autographs existed in the third century." "Very few of the old manuscript copies of the entire New Testament remain. Of those that have been discovered, the greater part contain the Gospels only. Very few have the Apocalypse. In the oldest specimens, several leaves are wanting, sometimes replaced in writing of much later date. All the manuscripts have obliterations and corrections; some made by the writer himself, others by persons of a subsequent time." The Alexandrian copy, said to have been brought from Egypt, is preserved in the British Museum. It is written on parchment, in Greek, and contains the Old Testament, in the Septuagint form, most of the New Testament, and the Epistles of Clement, Bishop of Rome, to the Corinthian church. Some date it from the close of the fourth century, others not till the latter half of the sixth. Some suppose that the most an-

o*

cient manuscript of the New Testament now existing is preserved at Cambridge University in England. It contains the Four Gospels, and the Acts of the Apostles, in Greek and Latin. The parchment is much torn and mutilated, and ten leaves are supplied by a later transcriber. Some say it was written in the second century, others in the fifth. Another copy, supposed to have been written in the fifth century, is preserved in the Vatican Library, at Rome. It originally contained the whole Bible in Greek.

SPURIOUS BOOKS.

The apocryphal Gospels and Epistles in circulation in the first centuries were numerous. Many of them were doubtless written by Gnostics; for it was their belief that any person endowed with the Gnosis was as perfect a medium of Divine truth as the Apostles themselves; and some considered themselves even more completely enlightened. There was the Gospel of Cerinthus; the Gospel according to the Twelve Apostles; the Gospel to the Egyptians; the Gospel of the Birth of Mary; Protevangelion, or First Gospel of the Birth of Christ, ascribed to James, "the Lord's brother;" the Gospel of the Infancy of Jesus, ascribed to the Apostle Thomas; the Gospel of Nicodemus, sometimes called the Acts of Pontius Pilate; the Acts of Paul and Thekla; the Book of Hermas, the Shepherd; the Doctrines of the Apostles; the Apocalypse of Peter; the Ascent of Isaiah; the Epistle of Barnabas; the Clementine Homilies; and many others. According to Origen, some classed the Ebionite Gospel of Matthew among them. Speaking of spurious books, he says: "There are some who place among them the Gospel according to the Hebrews; a volume with which Hebrew Christians are especially pleased."

Epiphanius supposed that Luke, in the introduction to his Gospel, alluded to the Gospel of Cerinthus; and Jerome conjectured the same concerning the Gospel of the Egyptians; suppositions which indicate the great antiquity of those books. About the end of the second century, when Gnostic sects were numerous, the fabrication of new Gospels, and alterations of the old, prevailed to a great extent; and it was a very common practice to write under the name of some Apostle, or other person eminent for holiness; by which means an extensive circulation was obtained, and responsibility, which might sometimes have proved dangerous, was avoided. It was not often easy to discover whence or how these manuscripts came into circulation. The early Fathers found them in existence, and revered by the people, and being exceedingly credulous, they sometimes received and quoted, without due examination, whatever tended to glorify Christ, or his Apostles.

The Gospel of the Birth of Mary is among the works preserved in Jerome's writings. It is said that some obscure sects, in the first centuries, believed it was written by Matthew. This Gospel declares that Mary was of the royal lineage of David. It states that an angel appeared to Joachim, her father, and to her mother Anna, and foretold to them the birth of a wonderful daughter. The Jews never had the custom of consecrating virgins to the temple, as was the case in many other countries. But the author of this Gospel states that the angel commanded them to carry their child to the temple, to be brought up there, devoted to the Lord, and carefully kept from all communication with the common people, that her character might be above all possibility of suspicion. The angelic vision was obeyed, and Mary was placed in the temple, as soon as she was weaned. There she had daily conversations with angels, and was so familiar with their glorious appearance, that she was never surprised to see her room suddenly filled with celestial light. When she was fourteen years old, a voice from the Mercy Seat ordered the High Priest to summon all the unmarried men of the lineage of David, to choose from among them a husband to the Virgin, by means of the prophecy of Isaiah: "There shall come forth a rod out of the stem of Jesse, and a flower shall spring out of its root." The High Priest therefore ordered them all to bring rods, resolving to bestow Mary on him whose rod blossomed when laid upon the altar. Joseph came among the rest; but being a very old man, he lingered behind the others, not wishing to enter into competition for the prize; whereupon, a dove alighted on his rod, and thus signally pointed him out, as the chosen of heaven.

In the Gospel of the Birth of Christ, which assumed to be written by the Apostle James the Less, Joseph is represented as reluctant to marry Mary, after he had been designated by the miracle of the dove and rod, saying: "I am an old man, and have children; but she is young, and I fear lest I should appear ridiculous in Israel." But the High Priest said to him: "Joseph, thou art the person chosen to take the Virgin of the Lord, to keep her for him;" and he reminded him that the judgments of the Lord descended upon those who refused to obey him. Joseph being afraid, took her home, and bidding her farewell, said: "I will leave thee in my house; but I must go and mind my trade of building." In this book it is stated that Jesus was born in a cave, three miles from Bethlehem, when Joseph was on his way to Jerusalem to be taxed. Tertullian and Origen probably borrowed the idea from this source; for they both speak of his having been born in a cave. The visit of the Wise Men from the East is described in this book. When Herod heard of them he inquired what sign they had seen, that brought them to Bethlehem. They answered: "We saw an extraordinary large star, shining among the stars of heaven; and it so outshone all the other stars, that they became invisible. We knew thereby that a great king was born in Israel; and therefore we are come to worship him." In consequence of this information, Herod ordered all the young children in and about Bethlehem to be slaughtered. This Gospel is described as written in Hebrew, and signed, "I, James, wrote this at Jerusalem." It was brought from the Levant, translated into Latin, and published in Switzerland, in 1552. It is said to have been publicly read in some of the Eastern churches.

The Gospel of the Infancy of Jesus, written under the name of the Apòstle Thomas, contains an accumulation of miracles. It declares that the cave where Jesus was born was filled with light at the moment of his birth; "greater than the light of lamps and candles, and greater than the light of the sun itself." The divine infant "spake from his cradle, and said to his mother Mary, 'I am Jesus, the Son of God; that Word, which thou didst bring forth, according to the declaration of the angel Gabriel; and my Father hath sent me for the salvation of the world.'" It is stated that when Joseph and Mary arrived in Egypt with their child, the great idol in the temple cried out: "'The unknown God hath come hither, who is truly God; nor is there any one beside him, who is worthy of divine worship.' At the same instant, the idol fell down; and at his fall, all the inhabitants of Egypt ran together." "The priest, who ministered to the idol, had a son three years old, who was possessed with a great multitude of devils. Going to the inn, he found Joseph and Mary. And when the Lady Mary had washed the swaddling clothes of the Lord Christ, and hung them out to dry upon a post, the boy possessed with the devil, took down one of them, and put it upon his head. And presently the devils began to come out of his mouth, and fly away in the shape of crows and serpents. From that time, the boy was healed by the power of the Lord Christ." When his father inquired concerning the matter, he replied: "'I went to the inn, and found there a very handsome woman, with a boy, whose swaddling-clothes she washed and hung on a post. I put one of them on my head, and immediately the devils fled away.' The father, exceedingly rejoiced, said, 'My son, perhaps this boy is the Son of the living God, who made the heavens and the earth; for as soon as he came among us, the idol was broken, and all the gods fell down.'" "Jesus was playing with other Hebrew boys, by a running stream; and he took soft clay from the banks, and formed of it twelve sparrows. A certain Jew, seeing what he was doing, went to his father Joseph, and said: 'Thy boy is playing by the river-side, and profaneth the Sabbath.' Then Joseph called to him and said: 'Why doest thou that which it is not lawful to do upon the Sabbath day?' Then Jesus, clapping the palms of his hands together, said to the sparrows: 'Fly away! and while ye live, remember me.' So the sparrows flew away with noise. And the Jews were astonished, and went and told their chief persons what a strange miracle they had seen wrought by Jesus." "A certain schoolmaster, named Zaccheus, said to Joseph, 'Thou hast a wise child. Send him to me, that he may learn to read.' When he sat down to teach Jesus the alphabet, he began with the first letter, Aleph; but Jesus pronounced the second, and the third, and said over the whole alphabet to the end. Then he opened a book, and taught his master the Prophets; and Zaccheus went home wonderfully surprised at so strange a thing."

This Gospel of the Infancy was much quoted in early times, and several of the stories it relates have ever since been believed by many members of the Catholic church. Eusebius and Athanasius both record that when Joseph and Mary arrived in Egypt, they took up their abode in Hermopolis, a city of Thebais, in which was a superb temple of Serapis. They visited this temple, carrying with them the infant Jesus. What was their astonishment to see the great idol, and all the inferior gods, fall prostrate before them! The priests fled with horror, and the whole city was filled with alarm. Sozomon, a Christian historian of the fifth century, likewise relates the story. It was cited as a remarkable verification of Isaiah's prophecy: "Behold the Lord rideth upon a swift cloud, and shall come into Egypt, and the idols of Egypt shall be moved at his presence, and the heart of Egypt shall melt in the midst of it."

Extracts in the first volume of this work show several striking points of resemblance between the ancient Hindoo and Hebrew Sacred Records. In some cases, even *names* are synonymous; the sons of Noah, for instance. The names of the first man and woman are Adim and Iva, in Sanscrit. In these spurious Gospels of Christianity, the observing reader will be reminded of the stories told of Crishna, in Sacred Books of Hindostan, quoted in the first volume of this work. Sir William Jones was so much struck with various coincidences, that he thought the Hindoos must have seen these spurious Christian Gospels, and copied from them. It does not seem to have occurred to him that the reverse might have been the case; and that Egyptian Christians, being frequently in communication with India, were very likely to become acquainted with Hindoo legends.

Many of the ancients supposed that the Book called The Shepherd of Hermas, was written by the Hermas whom Paul salutes, at the close of his Epistle to the Romans. Others assigned a later date, and attributed it to the brother of Pius, Bishop of Rome, in the second century. It consists of three books, occupied with a succession of visions, intended to convey instruction to the church, and to impress upon the mind the superior sanctity of celibacy. The following brief sample will serve to give some idea of it: " Behold I saw a great beast, as it were a whale; and fiery locusts came out of his mouth. The height of the beast was about a hundred feet. I began to weep, and to pray unto the Lord that he would deliver me from it. Then I called to mind the words I had heard: Doubt not Hermas! Wherefore, I delivered myself boldly unto the beast, which came on as if it could have devoured a city. I came near unto it; and the beast extended its whole length upon the ground, and put forth nothing but its tongue, nor once moved itself, till I had quite passed by. Now the beast had upon its head four colours; first black, then blood-red, then golden, then white. After I had passed by it, there met me a virgin well adorned, as if she had just come out of her bride-chamber; all in white, having a veil over her face, and covered with shining hair. I knew by my former visions that it was The Church; and thereupon I grew the more cheerful. She said: Did nothing meet you, O man? I replied: Lady, there met me such a beast as seemed able to devour a whole people; but, by the power and mercy of God, I escaped it. She replied: Thou didst escape it well, because thou didst cast thy whole care upon God. For this cause, the Lord sent his angel and stopped the mouth of the beast, that he should not devour thee. Go, therefore, and relate to the elect the great things God hath done for thee. And say unto them this beast is a figure of the trial about to come. If ye shall have prepared yourselves, if your hearts be pure and without spot, ye may escape it. Cast all your cares upon the Lord. He can turn away his wrath from you, and send you help and security. Wo to the doubtful! to those who shall hear these words and despise them. It would be better for them that they had not been born. Then I asked concerning the four colours upon the head of the beast. She said: The black denotes the world in which you dwell. The fiery red denotes that this age must be destroyed by fire and blood. Ye are the golden part, who have escaped out of it. For as gold is tried by the fire and made profitable, in like manner are ye tried, who live among the men of this world. The white colour denotes the time of the world which is to come, in which the elect of God shall dwell; because the elect shall be pure and without spot, unto life eternal. Wherefore, do not thou cease to speak these things in the ears of the saints." Hermas teaches that the Apostles descended into Hades, to baptize the pious personages of the Old Testament. He recommends frequent fasting, and adds: "Above all, exercise thy abstinence in this, to refrain both from hearing and from speaking what is wrong. Cleanse thy heart from all pollution, from all revengeful feelings, and from all covetousness. On the day thou fastest, content thyself with bread, vegetables, and water, and thank God for these. But reckon up what thy meal on this day would have cost thee, and give the amount to some widow or orphan, or to the poor. Happy for thee, if with thy children and whole household thou observest these things."

The Epistle which went under the name of Barnabas, companion of Paul, was known to the Alexandrian church in the second century. It contains singular specimens of the forced, allegorical mode of interpretation, which the Christian Fathers seem to have learned from Jewish Rabbins. It is therein stated that the Hebrew priests were ordered not to wash with vinegar the inwards of the goat offered in expiation for the sins of the people, in order to foreshadow that when Christ should offer his flesh "for the sins of a new people," they would give him vinegar to drink, mixed with gall. It was ordained by Moses, as a process of purification, that a red heifer should be burned; that a piece of scarlet wool and hyssop should be tied on a stick and dipped in the ashes, to sprinkle the people. The author of this Epistle says: "That heifer was Jesus Christ. And why was the wool put upon a *stick?* Because the kingdom of Jesus was founded upon the *cross;* and therefore they that put their trust in him shall live forever." According to the Greek method of notation the letter T signified three hundred, the letter I ten, and H eight; of which fact the following use is made in the Epistle of Barnabas: "Abraham circumcised three hundred and eighteen men of his house. What, therefore, was the mystery that was made known to him? The I H, which make eighteen, denote Jesus. And because the cross was that by which we were to find grace, he adds T, which is three hundred, and forms the figure of the cross. Wherefore, by three hundred and eighteen he signified Jesus and his cross." The ancient *Egyptian* cross was in the form of T. He adds: "He who has put the engrafted gift of his doctrine within us, knows that I never taught to any one a more certain truth; but I trust that ye are worthy of it." Again he says: "Why did Moses say, Ye shall not eat of the swine? He meant thou shalt not join thyself to such persons as are like unto swine; who while they live in pleasure forget their God." "He says also, Thou shalt not eat the eagle, nor the hawk, nor the kite, nor the crow; that is, thou shalt not keep company with such kind of men as know not how to get themselves food by their labour, but injuriously ravish away the things of others." "Neither shalt thou eat of the hyena; that is, Be not an adulterer, nor a corrupter of others. And wherefore so? Because that creature every year changes its kind, and is sometimes male and sometimes female." "Why might they eat such animals as clave the hoof? Because the righteous liveth in this present world, but his expectation is fixed upon the other. Behold, brethren, how admirably Moses commanded these things. Speaking as concerning meats, he delivered great precepts to them in the spiritual signification of those commands. They, according to the desires of the flesh, understood him as if he had only meant it of meats. But the Lord has circumcised our ears and our hearts, that we might know these things." This Epistle thus exhorts Christians to be in readiness for the second coming of Christ: "Be ye taught of God; seeking what it is the Lord requires of you, and doing it; that ye may be saved in the day of judgment. For the day is at hand in which all things shall be destroyed, together with the Wicked One."

The book called the Ascent of Isaiah was evidently written by some one imbued with Gnostic tendencies. It describes the progressive descent of Christ from his radiant home above, through "the seven heavenly spheres," gradually changing his form, during the journey, into the likeness of the inhabitants of each sphere; so that his superiority was always veiled. At last, he arrived on earth, and assumed the appearance of a mortal man.

A remarkable book, called the Clementine Homilies, was in general circulation, and had great celebrity. It professed to be written by Clement, Bishop of Rome, in the first century, and to give an account of his conversion, and of his travels with the Apostle Peter. But the name of Clement was assumed, on account of its authority with the church. Scholars say it can be clearly proved to have been written about a century after his death. At that period, Gentile Christians and Judaizing Christians were in opposition to each other; Gnostics were attacking Judaism; and Christians were contending with Gnostics. The book appears to have been written by some one who had combined Jewish, Gnostic, and Christian ideas, and who wished to present a common ground of conciliation to the conflicting parties. He adopts the idea of the Cabalists that the Wisdom of God was feminine. He called her by the Greek name Sophia, and said: "God himself rejoices in her alliance." His ideas concerning the First Adam and the Second Adam were also very similar to those entertained by many Jews. He describes Adam Kadman, the First Adam, as "Lord of All, existing before the worlds;" first manifested on earth in the form of Adam, afterward as Enoch, Abraham, and Moses. Lastly he took the form of Jesus, was crucified, and ascended to the heaven whence he came. "Changing the forms of his appearance, he passed through the course of ages, until reaching his own times, he was, by God's grace, anointed in recompense for his toils, and blessed with eternal repose." "The first prophet was Adam; in whom, if in any one, formed as he was immediately by the creative hand of God, that which is the immediate efflux of the Divine Spirit dwelt." "God, the alone good, bestowed every thing on the man created after his own image. Full of the divinity of his Creator, and as a true prophet, knowing all things, he revealed to his children an eternal Law, which has neither been destroyed by wars, nor corrupted by godless power, nor hidden in any particular place, but can be read of all men. The appearance neither of Moses nor of Jesus would have been necessary, if men had been willing of themselves, to come to a knowledge of what is right. But since this original revelation, which should have been transmitted by the living word, from generation to generation, was corrupted, over and over, by impure additions, proceeding from an Evil Principle, new revelations were requisite to counteract these corruptions, and restore that original revelation. And it was always that

Primal Spirit of Humanity, the Spirit of God in Adam, which reappeared, in manifold forms, and under various names." Supposing the Law of Moses to be a new revelation, to restore the primitive truths taught by Adam, this author exalted the Pentateuch above other books of the Hebrew Scriptures; but he maintained that it had been written many times over, and that many foreign elements had been introduced into it. The Father of Mankind appeared as Moses, to trust the Jews with the preservation of primal truths. He appeared as Jesus, for the especial purpose of delivering to his other children, the Gentiles, that pure primitive religion, which had been constantly handed down by a consecrated few among the Jews. The author of the Homilies says: "Jesus loved men, as none but the Father of the Human Race could love his own children. His greatest sorrow was that he must be striven against by those, in their ignorance, for whom he strove as his children. He loved them, though they hated him; he wept over the disobedient, he blessed them that blasphemed him, he prayed for his enemies; and these things he not only did himself, as a father, but also taught his disciples to pursue the same course of conduct toward men, as their brethren." "The same primitive religion is to be found in the pure doctrine of Moses and of Christ. He who possesses the former may dispense with the latter; and he who possesses the latter may dispense with the former; provided the Jew does not blaspheme Christ, whom he knows not, nor the Christian blaspheme Moses, whom he knows not. But he who is accounted worthy of attaining to the knowledge of both, to find in the doctrine announced by both but one and the same truth, is to be esteemed a man rich in God; one who has found in the old that which has become new, and in the new that which is old. The Jew and the Christian owe it entirely to the grace of God, that they have been led to a knowledge of the Divine will, by these revelations of the Primal Man, repeated under different forms, one by Moses, another by Christ." "He who is under no necessity of seeking for truth, who has no doubts, who *knows* the truth, by means of a higher Spirit, dwelling *within* himself, which is superior to all uncertainty, he alone obtains knowledge of the truth, and can reveal it unto others."

The reverence for apostolic traditions led to a collection of ecclesiastical laws, called Apostolical Constitutions and Apostolical Canons. These also were ascribed to Clement of Rome, whose acquaintance with Peter would enable him to receive them from high authority. Neander supposes them to have been formed gradually, out of different fragments, from the close of the second into the fourth century.

There was an ancient tradition that before the Apostles dispersed to proclaim Christ in all lands, they drew up a Confession of Faith, to which each one contributed an article. This has ever since been known under the name of the Apostles' Creed. In the early times, it was devoutly believed to be the work of their own hands; but this idea has long since been acknowledged to be without foundation. It cannot be traced beyond the fourth century, and the author is unknown. Before A. D. 600 it existed in the following form: "I believe in God the Father Almighty; and in Jesus Christ, his only Son, our Lord, who was born of the Holy Ghost and the Virgin Mary; was crucified under Pontius Pilate, and was buried; and the third day, he rose again from the dead, ascended into heaven, sitteth on the right hand of the Father; whence he shall come to judge the quick and the dead; and in the Holy Ghost; the Holy Church; the remission of sins; and the resurrection of the flesh. Amen." It was afterward altered, so as to read: "Who was *conceived* by the Holy Ghost, born of the Virgin Mary;" "I believe in the Holy *Catholic* church, and the *communion of saints.*" It was also added, that after Christ "was crucified, dead and buried, *he descended into hell.*"

Several of the spurious Gospels and Epistles were publicly read in the churches, and were often quoted by the Fathers, in a manner that implies they regarded them as of equal authority with canonical Scripture. The great number of church pictures illustrating those Gospels, and still revered in all Catholic countries, proves that their authority was very extensive. Perhaps none of the apocryphal books were held in higher estimation, in the first centuries, than the Shepherd of Hermas. Irenæus cites it as "the Scripture." Clement of Alexandria says: "The book of the Shepherd is disputed by some; on whose account it is not placed among the acknowledged books. But by others it is judged most necessary. For which reason, it is now publicly read in the churches, and I have understood that some of the most ancient writers used it." Origen says: "I think Hermas was the author of that book called the Shepherd. It seems to me a very useful writing, and, as I think, is divinely inspired. It is admitted into the church, but not acknowledged by all to be divine." Eusebius and Jerome say it was publicly read in the churches, though not esteemed canonical. Jerome praised it in his catalogue, but afterward pronounced it apocryphal and foolish. Rufinus expressly styles it "a book of the New Testament."

The Epistle of Barnabas was also much quoted by the Fathers; and some of them considered it genuine. Clement of Alexandria speaks of it as "read in most of the churches." Apparently it must have been extant in Justin Martyr's time; for it contains his statement that the effiacy of Moses' prayer was owing to his arms being extended in the form of a cross; and both of them speak of the cross as allegorically signified by every *stick*, *tree*, and *bit of wood* in the Old Testament.

NATIONS CONVERTED TO CHRISTIANITY.

In some countries, Christianity began to spread by means of Christian captives taken in war, who became missionaries among their conquerors; and when a king, queen, or other influential person, became a proselyte, the multitude followed their lead. The baptism of barbarians by hundreds and thousands, by no means implies that they understood the spirit of Christianity, or imbibed its principles. The crowd, as usual, followed the example of the powerful; and those who led them were often converted by some dream, or omen, the cure of a disease, or the fortunate event of a prayer or a vow. Miracles constantly wrought at the tomb of St. Martin, Bishop of Tours, were a fruitful source of additions to the church. The people of Gallicia, and the Suevic prince in Spain were converted by them. There were baptismal fonts near the Guadalquiver, which were miraculously replenished every year, on the evening before Easter. These caused many conversions.

The Goths were early converts to Christianity. When they made their first inroads into the Roman empire, they carried off many Christians among their captives; and the conquered gained spiritual ascendancy over the rude minds of their conquerors. As early as the time of Constantine, a Gothic bishop was sent as delegate to the Council at Nice. Bishops from those countries afterward visited Constantinople, at a time when Arianism was the religion of the emperor, and of nearly all the people in that city. Thus it happened that the Goths received Christianity in the Arian form, and so it was transmitted to the different branches of their nation. These Christianized barbarians were as fierce in their zeal to convert Catholics, as the Catholics had been to convert Arians. They fined, banished, and persecuted them in various and cruel forms. Long after Arianism was vanquished in other parts of the Christianized world, it remained in full force among various Gothic tribes; and this difference was the cause of perpetual and rancorous hostility. But finally, Goths gave in to the argument that all other nations had yielded to Catholic supremacy, and that they alone disturbed the unity of the church. One of their kings, who had consented to be baptized, was not deterred by being told that all his Pagan ancestors were undoubtedly in hell; but when the Catholic missionary assured him that all his Arian relatives must be damned

also, he drew back his foot after he had placed it in the
water.

When Clovis, king of the Franks, and founder of the
French monarchy, first heard an account of the death of
Christ, he exclaimed: "If I had been there, at the head
of my valiant Franks, I would have revenged him!" He
married Clotilda, a princess of Burgundy, who was a devout Catholic. For some time, he resisted her efforts to
convert him. He allowed their first child to be baptized;
but as the babe died soon after, he repented the concession
he had made, and said to his wife: "If he had been consecrated in the name of my Gods, he would not have died;
but being baptized in the name of your God, he could not
live." Clotilda was not discouraged by this unlucky event.
She availed herself of every opportunity to induce him to
relinquish the worship of idols. One day, when he was
going to battle, she said to him: "My lord, to insure victory, you must invoke the God of the Christians. He is
sole Ruler of the Universe, and he is styled the God of
Armies. If you address yourself to him with confidence,
nothing can resist you. Though your enemies were a
hundred against one, you would be sure to triumph over
them." The king came very near being defeated. When
he saw his cavalry flying in all directions, he spread out
his arms toward heaven, and exclaimed: "Oh Christ, whom
Clotilda invokes as Son of the Living God, I implore thy
assistance! I have called upon my gods, and I find they
have no power. Deliver me from my enemies, and I will
be baptized in thy name!" His troops rallied, fought desperately, and finally gained the victory. He was solemnly
baptized at Rheims, on the twenty-fifth of December, A. D.
496. According to the wish of the queen, it was made an
occasion of great pomp. There was a procession of bishops
and priests, with a long train of monks, carrying crosses,
and singing the liturgy. Immediately after baptism, he
was anointed, according to the mode of inaugurating Christian kings. It is recorded that the Holy Ghost, in the
form of a white dove, descended from heaven with a vial

of celestial oil for the occasion. His sister, and three thousand of his court and army, were baptized the same day. He soon after caused a whole line of princes to be assassinated, to make way for his ambition. But he spared no pains to secure the good-will of the clergy; and the Patriarch of Rome conferred on him the title of Most Christian Majesty, which the French kings have ever since retained.

The Burgundians and the Visigoths, who had been converted to Christianity by Arian bishops, had taken possession of some provinces in Gaul. Clovis said to his assembled warriors: "It grieves me to see the fairest portions of Gaul possessed by Arians. Let us march against them; and having vanquished the heretics, by God's aid, we will divide their fertile provinces among us." Clotilda approved of this resolution; and begged her husband to remember that donations for pious purposes would propitiate the Deity, secure the powerful prayers of his faithful servants the bishops, and bring down a blessing from heaven on his pious undertaking. Her words pleased the king, and he replied: "Wherever my battle-axe shall fall, there will I erect a church, and dedicate it to the Holy Apostles." And he hurled the axe from him with a strong arm. On his march to invade the Arians, he turned aside to visit the sepulchre of Martin of Tours. They were performing religious ceremonies in St. Martin's church, and Clovis charged his messenger to take particular notice what was chanted at the moment they entered. The words were of good omen; but to make success still more secure he offered prayers and costly oblations at the tomb. Among other things, he made a present of his favourite war-horse. He afterward wished to redeem the valuable animal with one hundred pieces of gold; but the miraculous power of the saint kept the horse enchanted in the stable, till he offered six hundred pieces.

Clotilda survived her warlike and victorious husband; and after her death, she was canonized by the church. She seems to have had a degree of worldly ambition rather inconsistent with saintly character. Her younger sons made war upon their eldest brother, and took his children captive. They so far respected the feelings of their aged mother, as to offer to spare her grandsons, provided they were devoted to monastic life. She passionately replied: "Better my descendants should be dead, than become shaven monks!" Two of the princes were stabbed. The third made his escape to a monastery, and afterward became the famous Saint Cloud.

Gaul, conquered by the orthodox Clovis, submitted to the Catholics. Spain, which had for awhile been Arian, under Gothic conquerors, was restored to the Catholic church by voluntary conversion of the Visigoths, under King Recared; who forthwith proceeded to persecute the Arians, and burn their books, as his predecessor had done toward the Catholics. He sent ambassadors to Gregory the Great, with costly offerings of gold and gems. The Pope received them graciously, and in return for their rich presents, conferred on Recared the title of Catholic Majesty, and sent him a small piece of the True Cross, a few hairs from the head of John the Baptist, and a key made of iron filings from the chain of St. Peter. The Lombards now remained the only Arian nation; but their queen was induced to aid Catholic missionaries to convert the people. Thus, after three hundred years of incessant wrangling, of mutual murders, and burning of each other's books and churches, the metaphysical controversy concerning the Trinity was hushed, and the unity of the Catholic church at last established.

In order to introduce Christianity into Scandinavian countries, missionaries deemed it necessary to make many concessions to their fierce converts. To eat horse-flesh in honour of Odin, and take as many wives as they chose, were their principal stipulations. Plurality of wives was granted, as a politic compromise; but horse-flesh was interdicted, on account of its association with idolatry. After they consented to be baptized, they had great carousals in honour of Christ, and the Apostles, and the martyrs, and all the saints. On these occasions, they drank horns full of strong liquor, as they had been accustomed to do in honour of their old gods; until at last, the Christian festivals became such scenes of tumultuous revelry, that the better sort of men avoided them. So superficial was their conversion, that the whole mass might have been easily turned back had any unlucky accident happened before there was time for the new worship to become fixed as a habit. While Catholic missionaries were holding conference with priests of Odin assembled in Iceland, a messenger brought tidings that a volcanic eruption had done great damage in a neighbouring district. The Icelandic priests at once said: "Odin has done this, to manifest his displeasure that there are men among us who propose to abandon his worship." A Christian convert reminded them that the soil on which they were then standing was formed of lava, from an eruption centuries ago. He inquired what it was that offended the gods then; and the priests were vanquished by his sensible argument. When Bishop Poppo tried to introduce Christianity into Jutland, he convinced the people of the truth of his doctrine by thrusting his hand into a red hot iron glove, and drawing it out uninjured. The people seeing this, rushed in crowds to be baptized by the worker of miracles. This circumstance is said to have introduced trial by ordeal into that country; the bishop's method of appeal to Heaven being considered as efficacious to ascertain the truth in legal disputes, as it had proved in theological.

When Gregory the Great wished to convert the English, a monk named Augustin was chosen for the purpose; he having already attained celebrity by raising the dead, restoring sight to the blind, and various other miracles. Accompanied by forty other monks, he went to Kent, where he was kindly received by Ethelbert the king, whose wife Bertha was a Christian. Augustin permitted no coercive measures to be used, but so great was the power of his miracles, that he is said to have baptized ten thousand converts in one day. His success was rewarded by being appointed Archbishop of Canterbury, with authority over all the English churches. There had been converts to Christianity in Wales, as early as the second century, and churches were established there, which had never submitted to the jurisdiction of Rome, but continued to follow many of the old customs of the Eastern churches. Augustin tried to induce the bishops to unite with the churches he had formed in England. But they answered that they could not lay aside their old customs, and conform to the ceremonies and institutions prescribed by Rome, without first obtaining the free consent of all the people. A synod was convened, where they agreed to meet Augustin. As he did not rise to receive them, or show them any mark of courtesy, they formed an idea that he was a proud ambitious man, and felt more than ever desirous to preserve their independence. They therefore declined his offers of alliance, and when he exhorted them to conform in the manner of observing Easter, and of administering baptism, they excused themselves; saying: "We owe no more to the Bishop of Rome than the love and brotherly assistance due to all who believe in Christ. But to our own bishop we owe obedience: and without his leave, we cannot alter any of the ordinances of the church." In consequence of this, Augustin proceeded to depose the bishops, without accusing them of any crime, and without the formality of a council. Not long afterward, twelve hundred Welsh monks were slaughtered, and their monastery destroyed, by the King of Northumberland; and suspicion rested upon Augustin as the instigator of the massacre. But he is described as "a most learned and pious man, an imitator of primitive holiness, frequent in watchings, fastings, prayers, and alms: earnest in rooting out Paganism; diligent in building and repairing churches; extraordinarily famous for the working of miracles, and cures among the people." He always walked when he visited his provinces, and often travelled barefoot. The skin on his knees had grown hard by perpetual kneeling at his devotions. Yet Gregory the Great felt it necessary to admonish him for being unduly puffed up, with the honours he received.

During the reign of Constantine, a woman named Nino, who had vowed herself to celibacy and prayer, fled from Armenia, because the Christians in that region were fiercely persecuted by the Persians, who were making a convulsive effort to restore and perpetuate the worship taught by Zoroaster. She took refuge in Iberia, a country of Asia now called Georgia. The people were rude and warlike, and, as usual with such tribes, they had an instinctive reverence for whoever devoted themselves to the service of the Deity, under circumstances of peculiar self-denial. The complete seclusion, the severe fasting, and continual prayers of the Armenian woman inspired respect and awe. It happened that a child belonging to the tribe was taken ill; and, acting under the influence of the universal belief in Asia, that whoever was holy could cure diseases, they brought the child to Nino. She told them she was not acquainted with any remedy for the disease, but she would pray to her God for help. She did so, and the child soon afterward recovered. The queen was informed of this, and when she was afflicted with severe illness, she sent for the devout Armenian. Nino declined the invitation, saying, with becoming humility, that she was no worker of miracles. The queen then insisted upon being carried to her, and besought prayers for her recovery. She complied with this request, and the invalid was soon after restored to health. The king wished to send a rich present; but his consort assured him that the Christian woman despised all earthly goods: that the only thing in which they could please her would be to join in worshipping her God. In the fulness of her gratitude, and perhaps hungering and thirsting for better spiritual food than had yet been offered to her, she listened eagerly to the instructions of her pious physician, and became a convert. Her husband also was greatly impressed by the cures the stranger had performed, which she reverently attributed to the power of the God in whom she believed; but he was held back by fear of

offending the old deities, and also by the danger of rendering himself unpopular among his subjects, who were bigoted worshippers of Aramazd, the Ormuzd of the ancient
Persians. One day when he was wandering alone through
a thick forest, he became enveloped in a dense fog, and was
unable to find his way. Awe-struck by the uncertain light,
and by the silent solitude of the place, he began to reflect
upon what he had heard of those Superior Spirits, who
guide the destinies of men. The thought passed through
his mind that if he should be safely restored to his companions, he might become a worshipper of the Christian's
God, of whom his wife told such marvellous things. At
that moment, the sun suddenly burst forth, and illumined
the foliage with a wondrous glory. The wavering mind
of the monarch hailed the beautiful omen. He saw in that
golden radiance a symbol of the light of truth, dispersing
all mists from the soul. He rejoined his companions, to
whom he related what had happened. He sent for the
Christian captive, and became converted by her. He began to instruct the men among his subjects, and the queen
the women. They sent to Rome for religious teachers, and
were baptized. The people were at first exceedingly averse
to a change in the national religion, but, after much opposition, the temple of Aramazd was pulled down, and a
Cross was raised upon its ruins. It is recorded that the
erection of the first Christian church was attended with
miracles. A heavy column of stone resisted all the efforts
of the workmen to raise it. But Nino spent the night in
praying that they might be assisted, and the next morning,
the pillar rose of its own accord, and stood erect. The
people, when they witnessed this, shouted in praise of the
Christian's God, and were generally baptized. The king
entered into alliance with Constantine the Great, who sent
him valuable presents, and a Christian bishop. The popular feeling toward the temple of Aramazd was transferred
to the Cross, the possession of which soon came to be regarded as the great safeguard of the nation.

Tiridates, king of Armenia, was a bigoted worshipper

mounted his horse, and for the slightest offence against the church, their subjects were forbidden to supply them with food, water, or fire, on pain of similar excommunication themselves.

The number of Catholics at the present time is estimated at about one hundred and forty millions.

SEPARATE CHURCHES.

GREEK CHURCH.—But neither the zeal of missionaries, nor the sword of kings, succeeded in making the Catholic church quite universal. The continual rivalship between the Patriarchs of Rome and Constantinople, at last terminated in open schism; and the adherents of the latter took the name of the Greek church. The point of doctrine on which they separated was concerning the mode in which the Holy Ghost came into existence. The church at Constantinople maintained that he proceeded from the Father *only;* but the Roman church decided that he proceeded from the Father *and* the Son. The Patriarch of Rome excommunicated the Patriarchs of Constantinople and Alexandria, in the fifth century. Various attempts to reunite were afterward made, but they were followed by renewed excommunications. The Greek church assumed entire independence, and were governed by their own Patriarch and bishops. In nearly all respects, their doctrines and ceremonies are like those of the Catholics. They accept the traditions of the Fathers as of equal authority with Scripture; believing them to have been orally transmitted from the Apostles. The lower order of their priests are allowed to marry once, provided it be not to a widow.

They invoke the Virgin and the saints, whose pictures abound in their churches and houses, sometimes set with precious stones. But they retain the opinion which caused the Iconoclast warfare, and allow no sculptured images. On the strength of this distinction, they express abhorrence of the Catholics, as idolaters.

Their numbers are computed at seventy millions.

P*

Theodosius suppressed Pagan worship by the sword, and dragged the gods of antiquity at his chariot-wheels. Justinian completed the work in the same spirit. The thousands who performed their ancient rites in secret were ferreted out, and allowed no choice between baptism and death. The same course was pursued toward the Samaritans. They resisted. Twenty thousand were slain; twenty thousand sold into slavery to Persians and East Indians; and the remainder saved their lives by consenting to be baptized. It has been computed that one hundred thousand Roman subjects were slaughtered in the course of Justinian's efforts to establish the unity of the Christian church. Charlemagne drove Paganism from Teutonic Europe at the point of his spear. In his attempts to force the Saxons into Christianity, which he doubtless did from motives of state policy, he incurred a war of thirty years' duration. At last, Wittikind the Great, Duke of Saxony, was compelled to submit. The only alternative allowed them was death or baptism; and he with his whole army submitted to the ceremony, which made them Christians. When the Saxons, under King Ethelwolf, fought with the Danes, they, in their turn, offered the same choice to those who were taken prisoners; and Danish vikings, or pirates, were baptized by hundreds on the battle fields, to escape the gallows, which was ready to receive them. King Olaf, who was afterward canonized, and became the patron saint of Norway, demolished the temples and altars of Odin, introduced Christianity among his subjects by an armed force, and allowed them no alternative but slaughter.

Every one knows how the wealth and power of the church went on increasing, until the Pope came to be universally acknowledged as the Vicegerent of God upon earth, the infallible medium of the Holy Ghost. When the empire broke up into independent nations, Rome became the ecclesiastical centre of the world, as it had formerly been of the civil power. So subservient were kings to priests, that princes held the Pope's stirrup while he

of the old gods of his country. He put in prison one of
his subjects who had become a Christian, and who refused
to offer sacrifices to Anaitis, a goddess resembling the
Venus of the Romans, and the Astarte of the Syrians.
Gregory the Christian languished in prison fourteen years.
Meanwhile, the king's sister had become converted; and
when a terrible pestilence broke out, she ventured to advise
that he should be released, as a means of arresting the plague.
The king, being himself afflicted with the deadly malady,
and greatly alarmed, accepted her counsel. He was cured
by Gregory, and the pestilence soon after abated. Believing this to be a sign of approval from Heaven, the monarch
consented to be baptized; and his example was soon after
followed by all his nobles and the people. Priests were
sent for from other countries; four hundred bishops were
consecrated, and churches erected everywhere; though
not without strenuous resistance. The Christian prisoner
who had effected all this, was appointed archbishop of the
kingdom, and became famous under the name of Gregory
the Illuminator. The Province of Dara, considered the
sacred region of Armenia, obstinately resisted the innovation, and fought desperately for the preservation of their
ancient altars and temples. Every Christian church erected
there was built under the protection of troops. The prolonged contest was at last decided by a bloody battle,
which was commemorated by the following inscription on
a monument:

> " The leader of the warriors was Argan,
> The Chief of the Priesthood,
> Who lies here in his grave,
> And with him one thousand thirty-eight men.
> This battle was fought for the god-head of Kisane,
> And for that of Christ."

This was the first war for the introduction of Christianity.
But it cannot with truth be said that Christianity made its
way by persuasion, and by appeals to the inward consciousness of men, except for the first three hundred years.

NESTORIANS.—The adherents of Nestorius, after they were excommunicated, sought protection in Persia, and gained proselytes in various Asiatic countries. The doctrine taught by Nestorius, that Christ had two natures, human and divine, was afterward received into the creed of the Catholic church; but as the Nestorians persisted in calling Mary the mother of Christ only, and refused to style her Mother of God, they remained excommunicated, and formed an independent establishment. Their doctrines, worship, and church government are like those of the Greek church; but they abominate pictures as well as images, and allow no image in their churches except the cross. When an image of the Virgin was presented to them by missionaries, they exclaimed: " We are Christians, not idolaters." It is supposed that some of them, when they fled from persecution, after the decision of the Council at Ephesus, took refuge in Hindostan; for churches maintaining the same faith and worship were found centuries afterward on the coast of Malabar. They were called Christians of St. Thomas, on account of a tradition that Thomas the Apostle travelled into India, carried the Gospel there, and became a martyr to the bigotry of the Bramins. But the tomb shown as his is now believed by many scholars to be the grave of a Nestorian bishop, by the name of Thomas. The Gospel of the Infancy of Jesus, mentioned among spurious books, as purporting to be written by the Apostle Thomas, is said to have been read in these churches on the Malabar coast as late as the sixteenth century. These Christians of St. Thomas united with other Nestorians in Mesopotamia and Syria, under one church government. The whole number is computed to be about three hundred thousand. They are generally called Syrian Christians, because they have the ancient Syrian version of the New Testament, and use the same language in their worship.

ARMENIANS.—Another independent church was formed in Armenia, which agreed with the Greek concerning "the procession of the Holy Ghost," but differed both from that and the Roman on the question whether Christ had one nature or two natures. They are the remains of the Monophysites, who so long kept up a warfare against the decree of the Council at Chalcedon. To this day they teach the doctrine of Eutyches, that Christ had but one nature, and that even his body was of a divine incorruptible substance. The Armenian church agrees with the Greek in believing that the Holy Ghost proceeded from the Father only. It was long before they became reconciled to images, but they now venerate images of the Virgin and the saints. Their Patriarch lives in a monastery on Mount Ararat, which is much resorted to as a place of pilgrimage. The number of Armenians is estimated at two millions. There are also Monophysite Christians remaining in Abyssinia, who retain many Jewish customs. They circumcise their children, keep Saturday as the Sabbath, and observe the laws of Moses concerning articles of food. They admit no one to the Lord's Supper till he is twenty-five years of age; maintaining that no one is accountable for sin before that time, and that all who die earlier are sure of salvation. In Egypt there is a small remnant of the disciples of Eutyches, called Copts. These and the Abyssinian Christians are all that remain of the once powerful churches in Africa, where Tertullian, Cyprian, and Augustine lived and laboured. Some travellers have mentioned a Gospel of Thomas, read in various Christian churches in Asia and Africa, and adopted by some as their only rule of faith. It seems likely that this is the apocryphal book mentioned under the title of The Infancy of Jesus; purporting to be written by the Apostle Thomas.

Christians of all churches are accustomed to offer their prayers in the name of Christ; and it is a prevailing belief that faith in the atonement of his blood will save the greatest sinner; even if he does not repent till he is on his death-bed. Among the titles commonly bestowed on Jesus, are "The Messiah; The Anointed One; The Holy Son of Mary; The Only Begotten Son of God; The Word of God; The God-man; God manifested in the flesh; God of God; The Mediator and Intercessor for the sins of mankind; The Lamb who was slain from the beginning; The Sacrifice for all sin; The Redeemer of the world."

The birth of Christ was not introduced as an era among the nations, until five hundred and twenty-seven years after that event. Dionysius Exiguus, abbot of a monastery in Rome, was the first author of it. In the beginning, there was considerable variation between the eras adopted by churches in different parts of the world; and differences of computation still remain. But nearly all Christian nations place the birth of Christ four thousand and four years after the Creation; in the seven hundred and fifty-third year of the building of Rome. Some learned men suppose it to have occurred two years earlier; others say four years. Not being introduced as an epoch until after several centuries had elapsed, it is not surprising that some discrepancies occur in the reckoning.

The entire number of Christians, of all denominations, is computed at about two hundred and fifty millions.

MOHAMMEDANISM.

"I ask myself if all that host,
 Whose turban'd marbles o'er them nod,
Were doomed, when giving up the ghost,
To die as those who have no God?
No, no, my God! They worshipped Thee;
 Then let no doubts my spirit darken,
That Thou, who always hearest me,
 To these, thy children too, didst hearken."

J. PIERPONT.

ACCORDING to Arabian traditions, when Hagar and her son were dying with thirst, and she implored God for relief, the angel Gabriel descended and stamped on the ground; whereupon, a fountain sprang forth in the desert, on the very spot where the city of Mecca now stands. Abraham loved Ishmael better than Isaac, and often visited him in his exile; being conducted by a miraculous horse, that enabled him to perform the journey in half a day. Nevertheless, when the boy was thirteen years old, he prepared to sacrifice him, having been thus commanded by God three times in a dream. Eblis, [the Devil,] wishing to prevent such an act of piety, gave warning to Hagar and her son; but they both replied: "If he believes it to be the will of Allah, let it be done." But when all was in readiness, Gabriel appeared with a ram, which he ordered Abraham to sacrifice instead of Ishmael. This ram was the same that Abel offered; and since that time it had been pastured in Paradise. The Jewish Talmud, in relating a similar story of Isaac, says an Angel brought the ram from Paradise, where it pastured under the Tree of Life, and drank from the rivers that flowed therefrom. Ishmael became a famous hunter and warrior, and married the daughter of a king in south Arabia. He had twelve sons, the founders of twelve tribes. Abraham, who took great interest in his prosperity, wished to have the worship of One Supreme God established among them. Allah had sent down from heaven a temple for Adam, but at the time of the Deluge, He had caused it to be again drawn up into heaven. Abraham prayed earnestly that the model of it might be revealed to him, and Gabriel brought it in answer to his prayer. He then assisted Ishmael in building a temple precisely like it, on the spot where he had prepared to sacrifice him to the Lord, close beside the miraculous fountain. The Angel appointed to prevent Adam from eating the forbidden fruit had been changed into a diamond for his neglect. The diamond had been given to Adam, but was afterward drawn up into heaven with his temple. When Gabriel brought the model to Abraham, this precious stone was also sent from Paradise for him to rest upon; and it was ever after preserved in the House of Prayer, which he and Ishmael erected.

The descendants of Ishmael were hunters and herdsmen, and, like their cousins the Israelites, lived thus for ages, without attracting the attention of more civilized portions of the world. It is recorded that Caab, son of Ishmael, was accustomed to assemble the people in the temple every Friday, and instruct them concerning the God taught by Abraham. Families that spread into the adjacent country built altars for themselves, but all were in the habit of repairing to the temple erected by Abraham, which was called the Caaba, from the name of the zealous preacher. Notwithstanding his constant exhortations, idolatry increased among his relatives; insomuch that when his grandson died, Mecca was the only place where the doctrine of One God was taught.

When Christianity became the established religion of the Roman empire, Arabians were in a condition which indicates that their opinions and customs had been principally derived from Chaldean and Egyptian sources; and such would be the natural result of traditional teaching, derived by Ishmael from his Chaldean father and Egyptian mother. A large majority of them worshipped Spirits of the Stars, whom they called "Sons of God" and "Daughters of God." They named the Supreme Being Allah Taaba, and considered the Spirits his subordinate agents in the creation and government of the world, and mediators between Him and mortals. Polytheism produced the same results there as elsewhere. The Supreme God became a mere abstract idea, and the inferior deities were the only objects of popular adoration. Opinions and customs varied in different parts of the country, but there was a general resemblance in doctrines and modes of worship. All professed to derive their system from Sabi, the son of Seth, and were therefore called Sabians. They prayed three times a day: at sunrise, at noon, and at sunset. They observed three annual fasts; offered sacrifices of men and animals; made a yearly pilgrimage to Mecca, where they performed many ceremonies; and occasionally made pilgrimages to Harran in Mesopotamia, rendered sacred by some connection with the history of Abraham. Some of them made devotional journeys into Egypt, where they sacrificed a cock and a black calf, offered prayers, and burned incense before the great pyramids, which they believed to be the sepulchres of Seth, and his sons Enoch and Sabi. The Arabians, from the most ancient times, universally practised circumcision, and abstained from pork. In some of the tribes, society was divided into castes. Some sects believed in the transmigration of souls, and some introduced into their worship the sexual symbols, which Hindoos and Egyptians reverenced as Emblems of Life. When a relative died, it was the general custom to sacrifice a camel on his grave, that he might have an animal to ride upon when his body rose from the dead. In the vicinity of Persia, the doctrines of Zoroaster had become considerably mixed with the old Arabian traditions. Some sects supposed that the souls of wicked men would be punished during nine thousand ages, and then all would be forgiven, and become good.

The seven days which constitute our week were successively appropriated to the worship of the seven Planetary Spirits, to each of whom a temple was erected. The one built at Mecca is said to have been originally consecrated to the Spirit of the planet Saturn. Each tribe considered itself under the especial protection of some tutelary deity. Therefore, one tribe peculiarly devoted itself to the Spirit of the Sun, another to Jupiter, another to Sirius, and another to the star in the Bull's eye. But the temple at Mecca, which contained the ancient Caaba within its enclosures, was the central place of worship for all the Sabians.

Jews had settled in different parts of Arabia long before the Christian era; and when Jerusalem was destroyed, large numbers of them took refuge there. They gained many proselytes, some of whom were powerful chiefs, whose example influenced whole tribes. This is not surprising, considering how much common ground there was between them and the descendants of Ishmael. Both reverenced Abraham as their ancestor; both received as sacred nearly the same accounts of the creation, the deluge, and the patriarchs; and both followed the Egyptian customs of circumcision and abstinence from pork.

When Nestorius was persecuted by the dominant Christian church, some of his adherents took refuge in Arabia, where they established churches, made some proselytes, and had a bishop. The followers of Eutyches, belonging to that branch of Monophysites called Jacobites, likewise found shelter there from the storm of persecution, and converted some of the natives to their form of Christianity. There were differences of opinion among the Arabian Christians. Some believed the soul died with the body, and would rise with it at the resurrection; others regarded that doctrine as a great heresy. Nestorians denied that Mary, a mortal woman, could be the mother of that portion of Christ's nature which was divine. But another Christian sect adored her as one of the Trinity; an idea which might have originated in the fact that some Jewish Christians represented the Holy Spirit as the *mother* of Christ.

Jews and Christians in Arabia competed with each other in proselyting the Sabians. Upon one occasion they challenged each other to a public discussion, which continued three days. Early Christian writers give a miraculous account of it. They say that on the third day of the disputation, the advocate of the Hebrew religion remarked: "If Jesus is really in heaven, and can hear the prayers of his worshippers, call upon him to appear, and then we shall be convinced." The Jewish portion of the audience cried out: "Yes; show us your Christ, and then we will believe that he is the Messiah." Whereupon, there came a loud clap of thunder, followed by vivid lightning; and Jesus appeared walking on a purple cloud, surrounded by rays of glory, crowned with a diadem, and bearing a sword in his right hand. He hovered over the assembly, and proclaimed, with a loud voice: "Lo, I appear in your sight! I am Jesus, whom your fathers crucified." When he had said this, he disappeared in the clouds. The Christians exclaimed: "Kyrie eleison!" which signifies, "O Lord, have mercy on us!" The Jews were struck blind by the vision, and did not recover their sight till they were all baptized.

But efforts to convert the Arabians were only partially successful. A great majority of the people continued to worship the Spirits of the Stars, under the form of images made to represent them. The Caaba contained three hundred and sixty images, either in human form, or in the shape of lions, eagles, bulls, and other creatures that represented the constellations. Three goddesses, named Al Lata, Al Uzzah, and Manah, were called "Daughters of God;" and their images were regarded with peculiar veneration. One of them held a babe in her arms, as the Egyptian Isis was represented with her infant Horus. Every family had images of household gods, to which prayers were offered in sickness or trouble, also when they set out on a journey, and when they returned. During the last month of every year, a great concourse of pilgrims travelled to Mecca, to offer vows and sacrifices, return thanks, and present images, or other gifts, to the temple. They put off their garments before entering on the consecrated ground, and walked naked round the Caaba seven times, throwing a stone each time, because they believed that Abraham drove away the Devil with seven stones, when he appeared on that spot and tried to tempt him not to sacrifice Ishmael, as the Lord had commanded. They reverently touched the stone which Gabriel had brought down for Abraham to rest upon; travelled seven times to the neighbouring mountains, looking on the ground, to imitate Hagar's search for water; drank from her miraculous fountain, and carried home some of the holy water. They sacrificed goats, sheep, and camels, part of which they ate, and distributed the remainder among the poor. Before they returned home, they cut off their hair and their nails, and burned them in the sacred valley of Mina. They wore amulets to protect them from evil, and had faith in the magical power of charms and talismans.

Such was the state of things in Arabia, when the celebrated Mohammed Ben Abdallah, commonly called Mahomet, was born at Mecca, five hundred and sixty-nine years after the birth of Christ. He was a lineal descendant from Ishmael, in a straight line, from eldest son to eldest son. He belonged to the Koreish, the most eminent of all the tribes. Ten of their principal men were hereditary governors of Mecca, and guardians of the Caaba. The family of Hashem, into which Mohammed was born, belonged to that honoured class. The offices they held involved responsibility, as well as credit; not only on account of the annual concourse of pilgrims, but because Mecca was a privileged place of sanctuary, like the Cities of Refuge appointed by Moses. Abdallah, the father of Mohammed, died without property, soon after the birth of his son. His mother Aminah, who was noted for her beauty, worth, and intelligence, died when he was six years old. His father's eldest brother, Abu Taleb, became guardian of the orphan. He was an upright man, and educated the boy conscientiously, according to the best ideas of his age and country. He was a merchant, engaged in inland trade, and as his nephew was destined to follow the same business, he frequently took him with him on distant excursions, while he was yet a lad.

In youth Mohammed was observable for integrity, thoughtfulness, and strictness in the performance of devotional exercises. He was rather taciturn, but when he did speak, it was with earnestness and sincerity. His companions were accustomed to call him Al Amin, The Faithful. He had large dark eyes, full of feeling, his complexion was fresh and glowing, his teeth brilliantly white, his mouth finely formed, and his whole countenance luminous with an expression of intelligence and frankness. He was above the medium stature, his limbs well-proportioned, and his movements graceful. By the influence of his uncle, he became agent of a widow with considerable property in Mecca, named Khadeejah. He managed her business with so much honesty and discretion, that he won her confidence and gratitude, which ripened into personal affection, cordially reciprocated by him. He was only twenty-five years old, and she was forty. She had been distinguished above all other women in Mecca for amiability and beauty; and though she had survived two husbands, her face was still handsome, and her figure graceful. This marriage placed Mohammed in easy circumstances. Little is recorded of him during the next fifteen years. He was constant in his affection for Khadeejah, very temperate in his habits, just in his dealings, scrupulous in keeping his word, kind and generous to his relatives, extremely liberal to the poor, and strict in the performance of religious exercises. The sacred stone, on which Abraham sat, was once stolen from the Caaba and carried off by a sect, who were in hopes of thereby attracting pilgrims to their city. They would not restore it for a long time, though the people of Mecca offered five thousand pieces of gold. But not succeeding in their project of attracting pilgrims, they finally sent it back; and the keepers of the Caaba proved its identity by its peculiar property of swimming on water. A dispute arose as to who should have the honour of replacing it in the temple; but the people manifested their respect for Mohammed by unanimously deciding that he was the most worthy.

All his relatives worshipped after the manner of the Sabians. How far he conformed to it, and what influences induced him to become dissatisfied with it, are not known. Jews were numerous, and much engaged in trade. In the course of his commercial expeditions he would be very likely to meet them, and to hear them express horror of idolatry. It is said he was on terms of intimacy with a learned Jew, and with a Persian named Salman, who having been converted to Judaism, and afterward to Christianity, in some form or other, finally became a Moslem. It is not improbable that he was likewise somewhat acquainted with the Nestorian and Jacobite Christians settled in Arabia, who seem not to have been in a very enlightened condition. When he was fourteen years old, travelling with his uncle to a Fair in Syria, he lodged with Bahira, a Nestorian monk, who had been a Jew; and some say he again spent the night with him, at a later period of his life. Whatever he learned must have been taught orally. During his lifetime, writing began to be introduced among the descendants of Ishmael; but when he was young, no Arab, not even the wealthiest and best educated, was taught to read or write; and it is supposed he always remained ignorant of those useful accomplishments. But Khadeejah had a cousin, named Warakah Ebn Nawfal, a proselyte to Christianity, who could read and write Arabic and Hebrew, and was tolerably well versed in the Scriptures. Mohammed had manifested devout tendencies from early youth; his mind was eager and inquisitive, and his memory remarkably retentive. Under such circumstances he could hardly fail to have heard much from Khadeejah's relative, which would make a deep impression on him, and form subjects of contemplation, to occupy his serious and thoughtful mind, during his jour-

neys through the deserts. The Arabs were in a very rude
state, and had many barbarous and superstitious customs.
Those not engaged in trade were generally herdsmen. In
many parts of the country, they were much addicted to
robbery and marauding excursions, as their cousins the
Israelites had been. Mohammed appears to have loved
those wild tribes, with the old Asiatic feeling for descendants from a common ancestor. He had heard how Moses
received communications from Jehovah, when he retired
to the sublime solitude of a mountain; how he was divinely
directed to lead the tribes of Israel away from the degrading
influences of idolatry, and teach them that the One Supreme God was the only suitable object of adoration; and
how those rude tribes, thus bound together by a common
faith, and a central place of worship, became a wealthy and
powerful nation. In this there was much to excite a fervid, energetic temperament. If God had listened to the
prayers of Moses, on Mount Sinai, and commissioned him
to be a great prophet to the descendants of Isaac, why
should He not also listen, on Mount Hera, to the earnest
entreaties of a descendant of Ishmael, who also derived his
existence from Abraham, a worshipper of the One True
God?

Through what states of preparation his soul passed is
unknown. It is only recorded that he strictly observed
the annual Arabian Lent, called the Fast of Ramadam,
which continued thirty days. On such occasions, he was
always accustomed to retire to a cave in Mount Hera, near
Mecca, and spend the month in solitude and prayer. No
one can tell whether severe fasting, and prolonged efforts
to concentrate all his thoughts on spiritual subjects, so
affected his nerves, as to produce vivid dreams, or apparent
visions. If so, he would honestly consider them miraculous, because that was the universal faith of the age in
which he lived. It was the old Sabian belief, corroborated
by the testimony of every Jew and Christian, with whom
he conversed.

In the fortieth year of his age, while fasting during the

month of Ramadam, in the cave on Mount Hera, he informed Khadeejah that the angel Gabriel had appeared to him, and told him he was appointed to be a prophet, to abolish idolatry, and teach the worship of One God.   Previous conversations had doubtless prepared his wife for this communication.   She listened with reverent joyfulness, and swore, by Him in whose hands her soul was, that she believed he was ordained to be the prophet of his people.   She soon communicated the tidings to her cousin, Warakah Ebn Nawfal, who was also ready to believe. He said Moses had predicted that a prophet like unto himself would arise, and that Jesus had promised not to leave his disciples alone, but to send them a Comforter.   He thought there was no reason to doubt that the same Angel, who had appeared to Moses, had been sent to Mohammed; but he did not live long to assist in propagating that belief.

From that time henceforth, Mohammed considered it his mission to destroy idolatry, and restore the worship of One God, as taught by Adam, Noah, Abraham, Moses, and Jesus; which religion he said both Jews and Christians had corrupted by their superstitions.   A favourite slave, named Zaid, believed his master was divinely inspired, and his faith was rewarded by immediate emancipation.   Not long after, Mohammed's cousin Ali, a fiery-hearted, spontaneous, generous lad, the son of Abu Tâleb, became a proselyte. The next convert was Abubeker, a man of high standing in the Koreish tribe, who soon gained over some other influential men in Mecca.   To them Mohammed preached, according to the communications he received from the angel Gabriel.   His two leading doctrines were the unity of God, and unquestioning submission to the Divine will; therefore he called his system Islam, which means submission.   Things went on in a quiet and rather private way for three years, during which he had only thirteen followers, including the members of his own family; but they all prayed incessantly that the faith might be extended, and they zealously devoted themselves to its advancement, in every possible way.   At the end of that time, he caused a banquet to be prepared, and invited forty relatives, all of them descendants of his great-grandfather Hashem, who had been a man of note in his day. When they had assembled, he told them of the visits of the Angel, and said: "God Almighty hath commanded me to call you unto him. I know of no man in all Arabia who can offer his kindred anything more excellent than I now offer you; happiness in this life, and felicity in that which is to come. Who among you will assist me in my mission? Who will be my brother, and vicegerent?" They all seemed doubtful what to think or say. The youthful Ali, then only fourteen years old, seeing them hesitate thus, started up, and exclaimed: "Oh prophet, I am the man! Whoever rises against thee, I will dash out his teeth, tear out his eyes, break his legs, and rip up his belly. O prophet, I will be thy brother and vicegerent." Mohammed embraced the ardent youth, and desired those present to listen to him, and obey him, as his deputy. Whereupon, many of them laughed, and told Abu Tâleb he must now prepare to submit to his son. The coldness of his kindred did not abate the zeal of Mohammed. He seized every opportunity to converse either with friends or strangers, concerning the doctrine of One Invisible God. He openly condemned or ridiculed some of the popular usages, rendered sacred by the sanction of ages. To those whom he saw worshipping after the manner of their country, he said: "You pray to idols, that you rub with oil and wax, and the flies stick to them. I tell you they are nothing but wood." The Koreish, supposing he assumed to be a prophet for the purpose of making money, offered to make a collection for him, to appoint him chief of the tribe, and marry him to any woman he wished, if he would desist from the course he was pursuing. His uncle, the beloved guardian of his childhood, besought him to keep silence, and not risk his own safety, and that of his relatives, by proclaiming such opinions. He burst into tears, and replied: "It is a faith approved by God, and He has appointed me to be its apostle. If they would put the sun in my right hand, and the

'moon in my left, and give me the whole earth for a possession, I could not disobey the commands of God."
When pilgrims arrived, or the people assembled on festival days, he delivered to them messages from the angel Gabriel against idolatry. His uncle Abu Tâleb sought to counteract these efforts, saying: "Citizens and pilgrims, do not listen to these impious novelties. Stand fast in the worship of Al Lata, and Al Uzzah." He had, however, a strong affection for his nephew, and did his utmost to protect him from his numerous enemies. Many of the Koreish were jealous of the influence exerted by the Hashem family, and this heretical teaching afforded them a good opportunity to seek to weaken it. They reproached Abu Tâleb for protecting his blasphemous relative; saying: "Thy nephew reviles our religion. He accuses our wise forefathers of ignorance and folly. Silence him quickly; lest he kindle discord and excite tumult in the city. If he perseveres, we will draw our swords against him and his adherents, and thou wilt be responsible for the blood of thy fellow-citizens." As the Prophet could not be induced to desist, they violently attacked him and his followers, and he was frequently obliged to change his residence, to save his life. Once, when he was proclaiming his prophetical mission to an assemblage of pilgrims, he was well nigh killed by the stones thrown at him. His uncle Abu Tâleb appears to have believed in his sincerity, though he had no faith in his mission. He encountered the enmity of his tribe by openly protecting him, and providing secret places of refuge when he could do no better. The more the danger increased, the more did the good Khadeejah strive to soothe and encourage her persecuted husband. She never doubted that he was indeed a prophet sent by God; and she felt as if she was performing a great duty in consecrating her property to his support and defence. Once, when he had been preaching to the people, and returned in the evening, the house was surrounded by furious men, who pelted it with stones and other missiles, and called upon him to appear, that they might kill the

man who blasphemed their gods. Khadeejah, perceiving there was no chance for him to escape, went forth into the midst of the mob, and demanded whether her countrymen had lost the Arabian sense of honour, that they could do so mean a thing as to attack the house of a woman. Her rebuke made them ashamed, and they dispersed without doing any further injury. But the animosity of the Koreish increased to such a degree, that the Prophet gave the more timid of his followers leave to withdraw from Mecca. In the fifth year of his mission, sixteen of them, among whom were one of his own daughters and her husband, took refuge in Abyssinia. The persecution continued to increase, and two years afterward they were followed by seventy or eighty more. They were all kindly received by Nejashy, king of that country, who was either partly or entirely a convert to Christianity. When they asked for his protection, they said: "We have been driven from Arabia because we believed in a prophet, whom God hath sent; the one whom Jesus promised. He forbids murder, robbery, gambling, oppression, and adultery. He enjoins us not to eat blood, or the flesh of any creature that died of itself. He commands us to worship One Invisible God, and no other; to pray often, and give a tenth of our income to the poor." Nejashy, highly pleased with this account, replied: "The Most High God sent Jesus with the same injunctions. What does your prophet say of *him?*" They answered: "He says Jesus was the Word of God, whom a virgin conceived by the breath of the Holy Spirit." "Prosperity be with you, and with him from whom you came!" exclaimed the king. "He must be that prophet on whom the Son of Mary pronounced blessings. If the duties of my royal station did not hinder me, verily I would go and assume the office of bearing his shoes. No one shall molest you." The Koreish sent to demand them, but he refused to give them up, and he afterward became a convert to the faith of Islam.

Persecution produced the usual effect. The new doctrines spread so rapidly among the tribes, that the exasperated Koreish entered into a league not to buy or sell, marry or give in marriage, or in any way hold intercourse with the descendants of Hashem, unless they would give up Mohammed to the vengeance of their offended deities. They entered into this covenant with solemn formalities, and to invest it with greater sacredness they placed a record of it in the Caaba. The relatives of Mohammed refused to renounce him; and the tribe divided into factions, which contended with each other during three years. At the end of that time, Mohammed told his uncle Abu Tâleb, leader of the Hashemites, that God had manifested his displeasure at the Koreish league, by causing a worm to eat every word out of the document placed in the Caaba, except His own sacred name. Abu Tâleb, being in some way convinced that the writing had actually disappeared, went to the leader of the Koreish and made a statement of it; declaring that if it proved false, he would deliver his nephew into their hands; provided they would agree to cancel the league, if it proved true. They acquiesced, and were much astonished to find the record obliterated, as he had said. But though their covenant was thus rendered void, animosity between the factions remained as strong as ever. That same year, which was the tenth of Mohammed's mission, his kind guardian Abu Tâleb died, at the age of eighty. Some say he embraced the faith of Islam on his death-bed; others deny it. Very soon afterward, Khadeejah died. She was sixty-five years old, and had lived with Mohammed a little more than twenty-four years; during which time she brought him two sons and four daughters. While she lived, no other woman shared his affections, and he never seemed to desire the acquaintance of any; a very remarkable fact, considering he was fifteen years younger than herself, and lived in a country where polygamy was sanctioned by law and universal custom. He buried her with his own hands; and that year was ever afterward named by him and his followers The Year of Mourning.

The animosity of the Koreish became more active after

he was deprived of the guardian uncle, who had so long loved and protected him. They intercepted supplies of water, and injured him and his adherents in so many ways, that he fled to Tayef, sixty miles from Mecca, accompanied by his favourite freed man Zaid. He was received coldly by the principal inhabitants, and when he had been there a month, the populace rose against him, while he was attempting to preach to them, and drove him from the city. He returned to Mecca, where he found his followers greatly disheartened by the unpromising aspect of his affairs. He kept up his courage, however, and continued to preach boldly to the pilgrims, and all others who would hear him. Six members of a Jewish tribe of Arabs, who lived at Yathreb thus became believers in his inspiration, and when they returned home, they warmly commended him and his doctrines.

In the twelfth year of his mission, he declared to his followers that he had made a journey from the temple in Mecca to Jerusalem, and had thence ascended through the seven heavens into the presence of God, and back again to Mecca, in one night. This excited so much distrust, that many left him. Others said if "Moses conversed with God face to face," they knew not why a similar privilege might not be granted to the prophet whom Moses had promised should be "like unto himself." The zealous convert Abubeker declared if Mohammed affirmed it, that was sufficient for him; he believed every word he uttered. His undoubting reliance confirmed some who were wavering; and the idea that Mohammed, who had heretofore received communications through the medium of the angel Gabriel, had been actually admitted to the Divine Presence, and taught by God himself, greatly increased the sacredness with which their faith invested him.

Meanwhile, the pilgrims, who had gone back to Yathreb favourably impressed with Mohammed's teaching, had sown some seeds of doctrine in that city. That same year twelve men came from thence, and had a meeting with the Prophet on a hill near Mecca. They took a solemn oath never to worship images, or kill their children, or steal, or commit fornication, or forge calumnies, and to obey the Prophet in all things reasonable. These proselytes, having received his blessing, were sent home with one of his experienced disciples, to give them still farther instruction in his doctrines. The next year, being the thirteenth of his mission, the Prophet met seventy-five more converts, in the night time, at the same place. He told them frankly that he had many and powerful enemies, and might soon be compelled to fly from his native city. If they sought to protect him, they might become involved in great dangers; therefore, unless they were very firmly persuaded in their own minds, they had better leave him to seek assistance elsewhere. They asked what reward they were to expect if they happened to be killed in defence of him and his doctrines. He told them they would thus make sure of the joys of Paradise; whereupon, with solemn formalities, they pledged themselves to his service. He chose twelve from among them, who were invested with the same authority that the Apostles of Christ had over the other disciples.

When the Koreish heard that his doctrines were thus extending abroad, and that he had formed a league with certain influential men in Yathreb, they resolved to prevent his leaving Mecca. It was agreed that a man should be selected from each of the forty tribes, and every one should pledge himself to plunge a knife in Mohammed's heart. This array of numbers was intended to prevent the Hashemites from revenging the murder of their kinsman; their power being altogether inadequate to a contest with all the tribes. The conspiracy came to the Prophet's knowledge. He said it was revealed to him by the angel Gabriel. He escaped by night in disguise, with his friend Abubeker. His generous-hearted cousin Ali assumed his garments, and laid himself down on the Prophet's couch to await the assassins. They came at the appointed hour; but they respected the nobleness of the action, and did him no injury. Meanwhile, the fugitives had concealed themselves in a cave, about three miles from Mecca. There they remained three days, and the son and daughter of Abubeker secretly conveyed them food. The Koreish sent scouts in every direction to search for them. One of these parties passed directly by the cave, but did not enter. As the sound of their trampling passed away, the trembling Abubeker remarked: "We are only two." "There is a third with us," replied Mohammed; "it is God himself." Some of the Prophet's followers say the Koreish were struck with sudden blindness, and could not see the cave. Others affirm that a spider was sent to spin a web across the entrance, and a pigeon was sent to weave a nest and lay two eggs. The pursuers, being deceived by those indications, took it for granted that no one could have recently entered there. Jews had a similar tradition concerning David; of whom the Talmud relates that the Most High sent a spider to weave a web across the mouth of the cave where he was hidden from the anger of Saul.

The fugitives remained in the cave three days. The pursuit having abated in that time, their friends furnished them with camels and a guide, and they escaped by night, through a rocky and desert country, to Yathreb, which was a hundred and seventy miles from Mecca. This is called the Hegira, which signifies Flight. It was the commencement of Mohammed's prosperous career as a prophet; therefore, his followers adopted it as their era. It occurred six hundred and twenty-two years after the birth of Christ, when Mohammed was fifty-three years old.

The wanderers met with a cordial reception from the believers at Yathreb. Mohammed bought a piece of ground, and built a small house and a place of worship; both characterized by extreme simplicity. There he stood and preached every Friday, leaning against a palm tree. It was several years before he indulged himself with the use of a chair. Afterward, a rude pulpit was made of rough timber. His fervour and eloquence gained converts rapidly. In a short time, there was scarcely a family to be found which did not contain more or less believers.

Before his flight from Mecca, the Prophet had always declared that he was appointed merely to preach One Invisible God, and the duty of submission to His decrees; that he had been invested with no authority to compel people to embrace the true religion. But after the Koreish attempted to murder him, he taught that it was highly meritorious to fight with unbelievers. It is said he was personally present in twenty-seven military expeditions, in nine of which he gave battle. On one of these occasions he was severely wounded, and narrowly escaped with his life. This somewhat shook the faith of his adherents; but he soon restored his authority by telling them the defeat was sent as a punishment for their sins, and to admonish them to be more zealous in the performance of religious duties. This, combined with the assurance that every one who died fighting for the faith of Islam was sure to go directly to Paradise, re-assured their faith and renewed their enthusiasm.

At the commencement of his career he strongly favoured the Jewish religion, and taught his followers to turn toward Jerusalem when they prayed. There are indications that he might have formed a friendly alliance with them, if they had not persevered in treating his claims with the utmost contempt. Three years after the Hegira, he led a band of his followers against the Jews of Koreidha, who had aided the Koreish against him. Nearly seven hundred men were dragged to the market-place in chains, massacred, and thrown into one common grave. The conquerors took possession of all their goods, and carried their women and children into bondage. He afterward took the principal Jewish city in Arabia, and completely subjugated all the descendants of Isaac in that region.

With success, his power over the minds of men increased of course. Though he lived with extremest simplicity in the midst of his followers, wore no pontifical robes, and assumed no regal state, he ruled them with the combined authority of pope and king. They believed everything he touched imbibed supernatural virtue. They reverently

picked up the hairs that fell from his head, and preserved
them as relics; and every one was eager to obtain some
of the water in which he had washed. His residence at
Yathreb rendered the city sacred; and it was thenceforth
called Medinat al Nabi, The City of the Prophet; known
to Europeans under the name of Medina. The most distinguished and venerated guardians of the holy Caaba had
never received a thousandth part of the homage accorded
to him. The shrine at Mecca was held so sacred by all
Arabians, that it was an object of importance to the Prophet to be allowed to make a pilgrimage thither with his
adherents, who fully believed that he was sent by God to
restore the religion of Abraham, as it had been originally
taught in that place. The animosity of the Koreish rendered such an attempt dangerous; but six years after the
Hegira his cause had acquired such strength, that he started
for Mecca, with an escort of fourteen hundred armed adherents. When he arrived at the boundary of the sacred
territory, the Koreish sent him orders not to enter the city.
He had determined to besiege the place, when an ambassador arrived, proposing a ten years' truce, on certain conditions. He and his followers were permitted to visit the
temple unarmed, and perform the customary rites of pilgrimage, with the agreement that they would all leave the
city at the expiration of the third day. Eighty of the
Koreish had entered Mohammed's camp in disguise, and
were discovered by the Prophet, who pardoned the spies,
and allowed them to return unmolested. It is said this
act of generosity occasioned the truce. But it is most
likely that the accounts they carried back served to intimidate his enemies, and that he had sufficient sagacity to
foresee such would be the result. For the ambassador,
who was sent to negotiate a treaty, returned, saying: "I
have seen the princes of Persia and the emperors of Rome;
but I have never seen a king among his subjects like Mohammed among his followers." The Koreish retired to
the neighbouring hills, while the pilgrims from Medina
performed their acts of worship within the consecrated ter-

ritory. Mohammed departed with his train on the third day; but during that time he succeeded in converting three influential men among the Koreish. The next year, the Prophet sent messages to various chiefs and princes, inviting them to embrace the only true religion. Some returned a respectful answer, accompanied with gifts. Others replied very contemptuously. One of his ambassadors, to a Grecian district in Syria, was put to death. He sent his freed man Zaid with three thousand men to revenge the insult. Victory was gained, after severe fighting, but Zaid was slain. The Prophet loved him, and had adopted him; for he had always been faithful and affectionate, and he was the first man who believed in his inspiration. When they told him Zaid was dead, he answered calmly: "He has done his master's work, and he has gone to his master. All is well with him." But when the corpse was brought home, the daughter of Zaid found the stern old warrior weeping over it like a sorrowing child. "What do I see!" she exclaimed, in astonishment. He answered: "You see a man weeping over his friend."

The Koreish having violated some articles of their treaty, Mohammed marched against Mecca with ten thousand troops. He ascended a hill near his native city, and prayed with a loud voice that Gabriel and three thousand angels might be sent to his assistance. Though these celestial auxiliaries were invisible, his followers had the most implicit faith that they were in attendance. They rushed furiously to the attack, and the Koreish, taken by surprise, offered slight resistance. The chiefs fell at the feet of their conqueror, who sternly demanded, "What right have you to expect mercy from a man whom you have so persecuted?" They answered: "We trust to the generosity of our kinsman." "You shall not trust in vain," he replied; and they received life and liberty, on condition of embracing the faith of Islam. Only ten in the city were condemned to die, and six of those were afterward pardoned. All the idols in the temple, and on the neighbouring mountains, were destroyed, to the great grief and dismay of their worshippers. The temple became a mosque, and the ancient Caaba the point toward which all believers in the Prophet turned when they prayed, as Jews did toward the Ark of the Covenant. The diamond from Paradise, on which Abraham rested, had long been known as "the black stone." Moslems say the frequent touch of Pagans had changed its colour, but its purity and lustre will one day be restored. The Prophet touched it, and thenceforth it became more sacred than it had ever been.

The man who began by saying he was merely sent to preach the truth, not to compel men to accept it, and who probably honestly thought so, while he was untempted by power, now began to announce that he was ordained to destroy monuments of idolatry everywhere, without regard to holy places, months, or days. He sustained himself by the example of Moses and Joshua, whom God had sent on a similar mission. He included Jews and Christians under the term idolaters. The first, because he said they styled Ezra "the Son of God." The second, because they worshipped Christ as God; prayed to the Spirits of Martyrs; paid homage to images, pictures, and relics; and in some cases believed the Virgin Mary to be one of the Trinity. Had the Jews treated him respectfully in the early days of his mission, when Jerusalem was his *kebla* for prayer, he would probably have made common cause with them; and very likely he might have done much toward verifying their ancient prophecy that they should conquer many nations, and finally subdue the whole earth. But he seems never to have forgiven the scorn with which they treated him. He had far greater aversion to them than to Christians. He often denounces them in the Koran, and during the latter part of his life he persecuted them with peculiar severity. But savage as were the Arab tribes, it must be admitted that they were somewhat less so, than the Hebrews had been under Joshua. In their efforts to extend what they believed to be the true religion, they were often cruel, tyrannical, and avaricious of plunder. Like their Hebrew

Q*

relatives, they seized "vineyards they had not planted," and "harvests they had not sowed," and said they did it in obedience to the commands of God. But they did not exterminate idolatrous tribes, with all their women and babes, without offering them a chance for escape. They always proffered the alternative of submission or battle. If they fought and were conquered, they could save their lives, and be admitted to equal privileges with their invaders, by assenting to their simple creed: "There is but One God, and Mohammed is his prophet." Exceptions were made in favour of those who received some Sacred Book for the guide of life; as did Jews and Christians. Such could purchase liberty to follow their own religion, by paying tribute; though they were deprived of many of the civil privileges enjoyed by "true believers," and were supposed to have no hopes of salvation in the world to come. This was done to express Mohammed's reverence for any laws which he believed to have been originally revealed from heaven, how much soever he supposed them to have been afterward corrupted.

Layard, in his very interesting book on the Remains of Nineveh, says: "One of the first acts of Mahomet, after he had established his power, was a treaty with the Nestorians, securing them protection and certain privileges. They were freed from military service, their customs and laws respected, their clergy exempted from tribute; and it was expressly declared that when a Christian woman entered into the service of a Mussulman, she should not be compelled to change her religion, to abstain from fasts, or to neglect her customary prayers and ceremonies. This document is rejected by some European critics as a forgery; but its authenticity was admitted by early Christian and Mahometan writers. A letter from the Patriarch Jesujabus is evidence of the Mahometan toleration of Nestorians. He writes: 'Even the Arabs, on whom the Almighty has in these days bestowed the dominion of the earth, are among us. They do not persecute the Christian religion; on the contrary, they commend our faith, and

honour the priests and saints of the Lord, conferring benefits upon his churches and convents.'" The Nestorians
were doubtless regarded with peculiar favour, because
they would never allow any picture or image to be placed
in their churches.

During twenty-four years, Mohammed lived with one
wife, devotedly attached to her, and her only. After her
death, he married twelve wives, all widows, except Ayesha, the daughter of his early and zealous friend Abubeker,
whom he espoused when she was only nine years old. In
addition to these, he had two handmaids; one of whom
gave birth to a son, named Ibraheem; the only child born
to him after the death of his first wife. The members of
this seraglio occupied separate apartments round his dwelling at Medina. His followers were not allowed to marry
more than four wives; the limit fixed by Jewish laws.
But he said he was himself exempted from that rule by
revelations from Gabriel, which are inserted in the Koran.
This extension of privilege was also in conformity to the
decisions of Jewish Rabbis, and was sustained by the example of David and Solomon; whom both Jews and Christians believed to be supernaturally guided and inspired.
He already had several wives, when he chanced to see the
wife of his freed man Zaid. She was very beautiful, and
he became violently enamoured. Zaid, who loved him
with strong personal affection, and reverenced him as the
chosen ambassador of the Most High, offered to divorce
her for his sake. Mohammed at first refused, and struggled a while with his passion. But a verse of the Koran
was revealed to him, which sanctioned the proceeding, and
he added the handsome Zaynab to his hareem. There was
no Nathan the prophet in Arabia, who dared to rise up
and rebuke him; and it must be confessed there were some
features in King David's treatment of Uriah even more
discreditable to a servant of God, than were Mohammed's
dealings with Zaid.

In the midst of all these irregularities, his good old
Khadeejah never seemed to lose her strong hold upon his

affections. After her death, he loved and trusted Ayesha more than any of his wives; partly on account of her youth and beauty, partly from his strong affection and gratitude for her father. Yet when this petted favourite, years after his first companion was in her grave, ventured to ask: "Do you not love me better than you did Khadeejah? She was old, and a widow. Am I not better than she was?" He replied warmly: "No; by Allah, there never *can* be a better woman than Khadeejah. She helped me when I was poor; she believed in me, when others despised me; she was devoted to me, when all men persecuted me." He was accustomed to say that there were four perfect women, who had more beautiful palaces in Paradise, than any other women. These were his wife Khadeejah, his daughter Fatima, the sister of Moses, and the mother of Jesus.

With the exception of voluptuous tendencies in the latter part of his life, and great fondness for perfumes, Mohammed was exceedingly frugal and temperate in all his habits. He never tasted of wine or intoxicating drinks. He sometimes ate animal food, and he was very partial to honey and milk; but his common diet was barley bread, dates, and water. Sometimes months passed without his eating anything that required fire for its preparation. A cloak spread on the ground served for his bed, and a skin filled with date leaves was his pillow. He rode on a blanket instead of a saddle, mended his own garments and sandals, milked the goats, and ate the same food as his servants, seated with them on the ground. He manifested an attentive kindness to children, and always gave the first salutation to whoever he met, even if it were the meanest beggar. He declared that he would always persist in doing such things, that they might thenceforth be deemed meritorious by those whom his example could influence. It was allowable for him to divide lands of the conquered, because God had given to him the possession of all the earth; and to take whatever he chose from the spoils of war, beside receiving a fifth part when division was made

Of course, an immense amount of wealth came into his
hands. But he was so generous to his friends, and so exceedingly liberal to the poor, that he never accumulated.
From the large sums that came to him, he reserved merely
enough to maintain his family; and even from that fund
he imparted so liberally to the necessities of others, that
the close of the year found him destitute. On one occasion, it is said he even gave away his last shirt. His followers have a tradition that an angel once appeared to
him, and offered to change the whole wilderness around
Mecca into gold for him. But he raised his hand toward
heaven, and said: "O Lord I desire to be filled one day,
and thank Thee, and be hungry another day, and suppli-
cate Thee." His followers placed implicit reliance on his
veracity and justice, which they declare was unimpeach-
able. His cruel treatment of the Jews of Koreidha was the
darkest stain upon his character. It cannot be excused,
even on the ground of mistaken theological zeal; for there
was great similarity in their opinions, and there was nothing in their practices to excite his animosity against image-
worship. With this exception, he was, on the whole, more
merciful than Asiatic conquerors have generally been.
Human nature is such a problem, that it is not easy to
decide how far his aggressions upon others might have
been sanctioned by the honest, though mistaken, convictions of his own conscience. He seems to have been sincerely persuaded that there was no salvation for those
whose faith was erroneous; certainly not if they were
idolaters. It is related of him that he went to visit his
mother's tomb. As he gazed upon it, he burst into a
flood of tears, and said: "I asked permission of God to
visit my mother's grave, and it was granted to me;
but when I asked leave to pray for her soul, it was
denied."

He was extremely devotional in his habits. He never
destroyed a piece of paper on which he knew that the name
of God was written in any language, or by the followers
of any religion. He was diligent in prayer. Ali has re

corded that he sometimes prayed all night, and that "from convulsive weeping his breast sounded like a boiling pot; so extreme was his awe of God." He fasted several days in every month, beside observing with great strictness the annual fast of Ramadam. He never mentioned the faults of others, or bestowed much praise. He often smiled, but never laughed. He was taciturn, as Arabians generally are; but he had an insinuating politeness, and was always courteous and affable, especially to inferiors. The Hashem family were distinguished by a large dark vein in the middle of the forehead, which swelled when they were excited. When Mohammed was angry, this became very prominent, and "the perspiration fell from his brow like pearls." But though naturally of a violent temper, he acquired great control over himself. It was one of his maxims that "he who can command his own soul is bravest of the brave." Returning from battle, he said he was going from a small contest to a great one. Being asked what he meant, he replied: "The conflict with our own souls, where we always have to encounter the worst of our enemies." He was never disturbed by the destruction of worldly goods, and was habitually gentle; but "if he heard that truth or equity had suffered, he was so angry for the Lord's sake, that no one could stand in his presence till the truth was vindicated." Though he dressed with such rude simplicity, associated daily with all sorts of men, and performed the most menial offices for himself, there was a dignity about him, which inspired veneration. The Persian Book of Traditions concerning him declares that "while he spoke, the company inclined toward him, and were silent and still, as if a bird were perched on their heads." "The Most High inspired such awe of him in the hearts of men, that notwithstanding his humility, condescension, and clemency, no one could look him directly in the face; and a trembling, which lasted two months, fell on every infidel and hypocrite who approached him." "Light radiated from his countenance, as from the full moon; and his smooth erect neck resembled a polished silver statue." He was of illustrious lineage, of unequalled nobleness, knowledge, and generosity; his words sweeter than honey; and for gracefulness a proverb." Of course, some allowance must be made for these accounts, considering the partial source whence they come. But a man who lived on an equality with his servants and soldiers, and yet impressed them with so much reverence, as to give rise to such traditions, must have been a remarkable character. To estimate him justly, it is necessary to remember that he was brought up among a fierce and ignorant people, and that he scarcely knew anything of the world beyond Arabia. His views concerning Christianity cannot surprise us, if we reflect what was its condition at that period; especially in the countries that came under his notice. Different sects persecuted each other even unto banishment and death; bishops contended for power, and were often unscrupulous about the means; the cross was considered an efficacious amulet to expel devils from haunted houses, and from the bodies of men; churches were filled with pictures and relics, before which the multitude prostrated themselves, praying for health and harvests; and in every house were images of apostles or martyrs, to which prayers were offered before and after a journey. It is not surprising that a religion without a priesthood to contend for wealth and power, with unadorned places of worship, few ceremonies, and a creed without abstruse doctrines, which merely taught belief in one God and submission to his decrees, should have impressed some minds favourably in comparison. Had Christianity been in harmony with the precepts and practice of its founder, the sword of Mohammed could not have displaced it in so many countries.

His system was a reproduction of old ideas, from various sources. He retained many of the Sabian traditions, and borrowed from Jews, Christians, and Persians. Judging from the quotations and allusions he makes, his knowledge of the Christian Scriptures was mostly confined to the Spurious Gospels, mentioned as having been in general use in the first centuries; which continued to be received and reverenced by churches in the East much longer than by those in the West.

As a reformer, Mohammed was most undoubtedly a benefactor to his country. All the changes he introduced were an improvement upon the state of things he found in Arabia. He abolished idolatry, and sacrifices, and firmly established the idea of one God. Daughters were considered a burden to a family, and a disgrace if they were not married; therefore, parents often drowned them, or buried them alive. But the Koran forbade this, as a great sin. Before his time, women were not allowed to inherit any share of a father's or husband's property, but he changed the laws, and inculcated justice and kindness toward widows and orphans. His example established the idea that no believer in the faith of Islam ought to hold a fellow believer in slavery. In the sale of captives, he prohibited the practice of separating mothers from their children. He ordained that masters and slaves should have the same food and clothing; and he rendered emancipation easy. The destitute were not trusted to casual charity. It was enacted that every man should give a tithe of his income for the support of the poor; and if he attempted to defraud, he was compelled to pay a fifth. The Arabians were much addicted to gambling and intoxication. Both of these were expressly forbidden. They were not even allowed to taste of wine or strong liquors. He did not abolish polygamy, which was the ancient custom of the country, and believed by him and his followers to be sanctioned by the example of the patriarchs; but he discouraged divorce, and passed several salutary and restraining laws on the subject. He continually urged honesty and veracity, as crowning virtues. The old custom of assembling on Friday to offer sacrifice and prayer had come to be used mainly as a convenience for trading purposes; but by his exhortations and laws it became invested with a devotional character. His rude countrymen already believed in a very sensual heaven and hell. The Koran diminished rather than increased this tendency. The voluptuous pictures, which Europeans are accustomed to quote, were mostly introduced by Books of Traditions, received as supplementary to the Koran, long after his death. He appointed the following prayer to be repeated by every one when he was about to leave his house: "Oh God, make me content with thy decrees, and bless me in that which thou hast destined. Help me not to wish the acceleration of what thou hast delayed, nor the delay of what thou hast accelerated; for all things are in thy power." He prescribed prayers five times in every twenty-four hours; at sunrise, noon, sunset, close of twilight, and before the first watch of the night. When some converts complained of this, as onerous, he replied: "Religion is nothing without prayer." He required that all these acts of devotion should be preceded by ablution, saying that without cleanliness no prayer could be acceptable to God. He taught his followers that prayer and fasting would carry them to the gate of Paradise, and benevolence to the poor would gain them admittance. He repeatedly disclaimed power to work any other miracle than producing the Koran. Whether he really believed he was in communication with the angel Gabriel, no mortal can ever know. The balance of evidence inclines a candid mind to the conclusion that he was a religious enthusiast, rather than an ambitious artful impostor.

Ten years after the Hegira, he made a pilgrimage to Mecca, with a splendid retinue of more than one hundred thousand followers. This was his last journey. The physical strength which had endured so much hardship, turmoil, and battle, had been failing for the last few years, in consequence of eating mutton, supposed to have been poisoned by a Jewish woman, in revenge for the injuries inflicted on her people. Soon after his return from Mecca, he was seized by fever, which at intervals deprived him of reason. He said to Ali: "Gabriel has every year recited the Koran to me once; but this year, he has done it twice. I think this is a sign that my departure is near." He emancipated all his slaves, and gave directions concerning his funeral. He was so poor, that he literally possessed nothing but one

camel; but he charged Ali to see that every debt was paid.
Until three days before his death, he continued his usual
practice of public exhortation and prayer. Weakness then
compelled him to ask his old friend Abubeker to perform
the duty for him. With a bandage bound tightly round
his throbbing head, and leaning on the shoulder of Ali, he
went to the mosque to bid his people farewell. "Oh, my
companions," said he, "what a prophet I have been unto
you! Did you not break my front teeth, throw dust on
my forehead, and cause blood to flow from my face, till
my beard was dyed with it? Have I not suffered distresses
and calamities through the ignorance of my people? Did
I not bind a stone on my stomach to allay the torment of
hunger, while aiding my followers?" They replied: "Yes,
O prophet of God. Verily you have endured much for
God's sake, and you have prohibited what was wrong.
May God reward you with the best of rewards, on our
account." He answered: "May God grant you the same.
The time is now very near when I shall be concealed from
you. Therefore, if any man has a claim on me, let him
declare it now." A voice from the crowd said: "You
owe me three drachms." He ordered them to be paid;
and added: "If I have done injury to any one, I adjure
him to rise and tell me." A man stood up, and said:
"Your staff struck me one day; but whether it was done
intentionally on your part, I do not know." He replied:
"God forbid that I should have done it intentionally;"
and he offered the man his staff, that he might return the
blow; saying: "It is better to be in shame now than at
the Day of Judgment." But he kissed the Prophet's body,
and forgave the accident. Mohammed said to the people:
"No one can hope for favour from God, but by obedience.
That alone can save us from the wrath of God. Verily, if
I should sin, I should go to hell. O Lord, I have delivered
thy message." He descended from the pulpit, and after
offering a brief prayer with the people, he returned to his
house. During his illness, he expressed undoubting confidence in the favour of God, and often repeated consoling

messages brought by the angel Gabriel, who was said to visit him every day and night. The only child he had left was Fatima, who had married her cousin Ali. He manifested the strongest affection for them, fervently blessed them and their children, and charged Ali to be always kind to his family. He had previously declared that tho Angel of Death would never be allowed to take his soul from the body till he received permission from himself. Gabriel informed him that the Angel was now in attendance, and would either take him, or go away, which ever he chose; adding: "Verily the Most High is desirous to meet you." Whereupon, Mohammed replied: "I have finished my mission, and am ready to join my fellow prophets in Paradise. Oh, Angel of Death, execute your orders!" He died with his head reclining in Ayesha's lap. His last broken words were: ",O God—pardon my sins— yes, my companions—I come."

The announcement of his departure was met with an outburst of clamorous grief. His friends exclaimed, "How *can* he be dead? He who was our witness and intercessor with God? By Allah, he *is* not dead! He is only wrapped in a trance, like Moses and Jesus; and he will speedily return to his faithful people." Omar, in his frenzy, unsheathed his scimitar, and declared he would strike off the head of any infidel, who said the Prophet was dead. But Abubeker rebuked them, saying: "Is it Mohammed you worship, or Him who created Mohammed? Verily Allah liveth forever; but his apostle was a mortal, like ourselves; and he has experienced the common fate of mortality, according to his own predictions." He died in the eleventh year of the Hegira, when he was sixty-three years old. People came from the surrounding country in great numbers to gaze upon his beloved countenance, and pronounce blessings over his bier. This ceremony lasted from Monday till Tuesday night. He had instructed Ali to build a very simple tomb, and enclose it with a wall. The possession of it rendered Medina a sacred city, thenceforth resorted to by many pilgrims.

SACRED BOOKS.—A belief prevailed among both Hebrews and Arabians that writings had been handed down
by Adam. Some Jewish Rabbis ascribed the ninety-second
Psalm to Adam. In some manuscripts, there was a Chal-
dee title, which declared: "This is a song of praise, repeated by the first man, for the Sabbath day." In the
Christian Scriptures, Jude alludes to prophecies by Enoch,
"the seventh from Adam." It was a current tradition
among Arabians that Adam received ten books from
heaven; that Abraham, in the course of his travels, found
a chest containing those books, together with others, written by Seth and Enoch; that ten others were afterward
communicated to him, among which was the Zend Avesta.
Books purporting to be written by Enoch and Seth still
exist in Asia. They are said to contain accounts of Star
Spirits, mediators between the Supreme and mortals, and
of love entertained by some of them for women on this
earth, by which different races of intermediate genii were
produced. At the time Mohammed appeared, the Book
of Seth was much revered by many of the Arab tribes.
They also had traditions concerning the creation, the deluge, and the descendants of Adam, which were very similar to the Hebrew, and which they traced to Abraham.
The Zend Avesta, also attributed to him, was regarded
with reverence, especially by tribes in the neighbourhood
of Persia. A knowledge of the Hebrew Scriptures, especially of the Rabbinical traditions which formed the Talmud, was introduced among tribes converted to Judaism.
They had much reverence for a book called Psalms of
David, to which were added prayers by Moses, Jonas and
others. Some of the numerous spurious Gospels afloat in
the first centuries, many of them from Gnostic sources, had
been introduced into Arabia by Christian sects; and it is
obvious that Mohammed, by some means or other, was
acquainted with them. The Koran seems to be composed
of fragments from all these sources; and this was in ac-
cordance with the teaching of Mohammed, who always
spoke of his own inspirations as "a confirmation of the

Scriptures which had been revealed before." He said ten books had been given to Adam, fifty to Seth, thirty to Enoch, and ten to Abraham. Afterward the Pentateuch was revealed to Moses, the Psalms to David, the Gospel to Jesus, and the Koran to him. He says: "We make no difference between that which God has taught *us*, and that which Abraham, Isaac, Ishmael, the twelve tribes, Moses, .and Jesus, have learned of the Lord." To restore religion .as it was taught by Abraham was especially his object. In the Koran it is written: "The Law and the Gospel were not sent down till after Abraham. He was neither a .Jew nor a Christian. But he was of the true religion; one resigned unto God, and not of the number of idolaters." Mohammed said the first hundred books revealed by God had all been entirely lost; that Jesus had carried his Gospel back with him to heaven; that the Pentateuch of Moses, the Psalms of David, and the Gospels received by Christians, had been so much altered, that, though they might retain some portions of truth, they were by no means to be relied on; the Koran was the last revelation that would ever be given; the only trustworthy standard; and angels had especial charge of it, to prevent its ever becoming corrupted, as other Sacred Books had been.

The Koran purports to have been revealed to Mohammed in portions, by the angel Gabriel, at different places, and successive periods, as various emergencies required, during the course of twenty three years. The Prophet being unable to write, employed a scribe to record these fragments. It is generally said that Ali was his principal amanuensis; but others were also employed. These fragments were left in a chest, in a very disorderly state, some written on skins, some on palm leaves, and some on shoulder-blades of mutton; for paper was not invented, and parchment was then rarely seen in Arabia. Two years after the death of Mohammed, his friend Abubeker collected them and had them copied into a volume; and it is said that some verses which had been committed to memory were added. It forms a printed book about

the size of the New Testament. Like the Pentateuch,
it constitutes the only civil code, as well as the religious
standard of the nation; and most of the laws are in fact
almost exact transcripts of the ordinations of Moses, and
the judicial decisions of Jewish Rabbis. It breathes also
the same spirit of extermination against idolaters, that
the Old Testament does against the Philistines. Hebrews
called their Sacred Books by the general term of The
Scriptures, or The Writings. Arabians named theirs Al
Koran, which signifies The Reading. The following extracts will serve to give some idea of its character: The
first chapter consists of a prayer, which all devout Moslems
pronounce before they begin to read anything, and as a
prelude to all important undertakings: " Praise be to God,
the Lord of all creatures; the Most Merciful, the King of
the Day of Judgment! Thee do we worship, and of thee
do we beg assistance. Direct us in the right way, in the
way of those to whom thou hast been gracious; not of
those against whom thou art incensed, nor of those who
go astray."

" God hath commanded that ye worship no one beside
him."

" There is no God but Allah, the living, the self-sub-
sisting. He hath sent down unto thee the book of The
Koran, with truth confirming that which was revealed before it. For he had previously sent down the Law and
the Gospel, as guides unto man. He had also sent down
the distinction between good and evil. Verily, those who
believe not the signs of God shall suffer a grievous punishment; for God is mighty, and able to revenge."

" Say God is one God; the eternal God. He begetteth
not, neither is he begotten; and there is not any one like
him."

" The Jews say Ezra is the Son of God, and the Christians
say Christ is the Son of God. This is their saying in their
mouths. They imitate the sayings of those who were unbelievers in former times. May God resist them! How
they are infatuated! They take priests and monks for

their lords, beside God, and Christ the son of Mary; although they are commanded to worship one God only. There is no God but him."

"When God shall say unto Jesus, at the Last Day, O Jesus, son of Mary, didst thou say unto men, take me and my mother for two gods, beside God? He shall answer, Praise be unto Thee! It is not for me to say that which I ought not. If I had said so, thou surely wouldst have known it. Thou knowest what is in *me*, but I know not what is in *Thee;* for thou art the knower of secrets. I have not spoken to them otherwise than what thou didst command me; namely, Worship God, who is *my* Lord, and *your* Lord."

"Verily Christ Jesus is the apostle of God; a Spirit proceeding from Him; the Word, which he conveyed into Mary. Believe, therefore, in God and his apostles; and say not there are three Gods. Forbear this. It will be better for you. God is but one God. Far be it from him that he should have a son! He alone governs the heavens and the earth. Christ doth not proudly disdain to be a servant unto God; neither do the angels, who approach near to his presence."

"Assuredly, they are infidels, who say, Verily, Christ, the son of Mary, is God; since Christ said, O children of Israel, serve God, my Lord, and your Lord. Whosoever giveth a companion unto God, God will exclude him from Paradise, and his habitation shall be hell-fire; and the ungodly shall have none to help them. They are certainly infidels, who say God is the third of three; for there is no God but one God. If they refrain not from what they say, a painful torment will surely be inflicted on them. Will they not, therefore, be turned unto God, and ask pardon of Him? since God is gracious and merciful. Christ, the son of Mary, was no more than an apostle. Other apostles preceded him. His mother was a woman of veracity. They both ate food."

"It is not allowable to the Prophet, nor to those who are true believers, that they pray for idolaters, although they be of kin, after it becomes known unto them, that they are inhabitants of hell. Abraham did not ask forgiveness for his father, otherwise than in fulfilment of a promise he had made unto him. And when it became known unto him that he was an enemy of God, he declared himself clear of him."

"Verily, repentance will be accepted with God, from those who do evil ignorantly, and repent speedily. Unto them will God be turned; for God is knowing and wise. But no repentance will be accepted from him who waits till death presents itself, and says: 'Verily I repent now;' nor from those who are unbelievers. For them is prepared a grievous punishment."

"Fight for the religion of God against those who fight against you; but transgress not by attacking them first; for God loveth not the transgressors. And kill them wherever ye find them; and turn them out of that whereof they have dispossessed you; for temptation to idolatry is more grievous than slaughter. Yet fight not against them in the holy temple, until they attack you therein; but if they attack you, slay them there."

"The sword is the key of heaven and of hell. A drop of blood shed in the cause of God, a night spent in arms, is of more avail than two months of fasting and prayer. Whosoever falls in battle, his sins are forgiven. At the day of judgment, his wounds shall be resplendent as vermillion, and odoriferous as musk; and the loss of his limbs shall be supplied by the wings of angels and cherubim."

"Whoever shall be slain unjustly, we have given his heir power to demand satisfaction. But let him not exceed the bounds of moderation, by putting to death the murderer in too cruel a manner, or by revenging his friend's blood on any other than the person who killed him."

"Verily, those who disbelieve our signs, we will surely cast to be broiled in hell-fire. So often as their skins shall be well burned, we will give them other skins in exchange, that they may have the sharper torment; for God is mighty and wise. But those who believe, and do that which is right, we will bring into gardens watered by rivers. Therein shall they remain forever, and there shall they enjoy wives free from all impurity; and we will lead them into perpetual shades."

"When the inevitable day of judgment shall come, it will abase some, and exalt others. Those on the left hand shall dwell amid burning winds, and scalding water, and in the shadow of black smoke. Those on the right hand shall approach near unto God. They shall dwell in gardens of delight, reposing on couches adorned with gold and precious stones. Youths, blooming with immortal beauty, shall wait upon them with whatsoever birds or fruits they may desire, and with goblets of wine, the drinking of which shall not disturb their reason, or cause their heads to ache. As a reward for that which they have wrought they shall have for companions fair damsels, resembling pearls hidden in their shells, and having large black eyes. They shall not hear any charge of sin, nor any vain discourse; but only the salutation, Peace! Peace!"

"He who shall appear with *good* works, shall receive a *tenfold* recompense for them; but he who shall appear with *evil* works, shall receive only an *equal* punishment for them."

"O Lord, give us the reward thou hast promised by thy apostles; and cover us not with shame on the day of resurrection. Their Lord answereth them, saying, I will not suffer the work of those among you who work righteously to be lost, whether ye are male or female; for the one of you is from the other."

"Surely those who are believers, and Jews also, and Christians, and Sabians, and all who believe in God, and the last day, and do that which is right, shall have their reward with the Lord. There shall come no fear upon them, neither shall they be grieved." Some commentators on the Koran admit that this text teaches the salvation of all men in their own religion, provided their faith is sin-

cere, and their works righteous. But they say it was soon
after abrogated by other revelations; especially by the
following message: "Whoever followeth any other religion than Islam, it shall not be accepted of him; and at
the last day, he shall be of those who perish."

"No man can die except by permission of God; according to what is written in his Book, which contains the
fore-ordination of all things."

"If ye hear that a mountain hath changed its place,
believe it; but if ye hear that a man has changed his disposition, believe it not." * * * * "He shall assuredly
return to that for which he was created."

"Freemen may marry as many as four wives, free or
servile; but no more." "Ye are to live chastely with
them, neither committing fornication, nor taking them for
concubines."

"O men, fear the Lord, who hath created you out of
one man, and out of him created his wife, and from those
two hath multiplied many men and women. Fear God,
by whom ye beseech one another. Respect women, who
have borne you; for God is watching over you. Give
orphans their substance when they come of age. Render
them not bad, in exchange for good; and devour not their
substance by adding it to your own; for this is a great sin.
If ye fear that ye shall not act righteously toward orphans
of the female sex, take in marriage such other women as
please you; two, or three, or four; but no more. If ye
fear that ye cannot act equitably toward so many, marry
one only; or the slaves ye shall have acquired. This will
be easier, that ye swerve not from righteousness."

"Men ought to have a part of what their parents and
kindred leave behind them, when they die; and women
ought also to have a part of what their parents and kindred
leave; whether it be little, or whether it be much, a deter-
minate part is due to them."

* "Show kindness unto your parents, whether one or both
of them attain to old age with thee. Say not unto them,
Fie upon you! neither reproach them. But speak respect-

fully unto them, and submit to behave humbly toward them, out of grateful affection; and say, O Lord, have mercy on them, and care tenderly for them, as they cared for me, when I was little."

"Give what is needful unto him who is of kin to you, also unto the poor and the traveller. Waste not thy substance profusely; for the profuse are brethren of the devils; and the Devil was ungrateful to his Lord. If thou turn away from giving to the needy, at least speak kindly to them, in expectation of the mercy thou hopest from God."

"Paradise is prepared for the godly, who give alms in prosperity and adversity; who bridle their anger, and forgive men. For God loveth the beneficent, and those who after having committed a crime, or dealt unjustly with their own souls, remember Him, and ask pardon for their sins, and persevere not in what they have done. Their reward shall be pardon from their Lord, and gardens wherein rivers flow. They shall remain therein forever."

"To endure and to pardon is the wisdom of life." "It is not righteousness that ye turn your faces in prayer toward the East and the West; but righteousness is of him who believeth in God and the last day, and the angels, and the Scriptures, and the prophets; who for the Lord's sake, giveth money unto his kindred, and unto orphans, and to the needy, and to strangers, and for the redemption of captives; who are constant in prayer, and in the giving of alms; who perform their covenant when they have covenanted; who behave patiently in times of violence, adversity, and hardship. Such are they who truly fear God."

"Unto such of your slaves as desire a written instrument, allowing them to redeem themselves, on paying a certain sum, write one, if ye know good in them; and impart to them of the riches of God, which He hath given you."

"If your maid-servants wish to live chastely, compel them not to prostitute themselves, in order that ye may gain the casual advantages of this present life."

"Walk not proudly in the land; for thou canst not

cleave the earth, neither canst thou equal the mountains in stature. All this is evil, and abominable in the sight of the Lord."

"O true believers, when ye are called to prayer on the Day of Assembly [Friday] hasten to the commemoration of God, and leave merchandizing. This would be better for you, if ye knew it. When prayer is ended, then disperse yourselves through the land as ye list, to seek gain from the liberality of God; but remember God frequently, that ye may prosper."

"Prayer is the pillar of religion, and the key of Paradise."

"Draw not near unto fornication; for it is wickedness, and an evil way."

"In wine and lots [gambling] there is great sin. In some respects they are of use unto men; but their sinfulness is greater than their use."

"God will not punish you for an inconsiderate word in your oaths; but he will punish you for what ye solemnly swear with deliberation. The expiation of such an oath shall be to feed ten poor men, or to clothe them, or to ransom a true believer from captivity. He who cannot find wherewith to perform one of these three things, shall fast for three days."

"Perform your covenant; for the performance of covenants shall be inquired into hereafter."

"When you measure aught, give full measure; and weigh with a just balance."

"One hour of equity is better than seventy years of devotion."

The accounts of Adam, Noah, and the patriarchs, which Arabs believed had been handed down by Abraham, are given in the Koran with less resemblance to the Pentateuch, than to Rabbinical traditions among the Jews. The following will serve for a sample: God is represented as saying to man, "We created you, and afterward formed you; and then said unto the angels, Worship Adam! And they all worshipped him except Eblis. God said,

What hinders thee from worshipping Adam, as I have commanded? He answered, I am more excellent than Adam; for thou hast created me of fire, and hast created him of clay. God said, Get thee down from Paradise; for it is not fitting to behave proudly therein. Get thee hence! Thou shalt be one of the contemptible. He said, Give me respite until the day of resurrection. God answered, Verily thou shalt be one of the respited. The Devil said, Because thou hast degraded me, I will lay wait for men in thy strait way. I will come upon them from before, and from behind, and from their right hand, and from their left. Thou shalt not find the greater part of them thankful. God said unto him, Get thee hence, despised and driven far away. Verily, whoever of them shall follow thee, I will surely fill hell with you all. As for thee, O Adam, dwell with thy wife in Paradise, and eat of the fruit thereof wherever ye will; but eat not of this tree, lest ye become of the number of the unjust. And Satan suggested to them both that he would discover unto them their nakedness, which was hidden from them. He said, Your Lord has not forbidden you this tree for any other reason but lest ye should become angels, or immortal. And he sware unto them, saying, Verily I counsel you aright; and through deceit, he caused them to fall. When they had tasted of the fruit, their nakedness appeared unto them; and they began to join together the leaves of Paradise to cover themselves. Their Lord called to them, saying, Did I not forbid you that tree? Did I not say unto you Satan is your declared enemy? They answered, O Lord, we have dealt unjustly with our own souls; and if thou art not merciful to forgive us, we shall surely perish. God said, Get ye down! the one of you an enemy to the other. Ye shall have a dwelling-place upon earth, and provision for a season. Therein shall ye live, and therein shall ye die; and from thence ye shall be taken forth at the resurrection."

The phrase, "Get ye *down*," implies that the Garden of Eden was supposed to be above this earth. Cyprian, and other Christian Fathers, believed that the souls of martyrs were waiting for the day of resurrection in the same Paradise from which Adam was expelled. Probably the idea of expulsion from Paradise grew out of the old oriental theory that the souls of human beings were originally angels, who were banished from their heavenly home for desiring too much knowledge, and were imprisoned in bodies on earth, made subject to death. In the sacred traditions of most nations, the *celestial* Paradise is described as having a Tree of Life in the midst, at the foot of which four rivers flowed.

The accounts of the birth of Christ in the Koran are obviously from some of the Spurious Gospels, described in the chapter on Christianity; and like them will remind the reader of Hindoo accounts of Crishna. The Gnostic idea that Jesus merely *appeared* to die is reproduced in the Koran, and of course universally believed by Moslems. A few extracts will serve to show this: "The angel said, O Mary, verily God sendeth thee good tidings. Thou shalt bear the Word proceeding from himself. His name shall be Christ Jesus, the Son of Mary. In this world he shall be honoured, and in the world to come he shall be one of those who approach near to the presence of God. He shall speak while he is yet in the cradle; and when he is grown up, he shall be one of the righteous. She answered, Lord, how shall I have a son, since a man hath not touched me? The angel replied, God creates whatever he pleases. When he decrees a thing, he says Be! and it is done. God will teach him wisdom, and the Scripture, and the Law, and the Gospel; and will appoint him an apostle to the children of Israel. He shall say, Verily, I come unto you with a sign from the Lord; for I will make before you the figure of a bird with clay, and when I breathe thereon it will become a bird, by permission of God. I will heal him that has been blind from his birth. I will cure the leper, and raise the dead, by permission of God. I come to confirm the Law, which was revealed before me. And I come unto you with a sign from your Lord; therefore, fear God and obey me."

"Zachariah, who had charge of Mary during her pregnancy with the immaculate child, being at that time officiating priest, suffered no one but himself to go into her chamber, or supply her with food; and he always locked seven doors upon her. Notwithstanding this precaution, he always found a plentiful table spread before her of summer fruits in winter, and winter fruits in summer."

"When Mary brought the babe to her people, they said, O Mary, now thou hast done a strange thing! Thy father was not a bad man, neither was thy mother a harlot. She made signs to the child to answer them. But they said, How shall he speak, who is but an infant in the cradle? Whereupon, the babe said, 'Verily, I am the servant of God. He hath given me the book of the Gospel, and appointed me to be a prophet. He hath commanded me to observe prayer, and to give alms so long as I shall live, and to be dutiful toward my mother. Peace be on the day whereon I was born, and the day whereon I shall die, and the day whereon I shall be raised to life.' This was Jesus, the son of Mary, the Word of truth, concerning whom they doubt. It is not meet for God that he should have any son. God forbid!" Certain Jews demanded, as a proof of Mohammed's mission, that they might see a book descend to him from heaven; or that he would produce one written in celestial characters, like the tables of Moses. In answer to this, the following verse was communicated for the Koran: "They who have received the Scriptures will demand of thee that thou cause a book to descend unto them from heaven. They formerly asked of Moses a greater thing than this; for they said, Show us God visibly. They have not believed in Jesus, and have spoken against Mary, which is a grievous calumny. They have said, Verily we have slain Jesus, the son of Mary, the apostle of God. Yet they slew him not, neither crucified him; for he was represented by one in his likeness. Verily, they who disagreed concerning him were in doubt as to this matter. They had no sure knowledge thereof, but

followed only an uncertain opinion. They did not really
kill him, but God took him up unto himself." * * * *
"The Jews devised a stratagem against Jesus, but God devised a stratagem against them. God was the best deviser
of stratagems, when he said, O Jesus, verily I will not have
thee to die, but I will deliver thee from the unbelievers,
and take thee up unto myself."

The sermon on the mount and the parables of Jesus are
not alluded to in the Koran. Whether Mohammed was
acquainted with them or not is a matter of uncertainty.
He never learned to read or write. His followers consider
this conclusive evidence that the Koran was produced by
direct inspiration; and they glory in calling him The Illiterate Prophet. The Koran gave this answer to those
who demanded miracles: "They say unless a sign be sent
down to him from his Lord, we will not believe. Answer,
Signs are in the power of God alone; and I am no more
than a public preacher. Is it not sufficient for them that
we have sent down unto thee the book of the Koran?
Thou couldst not read any book before this, neither couldst
thou write. Had it been otherwise, gainsayers might have
justly doubted the divine origin thereof."

All Asiatic languages lose much of their beauty and
majesty in the process of translation into modern tongues.
This is peculiarly the case with the Koran, because it was
written in a kind of chanting verse, the rhythm and ca-
dence of which were very musical to Arabian ears, but are
entirely lost in translation. To the English reader it
seems a confused medley of Chaldean, Persian, Arabian,
Jewish, and Christian traditions, with many excellent moral
maxims, and wearisome repetitions of promises and threat-
enings. Arabic and Hebrew have near relationship, being
derived from the same source; but Arabic is the richer
language, and has been styled "a more refined kind of
Hebrew." The Koreish spoke a dialect more polished
than the other tribes; and Mohammedans describe the
Koran as its purest and most beautiful specimen. The
following verse relating to the Deluge is quoted as pre-

eminently sublime: "O earth, swallow up thy waters!
and thou, O heaven, withhold thy rain! And immediately the water abated, and the decree was fulfilled."
They have a tradition that four unbelievers, most eminent
for eloquence, met at Mecca, to produce a book equal to
the Koran; but when they heard that sentence recited,
they gave up the attempt in despair. When poets produced anything of superior excellence, it was customary
to fasten it on the Caaba, by way of honourable distinction. But after that verse was revealed to Mohammed,
all the poets went to the temple at night, and removed
their specimens, lest they should be humbled by the comparison. When the inspired Imam Saduk listened to that
sentence, he exclaimed: "Verily, if men and genii were
purposely assembled to produce a book equal to the Koran, they could not produce one like unto it, though they
combined to assist each other." Their traditions likewise
declare that Mohammed once issued a challenge to the
learned everywhere, to disprove his claim to divine inspiration by composing a book equal to the Koran. "But
though the number of elegant writers exceeded the sands
of the desert, and all were eager to falsify the Prophet's
claims, yet their efforts were entirely vain." Mohammedan
writers say that "a sentence of the Koran inserted in any
other composition, however eloquent, is like a ruby, and
shines like a gem of most brilliant lustre. So inimitable
is its diction, as to be the subject of astonishment to all
learned men, ancient and modern." "Such is the innate
efficacy of the Koran, that it removes all pains of body
and sorrows of mind. It annihilates what is wrong in carnal desires, delivers from the temptations of Satan, from
external and internal fears, from enemies within and without. It removes all doubts raised by satanic influences,
sanctifies the heart, imparts health to the soul, and produces union with the Lord of Holiness. It moves hearts
that are heavy as mountains, causes rivers to flow from the
eyes, ploughs up the soil of careless bosoms, sows there the
seed of divine love, and like the trumpet of the archangel,

R*

re-animates those who are dead in pride." The Imam Saduk, being asked why it was that the more the Koran was read the newer it appeared, replied: "Because it was not sent for one particular age, but for all mankind, down to the judgment day." Some say that the proof of inspiration is not in the style, but in the remarkable and true prophecies it contains.

Jews believed that the Law of Moses was written before Adam was created; that it was coeval with the throne of Jehovah. The prevailing belief in Mohammedan countries is that the Koran was not written by any mortal; that it was the uncreated eternal Word, existing in the very essence of God; that every word of it was inscribed with a ray of light on the table of everlasting decrees, which stands near the throne of Allah; that a copy of it was written on parchment made of the skin of the ram, which Abraham sacrificed instead of Ishmael; that it was bound in silk, adorned with the gold and gems of Paradise, and brought by Gabriel to Mohammed. Portions of it were read to him from time to time, as occasions required; and once a year the entire volume was shown to him. All sects hold it in the greatest possible reverence. Like the Hindoos and the Jews, they never touch the Sacred Book without first washing their hands. Lest it should be done inadvertently, they place a label on the cover: "Let no one touch this, but those who are clean." They never hold it below their girdles; and never knowingly allow an unbeliever to possess a copy. On important occasions, they consult it as an oracle, taking the first verse they open upon as an inspired guide. They swear by it, carry it with them to war, inscribe sentences of it on their banners, and believe it will finally be established in every kingdom of the earth. The wealthy have copies of it enclosed in golden covers set with precious stones. In some places the entire volume is read through daily at the principal mosque, by relays of appointed readers, who take it up in succession. It is said there are some devotees who have read it seventy thousand times. All questions of life and property, as well as of doctrine, are decided by it. Having been in existence over twelve hundred years, it of course fails to meet all the wants of modern times, even where society is so very slightly progressive as in Asia. But they stretch its capacities by resorting to the same process that Hindoos did with the Vedas, and Jews with the Pentateuch; they give ingenious interpretations, and resort to allegorical significance where the literal meaning is unsatisfactory. An immense number of commentaries have been written upon it. It is supposed to require much learning to distinguish rightly between what was intended to be allegorical and what literal; to determine for what emergencies particular passages were written, and whether they were abrogated by succeeding passages. There have been various editions of the Koran; but they are all said to contain exactly the same number of words and letters; for, like the Jewish Rabbins, they take pains to count the letters, and even how many times each letter is used. It has been translated into many languages.

Jews formed the Talmud by collecting their prevalent traditions and oral laws, which became of equal authority with the Pentateuch. Christians received the Traditions of the Fathers as of equal authority with their Scriptures. Two hundred years after the death of Mohammed, traditions concerning him and his family, and a collection of canonical decisions made in the first ages of Islamism, were collected and published. The first of these volumes, called the Sonna was prepared under the supervision of Al Bochari, who from three hundred thousand traditions selected seven thousand two hundred and seventy five, believed to be authentic. To obtain divine direction in the process, he prayed for guidance each day in the temple at Mecca, having previously bathed in water from Hagar's sacred fountain. Each page, as it was written, was consecrated by being placed on the pulpit and on the tomb of Mohammed. This supplement to the Koran is received as sacred authority by a majority of Moslems, but not by all. After the death of the Prophet there was much quarrelling and fighting concerning who should preside over civil and ecclesiastical affairs. In the course of these contentions, Ali was assassinated. Mohammed had been accustomed to call him his brother, his vicegerent, his Aaron; and had given him his most beloved daughter in marriage. This, combined with his own honourable, generous, courageous, and poetic character, excited great veneration for his memory, and gave rise to a sect, who declared that Mohammed was the prophet of God, and Ali was the vicegerent of God. He, and the twelve Imans who succeeded him were believed to be inspired, and their sayings were invested with sacred authority. These followers of Ali rejected the Sonna, and collected another book of traditions called the Hyat ul Kuloob. The two volumes have many traditions in common; but Ali, Fatima, and their children are peculiarly glorified in the Hyat ul Kuloob. In the Koran, Mohammed repeatedly disclaims the power to work any other miracle than writing that sacred volume; but innumerable wonders are related of him in both the books of traditions. It is therein stated that his mother Aminah, previous to his birth was continually hearing benedictions pronounced upon her, from air, earth, and heaven. She told her husband Abdallah these prodigies, and he charged her to keep the matter secret. When her babe was born, a light beamed from his head, birds surrounded her, and a radiant angel took him in his arms, and made a mark between the shoulders with his signet ring; saying: "My Lord hath commanded me to breathe into thee the Holy Spirit. Blessed are they who obey thee, and woe unto those that oppose thee." Every idol in the Caaba fell on its face, as soon as he came into the world; and Lake Savah, which had been an object of worship, disappeared and became a salt plain. Sacred fires, which had not been extinguished for a thousand years, were quenched that night. The skill of soothsayers and magicians departed. Satan shrieked, and his infernal children drew near to inquire what new curse had fallen upon them. "Woe to you!" he cried. "Some great event has happened on earth unparalleled since Jesus ascended to heaven. Fly, to discover what it is!" In answer to his inquiries, Gabriel told him that Mohammed, the best of the prophets, was born, who would require men to worship God in the unity of his being. Whereupon, "the whole infernal crew cast the dust of degradation on their heads, and fled to the fourth sea, where they wept forty days." "The whole earth was illuminated that night. Every stone, and clod, and tree laughed for joy. All things in heaven and earth uttered praises to God." There was a monstrous fish called Tamoosa; probably another version of the Hebrew leviathan. He had seven hundred thousand tails. The same number of bullocks, each one larger than this world, walked up and down on his back; but, on account of the immensity of his size and strength, he was entirely unconscious of it. This huge creature, when he knew Mohammed was born, was "so agitated with joy, that if the Most High had not quieted him, he would surely have overturned the world." As soon as the wonderful babe came into the world, he prostrated himself in an attitude of worship; "with his luminous forehead on the floor, and his fore-finger pointing to heaven, while he pronounces, There is no God but Allah." "From his birth to his death, he was free from all sins, great and small, both of design and ignorance, and from all error." Jewish Rabbis declared that God created the world solely for the children of Israel, and on account of the merits of Moses. Moslems say the head and heart of Adam were formed from the sacred soil of Mecca and Medina; that God revealed to him the coming of Mohammed in the latter time, and said: "By my glory, I have created thee, and the whole world, only for his sake." When Eve was made, all the angels, and all the animals in Paradise, exclaimed: "Hail ye parents of Mohammed!" The Traditions represent Mohammed as saying: "I am Lord of all those who have been sent by God. This is no boast in me." "He who has seen me has seen God." "He who obeys me obeys God; and he who sins against

me sins against God." When unbelievers required that
he should prove his divine mission, by performing such
miracles as Abraham, and Moses, and Jesus did, he answered, My miracle is the Koran. I should not dare to
receive such verses from God, and then ask him to confirm
their inspiration by another miracle. Moreover, if I
should invoke miracles, and you should still remain unbelieving, they would bring judgments upon you." At
this juncture, Gabriel appeared and said to Mohammed:
"The Most High sends you salutation, and declares that
he will manifest whatever miracles they require to prove
your prophetical office; though after they have witnessed
them they will still remain in unbelief." His enemies demanded that the moon, which was then full, should be
divided into halves. The prophet raised his hand toward
heaven, saying, "Moon, part in twain!" and it was immediately done. He was then asked to restore the moon
to its former state, and it was forthwith accomplished.
The miracle was performed at Medina, but the prodigies
were seen at Mecca, and by travellers on their way from
Syria. Ebn Masood swore that the different portions of
the moon separated so far asunder, that he saw Mount
Hera between them. "When everything round Medina
was perishing from drought, he raised his blessed hand to
heaven, and prayed for mercy on the people; and before
he moved from his place, the rain fell in torrents." "A
man had his foot cut off in battle; but when Mohammed
applied some of his saliva, and joined it to the leg, the
limb was at once restored to its former condition." "He
was sent for to visit the son of a blind woman, and found
him dead; but as soon as he removed the cloth from his
face, the young man rose up and ate." "Once when he
was travelling through the wilderness asleep, a lote tree
which stood in his path, parted asunder for his camel to
pass through." It still remains in that state, and is called
The Prophet's Tree. People bind its leaves on sheep and
camels to protect them from harm. These Sacred Traditions declare that the moon rocked Mohammed, and no

insect ever lighted on him; that every tree bowed when
he passed, and every rock saluted him; that his forehead
was so luminous, it caused a reflection on the walls of the
house, like moonlight; that at night his steps were guided
by the light which radiated from his fingers; that his body
cast no shadow in the sunshine; that he saw behind as
well as before; heard when he was asleep as well as
awake; and knew what was concealed in the hearts of
men.

The story of the midnight journey to heaven is so
vaguely described in the Koran, that some commentators
think it was merely a dream, given for instruction. But
both the Books of Traditions amplify it greatly, and declare that it was performed when the Prophet was wide
awake, and that he was literally conveyed in the body, on
a steed sent from Paradise. In that blessed region, he saw
angels building palaces of gold, silver, and ruby blocks,
cemented with the soil, which was pure musk. Sometimes
they stopped, and being asked the reason, said they waited
to have expenses paid: which they explained by saying
that whenever true believers on earth exclaimed: "There
is no God but Allah! Praise be to Allah!" their work
went on; but when the voice of prayer ceased, they were
obliged to pause. Mohammed declared that the greater
part of the inhabitants of Paradise were those who had
been poor in this world; and that the gates were opened
for them five hundred years sooner than for the rich. On
the banks of celestial rivers he saw palaces prepared for
himself and his family, and his "pure women." In the
midst was the Tree of Happiness, of such immense size
that a bird could not fly round the trunk in seven hundred
years. Its branches, laden with fruit, and with baskets
full of silken garments, extended to every true believer.
From its roots flowed four rivers; water, milk, wine, and
honey. He also looked down into the hells, and saw
devils tearing sinners with red-hot pincers, and pouring
fire down their throats. The greater part of the tormented were women, suffering in one form or another for

having been disobedient to their husbands. One was
hung up by her hair, her brain boiling with excessive
heat, because she had not concealed her beautiful tresses
from the view of men. In the first heaven, he was introduced to Ishmael, who exclaimed: "Hail worthy brother
and prophet!" and all the angels laughed with joy. In
the second, John the Baptist and Jesus welcomed him
as worthy brother and prophet. In the sixth, Moses
saluted him, saying: "The children of Israel think I am
dearest to the Most High: but this man is dearer than I
am." In the seventh, Abraham blessed him as a worthy
son and prophet. Beyond that no angel or archangel was
allowed to go. But Mohammed left his companion Gabriel, and ascended to the throne of the Most High, who
placed his hand upon his shoulder, and promised to grant
everything he might ask for himself or his followers.

The Hyat ul Kuloob is full of glorifications of Ali and
his family. It is therein stated that Abraham, Moses,
Jesus, and all the archangels inquired so particularly after
Ali that Mohammed began to think his cousin was better
known in Paradise than he was himself. The Angel of
Death told him it was his office to take away the soul of
every human being, except his and Ali's; but the Most
High himself would take theirs away. The Prophet is
represented as declaring that himself and his daughter
Fatima, and her husband Ali, and their sons Hasan and
Husayn, were created ages before earth or heaven. When
asked how their existence commenced, he replied: "God
first uttered a word, and that word took the form of Light.
He uttered another word, which became Spirit. He then
tempered the light with the spirit, and formed me and
Fatima, and Ali, and Hasan and Husayn. We ascribed
praise to God, when there was no other existence to give
him glory. God afterward expanded my light, and formed
the empyrean; which, being created of my light, I am
more excellent than the empyrean. He next expanded
the light of Ali, and formed angels; therefore, he is superior to them. From the light of Fatima, he formed the

heavens and the earth; which are consequently inferior to her. He expanded the light of Hasan to form the sun and moon; so that he is superior to them. From the light of Husayn was formed Paradise and the Hoories; therefore he is more excellent than they." According to these traditions he told Ali that after his corpse was washed and perfumed, it would answer any questions he might ask. Accordingly "he taught Ali a thousand chapters of knowledge, from each of which a thousand more opened; and from these he learned all that would happen until the judgment day." Ali was also enabled to hear all that angels were saying to the spirit of Mohammed. It is said that angels were never sent down to the earth to announce the birth of any prophet, except Jesus and Mohammed; and that the pavilions of Paradise were never pitched for any woman but the Virgin Mary and Aminah. On the day that the Prophet was married to Khadeejah, all the angels sang a hymn of thanksgiving, and the Most High ordered Gabriel to go down and plant a banner of praise on the dome of the Caaba. Afterward, whenever he brought a message to Mohammed, he always left a respectful salutation for her. On one of these occasions, he stated that a palace built of precious stones had been prepared for her in Paradise.

The amours of the Prophet are described with Asiatic plainness on such subjects; and the joys of Paradise are much more minutely and glowingly painted than they are in the Koran. The gigantic Tree is described as hung with millions of baskets, each containing a thousand changes of garments of the richest silks and brocades. Beautiful damsels, called Hoories, are formed of the pure musk of Paradise. Their large dark eyes are full of melting tenderness, and they are so modest that they always remain hidden from public view in pavilions of pearl. Their bodies are so radiant, that they shine through seventy garments. If one of them were suspended between the sun and the earth, mortals would be willing to spare the orb of day. When true believers enter Paradise, they will be

as tall as Adam, who was sixty cubits high. They will be
endowed with the beauty of Joseph, the perfection of Jesus,
and the eloquence of Mohammed. At each meal, they
will be served with three hundred different kinds of food,
on plates of gold. Bells hanging on the Tree of Happiness will be set in motion by breezes from God's throne, as
often as they desire music. All their capacities for enjoyment will be a hundred fold greater than they were in this
life. Each one will have a hareem of seven thousand
Hoories, and eleven thousand women; the most perfect of
whom are more beautiful than the Hoories. When Saduk,
one of the twelve inspired Imams, was asked whether a
husband and wife, who were true believers, would resume
the matrimonial bond in another world, he replied, that if
the man was superior to the woman in excellence, he would
decide whether she should be of the number of his wives
or not; but if the woman was more excellent, she would
choose whether or not she would have him for a husband.

Some of the traditional sayings of Mohammed have
great moral excellence. The following, for example: "All
the sons of Adam are equal, like the teeth of a comb. One
has no preëminence over another, except that which is
imparted by a religious life." "Every good act is charity.
Giving water to the thirsty is charity. Putting a wanderer
in the right path is charity. Removing stones and thorns
from the road is charity. Exhorting your fellow men to
virtuous deeds is charity. Smiling in your brother's face
is charity. A man's true wealth hereafter is the good he
does in this world. When he dies, mortals will ask what
property he left behind him; but angels will inquire of
him: 'What good deeds hast thou sent before thee?'"
An aged woman and an African convert were once very
much troubled, because he told them there were no old
women in Paradise, and no black people; but they were
comforted by his afterward explaining that all the good
became eternally young and fair when they left this world.
It is related of his grandson, Hasan, that a slave who
upset on him a dish of boiling hot food, fell on his knees

in great fear, and repeated from the Koran: "Paradise is for those who bridle their anger." Hasan answered: "I am not angry." "And for those who forgive men," continued the slave. "I forgive you," was the mild response. The culprit finished the sacred sentence, by repeating: "For God loveth the beneficent." The master replied: "I give you your freedom, and four hundred pieces of silver."

SECTS.—Mohammed declared that revelations from God to man would cease with him; and he commanded that any one should be put to death who afterward claimed to be a prophet. He predicted that many such would arise, and that his followers would divide into many sects. It happened as he had very naturally foreseen. After his death, there were many who professed to be inspired messengers, and strove hard to equal his power over the minds of men. One said he was Moses returned in the flesh; another that he was John the Baptist. Their contending claims produced a great deal of disturbance and bloodshed. Several of the tribes manifested a strong tendency to return to idolatry; and considerable time elapsed before they were all united in one faith. After their power was consolidated, they divided into various sects. The first great division arose from political as well as religious causes. Those who asserted that Ali was the only legitimate successor of Mohammed, denied the authority of the caliphs who preceded him. To the simple creed, "There is no God but Allah, and Mohammed is the prophet of God;" they added "and Ali is the vicegerent of God." They reject the Sonna, and accuse their opponents of having expunged from the Koran many sentences favourable to the claims of Ali. The Sonnites retort upon them the charge of altering the Koran, and of publishing fabulous traditions to glorify Ali and his family. They call them Shiites, or Sheahs, which signifies Heretics; a name by which they have become generally known to Europeans. Their theological doctrines are the same. But when the

Sonnites perform ablution before prayers, they begin at the elbow and wash down to the fingers; whereas the Sheahs begin at the tips of the fingers and wash upward to the elbow. This has given rise to very hot controversies; being considered a question of as much importance as sprinkling and immersion among Christians. The animosity between these two sects is so great, that they consider it more meritorious to destroy each other, than to exterminate infidels. When Sheahs, on their pilgrimage to Mecca, pass through countries inhabited by Sonnites, they generally conform to their customs, and call themselves by their name; otherwise, scenes of violence and bloodshed occur continually. Both sects claim to be the only true interpreters of the Koran. Arabs, Turks, and Tartars are Sonnites. The Persians, and some East Indians, are adherents of Ali. The hostility between Turks and Persians is mainly caused by this sectarian feud. The Sonnites are divided into many sects. The four principal differ concerning some matters of practice, but agree on points of faith; therefore they do not deny to each other the possibility of salvation; which they all agree to do toward numerous minor sects deemed heretical.

There are seventy or eighty sects among the Sheahs. One small sect maintains that God was incarnated in the person of Ali; these do not perform pilgrimages to Mecca, but to Meschid, where Ali was buried; they neglect many of the purifications and fasts observed by orthodox Mohammedans, have no buildings for public worship, and perform their religious ceremonies in a very simple way. One small sect in Syria believe in the transmigration of souls, have consecrated plants and animals, and introduce the sexual emblems of Hindostan into their worship. The head of ecclesiastical and civil affairs in Persia was called the Imam. All the sects of Sheahs believe that Ali, and the twelve Imams who succeeded him, were directly inspired by God; therefore their decisions were to be accepted as permanent rules of life. Some asserted that the essence of God was incarnated in all of them. The last of these Imams was peculiarly celebrated for his sanctity, and was called Mahedi, which signifies The Guide. He retired to a cave near Bagdad, and the time and place of his death were unknown. This gave rise to a belief, still entertained by many, that he is living, and will appear in the last days, to establish the faith of Islam throughout the world. At different periods, a number of prophets have arisen claiming to be this Mohammedan Messiah.

A book called the Gospel of Barnabas is in great repute among them. It is supposed to be one of the Apocryphal Gospels, used by the Eastern churches, translated and modified by some Christian, who became a Moslem. It represents Christ as foretelling that God would send a prophet by the name of Mohammed, to perfect the dispensation he had brought to men. It declares that an unbelieving Jew, while watching Jesus to prevent his escape, was suddenly transformed into such an exact likeness of him, that even the Virgin Mary herself was deceived. This man was crucified, and Christ was taken up into heaven alive. But seeing his mother and his disciples so overwhelmed with grief, he appeared to them, and told them the stratagem God had devised. He foretold that a prophet greater than himself, named Mohammed, would be sent to lead men into the truth. He also promised to appear on earth again in the last days, and destroy a false prophet named Dejal, and a wild boar that would devastate the earth. He would burn the Christian Gospels, which ungodly priests had falsified, and the crosses they worshipped as gods, and help to subject the whole earth to Mohammed. In consequence of this communication, the Virgin Mary lived and died in the faith of Islam. It is the universal belief that when Mahedi appears, Jesus will come to his assistance; that he will perform his devotions in the mosque, will exterminate the Jews who rejected him, and the Christians who worshipped him as God; that he will marry and have children, and remain on the earth forty years, during which there will be universal peace and plenty. In the royal stable at Ispahan, two horses were always kept saddled; one for the use of Mahedi, the other for Jesus.

The idea of atonement for sin, by any kind of sacrifice, forms no part of the system of Mohammed; it being one of his favourite maxims that "a man cannot die for his neighbour." But in general, questions which excite controversy elsewhere have caused disputes among his followers. Some deny the personality of God; others affirm that he is in the likeness of a man. Mohammed said: "The heart of a believer is between the fingers of The Merciful." Some say that a preacher who should stretch forth his finger while he read that text would deserve to have it cut off; because he might thereby convey the idea that God had fingers. The doctrine of predestination is fully believed by orthodox sects. But it shocks the minds of many, who draw from it an inference that God is the author of evil; and this they are so reluctant to admit, that they are not even willing to say He created infidels. Out of this question has arisen much discussion whether the doctrine that infants are foredoomed to eternal punishment can be reconciled with the justice and mercy of God. The comparative importance of faith and works is another dividing topic. Some maintain that if a true believer in Mohammed commits a crime and dies without repentance, he must surely be damned to all eternity; though his punishment will be lighter than that of an infidel who commits the same crime. This is regarded as impious doctrine by the orthodox, who say God forgives everything but infidelity. Some sects maintain that this world will never be destroyed, and that there is no other heaven or hell. It is generally supposed that departed souls are waiting in some intermediate state, not very clearly defined. Some think they are with Adam in the lower heaven, because when the Prophet made his miraculous Night Journey, he said he saw souls destined to heaven on Adam's right hand, and those destined to hell on his left. The prevailing faith is that bodies will rise at the day of resurrection, and souls will be re-united with them. But some, who think man is merely a corporeal being, say the body only will rise; others believe the resurrection will be purely spiritual. The orthodox belief is that the Koran is the uncreated Word of God, and existed in his essence from all eternity. Some sects reject this doctrine, because it conveys to their minds the idea of two eternal beings. They are denounced as infidels, and in their turn denounce their opponents as idolaters. Men were scourged, imprisoned, and even put to death, for opinions on this point; until at last a law was passed allowing them to judge for themselves on the subject. Old theological ideas being strictly guarded by penal laws, as well as by habits of reverence, progressive minds found themselves in straitened circumstances; and, as usual, they made for themselves two doors of escape from inconvenient limitation. One class resorted to allegorical interpretation of the Koran; styling it half man and half beast, in reference to the spirit and the letter. Some scholars who had become enamoured with Aristotle, made use of metaphysical and logical subtleties to explain the literal sense. This mode, called Al Calam, or Science of Reason, excited strong abhorrence in orthodox minds. They said whoever resorted to this mode of interpretation ought to be impaled; while a public crier proclaimed through the streets: "This is the reward of those who forsake the Koran, and the Sacred Traditions, to follow the Science of Reason." A school of mysticism also arose among the Mohammedans, and took forms similar to the Hindoo and Platonic ideas. The complete union of the soul with God, and intuitive perceptions of divine things, thence derived, is taught by some as the highest wisdom and happiness. They convey this idea in glowing allegories concerning love and intoxication, which, like some Hindoo devotional writings, seem sensual to those who perceive only the external sense; but the initiated find in them an interior meaning. Their very dances have mystical significance; as is the case with the dance consecrated to the memory of Crishna. They carry about with them a small mirror as a religious symbol; which also was a custom among Egyptians, when they celebrated the Mysteries of Isis. This contemplative and mystical tendency of mind began to manifest itself decidedly among Mohammedans little more than a century after the Hegira, and has continually gained ground unto this day, especially among the superior class of minds in Persia. They became a distinct sect, known under the name of Sufis; which some learned men derive from the Arabic word Safi, meaning Pure; others from the Greek word Sophi, signifying Wise. Their saints believe that they receive immediate communications of truth from heaven into the interior of their minds, when they are completely abstracted from all earthly cares and wishes. They say it is mysteriously transmitted through the medium of Abubeker or Ali. But their doctrines are obviously of Hindoo origin, and bear no resemblance to the teachings of the Koran. Pantheism soon mingled with their system. Mohammed declared that God was not in anything, nor was anything in God; but devout Sufis believe they have become one with God; which Hindoos call absorption in Brahm. One of the Mohammedan poets says: "I am the world's soul." But these views are generally expressed in veiled language, lest they should give rise to a charge of blasphemy. One of their teachers, named Hosein al Hallaj, was put to death for making himself equal with God, by saying: "I am the Truth." Complete subjugation of the senses was of course intimately connected with this idea of mystical union with Deity. Hence the Sufis early formed monastic fraternities, which adopted very ascetic modes of life. It was the natural growth of the same foreign element which had been grafted upon Christianity, and produced monkism. Mohammed disapproved of celibacy, and declared he would have no monks in his religion. But three hundred years after the Hegira, Islam began to swarm with a class of men called Dervises, whose habits are very similar to Hindoo Fakirs, and Mendicant Monks. There are thirty-two religious orders of that kind in the Turkish empire; others in Persia and India. These Mohammedan monks have great reputation for miraculous power obtained by superior sanctity. People apply to them to interpret dreams, cure diseases, pray for the birth of children, for rain, harvests, and other blessings. People of the highest rank receive them at their tables, and the Imams are generally selected from their communities. The rosaries used by Dervises consist of ninety-nine beads, usually made of holy earth from Mecca or Medina. They pass these through their fingers at prayer, while they recount the ninety-nine qualities of God mentioned in the Koran.

A follower of Mohammed always calls himself a Moslem, which signifies a Believer. From the plural of this the European word Musulmân is formed. All sects entertain the greatest reverence for Mohammed. All their writings commence with a benediction on his name. They call him "The Lawgiver, The Prince of Men, Last and Best of the Prophets, The Most Noble of Apostles, The Refuge of Revelation, The Sanctified One, The Most Perfect of Created Beings, The Beloved of the Lord." They universally believe him to be the Prophet predicted by Moses, and the Comforter whom Jesus promised to send. They adduce passages from Apocryphal Gospels and from our Scriptures to prove it, and say that other texts, containing more positive evidence, have been fraudulently suppressed by Christians. The Crescent is the adopted emblem of their religion, because the new moon lighted him in his flight from Mecca. The country around that city swarms with pigeons, which they never kill, lest they should destroy some descendant of the sacred bird, sent by God to build a nest at the mouth of the cave where he was concealed. They have a similar feeling concerning spiders, because a spider spun a web across the entrance. Mohammed emancipated Zaid for believing in his mission; therefore, no Mohammedan ever holds a person of his own faith in slavery. The ancient fast of Ramadam is rendered still more holy by being associated with the first revelations he received from Heaven. During the entire month, they taste no food or drink between sunrise and sunset. They

abjure baths and perfumes, and shun the sight of women.
The fast is rendered void by inhaling the mere smell of
food; and some are so strict, they will not even swallow
the moisture in their mouths. As they reckon their
months by moons, the fast is moveable. When it occurs
at the sultry season of the year, the pious, especially those
who labour, often suffer very severely. Their teachers inculcate that fasting, to be of any avail, must include abstinence from worldly cares, evil thoughts, and impure ideas.
Many of the old opinions and customs were transferred
to the new religion; that being an invariable compromise
between the conservative and progressive tendencies of
man. The Caaba lost none of its sacredness. There is a
tradition that Mohammed said those who died without
visiting it might as well have died Jews or Christians.
The poorest Moslems often make great sacrifices to visit
Mecca once in their lives; and some go annually. On
their way, they almost invariably turn aside to visit the
tomb of their Prophet at Medina. Reverence for his
memory is reflected on all his descendants. The sover-
eignty of Mecca and guardianship of the Caaba is still
entrusted to them, and they take rank above princes. In
the lapse of centuries, they have become numerous, but
they all have honorary titles, take the highest seat in
company, receive a stipend from the public treasury, and
are distinguished by a turban or girdle of green, which is
a sacred colour.

Any system of religion or morals which did not profess
to be founded on the Koran would be taught at the peril
of life. All the sects study it in the light of either the
Sonnite or the Sheah Book of Traditions. In case of palpable contradictions, they say if a passage is not true in
one aspect it is in another, and that God can easily reconcile
what seems incongruous to the human mind. Some few
venture to declare that they receive only such traditions as
can be reconciled with reason; but such are regarded with
horror by orthodox believers.

The fundamental doctrines in which all agree are, that

God is One; that it is impious to divide his personality, or
to associate any other being with his worship; and that
Mohammed is the last and best of all the prophets He has
sent. Mohammedans adopt the old Persian ideas concerning Angels with ethereal bodies formed of celestial fire.
Each of the seven departments of Paradise is governed by
one of these radiant beings. They appoint others to various
offices; thus Gabriel is always sent with revelations; Az-
rael separates the souls and bodies of mortals at death;
and Israfil will sound the trumpet to summon bodies from
their graves, at the resurrection. Like the Persians and
other ancient nations, they believe that every human being
has two attendant angels from birth to death. One on his
right hand notes down his good actions, and the other, on
his left, records his evil deeds. The kindly angel has
control over the other. When man does a good deed he
writes it down, with delight, ten times; but when he commits any wickedness, he says to the angel on the left hand:
"Wait seven hours before you write it down. Perhaps he
may repent, and ask forgiveness." They say the dead are
visited in their graves by two dark angels, who cause them
to sit upright, while they question them concerning the
unity of God and the mission of Mohammed. If their
answers are satisfactory, they are left in peace to be refreshed by breezes from Paradise. Otherwise, they beat
them with iron maces, and leave them to be stung by
ninety-nine serpents, with seven heads each. This is believed so literally by many people, that it is a general custom to build tombs in such a manner that the dead can
easily sit upright. Some sects reject the account altogether;
others understand it allegorically; saying the serpents
represent remorse for sins. The good and evil words and
deeds of men, as recorded by their attendant Spirits, are said
to be given to Gabriel, who weighs them in a balance, and
dismisses souls to heaven or hell according to their merits.
All are obliged to pass over a bridge called Al Sirat, "fine
as the thread of a famished spider," with an edge sharp as
a scimitar. Beneath this bridge roar the flames of hell,

and beyond it are the regions of Paradise. True believers
are conveyed across like a flash of lightning; some will
pass with difficulty; and others will slip into hell. Those
who delight in spiritual interpretation, say this hair-breadth
bridge signifies the narrow and difficult path of piety in
this world. Some who are not good enough to pass directly
into Paradise, are supposed to remain in a place partitioned
off, until by acts of adoration they have more than balanced
the evil they have done, or the worship they have omitted. He who has wronged another will be obliged to make
over to the account of the injured party a proportionate
quantity of his own good works. If he has no such treasury to draw upon, he must be accountable for an equal
share of the sins of his victim. Moslems may have to wait
in some place of expiation from nine hundred to seven
thousand years, according to their degrees of guilt. But
because they have believed in the true faith, they will all
finally attain to Paradise, by help of their own prayers, and
the continual intercession of Mohammed. Hindoos and
Persians believed in seven ascending spheres of light and
happiness, above which dwelt the Supreme; and in seven
descending spheres of darkness and suffering. Mohammed
also taught that there were seven hells. Commentators
say the first is for sinful Moslems; the next is for Christians; the third for Jews; the fourth for Sabians and
Fire-Worshippers; the sixth for all those who worship a
plurality of gods, and have no Sacred Books; the seventh
and deepest is reserved for hypocrites of *all* religions. All
who disbelieve in Mohammed will be punished eternally,
in degrees proportioned to their obstinacy in rejecting him.
The tortures described are of various kinds. Excessive
hunger and thirst, intolerable stench, stinging serpents,
roasting over intense flames, and being shod with shoes of
fire, which will make the brains boil. In Paradise all that
delighted the soul or senses of man in this world will be
increased and refined beyond human imagination. These
joys are progressively multiplied and rendered more intense in the ascending regions of Paradise. Only martyrs

and great saints will attain to the pure spiritual bliss of daily communion with God which far transcends all other enjoyment. In the seventh and highest Paradise is the palace of Mohammed, and the Tree of Happiness. Immediately above this is the throne of the Most High.

On the subject of marriage and the forgiveness of injuries, the moral tone of Mohammedans is far below that of Christians. But they manifest more sincerity and earnestness in acting up to their standard. All travellers agree that they are remarkably characterized by honesty in their dealings; insomuch that at a distance from cities, it is a common custom to leave shops open without any person to tend them. Purchasers go in and take what goods they want, and leave on the counter the price marked on them. Exceeding liberality to the poor is another admirable trait; and in no Christian country are the chains of slavery so light, or so easily removed. The total abstinence from all intoxicating drink commanded by the Koran, is not unfrequently disobeyed; but devout believers never taste such liquors; they will neither buy nor sell them; nor will they consent to be supported with money obtained by such traffic. The estimate of women is very much lower than in Christian countries, but it is a mistake that they suppose them to have no souls. The Koran, and the Books of Traditions frequently allude to them as sharing the punishments of hell and the joys of Paradise. The majority of the people do not avail themselves of the license to marry four wives. The general tendency is to have but one. Friday, the ancient "Day of Assembly" among the Arabians, is the Mohammedan holy day. All go to the mosques to attend religious services, and when they have performed their devotions, they return to their customary business. They say creation was finished, and the resurrection will take place on that day. They call it the Prince of Days, and consider themselves peculiarly honoured, that God granted them the privilege of being the first to observe it. Some of the very strict consider it wrong to attend to worldly business during any

portion of the day. They have no priesthood. Reputable
and learned men are appointed to read and explain the
Koran and prayers, at prescribed seasons. The principal
interpreter of the Koran, to whose decision doubtful questions are referred, is called the Imam in Persia, and the
Grand Mufti in Turkey. They never make use of bells,
but in every town a public crier, called Muezzin, summons
the people to prayer, by proclaiming from the minarets or
steeples of the mosques: "God is great! To prayer! To
prayer!" This is repeated in a sort of chant consisting of
a few simple tones, and travellers describe it as producing
a very solemn effect. Though this is repeated five times a
day, every conscientious Moslem, as soon as he hears it,
washes himself and goes to the mosque to repeat a prayer.
If that is inconvenient, he spreads a cloth, turns his face
toward Mecca, and prostrates himself in the house, the
workshop, or the street, wherever he may happen to be;
for their Prophet said: "The whole world is a place of
prayer." At day-break, the Muezzin reminds all the people that prayer is better than sleep, and at noon he tells
them it is more salutary than food. They are as strict as
the ancient Hindoos and Persians in performing ablution
before worship. The spiritual class of commentators remind them that the requisite purification includes expung-
ing evil thoughts from the mind, as well as cleansing the
body from pollution. The Koran forbids believers ever
to declare the intention of doing anything without first
saying: "If it pleases God." To each chapter of the
Koran is prefixed: "In the name of the most Merciful
God;" and all Mohammedan books and writings copy this
example. When they took the Sacred Books of Jews
and Christians among the spoils of war, they never committed them to the flames; because they consider it impious
to destroy anything on which the name of God is written.
Omar, who ruled about twelve years after the Hegira, sent
armies into various countries to extend the faith. There
is a story that when Alexandria was taken, a question
arose whether the royal library might be spared; and

Omar replied: "The Koran contains all that is necessary; therefore, if those books agree with it, they are not needed; and if they contain anything contrary to it, they ought to be destroyed." It is said they were used to kindle fires in the baths, and that it took six months to destroy them. The Alexandrian Library had been pillaged by Christians, in the time of Theodosius, so that the shelves were left entirely empty. How so many volumes were afterward collected is not accounted for; and the story concerning Omar has latterly been much doubted.

Their places of worship called mosques are held in great reverence. There is always a fountain near by in which they wash before they enter. They take off their slippers, and ornaments, deeming it more reverent to the deity to enter his presence in plain apparel. Women say their prayers at home; it being supposed that their presence would tend to disturb a devotional frame of mind. Religious observances mingle with all the affairs of life. "There is no God but Allah" is constantly heard from Moslem lips; even when they answer the watchmen, they add "Allah Akbar," "God is Great." Of course the same inconsistencies occur among them, as among Christians. Constantine and Clovis prayed diligently and built churches, while they murdered sons and relatives. Aurungzebe murdered his father and brothers, and erected a magnificent mosque at Delhi in token of gratitude to Allah for success in the civil war. "He acted as High Priest at the consecration, and was in the habit of worshipping there in the humble dress of a Fakeer. He raised one hand to God, while with the other he signed warrants for the death of his nearest relatives."

The mosques are generally in the Moorish style of architecture, surmounted with crescent-crowned minarets, which have a light and elegant appearance, and are often richly ornamented. A quadrangular area, sometimes of very great extent, is enclosed by files of columns, supporting double rows of galleries. They contain no altars, images, paintings, or seats, except a chair for the Imam. In the direction of Mecca there is always an alcove called the Kebla, that worshippers may turn toward the sacred city, when they prostrate themselves in prayer. A good deal is expended on lamps, which form almost the only orna- ment of the interior, except sentences of the Koran inlaid in the walls, with mother-of-pearl, or other beautiful sub- stances, and often richly emblazoned.   Like the Jews, they never allow people of other religions to pass beyond the outer enclosure of their places of worship.   One of their most magnificent mosques was erected on the site of Solo- mon's temple, after they took possession of Jerusalem, which they visit as a holy city, next in importance to Mecca and Medina.   In the heart of Mecca is a large area enclosed with columns and galleries, including several small chapels, and the ancient Caaba in the centre.   The roof is covered with black damask embroidered with gold; an offering annually sent by the Sultan of Turkey.   It is sustained by a double file of columns, with rows of silver lamps, quaintly ornamented, suspended between them in festoons.   Within the Caaba is the celebrated black stone. Some suppose it was an aerolite, and thus acquired the reputation of having fallen from heaven.   It is set in silver now, and devoutly kissed by every pilgrim.   It is supposed that at the resurrection it will return to the angelic form it originally had, and will bear testimony in favour of all who have touched it in their pilgrimage.   This sacred enclosure also contains Hagar's Fountain, now called Zem Zem; and a white stone believed to mark the grave of Ishmael, which receives water from the roof by a golden spout.

Until recently, Christian writers have generally mani- fested a very uncandid spirit toward Mohammedans. They said pigeons were sacred at Mecca because the Prophet put grains of wheat into his ear, and trained a pigeon to pick them out; pretending that it was the Holy Spirit whisper- ing to him in the form of a dove.   This, and several other similar stories, are now acknowledged to be false.

Moslems have an insurmountable prejudice against mar-

rying with uncircumcised families; but they inherit their
Prophet's animosity to the Jews, whom they regard with
much more aversion than they do Christians. In consideration of their being believers in a Sacred Book; both
classes are allowed to retain their own places of worship
in countries conquered by Mohammedans, provided they
pay tribute, ring no bells, make no attempts at proselyting,
and do nothing to prevent their relatives from becoming
true believers. Contracts with them are subject to the
same laws that regulate the business-intercourse between
Moslems; but no promise or oath is binding, if made to
people who do not believe in a Sacred Book. The testimony of Christians is not received against Moslems, they
are not allowed to compete with them in their style of
living, and in the street, they must make way for the meanest follower of the Prophet. A more kindly state of feeling begins to manifest itself between the rival religions.
Christian writers have become more candid; and the Sultan of Turkey many years ago passed a law forbidding his
subjects to continue their practice of calling Christians dogs.
They both derive so much from Jewish fountains, that
Lessing calls them "Two litigating sons of the same father."

The extension of Mohammedanism, though occasionally
checked, has gradually increased ever since the Hegira.
Its professors are now estimated at one hundred and eighty
millions; nearly one-fifth of the whole human race.

s*

CONCLUDING CHAPTER.

"The word unto the Prophet spoken
Was writ on tablets yet unbroken;
The word by Seers or Sibyls told,
In groves of oak, or fanes of gold,
Still floats upon the morning wind,
Still whispers to the willing mind.
The heedless world hath never lost
One accent of the Holy Ghost."

R. W. EMERSON.

IN reviewing the contents of the preceding pages, every reflecting mind must be struck with the fact that "there have been but few voices in the world, and many echoes." How the same questionings, the same hopes, the same aspirations, have continually reappeared, in expressions varied by the climates and the ages! The same gamut, with infinite modifications of mode and time! In all ages and countries, the great souls of humanity have stood on the mountain peaks, alternately watching the clouds below, and the moonlight above, anxiously calling to each other: "Brethren, what of the night?" And to each and all an answer has returned, varying in distinctness: "Lo, the morning cometh."

If we would but look at the subject comprehensively, there is nothing in the history of man so interesting as the attempt to trace Infinite Wisdom making its way among the errors, the frailties, the passions, and the intense spiritual longings of finite souls. Everywhere the Divine Spirit takes form according to the capacity of reception. As this enlarges, old forms of thought and worship die, and the Spirit enters into new ones, which the previous growth has prepared. Thus is the Word of God forever incarnated, and dwelleth among men. Therefore, the very nature of a Written Revelation involves the necessity of ceasing to be adequate to the wants of society, sooner or later; for a Revelation must necessarily be adapted to the then present state of the public mind, and consequently be, in some degree, a measure of that mind. If it were entirely above the comprehension of the epoch, it could not *be* a Revelation. When it has done its destined work, and helped onward to a higher plane of perception, the soul begins to outgrow the Revelation, and can no longer receive it as a sufficient standard. Declining faith in the external letter always produces a reaction. The reverential tendency of man strives to resuscitate decaying forms by the infusion of spiritual significance. Then come elaborate and far-fetched explanations and allegories, by means of which the new thought is found in the old words; all of which is a patching and stretching of the worn-out garment, to make it cover the increasing stature. This habit of conservatism is wisely impressed upon our nature, to prevent abrupt and dangerous changes. But when the new garment is entirely prepared, the old one *will* drop off; and the attempt to stretch it merely cracks it in pieces.

Such periods of the world's growth are always sad to souls which have devout feelings and a limited vision. They need to be reminded of what the Athenian philosopher said to his disciple: "He may bury my *body;* but let him not think he buries *Socrates.*" No portion of truth ever did die, or ever can die. Its *spirit* is eternal, though its *forms* are ever changing. We cannot annul that law of our existence which forever makes the present a reproduction of all that was real in the past. Only inherited customs, in which men merely *seem* to believe, transmit no life. Every *genuine* belief helps to form future modes of thought; however absurd and fantastic the *form* of belief may appear to the future that looks back upon it.

Instead of considering our own religion the product of a gradual growth, to which the spiritual sunshine, air, and rain of previous centuries have contributed, it is the common tendency to speak of it as a gift suddenly dropped down from Heaven, for a chosen few, and unlike anything the world had ever received. The beautiful Night-blooming Cereus, with a pure light radiating from its deep centre, seems to have no relationship with the long dry stem, and the little shaggy buds of tufted tow; but the regal loveliness of the blossom could never have been produced, had not the long stem, and the uncouth bud, day after day, and month after month, conveyed to it nourishment from all the surrounding atmosphere.

The same is true of the world's religious growth. Dreamy contemplations of devout mystics in the ancient forests of Hindostan; the vague sublimity of Egyptian thought, born of vast deserts, and the solemn dimness of subterranean temples; the radiant army of Spirits, which illuminated the soul of the Persian, when with loving reverence he kissed his hand to the stars; Hebrew proneness to the supernatural, combined with the practical wisdom and equalizing system of Moses; moonlighted glimpses of the infinite, revealed to Plato; the Gospel of love and forgiveness preached by Jesus; all these are fused into our present modes of thought. We are told that wise men came from far countries, and offered jewels to the infant Christ. Figuratively, it might signify how all the nations added some gems to his crown of righteousness. Jews brought their fixed idea of the unity of God, their abhorrence of idolatry, their habitual thoughtfulness for the poor. Grecians imparted their free spirit and intellectual culture, to protect spiritual growth from a narrow and binding fanaticism. Romans brought their civil law, to restrain the selfishness of Christian proselytes, and help their imperfect sense of justice. Teutonic tribes brought their reverence for "the form *containing* woman," to aid the fulfilment of the prophecy, that there would be "neither male nor female in Christ Jesus." Those who laid down these offerings at the feet of Christ, did it in reverence for his divine doctrines of complete forgiveness of injuries, the universal brotherhood of man, and the all-pervading love of an ever-watchful Father.

This combination of goodness and truth, which we at the present time accept under the name of Christianity, resembles the threefold nature of man, described by ancient philosophers. The religious sentiment, reverential and humane, is the interior soul, in constant communication with God; intellectual culture, and powers of reflection, are the intermediate soul; and civil law is the material body. The soul forms the outline and expression of the body; but it is equally true that diseases of the body affect the state of the soul.

Preceding quotations from Greeks and Romans show the state of preparation existing in the Gentile world, previous to the ministry of Christ. The old Teutonic tribes, though comparatively rude in most respects, also imparted much that was valuable, in exchange for what they received. They had always been remarkable for the high consideration in which they held their women, and the respect with which they treated them. They were always allowed an equal share in religious ceremonies, and were habitually consulted in all the important affairs of war and government. Asiatic servitude and Roman profligacy were alike unknown to them. The best of the Romans acknowledged that, with regard to the dignity and purity of women, the sickly civilization of their own country was keenly rebuked by the more healthy tone of their barbarian conquerors. The introduction of this element had a very important influence on Christianity, in the Western portions of the world. The poor condition of churches in Asiatic countries, where Grecian culture, Roman law, and Teutonic intermixture, have *not* modified the growth of Christianity, indicates how much we owe to those collateral influences.

It is undeniable that with the good and the true from the past, there also came into Christianity much that was evil and false. But this is altogether inseparable from the imperfect condition of humanity. No man, not even the wisest, ever rises entirely above the opinions and customs

of the age in which he lives. The views of Socrates were
so far above those of the populace, that they cost him his
life. Yet one of his last acts was to enjoin the sacrifice of
a cock to Æsculapius. That Plato had very elevated views,
is shown by his placing *Goodness* above *Wisdom*, and both
above *Power*, in his attributes of the Deity; also by his
habit of regarding everything earthly as of little value, in
comparison with the immutable and eternal. Yet even he
would have had every one confined as a madman, who
refused to conform to the popular worship of the Gods.

When a traveller is whirled along on the rail-road, if
he toss a ball into the air, it returns again to his hand,
though the cars have gone ahead of the place whence it
was thrown; because it not only receives an upward tendency from the individual hand, but also a lateral impulse
from the motion of the train. Spiritual laws are in
correspondence with the natural. The highest aspirations
of an individual are inevitably modified by the social
atmosphere through which he is travelling; and the degree
of impetus given to his thought is according to the
progress of the age in which he is moving onward. If
a Revelation were dropped down directly from Heaven,
in all the languages of the world, at the end of a century it would be found to have produced quite different
systems of thought, and modes of action; because from
every community it would *take* quite as much as it would
give. This modifying power of external influences over
the interior aspirations of the soul, constitutes one of
the centripetal forces, by which God regulates the spiritual
condition of men.

If the Apostles had re-appeared in the sixth century,
would they have recognized the then existing Christianity,
as the doctrines *they* taught, and the worship *they* practised?
Constantine's colossal statue of Apollo was a very appropriate representation of it. The body of a Grecian god, the
head of the emperor, and rays of glory formed of nails said
to be taken from the cross of Christ, was a true image of the
Church at that period. Jewish converts had added to the

teaching of Jesus their own traditions, many of them drawn from Cabalistic sources; Grecian converts had breathed round it an atmosphere of Platonism; Gnostics mingled with it Persian and Buddhist theories, the tinge of which remained after Gnosticism itself had disappeared; and in them all was a pervading infusion of old Hindoo ideas, long ago transmitted through Egypt.

We are accustomed to speak of Christianity as entirely untinged with polytheistic notions; but *strictly* speaking, a purely monotheistic faith has never existed. Jews and Christians believed as distinctly in the active agency of Archangels, Angels, and Devils, as Grecians did in the numerous subordinate Spirits employed by Jove. Isis, the "Mother Goddess," was never more devoutly worshipped in Egypt, than is "The Mother of God," "The Queen of Heaven," by a large majority of Christians. The power almost universally attributed to Satan is quite equal to that which Persians ascribed to Arimanes. In the strict sense of the phrase, there are "Devil Worshippers" in all countries; that is, there are people, who, by prayers and ceremonies, seek to pacify a Powerful Spirit, whose vengeance they dread. In all religions, we find also a tendency to invest Deity with the feelings of human nature. This happens because no man can leap from his own shadow. In contrast with the intriguing, amorous gods of the lively, artistic Grecians, witness Tertullian's grim picture of the horrible games God would furnish at the Day of Judgment, for the triumph and delight of his faithful followers.

Among all people, except the Jews and Mohammedans, an intermediate object of worship, approaching nearer to human sympathies, has gradually superseded the more sublime and awful idea of the Supreme One. Thus Mithras eclipsed Ormuzd, and Crishna supplanted Brahma. The same craving for sympathy and mediation, led men to address more prayers to Christ, than to the Father; and eventually more to the Virgin Mary, than to either. Truly, it is somewhat discouraging to trace the progress of any great truth among existing prejudices, and antecedent institutions. One is continually reminded of Jean Paul's remark: "The progress of Mankind toward the City of God is like the walking of certain pilgrims to Jerusalem, who moved backward after every step forward."

The Fathers did the best they could to arrange the incongruous elements around them into an harmonious whole; and their decisions became established authority, under the name of apostolic tradition. They could not help lapping over their own old opinions upon the new; nor could they avoid having their theology more or less subject to modification from Jews, Gnostics, and philosophers, with whom they were in perpetual controversy. For while zealously combatting one error, they generally roused into activity the opposite extreme, and were compelled to sail between the two, as the only practicable course, though it might by no means be the one they would have chosen, if they had not been subject to counter currents. In order to estimate candidly the difficulties of their position, it would be necessary to stand, as they did, at a point of time, where all the old religions of the world were breaking up, and the Spirit of God was brooding over chaos, to produce new forms. We may smile at their credulity, but if we had been there, we should have been credulous also. And if we had great truths to defend from so many enemies, open and insidious, perhaps we should be more prone to imitate their theological intolerance, and occasional indirect statements, than we should be to manifest their unflinching courage, fervent piety, active benevolence, and unfailing sympathy with the poor and the oppressed.

I confess that the most powerful *external* testimony to the superior excellence of Christ's teaching, seems to me to be found in the fact that good men, and great men, and reflecting men, were irresistibly attracted toward it, notwithstanding the corruptions that early gathered round it, and all that Christians themselves did to bring disgrace upon the name. The secret of this power lay within itself.

Diluted as Christianity was, by conformity to existing institutions, and changed in its character and purpose, by the amalgamation of old traditions with new truths, it contained within itself living and universal principles, which no perversity of man could stifle. Through all the din and dissonance of polemics, the gentle, sympathizing words of Jesus sounded for ever, like a silver bell above the howlings of the storm. Earnest souls listened reverently to the all-pervading tones, and received therefrom a more child-like trust in the Heavenly Father, more humanity toward suffering brethren, and more assured hopes of life beyond the grave.

The explanation of the rapid spread of Christianity is to be found in its adaptation to the masses of mankind. The priesthood in Hindostan and Egypt, and the philosophers of Greece and Rome, had deemed it necessary to conceal their highest truths from the people, lest they should become perverted and desecrated by ignorance and grossness. They did not perceive a truth greater than all they taught; that there ought not to *be* any ignorant people; that knowledge should be diffused like the air, which every man may inhale, and into which every man may breathe. Moses took a great step in advance, when he sought to make of the Israelites "a nation of priests;" and Ezra wisely carried out his liberal views, when he erected synagogues, where all the people could hear the Law and the Prophets thrice a week. Socrates taught in the market-place, and distributed gems of wisdom in the workshops of mechanics. But this, noble as it was, was merely dissemination of *knowledge.* While the soul of Jesus, dwelling in a region of holiness, above the intellectual, "had compassion on the multitude;" was filled, to overflowing, with *sympathy* for the indigent, the afflicted, and the erring. It was reserved for *him* to "heal the broken-hearted," to "preach a Gospel to the poor," to say, "Her sins, which are many, are forgiven; for she loved much." Nearly two thousand years have passed away, since those words of love and pity were uttered; yet when I read them, my eyes often fill with tears. I thank thee, O Heavenly Father, for all the messengers thou hast sent to man; but above all, I thank thee for this, thy beloved son! Pure lily-blossom of the centuries, taking root deep in the muddy depths, and receiving the light and warmth of heaven into its golden heart! All that the pious have felt, all that poets have said, all that artists have done, with their manifold forms of beauty, to represent the ministry of Jesus, are but feeble expressions of the great debt we owe him, who is even now curing the lame, restoring sight to the blind, and raising the dead, in that *spiritual* sense in which all miracles are true. A friend writing to me, says: "That the nature of Jesus was gentle, affectionate, and feminine, is shown by his love for children, his tears for Lazarus, his shrinking from death. Yet, for the sake of substituting the good, the true, and the spiritual, for selfishness, falsehood, and formalism, he could live without genuine appreciation or sympathy, and calmly resign himself to an early and violent death. Theology and cant have half spoiled the Bible for us, so that I can scarcely make real to myself the spirit of Christ's words and life; but whenever I do so, I always find that it appeals powerfully to all that is deepest and best in my nature."

The few who possessed any knowledge had, for ages, trampled under their feet the ignorant multitude; either by laws of caste, as in Hindostan and Egypt, or by slavery, as in Greece and Rome. Among those generations of Egyptian peasants, there must have been many who gazed with mournful reverence at the star of Isis, and sometimes asked: "Why are the priests the only depositaries of thy mysteries? Why must we toil to build palaces for their dead bodies, while our own are so dishonoured while alive? Oh, Mother Goddess, if we are not of thy children, and may not learn thy laws, why hast thou sent us here, to labour, to suffer, and to die?" Yet most of those simple souls, after thus wrestling with the darkness that oppressed them, would go to the priests to seek atonement for the sin of their involuntary thoughts. And the poor Pariah, catching glimpses of the sacred Banian Groves from afar, and looking upward, half afraid of the bright Spirits who dwelt among the stars, could he otherwise than reproach them, that he by birth was excluded from the paths that led to light, while Bramins ruled on earth, and went to dwell in palaces above? Millions of such groans ascended from the oppressed earth, and still the ages rolled heavily on, and while the prophets of all nations promised a Messiah, the people imploringly exclaimed: "When will the deliverer appear?"

In the times immediately preceding our era, individual souls began to feel their deprivations and wrongs more distinctly; though as yet they had not reasoned concerning them. There was a state of preparation for the advent of Christ; the dawn of All Souls' Day. At that warm bright flush in the east, well might poor shepherds hear the angels sing! Well might the Holy Spirit appear to the populace in the form of a dove! Well might fishermen forsake their nets, to proclaim the glad tidings to all people! None but poor men, in sympathy with the poor, *could* have preached such a religion as the times demanded. The best among the rich and the educated heard in it the utterings of their own half-revealed consciousness of existing wrong; while to the poor, it was like opening prison doors, and letting in the light from heaven. The previous state of spiritual hunger is indicated by the rapid diffusion of the doctrines. Some, who are prone to look merely on the outside of things, have said that Christianity was embraced principally by the indigent, because it supplied them with food and raiment. Doubtless such motives influenced considerable numbers; but that reason is altogether insufficient to account for the general enthusiasm, which soon pervaded all ranks. The real attraction was of a more interior character. Never before had there been a strong spiritual tie between the educated and the ignorant, the rich and the poor. In Christian communities, the labouring man felt that he was a member of a large affectionate family, who sympathised with his sorrows, and rejoiced in his improvement. If beset with doubts or temptations, he could go to the church, as to a mother, who was ever ready to give him kindly counsel. If he had sinned, he could unburthen his heavy heart, and say: "Brethren, I have strayed from the right path. Help me to come into the fold again." Inexpressibly cheering and strengthening it must have been, to find it a recognized truth, that such as they had souls to be saved; souls of priceless worth, compared with which all the wealth of the world was as dross.

The civil relations of men remained the same; for there was a sincere reverence for government, as an institution ordained of God. Moreover, when the sect was comparatively pure it was too feeble to dictate to rulers. The democratic element *could* not take any other form than the religious. The church could control their own internal arrangements; and certainly they might have abolished slavery within their own limits. But many slaves to Pagan masters belonged to their communities, and the complicated relation required prudent management. Where slaves belonged to their own members, they could, in the *early* days, trust to Christian character, which really did, in good earnest, abolish all distinctions. This *spiritual* equality satisfied the requisitions of conscience, in times of primitive sincerity; and afterward, when professed Christians were often more selfish and tyrannical than many of the Pagans, the church had become too proud and politic to interfere with the wealthy, on any subject not connected with its own aggrandizement. Theological limitation also came in, to check expansive sympathy. To redeem only *Christians* from slavery, and of those only such as were in bondage to unbelieving masters, was merely an enlargement of the feeling which would lead a man to emancipate his own children, taken captive by strangers; still it *was* an enlargement, to acknowledge an extensive spiritual relationship, in addition to the bonds of nature. It was something gained, that every slave could by conversion become an object of this fraternal sympathy; that there was nothing to hinder him from being a priest; and if he had sufficient talent or virtue, he might eventually become a bishop; as was the case with Onesimus. It was also something gained, to have such eloquent outbursts against the whole institution of slavery, as were proclaimed from the pulpit by Gregory of Nyssa, and John of the Golden Mouth. Never had Pagan eloquence occupied itself with a theme so morally grand! No wonder the lowly and the ignorant reverenced, even to excess, those men of learning and talent, who laid aside worldly honours, to instruct them, and plead their cause with the powerful; and who proved the sincerity of their sympathy, by giving all they possessed to found hospitals, and establish orphan asylums. Never before had there been a class of teachers, who imparted regular instruction to the ignorant, and made it the business of their lives to protect the weak against the strong. Never had the aged and the helpless, the widows and the orphans, been so tenderly provided for, as they were by the Christian churches. Never in the world's history had there been such an earnest and extensive effort to inculcate the brotherhood of man, and to exemplify it by practice. Even when the sect became sufficiently numerous and powerful, to induce ambitious men to be its leaders, it long remained a matter of policy, with the worldly ones among the bishops, to manifest sympathy for the poor, that the character already established by the church might not be injured in the eyes of Pagans; for the argument Moses urged upon the Lord was obviously ever present to their minds: "If the people die by the way, the Egyptians will hear of it." But while some were influenced by this low motive, there were always, especially in the villages, many meek and pious clergymen, who relieved the suffering, and vindicated the oppressed, from their exceeding love and reverence for Jesus, who had said: "Inasmuch as ye have done it unto the least of these my brethren, ye have done it unto me."

Much of the preaching in those days would doubtless seem poor, if tried by our standard; but it was a great

advance in the condition of rude nations to have moral and
religious instruction of any kind offered to the whole people; and the benign countenance of Christ could never be
quite obscured by the clouds theology gathered round it.
It is true, the brotherhood of man was very imperfectly
acknowledged, or perceived. But good seed was sown in
the rough soil of human hearts, and in its growth it gradually modified or abolished many a barbarous custom; such
as the slaughter of prisoners taken in war, gladiatorial
combats, and contests with wild beasts, for the amusement
of the populace. It greatly aided previous influences,
which had prepared the way for improvement in human
affairs; especially in the condition of women. The Hebrew religion had always been very emphatic concerning
personal purity; and though polygamy was allowed, the
practice of it was an exception to the general rule. Teutonic tribes married but one wife, and fully acknowledged
the equality of men and women, in church and state. Romans prohibited polygamy by law. How far they had
advanced beyond Asiatic ideas on the subject, is indicated
by a remark of Cato the Censor, who lived two hundred
and thirty-two years before Christ. He was accustomed to
say: "They who beat wives or children lay their sacrilegious hands on the most sacred things in the world. For
myself, I prefer the character of a good husband, to that
of a great senator." The gentle and compassionate character of Christ was peculiarly attractive to the feminine nature; therefore, the number of proselytes was always much
greater among women than among men. The influence
they exerted over relatives was a constant theme of complaint and sarcasm among the Pagans. The orator Libanius reproached the patricians of Antioch with being
"governed by their wives, whom they ought to govern."
He inquires: "Why are you not guided by Pythagoras
and Plato, instead of appealing to your wives and mothers."
By proving such efficient missionaries with husbands, sons
and brothers, women acquired an importance in the church,
which they had never possessed in connection with the old *not true.*

worship. There was *spiritual* equality between slaves and patricians, between men and women. This religious sympathy and companionship greatly ennobled the idea of marriage. It does not appear that the wisest and best Pagan ever rose to such an elevated view of the subject, as Tertullian presents in his picture of a truly Christian union between the sexes.

The priesthood of Greece and Rome merely performed religious ceremonies to procure rain, preserve the crops, avert pestilence, and for other similar purposes. No such thing as moral teaching of the people was included in their office. Philosophers, who were the only preachers, appealed solely to reason, and systematically withdrew from the populace. Platonism, which was the most elevated form of philosophy, imparted a lunar light, beautiful but vague, and cold, because it came from intellect only. No roseate flush from the sentiments warmed its atmosphere. Plato preached a Gospel of Beauty, and endeavoured to form well-proportioned characters, like the harmonious structure of Grecian statues and temples. Hence, his constant allusions to music, as an essential element in education. But he did not embrace the poor and the ignorant within his sympathies. He had no word of strength or consolation to impart to sinful and contrite souls. The heaven he preached was only for those who "philosophized truly, and loved beautiful forms."

His followers, the New Platonists, taught that the Logos, who created the visible world, knew and loved only what was above him; and the Supreme, having no superior, knew and loved only himself. Such a God was not the Heavenly Father. And the future world could not have offered much that was palpable, even to the cultivated few, for whom it was partially unveiled in the Eleusinian Mysteries. The mind must have been bewildered in the long ascending and descending spiral of existences; the ever-evolving circles of manifested and reabsorbed spirit. In the eternal rotation of the infinite whole, an individual was but as dust thrown from the chariot wheel, in its perpetual circuit through the "orbit of necessity."

On the contrary, the most prominent feature in Christianity was the value and importance of individual man. For *him* was the world created, and all inferior creatures made; for *him* was heaven prepared; for *his* redemption the Son of God had given his life; over *his* repentance the church on earth, and the angels above, rejoiced. The resurrection of the *body*, to live a thousand years on *this earth*, renovated in beauty and purged of evil, was a far more tangible idea than that of a Grecian shade, waiting his appointed term in an unknown Elysium; for in all ages, people are much better acquainted with their bodies, than they are with their souls. Another exceedingly strong attraction, which Christianity presented, was the prospect of becoming completely purified from sin, and made sure of salvation, by the administration of baptism and the eucharist.

The alliance between Platonic philosophy and the old externals of worship satisfied conservative minds, who infused some life into the ceremonies, by investing them with allegorical significance. Plutarch compares Grecian mythology to a rainbow in relation to the sun. He says the light which formed it was from heaven, though it was broken by the medium. The facility with which the mind of man, in all ages and countries, contrives to adapt itself to whatever is held traditional and sacred, is remarkable. Mackay says truly: "A large mass of error is easily embalmed and perpetuated by a little truth." But conservatives of that period, as of all other periods, kept up old forms, not so much for themselves, as for the common people. Philosophers conformed to popular language concerning the gods, and practised outward ceremonies, long after they had inwardly set them aside, or given them a higher meaning. Growth was not considered dangerous, so long as it was confined to the initiated few; but it was supposed the safety of the state required that the populace should continue to regard as sacred old ideas in their old dress. We have no right to judge this very harshly, considering that the experience of revolving ages has not *yet* convinced mankind, that no dangers can possibly equal those arising from ignorance, and a suppression of the truth. But vain is the attempt to conserve a national faith in the hearts of the people, for any great length of time, after its hold upon thinking minds is weakened. A chain of unnoticed influences is always at work, by which the enlightened few affect the many, even when they do not intend it. Their zeal kindles others, and their coldness chills. The intermediate state between the old dying faith and the new birth has a paralyzing influence on the vitality of society, which manifests itself in religion, literature, and the Arts. All forms, that are kept up after they are felt to be empty, do in reality degenerate into image-worship, and greatly demoralize a people; whether it be nominal reverence for a mythology, or for days and seasons; for a statue, or a book. The early teachers of Christianity earnestly believed what they taught, and therefore they magnetized the multitude. New apple trees will not flourish where an old orchard has been. The Platonists taught much that was high and true, and furnished many noble examples. But they were offshoots from a decaying stock, which had drawn from the soil all the appropriate nourishment it had to impart; while Christianity was a fresh young tree, bearing different fruit, and deriving sustenance from other qualities of the earth.

If any one is disposed to doubt that Christianity contains within itself a vital element of progress, superior to any other spiritual influence by which God has yet guided the world, I think he will be convinced by comparing the practical results of different religious systems. All of them contain truth, all of them have produced, and are producing, greater or less degrees of good. But after making due deductions, on account of the iniquitous practices of Christendom, we are still compelled to admit that there only do we find sympathy, benevolence, and active exertion for the improvement of all mankind. Christianity is the only form of religion which has warmed up whole nations, to sacrifice time, talent, and wealth, for the benefit of remote and degraded classes of people, from whom no return of advantages could be expected. One instance will suffice for illustration. Where the slave trade and slavery have been abolished, it has not been done by policy of government. It has been the expansive force of Christian sympathy, compelling cold reluctant statesmen to move in obedience to the mighty pulsation of the popular heart. There was no fire to create such propelling steam in the Pagan religions; and in the Asiatic, the celestial spark smoulders under the heavy pressure of belief in irresistible fate.

In the Retrospective Chapter, a brief parallel has already been drawn between Buddhism and Christianity. As the formulas of the Christian church became established, the resemblance grew more and more striking. Witness invocations of the dead; temporary purification by fire after death, the term of which might be shortened by alms to monks, and donations to churches, offered by the living; pilgrimages to holy shrines; adoration of relics; self-torture of devotees; and the use of rosaries. The monastic institution is too exact a copy to be mistaken. There is nothing in the New Testament, which bears the slightest' resemblance to it; and there was nothing like it among the Hebrews, except the Egyptianized Jews called Therapeutæ, who lived in a land full of Hindoo customs. Buddhist countries have been little known to Europeans, until within the last century. As soon as they came in contact with each other, the close resemblance in many religious ideas, customs, and forms of worship, immediately attracted attention. Borri, a Jesuit missionary to Cochin China, says: "It looks as if the Devil had endeavoured among the Gentiles to represent the beauty and variety of religious orders in the Catholic church. The priests have chaplets and strings of beads about their necks. There are also among them persons resembling bishops, and abbots, and archbishops; and they use gilt staves, not unlike our croziers. If any man came newly into that country, he might easily be persuaded there had been Christians there in former times; so nearly has the Devil attempted to imitate us." It has been a favourite theory that Nestorian Christians sent missionaries, some thousand years ago, to Tartary, Northern Thibet, and Northern China; and that the Buddhists borrowed many ideas and customs from the churches they planted there. But the same similarities are found in Cochin China, Tonquin, and Japan, far beyond the bounds of any Nestorian missions. Moreover, there is not found in the religion of Thibet any tradition, any name, or any token whatsoever, indicating connection with Christianity. All, who are acquainted with human affairs, will acknowledge that the old rarely borrows from the new; especially in religious forms; while a new worship almost unavoidably becomes mingled with many things previously consecrated to the minds of men. The great antiquity of the Buddhist religion is proved, beyond all doubt, by the existence of Buddha's image in very ancient rock-temples in Hindostan, and by the allusion to his sect in the sacred poem called the Ramayana, written more than a thousand years before Christ. The same poem, and other still more ancient Sacred Books of Hindostan, mention anchorites, whose modes of asceticism and self-torture appear to have been very closely imitated by the disciples of St. Anthony. The religious associations of Bramins, in the forests, whose time was devoted to contemplation, a routine of prayers, and the instruction of young priests, greatly resemble the Christian monasteries, which did not come into existence till more than a thousand years later. Whether some of the early Gnostics, and other Christian teachers, were brought into direct contact with wandering Hindoo devotees; or with the Buddhist missionaries, who spread themselves all over the East; or whether they imbibed similar ideas and customs from Egypt, where they existed from very ancient times, is uncertain. But that India, by some process, direct or indirect, exerted great influence over early Christianity, appears too obvious to require argument.

All countries under European influences are subject to progression and change, from which even the most conservative states cannot entirely shield themselves. But in Asia, the depreciation of this visible world, and the universal belief in destiny, have produced an unchangeable lethargy. Therefore, those who visit Buddhist countries now, find them in very much the same condition that Christendom was before the Middle Ages. The Grand Lama is acknowledged as the central power of many nations, the same as the Pope was; monks with shaven heads are met everywhere, saying their prayers on rosaries; and crowds of pilgrims are constantly wending their way to the shrine of some celebrated relic, which they believe to be endowed with miraculous power to cure diseases, and bring good fortune. The account of Lamaseries in Thibet immediately suggests Mary Howitt's description of Christian Monasteries in the olden time:

> " And there they kept, the pious monks,
>   Within a garden small,
> All plants that had a healing power,
>   All herbs medicinal.
>
> And thither came the sick, the maimed,
>   The moonstruck and the blind,
> For holy flower, for wort of power,
>   For charmed root or rind."

Many resemblances in doctrine, and especially in forms of expression concerning Bouddha and Christ, will also strike every observing reader. It is expressly stated that Bouddha descended into the hells, to instruct and comfort the souls there. The same appears in the Apostles' Creed concerning Christ; but not until after the sixth century. In one sense, the followers of Bouddha regarded him as a redeemer. They viewed this world as a scene of illusions, in which men were kept enchanted, by reason of the soul's imprisonment in Matter. They saw no way of reconciling a material existence with spiritual life. Men must get *out* of the body, in order to be one with God. But though constantly tempted, nay compelled to sin, *in* the body, each offence must be atoned for, by an equivalent amount of suffering by somebody. Bouddha, while on earth, was described as inflicting severe penances upon himself, for the benefit of others. In the form of a beautiful fox, he allowed himself to be skinned alive, to invite tormenting insects, that he might in that way help to expiate the sins of mankind.

Christians taught the inherent transmitted sinfulness of all mortals; though the doctrine was not based on the same idea. They received from Jews the Cabalistic theory, that the germ of all human souls was in Adam; consequently all became infected with his sin; for which atonement must be made. It was a common idea that Christ's extreme agony in the garden was owing to the fact that he suffered for all the sins of all mankind.

Klaproth, a distinguished German Professor of the Asiatic Languages, says: "Next to the Christian religion, no one has contributed more to ennoble the human race, than the religion of Bouddha." Candour also requires the admission that the progress of Buddhism, though far more extensive than Christianity, has been more peaceful. There is no record that it was ever established in any country by force, nor have I met with any account of hostile sects slaying each other by hundreds.

Kindness toward animals, inculcated in all the Sacred Books, and everywhere practised as a religious duty, forms a lovely feature in the Asiatic religions, which Christianity would do well to imitate. True, it is founded on sympathy, produced by belief in the transmigration of souls, and it sometimes degenerates into fantastic excesses. But a friendly relation between men and animals is beautiful and good; and though Christians do not believe the soul of an ancestor may have passed into a horse, they might practise humanity from a higher motive. Tenderness toward the dumb creatures of God would harmonize with the spirit of the religion they profess; and to acquire it, they merely need to apply the first and most obvious rule of natural religion: "How should I like to be treated, if I were myself a horse?"

If Christians habitually looked at themselves, and at the followers of foreign religions, from the same point of view, there would be much less exultation over their own superiority. If the Koran declared that God said to Mohammed: "Smite Amalek. Destroy utterly all that they have, and spare them not; but slay man and woman, infant and suckling," the text would doubtless have been quoted thousands of times by theologians, to prove the cruelty of Moslems, and the improbability that such a command came by Divine inspiration.

The existence of caste in Hindostan has been a constant theme of disparaging comparison with Christianity. So far as relates to the teaching and example of Christ, such remarks are just; but in point of *practice*, the law of caste exists throughout Christendom. In most European countries, there is a caste, which derives its right to govern all the others from hereditary descent, without reference to talent or goodness. There is also a caste, who inherit high dignities, lucrative offices, and large landed estates, which cannot be sold to pay just debts to poor men. A member of this favoured caste sometimes possesses estates so extensive, that he could not ride over them in a week; while thousands of labourers cannot obtain land sufficient to raise food for their families. In the United States of America, there exists a degraded caste, amounting to more than four millions of people. They are taxed and punished by the laws, but are not allowed to vote for those who make them. They are confined to menial occupations; being excluded from all lucrative employments, all honourable offices, and from seminaries of education; except in a very few and recent instances. From cars, steamboats, and other public conveyances, they are either entirely excluded, or compelled to take the most unclean and uncomfortable places; by which the health of many is seriously injured. No amount of intelligence, or honourable conduct, can save them from this general proscription, to which they are condemned by birth. Many of them are pious Christians; some of them preachers of the Gospel; but they are required to worship in buildings by themselves. Where the numbers are not sufficient to form an isolated congregation, they are sometimes admitted into churches with the higher classes, on condition of sitting by themselves, far apart from others, and of not receiving the eucharist until all others have been served. It is not respectable to intermarry with them, or to eat at the same table. Even the dead bodies of these Christian Pariahs are regarded as a contamination, and are not allowed to be buried in the same enclosure with bones of the privileged classes. Similar customs in Hindostan are sanctioned by their Sacred Books, which enjoin a demarcation of castes; but the New Testament of the Christians expressly teaches the equality and brotherhood of mankind. In one case there is moral darkness; in the other, there is wilful disobedience to acknowledged light.

As a general thing, Christians have manifested very little kindness, or candour, in their estimate of other religions; but the darkest blot on their history is their treatment of the Jews. This is the more singular, because we have so much in common with them. We worship the same God, under the same name; we reverence their Scriptures; we make pilgrimages to their Holy City. Christ, and his Mother, and his Apostles, were Jews, and appear to have conformed to the established worship of the country; which we consequently claim as our sacred land. That the crucifixion occurred there was the fault of very few of the people. Only two of the tribes ever returned to Jerusalem, and of them merely a remnant. Their descendants scattered all over the Roman empire. They spoke a different language from their forefathers, and had little intercourse with Palestine. Doubtless thousands of them never heard of Jesus, till they were brought into collision with his followers, who increased Roman prejudice against them, by preaching the immediate establishment of the Messiah's kingdom on earth. It was not the benevolent and holy Jesus, consecrated to *our* hearts, whom *they* rejected. Palestine Jews described him to their brethren abroad, as the founder of an obscure sect, who was not strict in keeping the Sabbath, who associated with odious tax-gatherers and foreigners, who spoke disparagingly of their sacred traditions, called their men of prayer hypocrites, and was finally executed for attempting to make himself king. And even in Palestine, doubtless great numbers of the people never manifested any animosity toward him, and never in reality knew much about his character. His followers in Jerusalem, at the time of his death, numbered only one hundred and twenty; and the existence of so small a sect might easily be unknown in many parts of the country. Even those who were really his enemies acted with the blind bigotry so generally manifested by established churches toward non-conformists. The Christian Fathers themselves admit that the Jews were not *aware* of persecuting the Son of God; because both Christ and his Apostles sedulously *concealed* his divinity. But though so few were implicated in the cruel transaction, the Fathers were accustomed to speak of all Jews, in all parts of the world, as "murderers of Christ;" and they were everywhere hated and persecuted, as if each one of them had put him to death, knowing him to be the Son of God. For nearly two thousand years has this rancorous hostility been perpetuated, though it rests on such an unjust and irrational foundation. And men who branded all the Jews as outcasts, who plundered and slaughtered them, for an offence committed by a small number of their very remote ancestors, were accustomed to quote, as their standard, the prayer which Jesus offered for those who were the immediate causes of his death: "Father, forgive them; for they know not what they do."

Did a religion manifesting such a spirit offer anything lovely to the Jews, that they should be induced to embrace it? Do not noble souls naturally cling to ancient and consecrated usages, when men speak evil of them, and force is used to compel their relinquishment? If we looked at the subject candidly, I think we should acknowledge as heroic martyrs, those men and women, who resisted constant appeals to their fears and their selfishness, and at the cost of incredible sacrifices and sufferings, still set their faces steadfastly toward Jerusalem, and replied: "After this manner worship we the God of our fathers." Ever since I have reflected on the subject, I have never been able to do otherwise than reverence their firmness and their faith.

It has been the singular destiny of that extraordinary people to be objects of great exaggeration, both as ancients and moderns. When they were rude nomadic tribes, they had the narrowness and barbarity, which unavoidably characterize nations in that stage of civilization. But we regard them, at *that* time, as the only depositories of truth revealed by God to man; and the fragments of their barbarous history are quoted as sacred rules of life. The Jews of Rome and Alexandria, whom the Christian Fathers considered as deservedly accursed by men, and outcasts from God's mercy, were better, and far more enlightened, than those savage tribes of the desert, who went about slaughtering women and children, in the name of Jehovah, and who were nevertheless reverenced as the only people God had chosen for his own, on the face of the whole earth. Even on the borders of our own times, Moses Mendelssohn, the great and the good, would not have been allowed to purchase an acre of land in Christian countries, where Joshua is regarded as directly and constantly inspired by God, though he allured marauding tribes to conquer innocent people, by promises of "harvests they had not sowed, and vineyards they had not planted."

We owe the Jews an immense debt of gratitude, after deducting all exaggerations. Their great lawgiver cared for the poor, and instructed all the people; their prophets kept alive reverence for God, and abhorrence of idolatry; and their poets uttered solemn strains of penitence, through which contrite hearts have for ages poured out their sor-

rows and supplications before the Lord. These things
contributed very largely to form a basis on which to
build Christianity. Their Scriptures are exceedingly
valuable, as fragments of ancient history, which throw
light on our own religion. Their solemn rebukes of
sin, and their eloquent outbursts of devotional feeling,
render them venerable and dear to all religious souls.
But adapted, as some portions of them were, to savage
tribes, and others to semi-barbarous ages, they become a
positive obstacle to progress in humanity, when received
literally, by civilized nations, as a rule of life. How can
it be otherwise with books that authorize stoning people
to death for picking up sticks on Saturday; scalding a
man that scalds you; killing a son for disobedience; whip-
ping slaves as much as is consistent with their living over
two days; and cutting to pieces prisoners taken in battle?
Every abominable practice in Christendom has by turns
been sustained by arguments drawn from the Old Testament. True, other passages breathe a different spirit; but
that is because the volume is made up of fragments, composed at different epochs, and, by men of totally different
characters. The portion which may be made universally
applicable to all times is very small. Up to a certain
point, written Revelations aid the progress of nations; but
after the state of society for which they were written has
entirely passed away, they become a positive hindrance;
because the *habit* of reverence remains after the *life* has
gone. "It is only the *living*, who can bury the dead."
The Code of Menu and the Pouranas are the greatest of
all obstacles to the civilization of Hindostan; and the
progress of the Jews has been much impeded by the
Pentateuch and the Talmud. Men part slowly with old
established opinions and forms. Mental resistance to
change is as strong as the principle of inertia in mechanical science. When reason, in its manly growth, can no
longer be satisfied with the food that sustained its infancy,
imagination comes with a vase of ambrosial allegories. In
this way, Philo found the poetic system of Plato within

the practical and circumstantial laws of Moses. Ram-mohun Roy permeated the Vedas with the same refining element. And Christian Fathers found all the inward warfare of their souls in the wanderings and battles of the Israelites. But this process is resorted to only by reflective minds. The great majority venerate a doctrine, a book, or an institution, merely because it has *long* been venerated; and as Thomas Carlyle says: "It is truly surprising how long a rotten post may stand, provided it be not shaken." Dr. Lardner, the well-known ecclesiastical writer says: "No religion can be so absurd and unreasonable, especially when it has been established, and of a long time, that it will not find men of good abilities, not only to palliate and excuse, but also to approve and justify, and recommend its greatest absurdities."

But though it is unwise to expend vain efforts in galvanizing the dead, the body that once had life should be treated reverently. And we ought never to forget that forms, which are dead to us, may have been very much alive to others; that things may seem absurd merely because the *idea* they originally conveyed is lost. We turn with contempt from representations of Egyptian priests kneeling before a golden beetle. But five thousand years hence, similar feelings may be excited by pictures of a Catholic priest kneeling before an altar, on which is a lamb with a cross; because the meaning of the emblem may be forgotten. It is impossible for us to tell what spiritual truth the golden beetle represented to Egyptian minds. If we could be enabled to perceive the idea precisely as it appeared to them, perhaps the symbol would fill us with veneration, as the embodiment of some great mystery, connected with God and the soul. If in the long lapse of ages, a time should ever arrive, when men know as little about the ceremonies of the Christian church, as we know concerning those of Chaldea and Egypt, how would it seem to them to find an inscription somewhere, which recorded that men and women were accustomed to assemble on stated occasions to eat small morsels of bread, and sip a

few drops of wine, which the priest had previously consecrated by a form of prayer; that some deemed them the
veritable body and blood of God; and believed that the
salvation of the soul depended upon partaking of them?
If the significance of the ordinance were lost, how puerile
would the form appear! We consider the ancient religions absurd; but if we should ever become angels and
archangels, with a capacity of remembering our present
views concerning God and the soul, they will appear far
more external and childish, than do now those of the first
Hebrews in their tents, or the first Grecians in their caves.

And after all, there is more similarity in the leading
ideas of various ages and nations, than we have been accustomed to acknowledge. The seven Amshaspands of
Persia, the "seven mighty Princes" before the throne of
God, described by the Hebrew prophet, and the seven
Archangels in whom Christians believe, are certainly very
like each other. The Guardian Angels, so often pictured
by Christian artists, bear great resemblance to the winged
Archetype, which Grecians said every human being had
in the world of Spirits; a kind of Heavenly Elder Brother,
who was attracted toward him by the sympathy of spiritual relationship; who knew all his thoughts and actions,
and at death accompanied him to the Judges of the Dead,
and rendered an account of them. Certainly, Christians
invested Angels with a much higher and purer *character*,
than had belonged to Grecian Spirits. Thereby the progressive growth of the ages concerning Divine Natures was
expressed, and much was gained for the future. But all
human souls have been children of the same Father,
travelling toward the same home as ourselves; and therefore we must needs have much in common.

The great similarity in the prophecies, traditions, and
even emblems, of various ages and countries, will of course
strike every reader. In all parts of the world we find traditions of a time when the earth was spontaneously fruitful, when men were innocent, and lived to an immense age.
Everywhere, prophets have foretold that the Golden Age

would be restored by some holy and just man, or some incarnated deity, who would appear in the latter times. Everywhere, there have been predictions of the destruction of the world by fire, and accounts of its inundation by water. The Goddess Mother with her Child was pictured on Egyptian temples; veiled behind Chinese altars; consecrated in Druid groves; and glorified in Christian churches. People will explain these coincidences differently, according as the reverential or rational element prevails in character. Some will suppose that Hebrew Scriptures were the original source of all, and will consider everything a prophecy of Christ. Others will say that the same wants and aspirations in human nature produce similar manifestations in nations and times remote from each other; that the Past is always reproduced in the Present, and always prophesies the Future; as the child is prophetic of the man.

In the Retrospective Chapter, allusion was made to traces of animal magnetism among the ancients. Similar phenomena reappear in later times. Apollonius at Ephesus is described as perceiving things which happened at the same moment at Rome. Celsus speaks of it as a common thing for Egyptian magicians to make inanimate things move, as if they were alive, and so to influence uncultured men, as to produce in them whatever sights or sounds they pleased. Tertullian describes a Montanist woman, who cured diseases, perceived the thoughts of others, and held conversations with Spirits, which were taken down in writing, as inspired revelations. Hermits, reduced to a state of nervous excitability, by fasting and watchfulness, are said to have perceived the thoughts of people, to have cured diseases by laying on their hands, and even by transmitting written words to the invalid. The account of Theurgy among the New Platonists sounds like a modern description of clairvoyance. Early painters, in their pictures of the Virgin and saints curing diseases, sometimes represented streams of light radiating from their fingers.

With regard to the innumerable miracles recorded by all parties, there is doubtless very great allowance to be made for fabrication, exaggeration, and trickery; but after making all reasonable deductions from the accounts which have been handed down to us, it still seems likely that some remarkable things really did occur, and formed a basis for numerous reports. Perhaps some were unconsciously accomplished by means of that mysterious agency, which we call magnetism; and men finding themselves possessed of a power, which they could not explain, honestly supposed that some Spirit was working miracles through them. Whoever has been in the midst of a very excited crowd, has been aware of an influence which it is extremely difficult to resist; which seems to carry him out of himself, and renders it almost impossible to preserve the balance of his judgment. This sometimes happens even when there was originally little or no sympathy with the cause of excitement. What then must it be, where faith is at its highest pitch of exaltation, and the soul becomes a perfect medium of spiritual electricity? All earnestness is magnetic; and perhaps there never was a greater degree of enthusiasm, than pervaded early Christian assemblies; especially among the Montanists. How could it otherwise than operate powerfully on the nerves and imagination of an invalid, heated white-hot with the same fervour of faith? That diseases should actually be cured thereby, is no more incredible than the well known fact that the bed-ridden have been able to leap out of the windows, when their minds were excited to the highest degree, by a knowledge that the house was in flames. Lord Bacon says: "There has been very little inquiry, and not at all proportioned to the depth and importance of the subject, how far imagination, or thought, very fixed, and as it were exalted into a faith, can effect a change in the body of the imaginer."

At the present time, we begin to recognize the existence of laws connected with the relation of soul and body, and their action on each other; though as yet we have made no approach toward understanding them. But in those early centuries, no man dreamed of the existence of such laws. Everything was attributed to the *direct* agency of God. St. Anthony, Hilarion, and Simeon Stylites, might have really cured diseases, they knew not how, by reason of their own half disembodied state, and the undoubting faith of others. The peculiarities which are *induced* by any particular state of the world, are, by the necessity of spiritual laws, *adapted* to that state. What inspires reverence at one period, excites ridicule at another; and when faith in it has gone, it loses its magnetic power, for good or evil.

No doubt, many imputed miracles were merely natural experiments, or scientific phenomena, disguised under religious formulas, with which they had no connection. When the lamps used for Easter were replenished with water from the river, it was believed to be miraculously converted into oil by prayers of the bishop, and because he who poured it had strong faith in the power of Christ; but it is not likely he did anything more than most housewives have done, when they wished to raise the oil in their lamps. The Gymnosophist, who caused a tree to speak to Apollonius, was probably a ventriloquist. Perhaps the expelled Devils, who audibly acknowledged themselves to be Jupiter or Apollo, received similar aid; in fact the idea is suggested by a remark I have quoted from Justin Martyr. When Maximus, the Platonic philosopher, caused all the lamps in the temple to blaze instantly, by a form of words, there was doubtless gas in his proceedings. The Catholics, who talked after their tongues were cut out, have had parallels in modern times. The Academy of Science, in Paris, published, early in the eighteenth century, an account of a girl born without a tongue, who yet talked distinctly and easily. The statement was made by an eminent physician, who had carefully examined her mouth. A similar account was attested by them concerning a boy, who had lost his tongue by an ulcer.

The existence of very pious feelings, in conjunction with intolerance, cruelty, and selfish policy, has never ceased to surprise and perplex those who have viewed it calmly from a distance. Constantine, after he had manifested such zeal for bishops, and shown the greatest reliance on the efficacy of prayer, caused the death of his own son, and his sister's husband, and her son, from the fear that they might become formidable as rivals in the empire. Constantius, who was zealous for Christianity, pursued the same course with regard to his uncle and cousins. Theodosius, the most pious of them all, was relentless in his persecution of sects that differed in the slightest degree from the established church; and he ordered thousands of innocent people, including women and children, to be slaughtered, to gratify his resentment. From that time down to the present day, such instances abound; and it is common to explain them by the supposition of deliberate hypocrisy in religious professions. But I am convinced that piety toward God may be perfectly sincere in those who manifest great selfishness and violence toward their fellow creatures; because the two results proceed from different elements in man's nature, which must be harmoniously proportioned and combined to form a consistent religious character; but which, nevertheless, are often disproportioned, and even completely separated. Conscientiousness and reverence for the supernatural are distinct things; and either one or the other may predominate in character. I have known exceedingly conscientious and humane people, who would be uneasy for days, if they had struck a dog, or given a cent too little in change, or uttered an equivocation, who, nevertheless, could not be much impressed by the most solemn ceremonies of the church, or excited by the most fervent preaching. On the other hand, I have known extremely devotional people, who wept over the Bible, and could not live happily without frequent worship, who nevertheless abused animals, and dealt hardly with the poor, without being troubled by any degree of the remorse they would have felt, if they had fallen asleep for the night without uttering a prayer. John Newton was a memorable example to the point. He wrote in strains of the most affecting piety, spent much of his time in reading of Christ, and praying to him, and thankfully recorded "sweet seasons of communion with God," while he was carrying on the slave-trade on the coast of Africa. Extreme results of a similar nature occur in Italy, where devotional feelings are very strong, and moral principles generally flexible. Hired assassins will not kill their victim with a dagger whose handle is in the form of a cross. A ferocious bandit, who for a long time had rendered himself formidable to the police, was at last taken by means of his own piety. It was discovered that he had made a vow to do injury to no creature on Saturday; which the church had taught him was the birth-day of the Virgin Mary. They attacked him on that day, and as he offered no resistance, he was taken and executed; dying with a prayer on his lips.

In all ages, such melancholy discrepancies have been greatly increased by the tendency of the priesthood to substitute theology for religion. This troubled the waters of Christianity very near the fountain. Paul was one of the greatest and best among the messengers, whom God has sent to guide the human race. But he was brought up at the feet of a learned Jewish Rabbi, and of course breathed a polemical atmosphere. His whole soul was seized by the teachings of Christ, and, in his earnestness, he would fain have imparted his own faith and hope to all the world. But obstacles came in his way. Gentiles demanded a reason for his faith, and Jews insisted that he should sustain his hope by proofs brought from their prophecies and traditions. Thus he was forced into perpetual arguments, often of a metaphysical character. Christ preached a religion; Paul taught theology. Religion does not consist in *knowing;* it is a state of *feeling.* It was not the power of *doctrines,* that brought the Fathers into the church. It was a deep interior consciousness of the holiness and beauty. of Christ's example, and of his pure and gentle teaching. This they wished to embody in word and deed, and sow it widely in the seed-field of everlasting time. But theology encountered this devout consciousness, and piled up in its path the antecedent doctrines of the world, with subtle and totally unanswerable questions, which, nevertheless, would pertinaciously insist upon being answered. Thus the Fathers, especially the later ones, were drawn aside from religion to theology. Then followed sectarian warfare, and stormy councils; until the dominant church, aided by civil power, petrified all thought into formulas, and when hungry souls asked for bread, gave them a stone. Men who laboured for this result, and exulted in its completion, were not necessarily guided by ambition, or selfish policy. They were strongly impressed with the idea that to do good extensively, the church must be established; and that in order to be established, it must be one and indivisible in doctrines. In the process, errors of faith came to be regarded as more sinful, than the greatest moral delinquencies. The same stringent rule was applied even to external ceremonies. All must observe Easter on the same day; and the Gregorian Chants must be the universal standard for church music. In those chants, every singer must utter the same tone, in the same key. *Unison* of voices was the highest idea *theology* could attain to; but when *religion* can utter itself freely, worshippers sing a *harmony* of many different parts, and thus make music more pleasing to the ear of God, and more according to the pattern by which he created the universe.   .

In all forms of worship, and in all individual souls, religion diminishes in the same proportion that theology increases; for inquisitive thought always has a tendency to separate from the affections, in pursuit of mental abstractions. Intellect, in religious matters, has always proved like the horses of the Sun under the guidance of Phæton; rushing wildly among the stars, always descending in its course, and finally shattering the chariot, and extinguishing its warm radiance in the waters of this earth. From this frequent example, some draw the inference that it is wisest and safest to receive with unquestioning faith the opinions others have established; forgetting that the warmth was chilled, and the light well nigh extinguished, in the process of *becoming* established. There is another and a better lesson which the experience ought to teach; namely that religion does not consist in *doctrines* of any kind, but in *sentiments* of reverence toward God, and of justice and benevolence toward our fellow men.

It is impossible to exaggerate the evil work theology has done in the world. What destruction of the beautiful monuments of past ages, what waste of life, what disturbance of domestic and social happiness, what perverted feelings, what blighted hearts, have always marked its baneful progress! How the flowery meadow of childhood has been blasted by its lurid fires! Alas, what a world that was for infancy to open its wondering eyes upon, when exorcisms to cast out Devils were murmured over its innocent brow! When Pagan priests poured sacrificial wine into its tender stomach, and Christian deacons forced open its reluctant mouth, to pour in more wine, that the Devil might be expelled, which they supposed had taken possession of the poor little suffering lamb! What a spiritual atmosphere that was for childhood to breathe, when zealous mothers dragged their little ones, with hot haste, to the place of martyrdom, and taught them it was sinful to be attracted by birds and butterflies on the way! When monks scourged and nearly starved a little boy, to test whether his father had become sufficiently holy to witness their cruelty without any remains of human emotion!

Even if nothing worse than wasted mental effort could be laid to the charge of theology, that alone ought to be sufficient to banish it from the earth, as one of the worst enemies of mankind. What a vast amount of labour and learning has been expended, as uselessly as emptying shallow puddles into sieves! How much intellect has been employed mousing after texts, to sustain preconceived doctrines! Little or no progress toward truth is usually made, because passages of ancient books are taken up hundreds of years after they were written, and are used in a sense altogether foreign from the original intention, in order to sustain some opinion, or tradition of the then present time. And the human mind is not left free to pursue even *this* distorting process; but colleges of supervisors are appointed to instruct the young in what light everything *ought* to be viewed. One college covers the eyes of all its students with red spectacles, so that every object seems on fire. Another insists that blue spectacles are the only proper medium; consequently its pupils maintain that all creation is ghastly pale. Whereupon red spectacles rush to battle with blue spectacles, to prove that the whole landscape is flame-coloured. If one who uses his natural eyesight comes between them, and says, ever so gently: "Nay, my friends, you are both mistaken. The meadows are of an emerald green, and the sunshine is golden," he is rudely shoved aside, as an heretic, or an infidel. One party calls out to him: "Did you ever look at the landscape through red spectacles?" Another shouts: "Did you ever examine it by the only right method, which is through blue spectacles?" And if he cannot answer in the affirmative, they both vociferate: "Then you had better keep silence; for you are altogether incapable of forming a correct opinion on the subject."

Alas, what millions of men have been thus employed, in all countries, ever since the world began! What a blooming paradise would the whole earth be, if the same amount of intellect, labour, and zeal, had been expended on science, agriculture, and the arts! Polemical controversy must necessarily be useless, even if it were nothing worse; because it is always striving to settle infinite questions by the exercise of finite faculties. In this stage of existence, our Heavenly Father obviously intends that we should know very little concerning the destiny of our own souls, and their relations with Him and the universe. This inevitable limitation of our vision should teach us a lesson of humility with regard to our own views, and of respectful tenderness toward those of others. It is our duty to wait with hope and faith for the withdrawal of the screen, and to be thankful, meanwhile, that there are bright edges of light around the veil of the sanctuary, which give assurance of a glorious presence within.

Thousands of years ago, hermits in Hindostan inquired earnestly: "How does God exist? And whence came Evil?" And up to this day, there has been no approach made toward solving the problems. Here, we come up against the walls of limitation, with which the All Wise has circumscribed our vision. The answers to such queries are above finite comprehension. We cannot attain unto them; as the most sagacious elephant can never measure the distances of the stars, or calculate the return of the moon, though their solemn brightness may impress and overawe him, as vague conceptions of the Deity affect our own souls.

A wondrous want of faith in truth is constantly manifested by the jealous pains men take to regulate and control all inquiry into established formulas. The old writer Ludovicus Vives tells the story of a peasant who thought his donkey had drunk up the moon. Therefore, he killed the poor animal, in order to restore that luminary; thinking the world stood in much need of its light. Thus has bigotry, in its folly and madness, slain many a one, who was merely allaying spiritual thirst, by drinking from a pail of water, which reflected some beams of the moon, while the great planet itself serenely floated over all, and was reflected in a thousand streams. In the narrowness of our ignorance, we have been forever striving to limit the All Father's love. Hindoos thought themselves the sole depositaries of truth. Jews did the same. Christians, in their turn, denounced all but themselves, as "heathen," and "murderers of Christ," who must unavoidably burn in eternal fire. But while these successively asserted their exclusive claims, the Heavenly Father was lovingly and wisely guiding all, and renewing all. As no individual can monopolize sunshine, or water, so no nation, or sect, can appropriate to itself God's love or truth. If they think they have drunk up the sun, they are mistaken donkeys, who had but a dim reflection of it in their own small water-pail.

One of the most beautiful and sublime aspects of Divine Providence is the ethereal and infinite nature of all high truths and holy feelings. Religion, like music, cannot be compelled to express anything bad. Whatever words are appropriated to a tune, the tones preserve their purity. If there is evil done, the language must do it; the divine element of music has no share in the degrading office. A rough voice may mar its sweetness, a false ear may confuse the measure; but the true ear, that listens, perceives the inherent beauty, and the clear voice repeats it. In vain have theologians set rancorous words to a gentle tune. The *spirit* of Christ's teaching eludes their efforts; as he himself passed through the midst of those who would seize him, and went his way. Churches may anathematize each other; but above their discordant utterance, penitents hear the consoling voices of Mary Magdalen and the Prodigal Son, and the dying beggar smiles while he hears Lazarus call him to the gates of heaven.

It is true that mere theological tenets may do much and prolonged mischief. The abstract idea that Matter was the origin of Evil has produced.an immense amount of physical and moral disease in the world. Thousands and thousands have starved and lacerated their bodies, and stifled the kindliest emotions of human nature, in consequence of it. For centuries, it changed the entire social system, by banishing a very large proportion of men and women into convents. The influence of it to this day infects our ideas of love and marriage. A spiritual-minded woman once confessed to me she was greatly shocked by the news that Dr. Channing was about to be married; "because she had always considered him such a saint." The old Hindoo idea was lurking there, in the extremest form of Protestantism.

But even the most repulsive and fantastic forms of theology often embodied a high idea. The rage for celibacy which prevailed at one period of the world, was an excessive reaction from the tendency to bury the soul in material things; thus making the body a sepulchre instead of a temple, or a pleasant house. Augustine's doctrine, that a Christian should be *willing* to be damned for the glory of God, was only a very extreme form of expressing the beautiful idea of self-renunciation. The complicated Gnostic theories concerning Christ's derivation from the Supreme Being, through successive emanations, were but the utterance of the heart, stammering its homage through the imperfect medium of the intellect. Their wild poetic myths about Ennoia and Sophia Achamoth are obviously intended to represent the human soul, aspiring after the beautiful and the true, but snared by the temptations of life, chained by its necessities, mournfully conscious of its own degradation, forever striving to raise its fettered wings, and imploring aid from Higher Powers, to soar toward pure spiritual regions. Al Sirat, the hair-breadth bridge over flames of hell, placed before the entrance of Paradise, conveys to spiritual-minded Moslems a true picture of our earthly pilgrimage, where all human souls need good angels to help them across narrow bridges over gulfs of fire.

Always there is a saving power at work to guard the inner life from destruction. We are told that when Job was delivered to Satan, God stipulated that he should spare his life. The same reservation is made with regard to human hearts when they are made over to theology to be tormented. Human affections were given up to monasteries, to deal with them as they would; but kill them utterly they could not. Some vestiges of natural feeling remained in monks, and took refuge behind their consecrated symbols. Pictures of the "Queen of Heaven" often glowed with the sunlight of woman's tenderness, and fragrant memories of mothers and sisters were breathed around them, mingled at times with gentle visions of a wife that might have been. With all their stern stifling of nature, I doubt whether they could have worshipped the image of a man with such tender reverence. Nuns also, however orthodox their belief concerning original sin, and the unholiness of marriage, were doubtless attracted toward infant innocence in those pictures, and loved the child in that mother's arms, not always as an incarnated God, but as a human babe. In their visions of a spiritual bridegroom, nature sometimes mingled with grace, though the feeling lay concealed from their consciousness under a mystic veil. This is very observable in the ecstatic language of St. Theresa, concerning her union with Christ; portions of which would not have been altogether inappropriate, if addressed by Eloise to Abelard.

Even in the external observances and arbitrary power of the church there were many compensating influences. Images and pictures abounded, as they did in Pagan temples; but the *idea* they embodied was on a higher plane. Philosophers adored Beauty and Power in the statues of their gods. Christians venerated Purity, Gentleness, and Benevolence, in images of the Virgin and her Son. Whatever condition of things grows out of a certain state of society, must necessarily be in some degree best adapted to that state. Such a bishop as Ambrose could not rise up in England, or the United States. Obedience to such an one would be altogether a retrograde movement in society. But under the irresponsible despotism of Roman emperors, it was a positive blessing to mankind to have the civil power restrained by reverence for the ecclesiastical. The public penance imposed on the emperor Theodosius, for an act of barbarous injustice to the populace, was a salutary lesson to kings; and that a bishop was moved to do it, proved the increasing importance of the people's cause. The agents of Christianity, even when grasping at wealth and power, were employed by Providence to advance a democratic principle in the world, though they were generally unconscious agents. The universal custom of bequeathing large estates to the church did an immense amount of evil, in many ways. It encouraged men in the selfish and indolent idea of sinning while life and health lasted, and then purchasing salvation with money; it defrauded rightful heirs; and it rendered the church inordinately powerful, arrogant, and avaricious. But even this practice had some good results. To a considerable degree, monks were conveyancers of the wealth of rich robbers to the defrauded poor; for monasteries were asylums for homeless orphans and wandering beggars, hospitals for indigent invalids, and resting places for travellers. The old barriers of rank were likewise broken down by monasticism. Chrysostom, urging people to embrace it, says: "Even the sons of peasants and artificers, who enter this state of life, become so revered, that the first of the land are not ashamed to visit their cells, and consider it an honour to converse with them."

To a liberal soul, it is pleasant to find indications that, in the midst of fiercest controversy, the spirit of Christianity had not departed from the churches, and was not confined to them; that some, of all classes, paid voluntary homage to the good and the true. It is consoling to read of Christians, who thought Socrates and Plato might have been inspired by a portion of the Logos; and of Platonists, who acknowledged Jesus was one of the divine messengers sent by God to men. It is a beautiful picture, that of Christians in Carthage, risking their lives to tend Pagans smitten with the pestilence; and of Christians in Nicomedia, throwing open their granaries in time of famine, to feed the hungry multitude of unbelievers. It is cheering to read of Pagan magistrates, who evaded the laws, or stretched them to the utmost, to avoid inflicting penalties, and who were accustomed to give secret warning to Christians in time of danger. It makes one in love with human nature, to find Roman citizens refusing to be bound by the laws, during Diocletian's persecution, and acting from a higher law in their own hearts, which led them to risk their own property and personal safety, rather than betray fugitives, who had taken refuge with them. It is encouraging to all who wish to break down partition walls, to hear the orator Libanius pleading so earnestly in behalf of persecuted Christians, who had shown moderation in their day of power. It is touching to hear the much-wronged Israelites uniting their voices with Christians in Psalms of lamentation, at the funerals of good bishops. These things convey instructive lessons, which the world would do wisely to take to heart; for though nearly two thousand years have rolled away since the introduction of Christianity, men have not yet learned to view each other's religions with justice and candour.

While contending about the divinity of Christ's *person*, the divinity of his *example* has been comparatively neglected. The only real point of union for mankind, is in the acknowledgment of great moral principles. The *theology* of all religions is something extraneous and imperfect, which took shape from previous opinions, and peculiar circumstances of the time. It is, therefore, necessarily subject to change, and destined to pass away. But there is no occasion for alarm lest changes should come before the way is prepared for them. Conservatives may console themselves with Carlyle's wise remark: "The old skin never falls off, till a new one has formed under it." We may safely trust the preservation of truth to Him who guides the stars. Every particle of genuine life, contained within decaying forms of thought, will fall like ripe seed from a withered stem, and produce fresh plants, which will gradually develop with the progress of man, and ripen into spiritual flowers and fruit of more perfected varieties, than any the world has yet seen. The present *forms* of Christianity will vanish, and become traditional records, in the lapse of ages; but all that really makes it a *religion* will remain forever. As long as there are human souls, they will acknowledge Christ as a Son of God. Not because councils have decreed it; but because they will find in his example and precepts what they most desire to be, in their highest states of aspiration, when they are most filled with reverence for God, with compassion for the sufferings and faults of their fellow creatures, and with humility in view of their own deficiences. Because Jesus taught mankind to cast out the Demon Penalty, by means of the Angel Attraction, therefore shall all the ages honour and bless him. His precepts will be more and more venerated, the more they are examined in their own pure light, the more they are compared with other systems, and especially the more they are *practised*. Whether another great teacher will ever be sent to help us still further onward, it will be time enough to inquire when Christendom begins, in good earnest, to try the experiment of practical conformity to his religion. He has uttered the great diapason tone which would bring all discords into harmony. If only one nation would conscientiously obey his laws, in her internal and external regulations, she would be lifted up, and draw all the nations unto her. War and slavery, the gallows and prisons, would disappear from the earth. No miracles recorded in the wildest legends of the Middle Ages equal the power of Christian Faith to cast out Evil Spirits. No prophecies of a blissful future are too golden to describe the sunshine of universal Love.

On each individual soul devolves the duty of helping to produce this sublime result; and this can be done only by reverent obedience to inward convictions. God has not made conscience an infallible pope, to decide what is right or wrong, true or false; therefore, the most conscientious men may conform to a very imperfect, or even a wrong standard, on some subjects, while they adopt a very high standard with regard to others. This has been the case in all ages and countries, and under all forms of religion. It cannot be otherwise with beings who are formed by influences from two worlds. But it is an established law of our being that disobedience to our own consciences darkens the condition of our souls; while sincere reverence for that inward voice brings us gradually into greater and greater light. In this way, individuals who are true to their own convictions are always helping the public conscience to rise to a higher plane. A large majority of men, in all ages, are guided almost entirely by popular opinion; and that opinion derives its power of growth from individuals, who become mediums of Divine influence, by fearless obedience to their own internal light. The heroic old monk, who rushed into the amphitheatre to separate two gladiators, commanded to murder for the amusement of the

Roman populace, was put to death for obeying his own conscience, more enlightened than that of the people; but his voice afterward became the public voice, and gladiatorial combats were forbidden by law. Clarkson incurred much odium and persecution by denouncing a traffic, sanctioned by all the merchants of his time, licensed by the government, and not rebuked by the clergy; but eventually, the public conscience rose to his level, and Christian nations thenceforth branded the slave-trade as piracy. Once thoroughly impressed with the utter wickedness of the trade, he naturally came to the conclusion that a system originating in such monstrous violation of justice and humanity must also be wrong. His earnestness influenced other minds. Elizabeth Heyrick learned from them, and, with woman's spontaneous insight of the heart, added that if slavery was wrong, immediate and entire cessation from it was the only right way. The interior perceptions of these honest souls, fearlessly proclaimed, became the moral sentiment of the British nation; as they eventually will be of the whole world. In every village, there are a few individuals striving, on some subject or other, to live up to a standard higher than the community around them. Their truthful natures yield to a strong conviction that their own consciences ought to be obeyed, whatever men may say. Very often they see no further than this; and continue to labour, year after year, uncheered by hopes of changing the current of public opinion. But though they know it not, they are working for the ages. Each, in his own way, is a medium of the Holy Spirit.

While sincere and earnest individuals raise the standard of their own times, the age, improved by their efforts, educates other individuals, who, being thus raised to a higher point of view, can command a more extended vision than their predecessors. By obedience to a law within themselves, above the existing laws of society, such individuals help to raise the moral standard of succeeding ages to a plane still more elevated. By this mutual action and reaction between the public and private conscience, the world is slowly rolled onward toward its long-promised Golden Age. It is a glorious privilege to help it forward, even the hundredth part of an inch. It is a fearful responsibility to retard it, even a hair's breadth. Every one of us can aid in the great work, if we always look inward for our guide, and follow the voice of conscience, which to each one of us is truly the law of God.

> "Reverence for what's oldest, truest,
> Friendly welcome to the newest;
> Cheerful heart and purpose pure,
> So our onward way is sure."

LIST OF BOOKS USED IN THE PREPARATION
OF THESE VOLUMES.

The Works of Sir William Jones.
Ramohun Roy's Translation of the Vedas.
Heeren's Historical Researches.
Maurice's History of Hindostan.
Ramsay's Natural and Revealed Religion.
Priestly's Institutes.
La Vie Contemplative, Ascetique, et Monastique, chez les Indons et les Bouddhistes. Par J. J. Bochinger.
Oriental Memoirs. By Sir James Forbes.
Journal of a Residence in India. By Bishop Heber.
Herodotus.
Ancient Egyptians. By Sir J. Wilkinson.
Egypt's Place in Universal History. By C. J. Bunsen.
Denon's Travels in Egypt.
Belzoni's Travels in Egypt.
Eastern Lands, Past and Present. By Harriet Martineau.
Nineveh and its Remains. By Layard.
The Zend-Avesta. Translated into French. By Anquitil du Perron.
Confucius et Mencius. Par M. G. Pauthier.
Chinese Classics. By Rev. David Collie.
Duhalde's China.
Travels in Tartary, Thibet, and China. By M. Huc.
Plato. Translated by Taylor.
Sewall's Plato.
Potter's Antiquities of Greece.
Wordsworth's Greece.
Hesiod.
Homer.
Virgil.

Classical Museum.
Mayo's New System of Mythology.
Enfield's History of Philosophy.
Gray's Classical Ages.
Priestly's Philosophers.
Cicero Concerning the Nature of the Gods.
Dictionary of Greek and Roman Mythology. By Dr. W. M. Smith.
Smith's Classical Dictionary.
Prideaux's History of the Old and New Testament.
History of the Hebrew Monarchy. By Rev. Francis Newman.
De Wette on the Old and New Testament. Translated by Theodore Parker.
History of the Jews. By Josephus.
Lewis's History of the Hebrew Republic.
Warburton's Divine Legation of Moses.
Herder on Hebrew Poetry.
Milman's History of the Jews.
Mackay's Progress of the Intellect.
Library of the Fathers. Translated by members of the English church.
Book of the Fathers.
The Fathers of the Desert. By Henry Ruffner.
Lives of the Fathers, Martyrs and Saints. By Rev. Alban Butler.
Life of St. Chrysostom. Translated from the German of Dr. Neander by Rev. J. C. Stapleton.
Confessions of St. Augustine. Revised by Rev. E. B. Pusey.
Life of St. Anthony. From the Greek of St. Athanasius. Translated by Henry Ruffner.
Life of St. Hilarion. From the Latin of St. Jerome. Translated by Henry Ruffner.

Life of St. Paul the Simple. From Tillemont's Ecclesiastical History. Translated by Henry Ruffner.

Histoire de la Mère de Dieu. Par M. L'Abbé Orsini.

Ecclesiastical History. By Eusebius.

Mosheim's Ecclesiastical History.

Bingham's History of the Church.

Cave's Primitive Christianity.

Le Christianisme et L'Esclavage. Par M. L'Abbé Théron.

History of the Christian Religion. By Dr. Neander. Translated from the German, by Joseph Torrey.

History of Christianity. By Dr. Milman.

History of Early Opinions concerning Jesus Christ. By Dr. Priestly.

A Free Inquiry into the Miraculous Powers of the Christian Church. By Dr. Conyers Middleton.

A Free Inquiry into the Authenticity of the First Chapters of Matthew. By John Williams, LL. D.

Butler's Horæ Biblicæ.

Gibbon's History of the Decline and Fall of the Roman Empire.

The Apocryphal New Testament.

Life of Apollonius. Translated from the Greek of Philostratus, by Rev. Edward Berwick.

The Two First Books of Philostratus concerning Apollonius. Translated by Charles Blount.

Histoire Critique du Gnosticisme. Par M. Jacque Matter.

Histoire de L'Ecole D'Alexandrie. Par M. Jules Simon.

Sale's Translation of the Koran.

Life and Religion of Mohammed, as contained in the Hyat ul Kuloob.

Mohammedan Akhlak i Jalaly.

Bayle's Dictionary.

Conversations Lexicon.

Biblical Legends of the Musulmans. By Dr. G. Weil.

The Old and New Testament.

INDEX.

THE END.

Printed in the United States
83533LV00006B/1-24/A